2004

CLASSICS IN THE EDUCATION OF GIRLS AND WOMEN

by

Shirley Nelson Kersey

The Scarecrow Press, Inc.
Metuchen, N.J., & London
1981

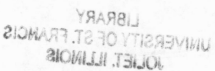
Library of Congress Cataloging in Publication Data

Main entry under title:

Classics in the education of girls and women.

1. Education of women—Philosophy—History—Collected works. I. Kersey, Shirley Nelson.
LC1707.C53   376   80-20711
ISBN 0-8108-1354-8

TO MY FATHER AND MOTHER,
who were committed to a university
education for their only daughter.

CONTENTS

PART VI: NINETEENTH CENTURY

ENGLAND

FRANCE

GERMANY

UNITED STATES

PREFACE

In response to a request from my department chairman at the University of Wisconsin—Milwaukee, I developed a course entitled History of the Education of Girls and Women in the Western World. An initial library search indicated that pertinent information is sparse, and that History of Education usually is synonymous with History of Male Education. I learned to be thankful when a chapter, an essay, a letter, a page, or even a paragraph contained knowledge germane to the History of Female Education.

To compensate for the lack of an available textbook, I wrote extensive handouts for classroom use. Also, I assigned the reading of original works which enabled students to perceive the essence of each historical period. Favorable student reaction to the content convinced me of the value of combining the selections in one volume to be available to a wide audience.

Dissimilarity of length among compositions chosen for this book is an inevitable consequence of the fragmentation, nature, and purpose of relevant literature. Perhaps this brief introduction to the subject matter might motivate persons to read entire works from which the excerpts have been chosen.

I am appreciative of the assistance, support, interest, and encouragement of students, colleagues, family, and friends who shared my conviction that this book should be written. I am especially grateful to Janet Wells, my son, David, and my daughter, Ann, who offered constructive criticism of the manuscript.

The Department of Cultural Foundations of Education at the University of Wisconsin—Milwaukee generously arranged for a valuable research assistant, Aileen Weber, to work with me. Kurt Behling provided efficient office service.

The extensive holdings of the library of the University of Wisconsin—Milwaukee facilitated my research. The knowledgeable, dependable, willing staff of the Interlibrary Loan Department was of inestimable aid to me.

Whether this volume is read independently or as an accompaniment to the textbook in process, I hope contributions of the thirty-five authors will bring both enjoyment and new information to each reader.

Shirley N. Kersey
University of Wisconsin—
Parkside
January 1980

INTRODUCTION

Horace Mann was the leading proponent of the Common School Movement, which was intended to provide tax supported equal educational opportunity for all persons in the United States. In 1848 he wrote that the principle of natural ethics

> ...proves the *absolute right* of every human being that comes into the world to an education; and which, of course, proves the correlative duty of every government to see that the means of that education are provided for all.*

Mann's intent is clear: education is the birthright of all individuals, irrespective of creed, color, family income and status, or, of foremost significance for the purpose of this book, sex. Historical accounts show that, although Mann's sentiment has not been the prevalent view toward female education throughout the past 2,500 years, in most time periods there have been a select few who have professed the desirability of formally educating girls and women. Essays, letters, and excerpts from lengthy works included in this volume were written by persons who did, in fact, alter educational circumstances for women of their day or for women of the future.

Twentieth-century women are indebted to the authors, philosophers, and educators who constituted a small minority among their contemporaries when they wrote boldly in favor of educational rights for girls and women. Selections in this volume appear in chronological order to reveal the slow, frustrating progression of equal educational opportunity for the female sex in Europe and the United States. It would be useful for the reader to peruse entries in sequence, to identify trends and influences, and to consider such topics as these: (1) obstacles to realization of equal male and female educational

---

*Lawrence Cremin. *The Republic and the School.* New York: Teachers College, Columbia University, 1957, p. 63.

opportunity, (2) European influences upon female education in the United States, (3) socio-economic effects upon female education, (4) positive and negative roles of religions, (5) changes in male and female attitudes toward the concept of an educated woman, (6) modifications in curriculum.

One definition of a classic is that it be of enduring interest, quality, or style. To conform with this interpretation, the final writings in this collection represent nineteenth-century educational practice and thought. Without the perspective of adequate historical distance, it is difficult to perceive accurately which written work from the current century will prove to be of permanent value.

As it does in many disciplines, Ancient Greece provides the logical starting point for a presentation of *Classics in the Education of Girls and Women.*

PART I: ANCIENT GREECE

The life-style of women in Ancient Greece varied significantly among the city-states. Spartan women received an extensive education in physical fitness, participated in athletic contests and contributed their views of family life and politics. Athenian women received no formal education, remained in specified rooms of the home, and rarely conversed with their husbands. However, hetaerae, mistress–companions whose lovers instructed them in literature, philosophy, and politics, were exceptions in Athens.

Leading philosophers shared the view of Aristotle who, in Book VI of *Politics,* stated that male rules over female. Conversely, Plato wrote favorably of women's intellectual capacities. He attributed the inferior reasoning power of females not to a lack of innate ability, but rather to inadequate education. Plato demonstrated advanced thinking when he assigned to women moral and intellectual equality with men; furthermore, he declared that women deserve equal political opportunity with men.

The first selection that follows is from Book V of Plato's *Republic,* which was written either in 411 or 412 B. C. The dialogue is between Socrates and a friend, Glaucon. The other of the Platonic excerpts reprinted here is from Book VII of *Laws,* Plato's final work, completed in approximately 348 B.C. The dialogue is between an intelligent Athenian and a dull Cretan named Clinias. In these two major works of Plato, the reader experiences a lone "voice crying in the wilderness" foreshadowing thought destined to become popular in the twentieth century.

PLATO (427–348 B. C.)

*REPUBLIC**

Book V

The aim of our theory was, I believe, to make our men as it were guardians of a flock.

Yes.

Let us keep on the same track, and give corresponding rules for the propagation of the species, and for rearing the young; and let us observe whether we find them suitable or not.

How do you mean?

Thus. Do we think that the females of watch-dogs ought to guard the flock along with the males, and hunt with them, and share in all their other duties; or that the females ought to stay at home, because they are disabled by having to breed and rear the cubs, while the males are to labour and be charged with all the care of the flocks?

We expect them to share in whatever is to be done; only we treat the females as the weaker, and the males as the stronger.

Is it possible to use animals for the same work, if you do not give them the same training and education;

It is not.

If then we are to employ the women in the same duties as the men, we must given them the same instructions.

Yes.

To the men we gave music and gymnastics.

Yes.

Then we must train the women also in the same two arts, giving them besides a military education, and treating them in the same way as the men.

---

*Reprinted from Davies, John Llewelyn, and Vaughan, David James (trans.). *The Republic of Plato*. London: Macmillan, 1898, pp. 156-163.

It follows naturally from what you say.

Perhaps many of the details of the question before us might appear unusually ridiculous, if carried out in the manner proposed.

No doubt they would.

Which of them do you find the most ridiculous? Is it not obviously the notion of the women exercising naked in the schools with the men, and not only the young women, but even those of an advanced age, just like those old men in the gymnasia, who, in spite of wrinkles and ugliness, still keep up their fondness for active exercises?

Yes, indeed: at the present day that would appear truly ridiculous.

Well then, as we have started the subject, we must not be afraid of the numerous jests which worthy men may make upon the notion of carrying out such a change in reference to the gymnasia and music; and above all, in the wearing of armour and riding on horseback.

You are right.

On the contrary, as we have begun the discussion, we must travel on to the rougher ground of our law, intreating these witty men to leave off their usual practice, and try to be serious; and reminding them that not long since it was thought discreditable and ridiculous among the Greeks, as it is now among most barbarian nations, for men to be seen naked. And when the Cretans first, and after them the Lacedaemonians began the practice of gymnastic exercises, the wits of the time had it in their power to make sport of those novelties. Do you not think so?

I do.

But when experience had shewn that it was better to strip than to cover up the body, and when the ridiculous effect, which this plan had to the eye, had given way before the arguments establishing its superiority, it was at the same time, as I imagine, demonstrated, that he is a fool who thinks anything ridiculous but that which is evil, and who attempts to raise a laugh by assuming any object to be ridiculous but that which is unwise and evil; or who chooses for the aim of his serious admiration any other mark save that which is good.

Most assuredly.

Must we not then first come to an agreement as to whether the regulations proposed are practicable or not, and give to any one, whether of a jocose or serious turn, an opportunity of raising the question, whether the nature of the human female is such as to

4 enable her to share in all the employments of the male, or whether she is wholly unequal to any, or equal to some and not to others; and if so, to which class military service belongs? Will not this be the way to make the best beginning, and, in all probability, the best ending also?

Yes, quite so.

Would you like, then, that we should argue against ourselves in behalf of an objector, that the adverse position may not be undefended against our attack?

There is no reason why we should not.

Then let us say in his behalf, 'Socrates and Glaucon, there is no need for others to advance anything against you: for you yourselves, at the beginning of your scheme for constructing a state, admitted that every individual therein ought, in accordance with nature, to do the one work which belongs to him.' 'We did admit this, I imagine: how could we do otherwise?' 'Can you deny that there is a very marked difference between the nature of woman and that of man?' 'Of course there is a difference.' 'Then is it not fitting to assign to each sex a different work, appropriate to its peculiar nature?' 'Undoubtedly.' 'Then if so, you must be in error now, and be contradicting yourselves when you go on to say, that men and women ought to engage in the same occupations when their natures are so widely diverse?' Shall you have any answers to make to that objection, my clever friend?

It is not so very easy to find one at a moment's notice: but I shall apply to you, and I do so now, to state what the arguments on our side are, and to expound them for us.

These objections, Glaucon, and many others like them, are what I anticipated all along; and that is why I was afraid and reluctant to meddle with the law that regulates the possession of the women and children, and the rearing of the latter.

To say the truth, it does seem no easy task.

Why no: but the fact is, that whether you fall into a small swimming-bath, or into the middle of the great ocean, you have to swim all the same.

Exactly so.

Then is it not best for us, in the present instance, to strike out and endeavour to emerge in safety from the discussion, in the hope that either a dolphin* may take us on his back, or some other unlooked-for deliverance present itself?

It would seem so.

---

*In allusion, probably, to the famous story of Arion. Herodotus, I. 24.

Come then, I continued, let us see if we can find the way out.
We admitted, you say, that different natures ought to have different occupations, and that the natures of men and women are different; but now we maintain that these different natures ought to engage in the same occupations. Is this your charge against us?

Precisely.

Truly, Glaucon, the power of the art of controversy is a very extra-ordinary one.

Why so?

Because it seems to me that many fall into it even against their will, and fancy they are discussing, when they are merely debating, because they cannot distinguish the meanings of a term, in their investigation of any question, but carry on their opposition to what is stated, by attacking the mere words, employing the art of debate, and not that of philosophical discussion.

This is no doubt the case with many: does it apply to us at the present moment?

Most assuredly it does; at any rate there is every appearance of our having fallen unintentionally into a verbal controversy.

How so?

We are pressing hard upon the mere letter of the dogma, that different natures ought not to engage in the same pursuits, in the most courageous style of verbal debate, but we have wholly forgotten to consider in what senses the words 'the same nature' and 'different natures' were employed, and what we had in view in our definition, when we assigned different pursuits to different natures, and the same pursuits to the same natures.

It is true we have not considered that.

That being the case, it is open to us apparently to ask ourselves whether bald men and long-haired men are of the same or of opposite natures, and after admitting the latter to be the case, we may say that if bald men make shoes, long-haired men must not be suffered to make them, or if the long-haired men make them, the others must be forbidden to do so.

Nay, that would be ridiculous.

Would it be ridiculous, except for the reason that we were not then using the words, 'the same' and 'different,' in a universal sense, being engaged only with that particular species of likeness and difference which applied directly to the pursuits in questions? For example, we said that two men who were mentally qualified for the medical profession, possessed the same nature. Do you not think so?

I do.

And that a man who would make a good physician had a different nature from one who would make a good carpenter.

Of course he has.

If, then the male and the female sex appear to differ in reference to any art, or other occupation, we shall say that such occupation must be appropriated to the one or the other: but if we find the difference between the sexes to consist simply in the parts they respectively bear in the propagation of the species, we shall assert that it has not yet been by any means demonstrated that the difference between man and woman touches our purpose; on the contrary, we shall still think it proper for our guardians and their wives to engage in the same pursuits.

And rightly.

Shall we not proceed to call upon our opponents to inform us what is that particular art or occupation connected with the organization of a state, in reference to which the nature of a man and a woman are not the same, but diverse?

We certainly are entitled to do so.

Well, perhaps it might be pleaded by others, as it was a little while ago by you, that it is not easy to give a satisfactory answer at a moment's notice; but that, with time for consideration, it would not be difficult to do so.

True, it might.

Would you like us then to beg the author of such objections to accompany us, to see if we can shew him that no occupation which belongs to the ordering of a state is peculiar to women?

By all means.

Well then, we will address him thus: Pray tell us whether, when you say that one man possesses talents for a particular study, and that another is without them, you mean that the former learns it easily, the latter with difficulty; and that the one with little instruction can find out much for himself in the subject he has studied, whereas the other after much teaching and practice cannot even retain what he has learnt; and that the mind of the one is duly aided, that of the other thwarted, by the bodily powers? Are not these the only marks by which you define the possession and the want of natural talents for any pursuit?

Every one will say yes.

Well then, do you know of any branch of human industry in which the female sex is not inferior in these respects to the male? or need we go the length of specifying the art of weaving, and the

manufacture of pastry and preserves, in which women are thought
to excel, and in which their discomfiture is most laughed at?

You are perfectly right that in almost every employment the one sex is vastly superior to the other. There are many women, no doubt, who are better in many things than many men; but, speaking generally, it is as you say.

I conclude then, my friend, that none of the occupations which comprehend the ordering of a state belong to woman as woman, nor yet to man as man; but natural gifts are to be found here and there, in both sexes alike; and, so far as her nature is concerned, the woman is admissable to all pursuits as well as the man; though in all of them the woman is weaker than the man.

Precisely so.

Shall we then hold, I imagine, that one woman may have talents for medicine, and another be without them; and that one may be musical, and another unmusical.

Undoubtedly.

And shall we not also say, that one woman may have qualifications for gymnastic exercises, and for war, and another be unwarlike, and without a taste for gymnastics?

I think we shall.

Again, may there not be a love of knowledge in one, and a distaste for it in another? and may not one be spirited, and another spiritless?

True again.

If that be so, there are some women who are fit, and others who are unfit, for the office of guardians. For were not those the qualities that we selected, in the case of the men, as marking their fitness for that office?

Yes, they were.

Then as far as the guardianship of a state is concerned, there is no difference between the natures of the man and of the woman, but only various degrees of weakness and strength.

Apparently there is none.

Then we shall have to select duly qualified women also, to share in the life and official labours of the duly qualified men; since we find that they are competent to the work, and of kindred nature with the men.

Just so.

And must we not assign the same pursuit to the same natures?

We must.

Then we are now brought round by a circuit to our former

8   position, and we admit that it is no violation of nature to assign music and gymnastic to the wives of our guardians.

Precisely so.

Then our intended legislation was not impracticable, or visionary, since the proposed law was in accordance with nature: rather it is in the existing usage, contravening this of ours, that to all appearance contravenes nature.

So it appears.

Our inquiry was, whether the proposed arrangement would be practicable, and whether it was the most desirable one, was it not?

It was.

Are we quite agreed that it is practicable?

Yes.

Then the next point to be settled, that it is also the most desirable arrangement?

Yes, obviously.

Very well; if the question is how to render a woman fit for the office of guardian, we shall not have one education for men, and another for women, especially as the nature to be wrought upon is the same in both cases.

No, the education will be the same.

LAWS*

Book VII

We are establishing gymnasia and all physical exercises connected with military training—the use of the bow and all kinds of missiles, light skirmishing and heavy-armed fighting of every description tactical evolutions, company-marching, camp-formations, and all the details of cavalry training. In all these subjects there should be public instructors, paid by the State; and their pupils should be not only the boys and men in the State, but also the girls and women who understand all these matters—being practised in all military drill and fighting while still girls and, when grown to womanhood, taking part in evolutions and rank-forming and the piling and shouldering of arms—and that, if for no other

*Reprinted from Bury, R.G. (trans.). *Laws*. Vol. II. London: William Heinemann Ltd., 1942, pp. 87, 89. By permission of The Loeb Classical Library (Harvard University Press: William Heinemann).

reason, at least for this reason, that, if ever the guards of the children and of the rest of the city should be obliged to leave the city and march out in full force, these women should be able at least to take their place; while if, on the other hand—and this is quite a possible contingency—an invading army of foreigners, fierce and strong, should force a battle round the city itself, then it would be a sore disgrace to the State if its women were so ill brought up as not even to be willing to do as do the mother-birds, which fight the strongest beasts in defense of their broods, but, instead of facing all risks, even death itself, to run straight to the temples and crowd all the shrines and holy places, and drown mankind in the disgrace of being the most craven of living creatures.

CLIN. By Heaven, Stranger, if ever this took place in a city, it would be a most unseemly thing, apart from the mischief of it.

ATH. Shall we, then, lay down this law,—that up to the point stated women must not neglect military training, but all citizens, men and women alike, must pay attention to it?

CLIN. I, for one, agree.

PART II: EARLY CHRISTIAN ERA

It is noteworthy that no writer in Early Rome produced a significant document which promoted the education of girls. Not even the famous educational theorist Quintilian, many of whose concepts appeared to be two thousand years in advance of the thinking of his time, stressed the need for increased formal education of females. Therefore, this book has a seven-hundred-year time lapse between the writing of Plato, who lived in pagan Athens, and the writing of St. Jerome, who lived in the Early Christian Era.

Jerome, whose given name was Sophronius Eusebius Hieronymus, was judged to have been the most learned man of his day. Born into a wealthy family, he set an example of asceticism by donating his property to the poor, then devoting his life to the service of others. The nature of Jerome's religious commitment differed distinctly from that of his counterparts because of his emphasis upon furthering the education of girls and women. He experienced extraordinary success in gathering recruits from among the ranks of wealthy Roman women, whom he persuaded to give their material possessions to the church, then to follow him to Bethlehem and dedicate their lives to serving God.

Paula, who contributed her enormous fortune to the church and established a nunnery in the Holy Land, was the most productive of these women. With the exception of one daughter, Eustochium, she left her children in Rome. Paula's grave is adjacent to that of Jerome, thus symbolizing her importance to him and to the Christian community.

Through his widely read books, Jerome made a long-lasting contribution to the education of girls. As late as the eighteenth century, Christians followed his simple curriculum for girls. This curriculum consisted of religion, reading, writing, grammar, and spinning. Jerome discouraged a high development of intellect in women because he feared this might lead them into temptation.

The first of Jerome's two letters excerpted here was written in 403 to Laeta, Paula's daughter-in-law. Laeta had written from Rome to ask Jerome's advice on raising her infant daughter as a Christian, though she lived in a Moslem environment as a result of an interfaith marriage. Laeta accepted his advice to send her daughter, Paula, to be supervised in Bethlehem by her Grandmother Paula and her Aunt Eustochium. Eventually, the young Paula succeeded her aunt as head of the nunnery founded by the elder Paula.

The second letter was written by Jerome in 413 to a child named Pacatula. He begins the letter with a discussion of the propriety of celibacy and chastity. He concludes with cautionary remarks about the dangers of contemporary worldliness. The brief excerpt reprinted in this volume contains specific advice for the education of girls.

Compayre, a prominent nineteenth-century French educator, judged these letters to be the most precious pedagogical documents of the Early Christian Era.

ST. JEROME (340–420)

LETTER CVII*

To Laeta

A Girl's Education

Thus must a soul be trained which is to be a temple of God. It must learn to hear nothing and to say nothing save what pertains to the fear of the Lord. It must have no comprehension of foul words, no knowledge of wordly songs, and its childish tongue must be imbued with the sweet music of the psalms. Let boys with their wanton frolics be kept far from Paula: let even her maids and attendants hold aloof from association with the worldly, lest they render their evil knowledge worse by teaching it to her. Have a set of letters made for her, of boxwood or of ivory, and tell her their names. Let her play with them, making play a road to learning, and let her not only grasp the right order of the letters and remember their names in a simple song, but also frequently upset their order and mix the last letters with the middle ones, the middle with the first. Thus she will know them all by sight as well as by sound. When she begins with uncertain hand to use the pen, either let another hand be put over hers to guide her baby fingers, or else have the letters marked on the tablet so that her writing may follow their outlines and keep to their limits without straying away. Offer her prizes for spelling, tempting her with such trifling gifts as please young children. Let her have companions too in her lessons, so that she may seek to rival them and be stimulated by any praise they win. You must not scold her if she is somewhat slow; praise is the best sharpener of wits. Let her be glad when she is first and sorry

*This and Letter CXXVIII (following) reprinted from Wright, F.A. (trans.). *Select Letters of St. Jerome*. London: William Heinemann, Ltd., 1933, pp. 345–349 and pp. 467–469, 475–477. By permission of The Loeb Classical Library (Harvard University Press: William Heinemann).

when she falls behind. Above all take care not to make her lessons distasteful; a childish dislike often lasts longer than childhood. The very words from which she will get into the way of forming sentences should not be taken at haphazard but be definitely chosen and arranged on purpose. For example, let her have the names of the prophets and the apostles, and the whole list of patriarchs from Adam downwards, as Matthew and Luke give it. She will then be doing two things at the same time, and will remember them afterwards.

For teacher you must choose a man of approved years, life and learning. Even a sage is not ashamed, methinks, to do for a relative or for a high-born virgin what Aristotle did for Philip's son, when like some humble clerk he taught him his first letters. Things must not be despised as trifles, if without them great results are impossible. The very letters themselves, and to the first lesson in them, sound quite differently from the mouth of a learned man, and of a rustic. And so you must take care not to let women's silly coaxing get your daughter into the way of cutting her words short, or of disporting herself in gold brocade and fine purple. The first habit ruins talk, the second character; and children should never learn what they will afterwards have to unlearn. We are told that the eloquence of the Gracchi was largely due to the way in which their mother talked to them as children, and it was by sitting on his father's lap that Hortensius became a great orator. The first impression made on a young mind is hard to remove. The shell-dyed wool—who can bring back its pristine whiteness? A new jar keeps for a long time the taste and smell of its original contents. Greek history tells us that the mighty king Alexander, who subdued the whole world, could not rid himself of the tricks of manner and gait which in his childhood he had caught from his governor Leonides. For it is easy to imitate the bad, and you may soon copy the faults of those to whose virtue you can never attain. Let Paula's foster-mother be a person neither drunken nor wanton nor fond of gossip; let her nurse be a modest woman, her foster-father a respectable man.

* * *

Paula must be deaf to all musical instruments, and never even know why the flute, the lyre, and the harp came into existence.

Let her every day repeat to you a portion of the Scriptures as her fixed task. A good number of verses she should learn by heart

14　in the Greek, but knowledge of the Latin should follow close after. If the tender lips are not trained from the beginning, the language is spoiled by a foreign accent and our native tongue debased by alien faults. You must be her teacher, to you her childish ignorance must look for a model. Let her never see anything in you or her father which she would do wrong to imitate. Remember that you are a virgin's parents and that you can teach her better by example than by words. Flowers quickly fade; violets, lilies, and saffron are soon withered by a baleful breeze. Let her never appear in public without you, let her never visit the churches and the martyrs' shrines except in your company. Let no youth or curled dandy ogle her. Let our little virgin never stir a finger's breadth from her mother when she attends a vigil or an all-night service. I would not let her have a favourite maid into whose ear she might frequently whisper: what she says to one, all ought to know. Let her choose as companion not a spruce, handsome girl, able to warble sweet songs in liquid notes, but one grave and pale, carelessly dressed and inclined to melancholy. Set before her as a pattern some aged virgin of approved faith, character, and chastity, one who may instruct her by word, and by example accustom her to rise from her bed at night for prayer and psalm singing, to chant hymns in the morning, at the third, sixth, and ninth hour, to take her place in the ranks as one of Christ's amazons, and with kindled lamp to offer the evening sacrifice. So let the day pass, and so let the night find her still labouring. Let reading follow prayer and prayer follow reading. The time will seem short when it is occupied with such a diversity of tasks.

Let her learn also to make wool, to hold the distaff, to put the basket in her lap, to turn the spindle, to shape the thread with her thumb.

* * *

Instead of jewels or silk let her love the manuscripts of the Holy Scriptures, and in them let her prefer correctness and accurate arrangement to gilding and Babylonian parchment with elaborate decorations. Let her learn the Psalter first, with these songs let her distract herself, and then let her learn lessons of life in the Proverbs of Solomon. In reading Ecclesiastes let her become accustomed to thread underfoot the things of this world; let her follow the examples of virtue and patience that she will find in Job. Let her then pass on to the Gospels and never again lay them down. Let her

drink in the Acts of the Apostles and the Epistles with all the will
of her heart. As soon as she has enriched her mind's storehouse
with these treasures, let her commit to memory the Prophets, the
Heptateuch, the books of Kings and the Chronicles, and the rolls of
Ezra and Esther. Then at last she may safely read the Song of
Songs: if she were to read it at the beginning, she might be harmed
by not perceiving that it was the song of a spiritual bridal expressed
in fleshly language. Let her avoid all the apocryphal books, and if
she ever wishes to read them, not for the truth of her doctrines but
out of respect for their wondrous tales, let her realize that they are
not really written by those to whom they are ascribed, that there are
many faulty elements in them, and that it requires great skill to look
for gold in mud. Let her always keep Cyprian's words by her, and
let her peruse the letters of Athanasius and the treatises of Hilary
without fear of stumbling. She may take pleasure in the learned
expositions of all such writers as maintain in their books a steady
love of the faith. If she reads others, let it be as a critic rather than
as a disciple.

You will answer: 'How shall I, a woman of the world living in
crowded Rome, be able to keep these injunctions?' Do not then
take up a burden which you cannot bear. When you have weaned
Paula as Isaac was weaned, and when you have clothed her as
Samuel was clothed, send her to her grandmother and her aunt. Set
this most precious jewel in Mary's chamber, and place her on the
cradle where Jesus cried. Let her be reared in a monastery amid
bands of virgins, where she will learn never to take an oath, and to
regard a lie as sacrilege. Let her know nothing of the world, but live
like the angels; let her be in the flesh and without the flesh, thinking
all mankind to be like herself. Thus, to say nothing of other things,
she will free you from the difficult task of watching over her and
from all the responsibility of guardianship. It is better for you to
regret her absence than every moment to be fearing what she is
saying, to whom she is talking, whom she greets and whom she likes
to see. Give to Eustochium the little child, whose very wailings are
now a prayer on your behalf; give her, to be her companion to-day,
to be the inheritor of her sanctity in the years to come. Let her gaze
upon and love, let her 'from her first years admire' one whose
words and gait and dress are an education in virtue. Let her
grandmother take her on her lap and repeat to her grandchild the
lessons she once taught her daughter. Long experience has taught
her how to rear, instruct, and watch over virgins, and in her crown
every day is woven the mystic hundred of chastity. O happy virgin!

16 O happy Paula, daughter of Toxotius! By the virtues of her grandmother and her aunt she is nobler in sanctity even than in lineage. Oh, if you could only see your mother-in-law and your sister, and know the mighty souls that dwell within their feeble bodies! Then I doubt not that you obey your innate love of chastity and come to them even before you daughter, exchanging God's first decree for the Gospel's second dispensation. You would surely count as nothing your desire for other children and would rather offer yourself to God. But inasmuch as 'there is a time to embrace and a time to refrain from embracing,' and 'the wife hath not power over her own body,' and 'every man should abide in the same calling wherein he was called' in the Lord, and because he who is under the yoke ought so to run as not to leave his companion in the mire, pay back in your children all that you defer paying in your own person. When Hannah had brought to the tabernacle the son whom she had vowed to God, she never took him back again, thinking it improper that a future prophet should grow up in the house of one who still desired to have other sons. In fine, after she had conceived and borne him, she did not venture to visit the temple and appear before God empty-handed, but first paid her debt, and then after offering her great sacrifice returned home, and having borne her first son for God was then given five children for herself. Do you wonder at the happiness of that holy woman? Then imitate her faith. If you will send us Paula, I undertake to be both her tutor and her foster-father. I will carry her on my shoulders, and my old tongue shall train her stammering lips. And I shall take more pride in my task than did the worldly philosopher; for I shall not be teaching a Macedonian king, destined to die by poison in Babylon, but a handmaid and bride of Christ who one day shall be presented to the heavenly throne.

LETTER CXXVIII

To Pacatula

Feminine Training

It is a difficult matter to write to a little girl who will not understand what you say, of whose mind you know nothing, and whose inclinations it would be dangerous to warrant. To use the

words of a famous orator's preface—in her case praise is based on
expectation rather than accomplishment. How can you urge self-control on a child who still craves after cakes, who babbles softly in her mother's arms, and finds honey sweeter than words? Can she pay attention to the deep sayings of the apostle, when she takes more pleasure in old wives' tales than in them? Can she heed the dark riddles of the prophets when her nurse's frown is sufficient to frighten her? Can she appreciate the majesty of the Gospel when its lightnings dazzle all men's senses? How can I bid her to be obedient to her parents, this child who beats her mother with baby hand? So my little Pacatula must read this letter herself in days to come; and in the meantime learn her alphabet, spelling, grammar, and syntax. To get her to repeat her lessons in her little shrill voice she must have a prize of a honey cake offered to her. She will do her work quickly if she is going to receive as reward some sweetmeat, or bright flower, or glittering bauble, or pretty doll. Meanwhile, too, she must learn to spin, drawing down the threads with tender fingers; and though at first she may often break the yarn, she will one day cease to do so. Then, when work is over, she may indulge in play, hanging on her mother's neck and snatching kisses from her relations. Let her be rewarded for singing the psalms aloud, so that she may love what she is forced to do, and it be not work but pleasure, not a matter of necessity but one of freewill.

* * *

Females should only mix with their own sex; they should not know how to play with boys, nay, they should be afraid to do so. A girl should have no acquaintance with lewd talk, and if amid the noisy bustle of a household she hears an unclean word, she should not understand it. Her mother's nod should be as good as speech, her mother's advice equivalent to a command. She should love her as her parent, obey her as her mistress, fear her as her teacher. At first she will be but a shy little maid without all her teeth, but as soon as she has reached her seventh year and has learned to blush, knowing what she should not say, and doubting what she should say, she should commit the psalter to memory, and until she is grown up she should make the books of Solomon, the Gospels, the apostles, and the prophets the treasure of her heart. She should not appear in public too freely nor always seek a crowded church. Let her find all her pleasure in her own room. She must never look at foppish youths or curled coxcombs, who wound the soul through

18   the ears with their honeyed talk. She must be protected also from the wantonness of other girls. The more freedom of access such persons have, the more difficult they are to shake off; the knowledge they have acquired they impart in secret and corrupt a secluded Danae with vulgar gossip. Let her teacher be her companion, her attendant her guardian, and let her be a woman not given to much wine, one who, as the apostle says, is not idle nor a tattler, but sober, grave, skilled in spinning, saying only such words as will train a girl's mind in virtue. For as water follows behind a finger in the sand, so soft and tender youth is pliable for good or evil, and can be drawn wherever you guide it.

PART III: RENAISSANCE

The Christian Era of Jerome blended into the Middle Ages, which dated from the sixth through the thirteenth centuries. Medieval nunneries served as a haven and, of course, provided religious study. The curriculum focused on Latin, Greek, and intricate needlework. Throughout the Middle Ages the influence of the Roman Catholic Church continued to dominate education of both sexes, while the influence of the Royal Courts added a new dimension with the Establishment of court schools.

Charlemagne brought from England the renowned educator Alcuin, who established a court school attended by male and female members of the Frankish court. Curiously, neither Alcuin nor any of the highly regarded nun-educators left written work which detailed educational practice and theory concerning girls. For this reason there is an absence of significant female educational classics between the time of Jerome and the beginning of the Renaissance in the fourteenth century.

The Renaissance milieu tended to be conducive to educational advancement of women. In Italy, for example, women were presumed to possess intellectual capacity equal to that of men. Several women lectured behind opaque screens in order that they not distract the male students! Members of both sexes were affected by the prevailing philosophy, Humanism, which brought to education a revival of classical scholarship.

The distinguished humanist Vittorino da Feltre was influential in the intellectual advancement of women through his active life as a teacher and a tutor. Unfortunately, he wrote nothing stating his educational philosophy for girls and women. Bruni, Erasmus, and Vives wrote eloquently on the subject as is apparent in the following entries of these three revered humanists.

LEONARDO BRUNI (ca. 1370-1444)

Bruni D'Arezzo was Chancellor of the Republic of Florence from 1427 to 1444, but his lasting fame was a result of his Latin and Greek translations. His *History of Florence* was known as the first modern history book because of its break from medieval historical methodology.

Bruni's 1405 or 1406 letter to Baptista Malatesta was the earliest humanist educational tract dedicated to a lady. This dedication demonstrated his serious respect for the intellectual capabilities of Italian women. Baptista, with an interest in poetry, ancient literature, Latin, and philosophy, exemplified the character of intellectual Renaissance women. In this letter Bruni specifies desirable studies for women, and makes obvious his high regard for the mental capacity of women.

LEONARDO D'AREZZO CONCERNING THE STUDY OF LITERATURE*

A Letter Addressed to the Illustrious Lady, Baptista Malatesta.

I am led to address this Tractate to you, Illustrious Lady, by the high repute which attaches to your name in the field of learning; and I offer it, partly as an encouragement to further effort. Were it necessary I might urge you by brilliant instances from antiquity: Cornelia, the daughter of Scipio, whose Epistles survived for centuries as models of style; Sappho, the poetess, held in so great honour for the exuberance of her poetic art; Aspasia, who learning and eloquence made her not unworthy of the intimacy of Socrates. Upon these, the most distinguished of a long range of great names,

---

*From Woodward, William Harrison. *Vittorino da Feltre and Other Humanist Educators.* Cambridge: At the University Press, 1897, pp. 123-133.

I would have you fix your mind; for an intelligence such as your own can be satisfied with nothing less than the best. You yourself, indeed, may hope to win a fame higher even than theirs. For they lived in days when learning was no rare attainment, and therefore they enjoyed no unique renown. Whilst, alas, upon such times are we fallen that a learned man seems well-nigh a portent, and erudition in a woman is a thing utterly unknown. For true learning has almost died away amongst us. True learning, I say: not a mere acquaintance with that vulgar, threadbare jargon which satisfies those who devote themselves to Theology, but sound learning in its proper and legitimate sense, vix., the knowledge of realities—Facts and Principles—united to a perfect familiarity with Letters and the art of expression. Now this combination we find in Lactantius, in Augustine, or in Jerome; each of them at once a great theologian and profoundly versed in literature. But turn from them to their successors of to-day: how much we blush for their ignorance of the whole field of Letters!

This leads me to press home this truth—though in your case it is unnecessary—that the foundations of all true learning must be laid in the sound and thorough knowledge of Latin: which implies study marked by a broad spirit, accurate scholarship, and careful attention to details. Unless this basis be secured it is useless to attempt to rear an enduring edifice. Without it the great monuments of literature are unintelligible, and the art of composition impossible. To attain this essential knowledge we must never relax our careful attention to the grammar of the language, but perpetually confirm and extend our acquaintance with it until it is thoroughly our own. We may gain much from Servius, Donatus and Priscian, but more by careful observation in our own reading, in which we must note attentively vocabulary and inflexions, figures of speech and metaphors, and all the devices of style, such as rhythm, or antithesis, by which fine taste is exhibited. To this end we must be supremely careful in our choice of authors, lest an inartistic and debased style infect our own writing and degrade our taste; which danger is best avoided by bringing a keen, critical sense to bear upon select works, observing the sense of each passage, the structure of the sentence, the force of every word down to the least important particle. In this way our reading reacts directly upon our style.

You may naturally turn first to Christian writers, foremost amongst whom, with marked distinction, stands Lactantius, by common consent the finest stylist of the post-classical period.

22   Especially do I commend to your study his works, *'Adversus falsam Religionem,' 'De via Dei,'* and *'De opificio hominis.'* After Lactantius your choice may lie between Augustine, Jerome, Ambrose, and Cyprian; should you desire to read Gregory of Naxianzen, Chrysostom, and Basil, be careful as to the accuracy of the translations you adopt. Of the classical authors Cicero will be your constant pleasure: how unapproachable in wealth of ideas and of language, in force of style, indeed, in all that can attract in a writer! Next to him ranks Vergil, the glory and the delight of our national literature. Livy and Sallust, and then the chief poets, follow in order. The usage of these authors will serve you as your test of correctness in choice of vocabulary and of constructions.

    Now we notice in all good prose—though it is not of course obtrusive—a certain element of rhythm, which coincides with and expresses the general structure of the passage, and consequently gives a clue to its sense. I commend, therefore, to you as an aid to understanding an author the practice of reading aloud with clear and exact intonation. By this device you will seize more quickly the drift of the passage, by realising the main lines on which it is constructed. And the music of the prose thus interpreted by the voice will react with advantage upon your own composition, and at the same time will improve your own Reading by compelling deliberate and intelligent expression.

    The art of Writing is not limited to the mere formation of letters, but it concerns also the subject of the diphthongs, and of the syllabic divisions of words; the accepted usages in the writing of each letter, singly and in cursive script, and the whole field of abbreviations. This may seem a trivial matter, but a knowledge of educated practice on these points may fairly be expected from us. The laws of quantity are more important, since in poetry scansion is frequently our only certain clue to construction. One might ask, further, what capacity in poetic composition or what critical ability or taste in poetical literature is possible to a man who is not first of all secure on points of quantity and metre? Nor is prose, as I have already hinted, without its metrical element; upon which indeed Aristotle and Cicero dwelt with some minuteness. A skilful orator or historian will be careful of the effect to be gained by spondaic, iambic, dactylic or other rhythm in arousing differing emotions congruous to his matter in hand. To ignore this is to neglect one of the most delicate points of style. You will notice that such refinements will apply only to one who aspires to proficiency in the finer shades of criticism and expression, but such a one must

certainly by observation and practice become familiar with every
device which lends distinction and adornment to the literary art.

But the wider question now confronts us, that of the subject matter of our studies, that which I have already called the realities of fact and principle, as distinct from literary form. Here, as before, I am contemplating a student of keen and lofty aspiration to whom nothing that is worthy in any learned discipline is without its interest. But it is necessary to exercise discrimination. In some branches of knowledge I would rather restrain the ardour of the learner, in others, again, encourage it to the uttermost. Thus there are certain subjects in which, whilst a modest proficiency is on all accounts to be desired, a minute knowledge and excessive devotion seem to be a vain display. For instance, subtleties of Arithmetic and Geometry are not worthy to absorb a cultivated mind, and the same must be said of Astrology. You will be surprised to find me suggesting (though with much more hesitation) that the great and complex art of Rhetoric should be placed in the same category. My chief reason is the obvious one, that I have in view the cultivation most fitting to a woman. To her neither the intricacies of debate nor the oratorical artifices of action and delivery are of the least practical use, if indeed they are not positively unbecoming. Rhetoric in all its forms,—public discussion, forensic argument, logical fence, and the like—lies absolutely outside the province of woman.

What Disciplines then are properly open to her? In the first place she has before her, as a subject peculiarly her own, the whole field of religion and morals. The literature of the Church will thus claim her earnest study. Such a writer, for instance, as St Augustine affords her the fullest scope for reverent yet learned inquiry. Her devotional instinct may lead her to value the help and consolation of holy men now living; but in this case let her not for an instant yield to the impulse to look into their writings, which, compared with those of Augustine, are utterly destitute of sound and melodious style, and seem to me to have no attraction whatever.

Moreover, the cultivated Christian lady has no need in the study of this weighty subject to confine herself to ecclesiastical writers. Morals, indeed, have been treated of by the noblest intellects of Greece and Rome. What they have left to us upon Continence, Temperance, Modesty, Justice, Courage, Greatness of Soul, demands your sincere respect. You must enter into such questions as the sufficiency of Virtue to Happiness; or whether, if Happiness consist in Virtue, it can be destroyed by torture, imprisonment or exile; whether, admitting that these may prevent a man from being happy, they can be further said to make him miserable. Again, does Happiness consist (with Epicurus) in the presence of pleasure and the absence of pain: or (with Xenophon) in the consciousness of uprightness: or (with Aristotle) in the practice of Virtue? These inquiries are, of all others, most worthy to be pursued by men and women alike; they are fit material for formal discussion and for literary exercise. Let religion and morals, therefore, hold the first place in the education of a Christian lady.

But we must not forget that true distinction is to be gained by a wide and varied range of such studies as conduce to the profitable enjoyment of life, in which, however, we must observe due proportion in the attention and time we devote to them.

First amongst such studies I place History: a subject which must not on any account be neglected by one who aspires to true cultivation. For it is our duty to understand the origins of our own history and its development; and the achievements of Peoples and of Kings.

For the careful study of the past enlarges our foresight in contemporary affairs and affords to citizens and to monarchs lessons of incitement or warning in the ordering of public policy. From History, also, we draw our store of examples of moral precepts.

In the monuments of ancient literature which have come down to us History holds a position of great distinction. We specially prize such authors as Livy, Sallust and Curtius; and, perhaps even above these, Julius Caesar; the style of whose Commentaries, so elegant and so limpid, entitles them to our warm admiration. Such writers are fully within the comprehension of a studious lady. For, after all, History is an easy subject: there is nothing in its study subtle or complex. It consists in the narration of the simplest matters of fact which, once grasped, are readily retained in the memory.

The great Orators of antiquity must by all means be included. Nowhere do we find the virtues more warmly extolled, the vices so fiercely decried. From them we may learn, also, how to express consolation, encouragement, dissuasion or advice. If the principles which orators set forth are portrayed for us by philosophers, it is from the former that we learn how to employ the emotions—such as indignation, or pity—in driving home their application in individual cases. Further, from oratory we derive our store of those elegant or striking turns of expression which are used with so much effect in literary compositions. Lastly, in oratory we find that wealth of vocabulary, that clear easy-flowing style, that verve and force, which are invaluable to us both in writing and in conversation.

I come now to Poetry and the Poets—a subject with which every educated lady must shew herself thoroughly familiar. For we cannot point to any great mind of the past for whom the Poets had not a powerful attraction. Aristotle, in constantly quoting Homer, Hesiod, Pindar, Euripides and other poets, proves that he knew their works hardly less intimately than those of the philosophers. Plato, also, frequently appeals to them, and in this way covers them with his approval. If we turn to Cicero, we find him not content with quoting Ennius, Accius, and others of the Latins, but rendering poems from the Greek and employing them habitually. Seneca, the austere, not only abounds in poetical allusions, but was himself a poet; whilst the great Fathers of the Church, Jerome, Augustine, Lactantius and Boethius, reveal their acquaintance with the poets in their controversies and, indeed, in all their writings. Hence my view that familiarity with the great poets of antiquity is essential to any claim to true education. For in their writings we find deep speculations upon Nature, and upon the Causes and Origins of things, which must carry weight with us both from their antiquity and from their authorship. Besides these, many important truths upon matters of daily life are suggested or illustrated. All this expressed with such grace and dignity as demands our admiration. For example, how vividly is the art of war portrayed in Homer: the duties of a leader of men: the chances of the field: the varying temper of the host! Wise counsel, too, is not wanting, as when Hector upbraids Aeneas for too rashly urging the pursuit. Would, indeed, that in our own day our captains would deign to profit by this ancient wisdom, to the security of the commonwealth and the saving of valuable lives! Consider, again, how fitly Iris, descending upon Agamemnon in his sleep, warns against the sloth of rulers—could Socrates, Plato or Pythagoras more pointedly exhibit the responsibility of a kind of men? There are the precepts also, not fewer nor less weighty, which pertain to the arts of peace. But it is time to pass to our own Poets, to Vergil, who surpasses, it seems to me, all philosophers in displaying the inner secrets of Nature and of the Soul:

> "Know first, the heaven, the earth, the main,
> The moon's pale orb, the starry train,
>   Are nourished by a soul,

A bright intelligence, whose flame
Glows in each member of the frame
   And stirs the mighty whole.
Thence souls of men and cattle spring,
And the gay people of the wing,
And those strange shapes that ocean hides
Beneath the smoothness of the tides.
A fiery strength inspires their lives,
An essence that from heaven derives,
Though clogged in part by limbs of clay
And the dull 'vesture of decay.*'"

Nor can we deny a certain inspiration to a poet who, on the very eve of the Redeemer's birth, could speak of 'the Virgin's return,' and 'the Divine offspring sent down from on High.' So thought Lactantius, who held that the Sibyl here alludes directly to the Saviour. Such power of reading the future is implied in the name 'vates,' so often given to the true poet, and we must all recognise in such one a certain 'possession,' as by a Power other and stronger than himself.

We know, however, that in certain quarters—where all knowledge and appreciation of Letters is wanting—this whole branch of Literature, marked as it is by something of the Divine, and fit, therefore, for the highest place, is decried as unworthy of study. But when we remember the value of the best poetry, its charm of form and the variety and interest of its subject-matter, when we consider the ease with which from our childhood up it can be committed to memory, when we recall the peculiar affinity of rhythm and metre to our emotions and our intelligence, we must conclude that Nature herself is against such headlong critics. Have we not often felt the sudden uplifting of the Soul when in the solemn Office of the Mass such a passage as the 'Primo dierum omnium' bursts upon us? It is not hard for us, then, to understand what the Ancients meant when they said that the Soul is ordered in special relation to the principles of Harmony and Rhythm, and is, therefore, by no other influence so fitly and so surely moved. Hence I hold my conviction to be securely based; namely, that Poetry has, by our very constitution, a stronger attraction for us than any other form of expression, and that anyone ignorant of, and indifferent to, so valuable an aid to knowledge and so ennobling a source of pleasure can by no means be entitled to be called educated. If I seem to have dwelt at undue length upon this matter, please believe that my difficulty has rather

---

*Vergil, *Aeneid* VI. (Conington's version).

been to restrain myself, so keenly do I feel upon it. I do not forget that one of your own House has expressly taken up a position in a contrary sense. He, indeed, justly commands the respect of all. But there are disputants of another class. Their attitude is merely this: 'the themes of the ancient poets are chosen from stories of love and sin.' But I point to the tale of Penelope and Ulysses, of Alcestis and Admetus, which are but typical of many others, and I ask, 'Where can you find nobler examples of constancy and devotion, or more pointed lessons in the highest virtues of womanhood?' 'True,' it is replied, 'but there are stories of a different kind, of Phoebus and Danae, of Vulcan and Venus.' But who can fail to understand that such fictions are not to be read literally, that such episodes are insignificant in number as compared with that great array of noble figures which stand forth from the pages of Vergil and Homer, and that it is unjust criticism to ignore the beauties of any work of art and to call attention only to its blemishes? 'Yes, but, like Cato, we are willing to sacrifice the beauties so we be not soiled by the blots: hence we would neither read the poets ourselves nor put them into the hands of others.' Plato and Aristotle, however, studied the poets, and I decline to admit that in practical wisdom or in moral earnestness they yield to our modern critics. They were not Christians, indeed, but consistency of life and abhorrence of evil existed before Christianity and are independent of it. Suppose we turn to the Scriptures. We must admit that they contain not a few narratives which compare unfavourably with any treated by the poets, but we do not for that reason prohibit the Bible. When I read the loves of Aeneas and Dido in the *Aeneid* I pay my tribute of admiration to the genius of the poet, but the matter itself I know to be a fiction, and thus it leaves no moral impression: and so in other instances of the kind, where literal truth is not the object aimed at. The Scriptures, on the other hand, whose literal accuracy no one questions, not seldom cause me misgivings on this head.

But I am ready to admit that there are two types of poet: the aristocracy, so to call them, of their craft, and the vulgar, and that the latter may be put aside in ordering a woman's reading. A comic dramatist may season his wit too highly: a satirist describe too bluntly the moral corruption which he scourges: let her pass them by. Vergil, on the other hand, Seneca, Statius, and others like them, rank with the noblest names, and may, nay must, be the trusted companions of all who aspire to be called cultivated.

To sum up what I have endeavoured to set forth. That high standard of education to which I referred at the outset is only to be reached by one who has seen many things and read much. Poet, Orator, Historian, and the rest, all must be studied, each must contribute a share. Our learning thus becomes full, ready, varied and elegant, available for action or for discourse in all subjects. But to enable us to make effectual use of what we know we must add to our knowledge the power of expression. These two sides of learning, indeed, should not be separated: they afford mutual aid and distinction. Proficiency in literary form, not accompanied by broad acquaintance with facts and truths, is a barren attainment; whilst information, however vast, which lacks all grace of expression, would seem to be put under a bushel or partly thrown away. Indeed, one may fairly ask what advantage it is to possess profound and varied learning if one cannot convey it in language worthy of the subject. Where, however, this double capacity exists —breadth of learning and grace of style—we allow the highest title to distinction and to abiding fame. If we review the great names of ancient literature, Plato, Democritus, Aristotle, Theophrastus, Varro, Cicero, Seneca, Augustine, Jerome, Lactantius, we shall find it hard to say whether we admire more their attainments or their literary power.

But my last word must be this. The intelligence that aspires to the best must aim at both. In doing so, all sources of profitable learning will in due proportion claim your study. None have more urgent claim than the subjects and authors which treat of Religion and of our duties in the world; and it is because they assist and illustrate these supreme studies that I press upon your attention the works of the most approved poets, historians and orators of the past.

DESIDERIUS ERASMUS (1466–1536)

Perhaps the most universally recognized spokesman for the Renaissance, Erasmus conveyed the essence of the period through his writing, in which he advocated a return to the study of classical literature. Erasmus, a Dutch celibate monk, was influenced by early work of the Spanish humanist Vives, with whom he established steadfast correspondence. They consistently read one another's books, and grew in mutual respect.

Exposure to the home of Sir Thomas More convinced Erasmus that women were entitled to receive a liberal education, and that their attainment of advanced learning would benefit the family and society. In fact, Erasmus became contemptuous of the prevalent education of girls. He encouraged women to study whatever would assist them in educating their own children and in becoming intellectual companions to their husbands. He not only approved light literature for girls, but even wrote for them.

Among his *Colloquies* is "The Abbot and the Learned Lady," which features an ignorant abbot giving time-worn arguments used by the common people who opposed education of women. The competent debater is a young lady, Magdalia, who undoubtedly represents the intellectually able Margaret More Roper, daughter of Sir Thomas More. This clever dialogue was written in 1524.

THE ABBOT AND THE LEARNED LADY*

Antronius, Magdalia

ANTRONIUS. What furnishings do I see here?

MAGDALIA. Elegant, aren't they;

*Reprinted from Thompson, Craig R. (trans.). *The Colloquies of Erasmus.* Chicago: University of Chicago Press, 1965, pp. 219-223. By permission of the publisher.

ANT. How elegant I don't know, but certainly unbecoming both to a young miss and a married woman.

MAGD. Why?

ANT. Because the whole place is filled with books.

MAGD. Are you so old, an abbot as well as a courtier, and have never seen books in court ladies' houses?

ANT. Yes, but those were in French. Here I see Greek and Latin ones.

MAGD. Are French books the only ones that teach wisdom?

ANT. But it's fitting for court ladies to have something with which to beguile their leisure.

MAGD. Are court ladies the only ones allowed to improve their minds and enjoy themselves?

ANT. You confuse growing wise with enjoying yourself. It's not feminine to be brainy. A lady's business is to have a good time.

MAGD. Shouldn't everyone live well?

ANT. Yes, in my opinion.

MAGD. But who can have a good time without living well?

ANT. Rather, who can enjoy himself if he *does* live well?

MAGD. So you approve of those who live basely if only they have a good time?

ANT. I believe those who have a good time are living well.

MAGD. Where does this good time come from? From externals or from within?

ANT. From externals.

MAGD. Shrewd abbot but stupid philosopher! Tell me: how do you measure good times?

ANT. By sleep, dinner parties, doing as one likes, money, honors.

MAGD. But if to these things God added wisdom, you wouldn't enjoy yourself?

ANT. What do you mean by wisdom?

MAGD. This: understanding that a man is not happy without the goods of the mind; that wealth, honors, class make him neither happier nor better.

ANT. Away with that wisdom!

MAGD. What if I enjoy reading a good author more than you do hunting, drinking, or playing dice? You won't think I'm having a good time?

ANT. *I* wouldn't live like that.

MAGD. I'm not asking what *you* would enjoy most, but what *ought* to be enjoyable.

ANT. I wouldn't want my monks to spend their time on books.

MAGD. Yet my husband heartily approves of my doing so. But exactly why do you disapprove of this in your monks?

ANT. Because I find they're less tractable; they talk back by quoting from decrees and decretals, from Peter and Paul.

MAGD. So your rules conflict with those of Peter and Paul?

ANT. What *they* may enjoin I don't know, but still I don't like a monk who talks back. And I don't want any of mine to know more than I do.

MAGD. You could avoid that by endeavoring to know as much as possible.

ANT. I haven't the leisure.

MAGD. How come?

ANT. Because I've no free time.

MAGD. No free time to grow wise?

ANT. No.

MAGD. What hinders you?

ANT. Long prayers, housekeeping, hunts, horses, court functions.

MAGD. So. These are more important to you than wisdom?

ANT. It's what we're used to.

MAGD. Now tell me this: if some heavenly power enabled you to turn your monks and yourself too into any animal whatever, would you change them into hogs and yourself into a horse?

ANT. Not at all.

MAGD. But by doing so you'd prevent anybody's being wiser than you.

ANT. I shouldn't much care what sort of animal the monks were, provided I myself were a human being.

MAGD. Do you think one is human if he's neither wise nor wants to be wise?

ANT. I'm wise enough—so far as I'm concerned.

MAGD. And swine are wise enough so far as *they're* concerned.

ANT. You strike me as a sophistress, so keenly do you dispute.

MAGD. I won't say how you strike me! But why do these furnishings displease you?

ANT. Because distaff and spindle are the proper equipment for women.

MAGD. Isn't it a wife's business to manage the household and rear the children?

ANT. It is.

MAGD. Do you think she can manage so big a job without wisdom?

ANT. I suppose not.

MAGD. But books teach me this wisdom.

ANT. Sixty-two monks I have at home, yet you won't find a single book in my cell.

MAGD. Those monks are well provided for!

ANT. I could put up with books, but not Latin ones.

MAGD. Why not?

ANT. Because that language isn't fit for women.

MAGD. I want to know why.

ANT. Because it does little to protect their chastity.

MAGD. Therefore French books, full of the most frivolous stories, do promote chastity?

ANT. There's another reason.

MAGD. Tell me plainly, whatever it is.

ANT. They're safer from priests if they don't know Latin.

MAGD. Very little danger from you in that respect, since you take such pains not to know Latin!

ANT. The public agrees with me, because it's a rare and exceptional thing for a woman to know Latin.

MAGD. Why cite the public, the worst possible authority on conduct? Why tell me of custom, the mistress of every vice? Accustom yourself to the best; then the unusual will become habitual; the harsh, enjoyable; the apparently unseemly, seemly.

ANT. I hear you.

MAGD. Is it fitting for a German woman to learn French?

ANT. Of course.

MAGD. Why?

ANT. To talk with those who know French.

MAGD. And do you think it unsuitable for me to know Latin in order to converse daily with authors so numerous, so eloquent, so learned, so wise; with counselors so faithful?

ANT. Books ruin women's wits—which are none too plentiful anyway.

MAGD. How plentiful *yours* are, I don't know. Assuredly I prefer to spend mine, however slight, on profitable studies rather than on prayers said by rote, all-night parties, and heavy drinking.

ANT. Bookishness drives people mad.

MAGD. The company of boozers, jesters, and mimes doesn't drive you mad?

ANT. Not at all. It relieves boredom.

MAGD. Then how could such delightful companions as mine drive me mad?

ANT. That's what people say.

MAGD. But the plain fact of the matter says something else. How many more we see driven mad through intemperate wining and dining, night-long bouts of drunkenness, uncontrolled passions!

ANT. I'm sure I wouldn't want a learned wife.

MAGD. But I congratulate myself on having a husband different from you. For learning renders him dearer to me, and me dearer to him.

ANT. Learning costs immense toil, and after all you must die.

MAGD. Tell me, my dear sir: if you had to die tomorrow, would you rather die more foolish or more wise?

ANT. If wisdom came without hard work—

MAGD. But man gets nothing in this life without hard work. And yet whatever he does win, with however much labor, must be left behind. Why should we hesitate to take pains in the most precious thing of all, the fruits of which accompany us to another life also?

ANT. I've often heard the common saying, "A wise woman is twice foolish."

MAGD. That's commonly said, yes, but by fools. A woman truly wise is not wise in her own conceit. On the other hand, one who thinks herself wise when she knows nothing is indeed twice foolish.

ANT. I don't know how it is, but as packsaddles don't fit an ox, so learning doesn't fit a woman.

MAGD. But you can't deny that packsaddles would fit an ox better than a miter would fit an ass or a swine.—What's your feeling about the Virgin Mother?

ANT. I reverence her.

MAGD. Didn't she read books?

ANT. Yes, but not these.

MAGD. What did she read, then?

ANT. The canonical Hours.

MAGD. According to which use?

ANT. The Benedictine.

MAGD. Very likely! What about Paula and Eustochium? Didn't they read the Sacred Scriptures?

ANT. But that's rare nowadays.

MAGD. So was an unlettered abbot a rare bird once upon a time! Nowadays nothing's more common. Once upon a time princes and emperors excelled as much in learning as in might. But even now this isn't so rare as you suppose. In Spain and Italy there are not a few women of the highest rank who can rival any man. In England there are the More girls, in Germany the Pirckheimer and Blauer girls. If you're not careful, the net result will be that we'll preside in the theological schools, preach in the churches, and wear your miters.

ANT. God forbid!

MAGD. No, it will be up to *you* to forbid. But if you keep on as you've begun, geese may do the preaching sooner than put up with you tongue-tied pastors. The world's a stage that's topsy-turvy now, as you see. Every man must play his part or—exit.

ANT. How did I run across this woman? When *you* come calling on *us,* I'll treat you more politely.

MAGD. How?

ANT. We'll dance, drink as much as we please, hunt, play games, and laugh.

MAGD. For my part, I feel like laughing even now.

JUAN LUIS VIVES (1492–1540)

Born to a family of noble status, Vives received an early education from his gifted mother. Subsequently, he studied in Paris, then earned a Doctor of Law degree from Oxford, where he became a lecturer in philosophy.

Vives was in theoretical agreement with Bruni and Erasmus; indeed, he acknowledged Erasmus' influence upon his own learning theory. As did Erasmus, he opposed Scholasticism, the medieval philosophy which stressed adherence to church doctrine. This opposition led Vives to attempt to combine the principles of Christianity and Humanism.

Certainly not a total revolutionary, Vives encouraged women to engage in prayer, and urged them not to participate in such customs as dancing, face painting, hair bleaching, or wearing clothing of extreme style. He recommended that hard work be accompanied by a diet of cold water and vegetables. He reminded girls of their obligation to care for sick family members and to cook for the household.

However, Vives broke with tradition sufficiently to have been acclaimed the first great modern student of educational theory. Aware of the prevailing inadequate preparation of teachers, he proposed a type of Normal School education. He recommended that girls receive a classical education combined with domestic science, on the assumption that scientific study would enhance cooking and nursing skills.

Vives influenced education both in the French Royal Court and in the English Royal Court. Catherine of Aragon summoned him to tutor Mary, her daughter by King Henry VIII. It was this Mary who would become known as Bloody Mary during her reign as Queen of England.

In agreement with the teaching of Quintilian, Vives advanced the notion that a mother must nourish not only the body but also the mind of her child.

The following partial reproduction is from a 1524 essay, "The Instruction of a Christian Woman," which is believed to have been the first post-medieval literary tribute by an author to his mother.

THE INSTRUCTION OF A CHRISTIAN WOMAN

"Of the lernyng of maydes," Chapter iv

Of maides some be but lyttell mete for lernynge. Lyke wyse as some men be unapte, agayne some be even borne unto it, or at leste not unfete for it. Therfore they that be dulle are not to be discoraged, and those that be apte, shulde be hartened and encoraged. I perceive that lerned women be suspected of many: as who sayth, the subtylitie of lerning shulde be a norisshement for the malitiousnes of their nature. Verely I do not alowe in a subtill and a crafty woman suche lerning, as shulde teche her disceite, and teche her no good maners and vertues: Not withstandinge the preceptes of living, and the examples of those that have lived well, and had knowlege to gether or holines, be the kepers of chastite and purenes, and the copies of vertues, and pryckes to pricke and to move folkes to continue in them. Aristotel asketh a question, why trompettes and minstrelles, that play at festes for wages, and resortynges and gatherynges of people, whome the Grekes call in their language, as ye wold say, Bacchus servantes, be ever gyven unto pleasures, and no goodnesse at all, but spend out their thrifte, and their lyfe in noughtynes. He maketh answere hym selfe, that it is so, bycause they be ever among volupties and pleasures, and bankettynge, nor here any tyme the preceptes of good living, nor regard any man that lyveth wel, and therefore they can lyve none other wyse, than they have lerned, eyther by seing or heryng. No have they heard, nor sene, neither used any thing, but pleasure and beastlines, among uncomely cryeng and shouttynge, amonge dauncers and kyssers, laughers and eaters, drunkerdes and spewers, amonge folke drowned in excedynge overmuche joye and gladnes, all care and mynde of goodnes laid aparte. Therfore must they nedes shew such thinges in their conditions all their lyfe. But you shal not lightly fynde an evyll womanne, excepte it be suche one, as eyther knoweth not, or at leste way considereth not what chastite and honesty is worth, nor seeth what mischiefe she doeth, when she

---

*From the translation by Richard Hyrde. London: T. Berthelet, 1540, pp. 6-10.

forgoeth it, nor regardeth how great a treasure, for howe fowle, for howe light, and transitory an image of pleasure she changeth, what a sort of ungratiousness is she letteth in, what tyme she shutteth forthe chastyte, nor pondreth what bodily pleasure is, how vayne and foolyshe a thinge, which is not worthe the turnynge of an hande, not only unworthy, wherefore she shulde caste away that which is the most goodly treasure, that a woman can have. And she that hath lerned in bookes to caste this and such other thinges, and hath furnyshed and fenced her mynde with holy counsayles, shal never fynd to do any vylany. For if she can fynd in her harte to do naughtyly, havyng so many preceptes of vertue to kepe her, what shulde we suppose she shuld do, havyng no knowleg of goodnes at all? And truly if we wold call the old world to remembrance, and reherse their tyme, we shall fynde no lerned woman that ever was evyll, where I coude brynge forth an hundred good, as Cornelia the mother of Gracchus, which was an example of all goodnes and chastite, and taught her children her owne selfe. And Portia, the wyfe of Brutus, that tooke of her fathers wysedome. And Cleobula, daughter of Cleobulus, one of the seven wyse men, which Cleobula was to gyven unto lernynge and philosophie, that she clerely dispised all pleasure of the body, and lived perpetually a mayde, at whome the daughter of Pithagoras the philosopher tooke example, which after her fathers dethe was the ruler of his schoole, and was made the maystress of the college of virgins. Also Theaneo, one of the same secte and schoole, daughter unto Metapontus, whiche had also the gift of prophesy, was a woman of singular chastite. And saint Jeromme sayth, that the ten Sibilles were virgins. Also Cassandra, and prophetes of Appollo, and Juno at Crissa, were virgins. And that was a common thing, as we rede, that those women that were prophetes, were virgins. And she that answered such as came to aske any thinge of Appollo in Delphis, was ever a virgine, of whom the first was Phemone, which firste found verse royal. Also Sulpitia, wyfe unto Caleno, lefte behynde her holy preceptes of matrimony, that she had used in her lyvinge herselfe, of whome the poet Martiall writeth on this wyse.

Redeth Sulpitia all yonge women,
That cast youre mynde to please one man.
Redeth Sulpitia also all men
That do entende to please one woman.
Of honest and vertuous love, doth she tell,
Chaste pastymes, playes, and pleasure,

Whole bookes who so considereth well,
Shall say ther is none holyer.

(Martial, Book X, Epigram 35, *De Sulpitia*)

And it is playnely knowen, that no man in that tyme was more happy wyfe than was Caleno of Sulpitia. Hortentia, the daughter of Hortentius the oratour, did so resemble her fathers eloquence, that she made an oration unto the judges of the cyty for the women, which oration the successours of that tyme dyd rede, not only as a laud and prayse of womens eloquence, but also to lerne counnynge of it, as well as of Cicero or Demosthenes orations. Edesia of the city of Alexandre, kinswoman unto Sirian the philosopher, was of so great lernynge and vertuous disposition, that she was a woundre unto all the worlde in her tyme. Corinna Theia, a vertuous woman, over came the poete Pindar five tymes in verses. Paula, the wyfe of Seneca, enfourmed with the doctrine of her husband, folowed also her husband in conditions. And Seneca hym selfe maketh sorowe that hys mother was not wel lerned in the preceptes of wyse men, whiche she had ben entred in at her husbandes commandement. Argentaria Polla, wyfe unto the poet Lucan, whiche after her husbandes dethe corected his bookes, and it is sayde, that she helped hym with the makynge, was a noble woman of birthe, ryche, and excellent of beautie, and wyt, and chastite, of whome Calliope in Statius, speaketh thus unto Lucan.

I shall not gyve the onely excellence in makynge,
But also bynde a mariage, thee unto
One mete for thy wytte and great counnyng,
Suche as Venus wold give, or the goddes Juno,
In beauty, symplicite, and gentilnes,
In byrthe, grace, favour, and riches.

(Statius, *Sylvae,* Book ii, VII, 81 and following)

Also Diodorus the logitian had five doughters excellent in lernynge and chastite: of whome Philo mayster unto Carneades, writeth the history. Zenobia, the queene of Palmyra, was lerned both in Latyne and Greke, and wrote an history, of whome, with other more in the nexte booke, I shall tell the marvaylous chastite. I nede not to reherse the Christen women, as Tecla, disciple of Paule, a scholer mete for suche a noble mayster, and Cateryne of Alexandria, doughter unto Costus, whiche overcame in disputations the greattest and moste exercised philosophers. There was one of the same name Catheryne Senensis, a wondrous counnynge mayde, which hath lefte behynde her examples of her witte: in the whyche doth appere the purenes of her moste holy mynde. Nor we nede not to envy the pagans for their poetes, whiche have in one house foure maydes all poetes, all doughters of Philippe. And in saynt Jeromes tyme all holy women were very well lerned. Wolde god that nowe a dayes, many olde men were able to be compared unto them in counnynge. Saynt Jerome wryteth unto Paula, Leta, Eustachium, Fabiola, Marcella, Furia, Demetrias, Salma, and Hierontia: Saynt Ambrose unto other: Saynt Augustyne unto other, and all marvelous wytted, well lerned, and holy. Valeria Proba, whiche loved her husbande syngularly well, made the lyfe of our lorde Christe out of Virgils verses. Wryters of Cronicles say, that Theodosia, doughter unto Theodosius the yonger, was as noble by her lernynge and vertue, as by her Empire, and the makynges that be taken out of Homer named Centones be called hers. I have red epistoles and counnyng workes of Hildegard, a mayde of Almayne. There hath bene sene in our time the foure doughters of quene Isabel, of whom I spake a lytell before, that were well lerned all. It is tolde me with great preise and marvayle in many places of this countre, that dame Joanne, the wyfe of kinge Philippe, mother unto Carolus that nowe is, was wont to make answere in Latyne, and that without any study unto the orations that were made after the custome in townes, unto new princes. The same sayth every body by the other two systers, which be dead in Portugal. Than which foure systers there were no more quenes by any mannes remembrance more chaste of body thanne they, none of better name, none better loved of their subjectes, nor more favored, nor better loved their husbandes, none that more lawely did obey them, nor that kepte bothe theym and all theirs, better without spotte of vilany; there were none that more hated filthynes and wantonnes, none that ever did more perfectly fulfyll all the poyntes of a good woman.

Nowe if a man may be suffered among quenes to speke of more mean folkes, I wold reken amonge this sort the daughters of S. T. M. kn: M. E. and C, and with them their kynnes woman, M. G.*
whome their father, not content only to have them good and very chast, wold also they shuld be well lerned, supposynge that by that meane they shuld be more truly and surely chast. Wher in neyther that great wyse man is disceyved, nor none other that are of the same opinion. For the study of lerning is such a thing, that it

---

*Sir Thomas More Knight: Margaret, Elizabeth, Cecilia; and Margaret Giggs.

occupieth ones mind holly, and lifteth it up unto the knowlege of most goodly matters, and plucketh it from the remembraunce of such thinges as be foul. And if any such thought come in to their mynd, eyther the mynde, well fortified with the preceptes of good lyvynge, avoydeth them away, or els it gyveth none hede unto those thynges that be vyle and foule, when it hath other most goodly and pure pleasure, where with it is delyted. And therfore I suppose that Pallas, the goddes of wysedome and counyng, and all the Muses, were feyned in olde tyme to be virgyns. And the mynde, set upon lernynge and wysedome, shall not only abhore from foul luste, that is to saye the moste whyte thinge from soot, and most pure from spottes. But also they shall leave all suche lyght and triflynge pleasures, wherin the lyght fantasies of maydes have delite, as songes, daunces, and suche other wanton and peevyshe playes. A woman, saythe Plutarche, given unto lerning, wyll never delyte in daunsynge. But here paraventure a man wolde aske, what lernynge a woman shuld be set unto, and what shall she study: I have tolde you. The study of wisdome, the which doth enstruct their maners, and enfourme their lyving, and teacheth them the waye of good and holy lyfe. As for eloquence, I have no great care, nor a woman nedeth it not, but she nedeth goodnes and wysedome. Nor it is no shame for a woman to holde her peace, but it is shame for her and abomynable to lack discretion, and to lyve yll. Nor I wyll not here condempne eloquence, which both Quintilian, and saint Jerome folowyng hym, say, was preysed in Cornelya, the mother of Gracchus, and in Hortentia, the doughter of Hortentius. If there may be founde any holy and well lerned woman, I had rather have her to teach them. If there be none, let us chose some man either well aged, or els very good and vertuous, which hathe a wyfe, and that right faire enoughe, whome he lovethe well, and so shall he not desire other. For these thinges oughte to be sene unto, for as muche as chastite in bringinge up a woman requireth the most dilygence, and in a maner all to gether. When she shal be taught to rede, let those bookes be taken in hand, that may teche good maners. And whan she that lerne to wryte, let not her example be voyd verses, nor wanton or triflynge songes, but some sad sentence, prudent and chaste, taken out of holy scripture, or the sayenges of philosophers, which by other wrytyng she may fasten better in her memory. And in lernynge, as I poyntenone end to the manne, no more I doo to the woman: saying it is mete that the man have knowlege of many and divers thinges, that may both profit hym selfe and the comon welthe, bothe with the use and increasinge of lernyng. But I wold the woman shuld be al to gether in that parte of philosophy that takethe upon it to enfourme, and teche, and amende the conditions. Finally, let her lerne for her selfe alone and her yonge children, or her systers in our lorde. For it neyther becometh a woman to rule a schole, nor to lyve amonge men, or speke abrode, and shake off her demurenes and honesty, eyther all together or els a great parte: which if she be good, it were better to be at home within and unknownen to other folkes. And in company to hold her tonge demurely. And let fewe see her, and none at all here her. The apostle Paule, the vessell of election, enfourming and teachynge the churche of the Corinthis with holy preceptes, saythe: Let youre women holde their tonges in congregations, nor they be not allowed to speake but to be subjecte as the lawe biddeth. If they wolde lerne any thing, lette them aske their husbandes at home. And unto his disciple, Timothe, he wrytethe on this wyse: Let a woman lerne in sylence with a subjection. But I gyve no lycence to a woman to be a techer, nor to have authorite of the man, but to be in silence. For Adam was the fyrst made: and after Eve, and Adame was not betrayed, the woman was betrayed in to the breche of the commandement. Therfore bycause a woman is a frayle thinge, and of weake discretion, and that may lightly be disceyved, whiche thinge our fyrste mother Eve sheweth, whome the dyvell caught with a lyght argument. Therfore a woman shuld not teache, leste when she hath taken a false opinion and belove of any thyng, she spred it in to the herars, by the authorite of maystershypp, and lyghtly bringe other in to the same errour, for the lerners commonly do after the teacher with good wyll.

PART IV: REFORMATION

The classical, humanistic milieu of the Renaissance gave way to the more practical education of the sixteenth and seventeenth centuries—the Reformation, which was ushered in by religious upheaval. The widespread closing of nunneries substantially diminished opportunities for girls and women to receive a formal education, but Martin Luther advanced the notion of individual interpretation of the Bible. This concept induced the public to recognize a need for universal literacy.

An increase in world trade signalled the rise of a class of merchants who needed to read and write in the vernacular, not in Latin and Greek; public primary schools responded to this need. This situation reflected a necessity for educational change for girls as well as for boys, because significant numbers of women shared business responsibilities with their merchant-husbands.

Prominent men in Europe took an active interest in the education of women, while women themselves followed this lead. Evidence of this involvement is apparent in the fact that the first female author whose work is included in this volume lived during the Reformation. Moreover, Cresacre More, the first male Reformation author quoted here, was chosen for representation in his collection not for his own accomplishments, but because of the scholarly achievements of his female ancestors.

CRESACRE MORE (1572–1649)

In 1626 Cresacre More, an English theologian and author, wrote *The Life and Death of Sir Thomas More,* a biography of his great-grandfather.

Thomas More (1478-1535) has been praised lavishly for the distinguished educational achievements of his one son and three daughters, who were taught by More and by tutors. Having provided a thorough academic foundation, More persisted in expanding their knowledge and use of literary skills, primarily through encouraging them to write daily letters to him when they were apart. His eldest daughter, Margaret, was his favorite as well as the most intellectually gifted of the girls. Proficient in Latin and Greek, she wrote and translated in three languages. She corresponded with Erasmus, who referred to the More household as an academy.

The following letters written by Thomas More to his daughter Margaret provide an example of his abiding influence upon her academic performance as well as an indication of his enlightened views on female education. Cresacre More's commentary further clarifies recognition awarded Margaret.

THE LIFE AND DEATH OF SIR THOMAS MORE*

Another epistle of Sir Thomas More to his Children. Thomas More to his whole schoole sendeth greetinge: Beholde how I have found out acompendious way to salute you all, and make spare of time and paper, which I must needes have wasted in saluting everie one of you particularly by your names; which would be verie superfluous, because you are all so deare unto me, some in one respect, some in another, that I can omitt none of you unsaluted. Yet, I knowe not, whether there can be anie better motive, why I

*Reprinted from More, Cresacre, *The Life and Death of Sir Thomas More.* England: Scolar Press, Ltd., 1630; Mentston, Yorkshire, England: The Scolar Press, Ltd., 1971, pp. 173-192. By permission of the publisher.

44   should love you, then because you are schollars, learning seeming
to binde me more strayely unto you, then the nearenesse of bloud.
I rejoyce therefore that *Mr. Drue* is returned safe, of whose safetie
you knowe I was carefull. If I loved you not exceedingly, I should
envie this your so great happinesse, to have had so manie great
schollars for your maisters. For I thinke *Mr. Nicolas* is with you
also, and that you have learned of him much astronomie; so farre
in this science, that you now knowe not only the pole-starre, or
dogg, and such like of the common Constellations, but also, which
argueth an absolute and cunning astronomer, in the chiefe planetts
themselves: you are able to discerne the sunne from the moone; goe
forward therefore with this your new and admirable skill, by which
you do thus climbe up to the starres, which whilst you daily admire,
in the meane while I admonish you also to thinke of this holie fast
of Lent, and lett that excellent and pious song of *Boethius* sound in
your eares, whereby you are taught also with your mindes to
penetrate beauten, least when the bodie is lifted upon high, the
soule be driven downe to the earth with the brute beasts. Farewell.
From the Court this 23th of March.

   Another. Thomas More to his beloved Children, and to
Margarett Gigs, whome he numbreth amongst his owne, sendeth
greeting: The merchant of *Bristow* brought unto me your letters, the
next day after he had receaved them of you, with which I was
exceedingly delighted. For there can come nothing, yea though it
were never so rude, never so meanely polished, from this your
shoppe, but it procureth me more delight than anie other mens
workes, be they never so eloquent; your writing do so stirre up my
affection towards you; but excluding these your letters may also
very well please me for their owne worth, being full of fine witt, and
of a pure Latine phrase. But therefore none of them all, but joyed
me exceedingly, yet to tell you ingeniously what I thinke, my sonne
John's letter pleased me best, both because it was longer than the
other, as also for that he seemeth to have taken more paynes than
the rest. For he not only paynteth out the matter decently, and
speaketh elegantly, but he playeth also pleasantly with me, and
returneth my jeastes upon me againe very wittily; and this he doth
not only pleasantly, but temperately withall, shewing that he is
mindefull with whome he jeasteth, to witt, his father, whome he
endeavoureth so to delight, that he is also afeared to offende.
Hereafter I expect everie day letters from everie one of you; neither
will I accept of such excuses, as you complaine of, that you have no
leasure, or that the Carrier went away suddenly, or that you have

no matter to write; John is not wont to alleage anie such things; nothing can hinder you from writing, but manie things may exhort you thereto, why should you lay anie faulte upon the Carrier, seing you may prevent his coming, and have them readie made up, and sealed two daies before anie offer themselves to carrie them. And how can you want matter of writing unto me, who am delighted to heare eyther of your studies, or of your play: whome you may even then please exceedingly, when have nothing to write of, you write as largely as you can of that nothing, then which nothing is more easie for you to doe, especially being women, and therefore pratlers by nature, and amongst whome daily a great storie riseth of nothing. But this I admonish you to doe, that whether you write of serious matters, or of trifles, you write with diligence and consideration, premeditating of it before; neither will it be amisse, if you first indite it in English, for then it may more easily be translated into Latine, whilst the minde free from inventing is attentive to finde apt and eloquent wordes. And although I putt this to your choice, whether you will do so or no: yet I enjoyne you by all meanes, that you diligently examine what you have written, before you write it over fayre againe; first considering attentively the whole sentence, and after examine everie parte thereof, by which meanes you may easily finde out, if anie solecismes have escaped you: which being putt out, and your letter written fayre, yet then lett it not also trouble to examine it over againe; for sometimes the same faultes creepe in at the second writing, which you before had blotted out. By this your diligence you will procure, that those your trifles will seeme serious matters. For as nothing is so pleasing but may be made unsavorie by prating garrulitie; so nothing is by nature so unpleasant, that by industrie may not be made full of grace and pleasantnesse. Farewell my sweetest Children. From the Court this 3. of September.

Another letter to his daughter Margarett only: Thy letters (dearest *Margarett*) were gratefull unto me, which certified me of the state of Shaw; yet would they have bene more gratefull unto me, if they had tolde me, what your and your brother's studies were, what is read amongst you everie day, how pleasantly you conferre togeather, what themes you make, and how you passe the day away amongst you in the sweete fruits of learning. And although nothing is written from you, but it is most pleasing unto me, yet those things are most sugred sweete, which I cannot learne of but by you or your brother. *And in the ende:* I pray thee, *Megg,* see that I understande by you, what your studies are. For rather then I would suffer you, my children, to live idely, I would my self looke unto you, with the losse of my temporall estate, bidding all other cares and businesses Farewell, amongst which there is nothing more sweete unto me, then thyself, my dearest daughter. Farewell.

It seemeth also by another letter of his, how careful he was that his children might be learned and diligent, and he prayseth them for it thus: Thomas More sendeth greeting to his most deare daughters *Margarett, Elizabeth* and *Cecilie;* and to *Margarett Gigs* as deare to him as if she were his owne. I cannot sufficiently expresse, my best beloved wenches, how your eloquent letters have exceedingly pleased me; and this is not the least cause, that I understande by them, you have not in your journeys, though you change places often, omitted anie thing of your custome of exercising yourselves, either in making of Declamations, composing of verses, or in your Logike exercises; by this I perswade my selfe, that you dearely love me, because I see you have so great a care to please me by your diligence in my absence, as to perfourme these things, which you knowe how gratefull they are unto me in my presence. And as I finde this your minde and affection so much to delight me, so will I procure that my returne shall be profitable unto you. And perswade yourselves that there is nothing amongst these my troublesome & carefull affaires that recreateth me so much, as when I reade somewhat of your labours, by which I understande those things to be true, which your most loving maister writeth so lovingly of you, that unlesse your owne epistles did shew evidently unto me, how earnest your desire is towards learning, I should have judged that he had written of affection then according to the truth: but now by these that you write, you make him to be believed, and me to imagine those things to be true of your wittie and acute dispistacions, which he boasteth of you almost above all beliefe; I am therefore marvelous desirous to come home, that we may heare them, and sett our schollar to dispute with you, who is slowe to believe, yea out of all hope or conceipt to finde you able, to be answerable to your master's prayses. But I hope, knowing how steadfast you are in your affections, that you will shortly overcome your maister, if not in disputing, at least in not leaving of your strife. Farewell, deare wenches.

And thus you may conjecture how learned his daughters were; to whome for this respect Erasmus dedicated his Commentarie upon Ouide de nuce. Lewis Vives also writeth great commendations of this schoole of Sir Thomas More's in his booke to Q. Catherine of England. And both Erasmus dedicated Aristotle in Greeke, and Simon

Grineus, who although an heretike, yet in respect of his learning had *bene kindely used by Sir Thomas More, as he writeth himself, did* *dedicate Plato and other bookes in Greeke unto my grandfather John* *More as to one that was also very skillful in that toung. See what* *Grineus speaketh unto him:* There was a great necessitie, why I should dedicate these books of *Proclus* full of marvelous learning, by my paynes sett out, but not without the singular benefitt of your father effected, unto you, to whome by reason of your father-like vertues all the fruite of this benefitt is to rebounde, both because you may be an ornamet unto them, and they also may doe great good unto you, whome I knowe to be learned, and for these grave disputacions sufficiently provided and made fitt, by the continued conversation of so worthie a father, and by the companie of your sisters, who are most expert in all kinde of sciences. For what Authour can be more gratefull to those desirous mindes of most goodlie things, such as you and the Muses your sisters are, whome a divine heate of spiritt to the admiration and a new example of this our age, hath driven into the sea of learning so farre, and so happily, that they see no learning to be above their reache, no disputations of philosophie above their capacities: And none can better explicate engangled questions, none sifte them more profoundly, nor none conceave them more easily, then this authour.

Lett us see another letter to his daughter Margarett only: You aske monye, deare *Megg,* too shamefully & fearefully of your father, who is both desirous to give it you, and your letter hath deserved it, which I could finde in my hart to recompence, not as *Alexander* did by *Cherilus,* giving him for everie verse a Philippine of golde; but if my abilitie were answerable to my will, I would bestowe two Crownes of pure golde for everie fillable thereof. Here I sende you as much as you requested, being willing to have sent you more; but that as I am glad to give, so I am desirous to be asked and fawned on by my daughters, thee especially, whome vertue and learning hath made most deare unto me. Wherefore the sooner you have spent this money well as you are wont to doe, and the sooner you aske for more, the sooner knowe you will doe your father a singular pleasure. Farewell my most beloved daughter.

This daughter was likest her father as well in favour as witt, and *proved a most rare woman for learning, sanctitie, and secrecie, and* *therefore he trusted her with all his secretts. She wrote two Declama-* *tions in English, which her father and she turned into Latine so* *elegantly, as one could hardly judge, which was the best. She made* *also a treatise of the Foure Last things; which her father sincerely protested, that it was better than his, and therefore, it may be, never finished his. She corrected by her witt a place in S. Cyprian, corrupted, as Pamelian and John Coster testifye, in steede of nisi vos sinceritatis, rectoring nervos sinceritatis. To her Eramus wrote an epistle, as to a woman not only famous for manners, and vertue, but most of all for learning. We have heretofore made mention of her letter that Cardinal Poole so liked, that when he had read it, he would not believe it could be anie womans; in answer whereof Sir Thomas did sende her the letter, some parte whereof we have seene before; the rest is this, which though there were no other testimonie of her extraordinarie learning, might suffice:* In the meanetime, *saith her father,* I thought with my self how true I found that now, which once I remember I spoke unto you in jeaste, when I pittied your hard happe, that men that read your writings, would suspect you to have had helpe of some other man therein, which would derogate somewhat from the praises due to your workes; seing that you of all others deserved least to have such a suspition had of you, for that you never could abide to be decked with the plumes of other birds. But you, sweete *Megg,* are rather to be praised for this, that seing you cannot hope for condigne praise of your labours, yet for all this you goe forward with this your invincible courrage, to joyne with your vertue the knowledge of most excellent sciences: and contenting yourself with your owne pleasure in learning you never hunte after vulgar praises, nor receave them willingly, though they be offered you; And for your singular pietie and love towards me, you esteeme me and your husband a sufficient and ample theater for you to content you with; who in requitall of this your affection beseech God and our Ladie, with as hartie praiers as possible we can powre out, to give you an easie and happie childbirth, to encrease your familie with a child most like yourself, except only in sexe; yet if it be a wench, that it may be such a one, as would in time recompece by imitation of her mothers learning and vertues, what by the condition of her sexe may be wanting; such a wenche I should preferr before three boys. Farewell, dearest daughter.

But see, I pray you, how a most learned bishopp in England was ravished with her learning and witt, as it appeareth by a letter, which her father wrote unto her to certifye her thereof. Thomas More sendeth hartie greeting to his dearest daughter *Margarett:* I will lett passe to tell you, my sweetest daughter, how much your letter delighted me; you may imagine how exceedingly it pleased your father, when you understande what affection the reading of it raysed in a stranger. It happened me this evening to sitt witt *John*

Lo: Bishopp of *E'xeter,* a learned man, and by all mens judgement, a most sincere man: As we were talking togeather, and I taking out of my pockett a paper, which was to the purpose we were talking of, I pulled out, by chace, therewith your letter. The handwriting pleasing him, he tooke it from me and looked on it; when he perceaved it by the salutacion to be a womans, he beganne more greedily to read it, noveltie inviting him thereunto: but when he had read it, and understood that it was your writing, which he never could have believed, if I had not seriously affirmed it; such a letter, I will say no more; yet why should not I reporte that which he sayd unto me? So pure a stile, so good Latine, so eloquent, so full of sweete affections; he was marvelously ravished with it; when I perceaved that, I brought forth also an Oration of yours, which he reading, and also manie of your verses, he was so moved with the matter so unlooked for, that the verie countenance and gesture of the man free from all flatterie and deceipt, bewrayed that his minde was more than his words could utter, although he uttered manie to your greate praise; and forthwith he drew out of his pocket a portegue, the which you shall receave enclosed herein. I could not possibly shune the taking of it, but he would needes send it unto you, as a signe of his deare affection towards you, although by all meanes I endeavoured to give him againe; which was the cause I shewed him none of your other sisters workes; for I was afeared least I should have bene thought to have shewed them of purpose, because he should bestowe the like courtesie upon them; for it troubled me sore, that I must needes take this of him. but he is so worthie a man, as I have sayd, that it is a happinesse to please him thus; write carefully unto him and as eloquently as you are able, to give him thankes therefore. Farewell; from the Court this 11th of Septemb. even almost at midnight.

She made an oration to answer Quintilian, defending that rich man, which he accuseth for having poysoned a poore mans bees, with certaine venemous flowers in his garden, so eloquent and wittie that it may strive with his. She translated Eusebius out of Greeke, but it was never printed, because Christopherson at that time had donne it exactly before. Yet one other letter will I sett downe of Sir Thomas to his daughter, which is thus: Thomas More sendeth greeting to his dearest daughter Margarett: There was noe reason, my dearest daughter, why thou shouldst have differred thy writing unto me one day longer, for feare that thy letters being so barren, should not be read of me without loathing. For though they had not been most curious, yet in respect of thy sexe, thou mightest have bene pardoned by anie man; yea eve a blemish in the childe's face, seemeth often to a father beautifull. But these your letters, *Megg,* were so eloquently polished, that they had nothing in them, not only why they should feare the most indulgent affection of your father *More* but also they needed not have regarded even *Momus* his cesure, though never so teastie I greatly thanke. *Mr. Nicholas* our deare friend (a most expert man in astronomie) and doe congratulate your happinesse, whome it may fortune within the space of one moneth with a small labour of your owne to learn so manie and such high wonders of that mightie and eternall workman, which were not found but in manie ages, by watching in so manie cold nights under the open skyes, with much labour and paines, by such excellent and above all other mens understanding witts. This which you write, pleaseth me exceedingly, that you had determined with yourself to studie philosophie so diligently, that you will hereafter recompence by your diligence, what your negligence hath heretofore lost you. I love you for this, deare *Megg,* that where as I never have found you to be a loyterer (your learning, which is not ordinarie, but in all kinde of sciences most excellent, evidently shewing, how painefully you have proceeded therein) yet such is your modestie, that you had rather still accuse yourself of negligence, then vainely boaste of diligence; except you meane by this your speach that you will be hereafter so diligent, that your former endeavours, though indeed they were great and praise worthie, yet in respect of your future diligence, may be called negligence. If it be so that you meane, (as I doe verily thinke you do), I imagine nothing can happen to me more fortunate, nothing to you, my dearest daughter, more happie; For as I have earnestly wished that you might spende the rest of your life in studying physicke and holie Scriptures, by the which there shall never be helpes wanting unto you, for the ende of mas life; which is, to endeavour that a sounde minde be in a healthfull bodie, of which studies you have alreadie layde some foundations, and you shall never want matter to builde thereupon; so now I thinke that some of the first yeares of your youth yet flourishing may be very well bestowed in humane learning & the liberall Arts, both because your age may best struggle with those difficulties, and for that it is uncertain, whether at anie time else we shall have the comoditie of so carefull so loving and so learned a maister: to lett passe, that by this kinde of learning our judgements are either gotten, or certainly much helped thereby. I could wishe, deare *Megg,* that I might talke with you a long time about these matters, but beholde they which

bring in supper, interrupt me and call me away. My supper cannot 51
be so sweete unto me, as this my speach with you is, if I were not
to respect others more than myself. Farewell, dearest daughter, &
commende me kindely to your housband, my loving sonne, who
maketh me rejoyce for that he studieth the same things you doe;
and whereas I am wont alwaies to counsell you to give place to your
husband, now on the other side I give you license to strive to
maister him in the knowledge of the sphere. Farewell againe &
againe. Commende me to all your schoole-fellowes, but to your
maister especially.

RICHARD MULCASTER (1530–1611)

Mulcaster was one of the most important of the early English schoolmasters. He was headmaster of the Merchant Taylors' School from its founding in 1561 to the year 1568, and was headmaster of St. Paul's Cathedral School from 1568 to 1608.

A true educator of the Reformation, he promoted the use of the vernacular in schools because he saw only limited value in a knowledge of Latin and Greek. He differed from the majority of Reformation theorists, however, when he demanded that education be made pleasurable.

Mulcaster offers specific advice in the essay "Education of Girls," which was included in his *Positions* (1581).

POSITIONS*

Chapter 38, "Education of Girls"

THAT YOUNG MAIDENS ARE TO BE SET TO LEARNING, WHICH IS PROVED, BY THE CUSTOME OF OUR COUNTREY, BY OUR DUETIE TOWARDES THEM, BY THEIR NATURALL ABILITIES, AND BY THE WORTHY EFFECTES OF SUCH AS HAVE BENE WELL TRAINED. THE ENDE WHERUNTO THEIR EDUCATION SERVETH WHICH IS THE CAUSE WHY AND HOW MUCH THEY LEARNE. WHICH OF THEM ARE TO LEARNE, WHEN THEY ARE TO BEGIN TO LEARNE. WHAT AND HOW MUCH THEY MAY LEARNE. OF WHOM AND WHERE THEY OUGHT TO BE TAUGHT.

*From Quick, Robert Hebert. *Positions by Richard Mulcaster.* London: Longmans, Green, and Co., 1888, pp. 166–182.

When I did appoint the persons, which were to receive the benefit of education: I did not exclude young *maidens,* and therefore seeing I made them one braunche of my division, I must of force say somewhat more of them. A thing perhaps which some will thinke might wel enough have bene past over with silence, as not belonging to my purpose, which professe the education of boyes, and the generall traine in that kinde. But seeing I begin so low as the first *Elementarie,* wherin we see that young *maidens* be ordinarily trained, how could I seeme not to see them, being so apparently taught?

And to prove that they are to be trained, I finde foure speciall reasons, whereof any one, much more all may perswade any their most adversarie, much more me, which am for them toothe and naile. 1. The first is the *maner* and *custome* of my countrey, which allowing them to learne, will be lothe to be contraried by any of her countreymen. 2. The second is the *duetie,* which we owe unto them, whereby we are charged in conscience, not to leave them lame, in that which is for them. 3. The third is their owne *towardnesse,* which God by nature would never have given them to remaine idle, or to small purpose. 4. The fourth is the excellent *effectes* in that sex, when they have had the helpe of good bringing up: which commendeth the cause of such excellencie, and wisheth us to cherishe that tree, whose frute is both so pleasaunt in taste, and so profitable in triall. What can be said more? our *countrey* doth allow it, our *duetie* doth enforce it, their *aptnesse* calls for it, their *excellencie* commandes it: and dare private *conceit,* once seems to withstand where so great, and so rare circumstances do so earnestly commende.

But for the better understanding of these foure reasons, I will examine everie of them, somewhat nearer, as inducers to the truth, ear I deale with the traine. For the first: If I should seeme to enforce any noveltie, I might seeme ridiculous, and never se that thing take place, which I tender so much: but considering, the *custome* of my countrie hath delivered me of that care, which hath made the *maidens* traine her owne approved travell, what absurditie am I in, to say that is true, which my countrie dare avow, and daily doth trie? I set not young *maidens* to publike grammar scholes, a thing not used in my countrie, I send them not to the universities, having no president thereof in my countrie, I allow them learning with distinction in degrees, with difference of their calling, with respect to their endes, wherefore they learne, wherein my countrie confirmeth my opinion. We see young *maidens* be taught to read and write, and can do both with praise: we heare them sing and playe:

and both passing well, we know that they learne the best and finest of our learned languages, to the admiration of all men. For the daiely spoken tongues and of best reputation in our time, who so shall denie that they may not compare even with our kinde in the best degree, they will claime no other combate, then to talke with him in that verie tongue, who shall seeke to taunt them for it. These things our country doth stand to, these qualities their parentes procure them, as either opportunitie of circumstance will serve, or their owne power will extend unto, or their daughters towardnesse doth offer hope, to be preferred by, for singularitie of endowment, either in marriage, or some other meane. Nay do we not see in our countrey, some of that sex so excellently well trained, and so rarely qualified, either for the toungues themselves, or for the matter in the toungues: as they may be opposed by way of comparison, if not preferred as beyond comparison, even to the best *Romaines* or *Greekish paragonnes* be they never so much praised: to the *Germaine* or *French* gentlewymen, by late writers so wel liked: to the *Italian* ladies who dare write themselves, and deserve fame for so doing? whose excellencie is so geason, as they be rather wonders to gaze at, then presidents to follow. And is that to be called in question, which we both dayly see in many, and wonder at in some? I dare be bould therefore to admit young *maidens* to learne, seeing my countrie gives my leave, and her *custome* stands for me.

For the second point. The duetie which we owe them doth straitly commaund us to see them well brought up. For what be young *maidens* in respect of our sex? Are they not the seminary of our succession? the naturall frye, from whence we are to chuse our naturall, next and most necessarie freindes? The very selfe same creatures, which were made for our comfort, the onely good to garnish our alonenesse, the nearest companions in our weale or wo? the peculiar and priviest partakers in all our fortunes? borne for us to life, bound to us till death? And can we in conscience but carefully thinke of them, which are so many wayes linked unto us? Is it either nothing, or but some small thing, to have our childrens mothers well furnished in minde, well strengthened in bodie? which desire by them to maintaine our succession? or is it not their good to be so well garnished, which good being defeated in them by our indiligence, of whom they are to have it, doth it not charge us with breache of duetie, bycause they have it not? They are committed and commended unto us, as pupilles unto tutours, as bodies unto heades, nay as bodies unto soules: so that if we tender not their education duetifully, they maye urge that against us, if at any time

either by their owne right, or by our default, they winne the upper
roome and make us stand bare head, or be bolder with us to.

They that write of the use of our bodies, do greatly blame such parents, as suffer not their children to use the left hand, as well as the right, bycause thereby they weaken their strength and the use of their limmes: and can we be without blame, who seeke not to strengthen that, which was once taken from us, and yet taryeth with us, as a part of us still: knowing it to be the weaker? Or is there any better meane to strengthen their minde, then that knowledge of God, of religion, of civil, of domesticall dueties, which we have by our traine, and ought not to denie them being comprised in bookes, and is to be compassed in youth?

That some exercise of bodie ought to be used, some ordinarie stirring ought to be enjoyned, some provision for private and peculiar trainers ought to be made: not onely the ladies of *Lacedaemon* will sweare, but all the world will sooth, if they do but wey, that it is to much to weaken our owne selves by not strengthening their side. That cunning poet for judgement in matter, and great philosopher for secrecie in nature, our well knowen *Virgill,* saw in a goodly horse that was offered unto *Augustus Caesar* an infirmitie unperceaved by either looker on or any of his stable, which came as he said by some weakness in the damme, and was confessed to be true. *Galene* and the whole familie of Physicians ripping up our infirmities, which be not to be avoided, placeth the seminarie and originall, engraffed in nature, as our greatest and nearest foes. And therefore to be prevented by the parentes, thorough considerate traine, the best and fairest meane, to better weake nature: so that of *duety* they are to be cared for. And what care in *duetie* is greater, then this in traine?

3. Their *natural towardnesse* which was my third reason doth most manifestly call upon us, to see them well brought up. If nature have given them abilities to prove excellent in their kinde, and yet thereby in no point to let their most laudable dueties in marriage and matche, but rather to bewtifie them, with most singular ornaments, are not we to be condemned of extreme unnaturallnes, if we gay not that by discipline, which is given them by *nature?* That naturally they are so richly endowed, all *Philosophie* is full, no *Divinitie* denyes, *Plato** and his *Academikes* say, that all vertues be indifferent, nay all one in man and woman: saving that they be more strong and more durable in men, weaker and more variable in

*Proclus upon Platoes common weale, and Theodorus Asinaeus upon the question, whether men and wymen have all vertues common.

wymen. *Xeno* and his *Stoikes* though they esteeme the ods betwene man and woman naturally to be as great as the difference, betwene an heavenly and an earthly creature, which *Plato* did not, making them both of one mould, yet they graunt them equalitie and samenesse in vertue, though they deliver the strength and constancie over unto men, as properly belonging unto that side. *Aristotle* and his *Peripatetikes* confessing them both to be of one kinde, though to different uses in *nature,* according to those differences in *condition,* appointeth them differences in *vertue,* and yet wherin they agree: alloateth them the same. When they have concluded thus of their natural abilities, and so absolutely entitled them unto all vertues, they rest not there, but procede on further to their education in this sorte. That as naturally every one hath some good assigned him, whereunto he is to aspire, and not to cease until he have obtained it, onlesse he will by his owne negligence reject that benefit, which the munificence of *nature* hath liberally bestowed on him: so there is a certaine meane, whereby to winne that perfitly, which *nature* of her selfe doth wish us franckly. This meane they call *education,* whereby the naturall inclinations be gently caryed on, if they will curteously follow, or otherwise be hastened, if they must needes be forced, until they arrive at that same best, which *nature* bendeth unto with full saile, in those fairer, which follow the traine willingly, in those meaner, which must be bet unto it. And yet even there where it is sorest laboured, it worketh some effecte unworthy of repentaunce, and is better forced on in youth, then forgon in age: rather in children with feare, then not in men with griefe. Now as the inclinations be common to both the kindes, so they devide the meane of education indifferently betwene both. Which being thus, as both the truth tells the ignorant, and reading shewes the learned, we do wel then perceave by *naturall men,* and *Philosophicall reasons,* that young *maidens* deserve the traine: bycause they have that treasure, which belongeth unto it, bestowed on them by *nature,* to be bettered in them by *nurture.* Neither doth *religion* contrarie religious *nature.* For the *Lorde* of *nature,* which created that motion to continue the consequence of all living creatures, by succession to the like, by education to the best, appointing either kinde the limittes of their duetie, and requiring of either the perfourmaunce thereof, alloweth all such ordinarie and orderly meanes, as by his direction in his word may bring them both from his appointment to their perfourmaunce, from the first starting place, to the outmost gole: that is unto that good, which he hath assigned them, by such wayes, as he hath willed them: so that both by *nature* the most obedient servant, and by the *Lorde* of *nature* our most bountifull *God,* we have it in commandement not onely to traine up our owne sex, but also our female, seeing he hath to require an account for naturall talentes of both the parties, us for directing them: them for perfourmance of our direction.

4. The excellent effectes of those women, which have bene verie well trained, do well declare, that they deserve the best training: which reason was my last in order, but not my least in force, to prove their more then common excellencie. This is a point of such galancie, if my purpose were to praise them, as it is but to give precept, how to make them praiseworthie, as I might soner weary my selfe with reckoning up of writers, and calling worthie wymen to be witnesses in their owne cause then worthely to express their weight and worth, bycause I beleeve that to be most true, which is cronicled of them. I will not medle with any moe writers to whom wymen are most bound, for best speaking of them, and most spreading of their vertues, then with one onely man a single witnes in person, but above all singularitie if profe: the learned and honest *Plutarch,* whose name emporteth a princis treasure, whose writings witnes an unwearied travel, whose plaine truth was never tainted. Would he so learned, so honest, so true, so sterne, have become such a trumpet for their fame, to triumph by, so have gratified that sex, whom he stood not in awe of: so have beutified their doings, whom he might not have medled with, so have avaunced their honoured, to hasard his owne sex, by setting them so hie, if he had not resolutely knowne the truth of his subject? he durst be so bould with his owne Emperour the good *Traian,* to fore his scholer, in his epistle to him before his booke of governing the common weale, as to say and call his booke to witnes thereof, that if he went to governe, and overthrew the state, he did it not by the authoritie of *Plutarch,* as disavowing his scholer, if he departed from his lessons. And would that courage have bene forced to frame a false argument? or is so great a truth not to have so great a credit? howsover some of the lighter heades have lewdly belyed them, or vainly accused them: yet the verie best and gravest writers thinke worthely of them, and make report of them with honour. *Ariosto* and *Boccacio* will beloth to be tearmed light, being so great doctours in their divinite, yet they be somwhat over heavie to wymen, without any great weight as in generall the *Italian* writers be, which in the middest of their loving levities still glaunce at their lightnes, and that so beyound all manhoode, as they feele their owne fault, and dispaire of reconcilement, though they crie still for

58   pardon. As those men know well, which will rather mervell, that I have red those bookes, then mistrust my report, which they know to be true. In all good and generally authorised histories, and in many particuler discourses, it is most evident, that not onely private and particular wymen, being very well trained, but also great princesses and gallant troupes of the same sex have shewed fourth in them selves marvelous effectes of vertue and valure. And good reason why. For where naturally they have to shew, if education procure shew, is it a thing to be wondered at? Or is their singularitie less in nature, bycause wymen be lesse accustomed to shew it, and not so commonly employed, as we men be? Yet whensoever they be, by their dealinges they shew us that they have no dead flesh nor any base mettle. Well, I will knit up this conclusion and burne day light no longer, to prove that carefully, which all men may see clearely, and their adversaries grieve at, bycause it confutes their follie, which upon some private errour of their owne, to seeme fautles in wordes, where they be faithles in deedes, blame silly wymen as being the onely cause why they went awrie.

That young *maidens* can learne, nature doth give them, and that they have learned, our experience doth teach us, with what care to themselves, them selves can best witnes, with what comfort to us, what forraine example can more assure the world, then our diamond at home? our most deare soveraine lady and princesse, by nature a woman, by vertue a worthy, not one of the nyne, but the tenth above the nyne, to perfit in her person that absolute number, which is no fitter to comprehend all absolutnes in Arithmetike, then she is knowne to containe al perfections in nature, all degrees in valure, and to become a president: to those nyne worthy men, as *Apollo** is accounted to the nyne famouse wymen, she to vertues and vertuous men, he to muses, and learned wymen: thereby to prove *Plutarches* conclusion true, that oppositions of vertues by way of comparison is their chiefe commendation. Is *Anacreon* a good poet, what say you to *Sappho?* Is *Bacis* a good prophet, what say you to *Sibill?* was *Sesostris* a famous prince, what say you to *Semiramis?* was *Servius* a noble king, what say you to *Tanaquill?* was *Brutus* a stowt man, what say you to *Porcia?* Thus reasoneth *Plutarch,†* and so do I, is it honorable for *Apollo* a man to have the presidencie over nyne wymen, the resemblers of learning? then more honorable it is for our most worthy *Princesse* to have the

---

*Philo Iudaeus in his discours of the ten commaundementes rips out the perfitnes of that number.
†Plutarch in his booke of wymens vertues.

presidencie over nyne men, the paragons of vertue: and yet to be so familiarly acquainted with the nyne *muses,* as they are in strife who may love her best, for being best learned? for whose excellent knowledge and learning, we have most cause to rejoyce, who tast of the trute: and posteritie to praise, which shall maintaine her memorie: though I wish their memorie abridged, to have our tast enlarged: our proving lengthened, to have their praising shortened: to be glad that we have her, not to greve, that we had her: as that omnipotent god, which gave her unto us, when we had more neede of such a prince, then shee of such a people, will preserve her for us, I do nothing dout, that we both may serve him, she as our carefull soveraine, to set forth his glory, we as her faithfull subjects, to submit our selves to it.

If no storie did tell it, if no state did allow it, if no example did confirme it, that young *maidens* deserve the trayning, this our owne myrour, the majestie of her sex, doth prove it in her owne person, and commendes it to our reason. We have besides her highness as undershining starres, many singuler ladies and gentlewymen, so skilfull in all cunning, of the most laudable, and loveworthy qualities of learning, as they may well be alleadged for a president to prayse, not for a pattern to prove like by: though hope have a head, and nature be no nigard, if education do her dutie, and will seeke to resemble even where presidentes be passing, both hope to attaine to, and possibilitie to seeme to. Wherefore by these profes, I take it to be very clear, that I am not farre overshot, in admitting them to traine being so traineable by nature, and so natable by effectes.

But now having graunted them the benefit and society of our education, we must assigne the end, wherefore their traine shall serve, whereby we may apply it the better. Our owne traine is without restraint for either matter or maner, bycause our employment is so generall in all thinges: theirs is within limit, and so must their traine be. If a young *maiden* be to be trained in respect of marriage, obedience to her head, and the qualities which looke that way, must needes be her best way: if in regard of necessitie to learne how to live, artificiall traine must furnish out her trade: if in respect of ornament to beawtifie her birth, and to honour her place, rareties in that kinde and seemly for that kinde do best beseeme such: if for government, not denyed them by God, and devised them by men, the greatnes of their calling doth call for great giftes, and generall excellencies for generall occurrences. Wherefore having these different endes always in eye, we may point them their traine in different degrees. But some *Timon* will say, what should wymen do with learning? Such a churlish carper will never picke out the best, but be alway ready to blame the worst. If all men used all pointes of learning well, we had some reason to alleadge against wymen, but seeing misuse is common to both the kinds, why blame we their infirmitie, whence we free not our selves? Some wymen abuse writing to that end, some reading to this, some all that they learne any waye, to some other ill some waye. And I praie you what do we? I do not excuse ill: but barre them from accusing, which be as bad themselves: unlesse they will first condemne themselves, and so proceede in their plea with more discretion after a repentant discoverie. But they will not deale thus, they will rather retire for shame and prove to be nonsuite, then confesse themselves faulty and blush for their blaming. Wherfore as the communitie of vertues, argueth the communities of vices naturally in both: so let us in that point enterchaunge forgivenesse, and in hope of the vertues direct to the best, not for feare of the vices, make an open gap for them. Wherefore in directing of that traine, which I do assigne unto young maidens, I will follow this methode, and shew which of them be to learne, and when, what and how much, where and of whom.

As concerning those which are to be trained, and when they are to begin their traine, this is my opinion. The same restraint in cases of necessitie, where they conveniently cannot, and the same freedom in cases of libertie, when they commodiously may, being reserved to parentes in their daughters, which I allowed them in their sonnes, and the same regard to the weaknesse and strength of their witts and bodies, the same care for their womanly exercises, for helpe of their health, and strength of their limmes, being remitted to their considerations, which I assigned them in their sonnes, I do thinke the same time fit for both, not determinable by yeares, but by ripenesse of witte to conceive without tiring, and strength of bodies to travell without wearying. For though the girles seeme commonly to have a quicker ripening in witte, then boyes have, for all that seeming, yet it is not so. Their naturall weaknesse which cannot holde long, delivers very soone, and yet there be as pratling boyes, as there be pratling wenches. Besides, their braines be not so much charged, neither will weight nor with multitude of matters, as boyes heades be, and therefore like empty caske they make the greater noise. As those men which seeme to be very quicke witted by some sudden pretie aunswere, or some sharp replie, be not always burthened, neither with letters, nor learning, but out of small store, they offer us still the floore, and holde most of the mother. Which sharpnesse of witte though it be within them, as it bewraeth it selfe: yet it might dwell within them a great while, without bewraying of it selfe, if studie kept them still, or great doinges did dull them: as slight dealinges and imperious, do commonly maintaine that kinde of courage. Boyes have it alwaye, but oftimes hide it, bycause their stuffe admitteth time: wenches have it alwaye, and alwaye bewray it, bycause their timber abides no tarying. And seeing it is in both, it deserves care in both, neither to timely to stirre them, nor let them loyter to long. As for bodies the *maidens* be more weake, most commonly even by nature, as of a moonish influence, and all our whole kinde is weake of the mother side, which when she was first made, even then weakened the mans side. Therefore great regard must be had to them, no lesse, nay rather more then to boyes in that time. For in process of time, if they be of worth themselves, they may so matche, as the parent may take more pleasure in his sonnes by law, then in his heires by nature. They are to be the principall pillers in the upholding of housholdes, and so they are likely to prove, if they prove well in training. The dearest comfort that man can have, if they encline to good: the nearest corrosive if they tread awry. And therfore charilie to be cared for, bearing a jewell of such worth, in a vessel of such weaknesse. Thus much for there persons whom I turne over to the parentes abilitie for charge: of their owne capacitie for conceit: in eche degree some, from the lowest in menaltie, to the highest in mistriship.

The time hath tied it selfe to strength in both parts, for the bodie to travell, for the soule to conceive. The exercises pray in no case to be forgot as a preservative to the body, and a conserve for the soule.

For the matter what they shall learne, thus I thinke, following the custome of my countrie, which in that that is usuall doth lead me on boldly, and in that so which is most rare, doth shew me my path, to be already troden. So that I shall not neede to erre, if I marke buy my guide wel. Where rare excellencies in some wymen, do but shew us some one or two parentes good successe, in their daughters learning, there is neither president to be fetcht, nor precept to be framed. For preceptes be to conduct the common, but these singularities be above the common, presidentes be for hope, those pictures passe beyond al hope. And yet they serve for profe to proceede by in way of argument, that wymen can learne if they will, and may learne what they list, when they bend their wittes to it. To learne to read is very common, where convenientnes doth serve, and *writing* is not refused, where oportunitie will yeild it.

Reading if for nothing else it were, as for many thinges else it is, is verie needefull for religion, to read that which they must know, and ought to performe, if they have not whom to heare, in that matter which they read: or if their memorie be not stedfast, by reading to revive it. If they heare first and after read of the selfe same argument, reading confirmes their memorie. Here I may not omit many and great contentmentes, many and sound comfortes, many and manifoulde delites, which those wymen that have skill and time to reade, without hindering their houswifery, do continually receive by reading of some comfortable and wise discourses, penned either in forme of historie, or for direction to liue by.

As for *writing,* though it be discommended for some private carriages, wherein we men also, no lesse then wymen, beare oftentimes blame, if that were a sufficient exception why we should not learne to write, it hath this commoditie where it filleth in match, and helpes to enrich the goodmans mercerie. Many good occasions are oftentimes offered, where it were better for them to have the use of their pen, for the good that comes by it, then to wish they had it, when the default is felt: and for feare of evill, which cannot be avoided in some, to avert that good, which may be commodious to many.

Musicke is much used, where it is to be had, to the parentes delite, while the daughters be yong, more then to their owne, which commonly proveth true, when the yong wenches become yong wives. For then lightly forgetting *Musicke* when they learne to be mothers, they give it in manifest evidence, that in their learning of it, they did more seeke to please their parentes, then to pleasure themselves. But howsoever it is, seeing the thing is not rejected, if with the learning of it once, it may be retained still (as by order it may) it is ill let go, which is got with great paines, and bought with some cost. The learninge to sing and plaie by the booke, a matter soone had, when *Musike* is first minded, which still preserve the cunning, though discontinuance disturbe. And seeing it is but little which they learne, and the time as litle wherein they learne, bycause they haste still on toward husbandes, it were expedient, that they learned perfitly, and that with the losse of their pennie, they lost not their pennieworth also, besides the losse of their time, which is the greatest losse of all. I medle not with *nedles,* nor yet with *houswiferie,* though I thinke it, and know it, to be a principall commendation in a woman: to be able to governe and direct her

houshold, to looke to her house and familie, to provide and keepe
necessaries, though the goodman pay, to know the force of her
kitchen, for sicknes and health, in her selfe and her charge: bycause
I deale onely with such thinges as be incident to their learning.
Which seeing the custome of my country doth permit, I may not
mislike, nay I may wish it with warrant, the thing being good and
well beseeming their sex. This is the most so farre as I remember,
which they commonly use in youth, and participate with us in. If
any parent do privately traine up his children of either sex in any
other private fantsie of his owne, I cannot commend it, bycause I do
not know it, and if it fortune to die within his private walles, I
cannot give it life by publike rehearsall. The common and most
knowne is that, which I have saide.

The next pointe *how much,* is a question of more enquirie, and
therefore requireth advised handling. To appoint besides these
thinges, which are already spoken of, how much further any *maide*
maye proceede in matter of learning and traine, is a matter of some
moment, and concerneth no meane ones. And yet some petie
lowlinges, do sometimes seeke to resemble, where they have small
reason, and will needes seeme like, where their petieship cannot
light, using shew for a shadow, where they have no fitter shift. And
therfore in so doing, they passe beyond the boundes both of their
birth, and their best beseeming. Which then discovereth a verie
meere follie, when a meane parent traineth up his daughter hie in
those properties, which I shall streight waye speake of, and she
matcheth lowe, but within her owne compasse. For in such a case
those overraught qualities for the toyousnesse thereof being mis-
placed in her, do cause the young woman rather to be toyed withall,
as by them giving signe of some idle conceit otherwise, then to be
thought verie well of, as one wisely brought up. There is a
comlynesse in eche kinde, and a decentnesse in degree, which is best
observed, when eche one provides according to his power, without
overreaching. If some odde property do worke preferrement
beyond proportion, it commonly stayes there, and who so shootes
at the like, in hope to hit, may sooner misse: bycause the wayes to
misse be so many, and to hit is but one, and wounders which be but
onse seene, be no examples to resemble. Every *maide* maye not hope
to speede, as she would wishe, bycause some one hath sped better
then she could wishe.

Where the question is *how much* a woman ought to learne, the
aunswere may be, so much as shall be needefull. If that also come
in doubt, the returne may be, either so much as her parentes

64   conceive of her in hope, if her parentage be meane, or provide for her in state, if her birth beare a saile. For if the parentes be of calling, and in great account, and the daughters capable of some singular qualities, many commendable effects may be wrought therby, and the young maidens being well trained are verie soone commended to right honorable matches, whom they may well beseeme, and aunswere much better, their qualities in state having good correspondence, with their matches of state, and their wise-doms also putting to helping hand, for the procuring of their common good. Not here to note, what frute the common weale may reape, by such witts so worthily advaunced, besides their owne private. If the parentes be meane, and the *maidens* in their training shew forth at the verie first some singular rarenesse like to ensue, if they florish but their naturall, there hope maye grow great, that some great matche may as well like of a young maiden excellently qualified, as most do delite in brute or brutish thinges for some straunge qualitie, either in nature to embrase, or in art to marvell. And yet this hope may faile. For neither have great personages alwaye that judgement, nor young *maidens* alwaye that fortune, though the *maidens* remaine the gainers, for they have the qualities to comfort their mediocrity, and those great ones want judgement to set forth their nobilitie.

This *how much* consisteth either in perfiting of those fornamed foure, *reading* well, *writing* faire, *singing* sweete, *playing* fine, beyond all cry and above all comparison, that pure excellencie in things but ordinarie may cause extraordinarie liking: or else in skill of languages annexed to these foure, that more good giftes may worke more sounder. "For meane is a maime where excellencie is the marvell." To hope for hie mariages, is good meat, but not for mowers, to have leasure to take delite in these gentlewomanly qualities, is no worke for who will: Nay to be a paragon among princes, to use such singularities, for the singular good of the general state, and the wonder of her person, were a wish in dispaire, were not true proofe the just warrant, that such a thing may be wished, bycause in our time we have found it, even then, when we did wish it most, and in the ende more marvellous, then at first we durst have wished. The eventes in these wymen which we see in our dayes, to have bene brought up in learning, do rule this conclusion. That such personages as be borne to be princes, or matches to great peeres, or to furnish out such traines, for some peculiar ornamentes to their place and calling, are to receive this kinde of education in the highest degree, that is convenient for their kinde. But princely *maidens* above all: bycause occasion of their height standes in neede of such figtes, both to honour themselves, and to discharge the duetie, which the countries, conmitted to their hands, do daily call for, and besides what matche is more honorable, then when desert for rare qualities, doth joine it selfe, with highnesse in degree? I feare no workmanship in wymen to give them *Geometrie* and her sister sciences: to make them *Mathematicalls,* though I meane them *Musicke:* nor yet barres to plead at, to leave them the lawes: nor urinalls to looke on, to lend them some Physicke, though the skil of herbes have bene the studies of nobilite, by the *Persian* storie, and much commended in wymen: nor pulpittes to preach in, to utter their *Divinitie:* though by learning of some language, they can talke of the lining: and for direction of their life, they must be afforded some though not as preachers and leaders; yet as honest perfourmers, and vertuous livers. *Philosophie* would furnish their generall discourses, if their leasure could entend it: but the knowledge of some toungues, either of substaunce in respect of deeper learning, or account for the present time may verie well be wisht them: and those faculties also, which do belong to the furniture of speache, may be verie well allowed them, bycause toungues be most proper, where they do naturally arme. If I should allow them the *pencil* to draw, as the penne to write, and thereby entitle them to all my Elementarie principles, I might have reason for me. For it neither requireth any great labour to fraye young maidens from it, and it would helpe their nedle, to beautifie their workes: and it is maintainable by very good examples even of their owne kinde. *Timarete** the vertuous, daughter to *Mycon: Irene,* the curteous, daughter to *Cratinus: Aristarete* the absolute, daughter to *Nearchus: Lala* the eloquent, and ever maide of *Cyzicus: Martia* the couragious, daughter to *Varro* the best learned and most loved of any *Romain,* and many mo besides, did so use the *pencill,* as their fame therefore is so much the fairer, bycause the fact in that sex is so seldom and reare.

And is not a young gentlewoman, thinke you, thoroughly furnished, which can reade plainly and distinctly, write faire and swiftly, sing cleare and sweetly, play wel and finely, understand and speake the learned languages, and those toungues also which the time most embraseth, with some *Logicall* helpe to chop, and some *Rhetoricke* to brave. Besides the matter which is gathered, while these toungues be either learned, or lookt on, as wordes must have seates, no lesse then rayment bodies. Were it any argument of an

---

*Plin. lib. 35. cap. II.

unfurnished maiden, besides these qualities to draw cleane in good proportion, and with good symmetrie? Now if she be an honest woman, and a good housewife to, were she not worth the wishing, and worthy the shryning? and yet such there be, and such we know. Or is it likely that her children shalbe eare a whit the worse brought up, if she be a *Laelia,* an *Hortensia,* or a *Cornelia,* which were so endued and noted for so doing? It is written of *Eurydice* the *Epirote,* that after she began to have children, she sought to have learning, to bring them up skilfully, whom she brought forth naturally. Which thing she perfourmed in deede, a most carefull mother, and a most skilfull mistresse. For which her well doing, she hath wonne the reward, to be enrowled among the most rare matrones.

Now there is nothing left to ende this treatise of young *maidens,* but where and under whom, they are to learne, which question will be sufficiently resolved, upon consideration of the time how long they are to learne, which time is commonly till they be about thirtene or fouretene years old, wherein as the matter, which they must deale with all, cannot be very much in so litle time, so the perfitting thereof requireth much travel, though their time be so little, and there would be some shew afterward, wherein their trayning did availe them. They that may continue some long time at learning, thorough the state and abilitie of their parentes have also their time and place sutably appointed, by the foresight of their parents. So that the time resting in private forecast, I can not reduce it to generall precept, but onely thus farre, that in perfitnes it may shew, how well it was employed.

The places wherein they learne be either *publike,* if they go forth to the *Elementarie* schole, or *private* if they be taught at home. The teacher either of their owne sex or of ours.

For *publike* places, bycause in that kinde there is no publike provision, but such as the professours of their training do make of them selves, I can say little, but leave them to that and to their parentes circumspection, which both in their being abroad, during their minority, and in bringing them up at home after their minoritie, I know will be very diligent to have all thinges well. For their teachers, their owne sex were fittest in some respects, but ours frame them best, and with good regard to some circumstances will bring them up excellently well, specially if their parentes be either of learning to judge, or of authoritie to commaund, or of both, to do both, as experience hath taught us in those, which have proved so well. The greater borne Ladyes and gentlewymen, as they are to enjoy the benefit of this education most, so they have best meanes

to prosecute it best, being neither restrained in wealth, but to have
the best teachers, and greatest helpes: neither abbridged in time, but
to ply all at full. And thus I take my leave of young maidens and
gentlewymen, to whom I wish as well, as I have saide well of them.

JOHN DURY (1596–1680)

John Dury, an Englishman, labored to unify evangelical churches in Sweden, Denmark, and Germany. Also, he was instrumental in bringing about educational changes during the Reformation.

Dury's educational philosophy resembled that of the eminent Moravian bishop, Comenius (1592–1670). A notable agreement was their promotion of a practical curriculum.

In his book, *The Reformed School* (ca. 1649), Dury proposed a universal, publicly financed school system for all children aged eight through fourteen. The brief selection which follows makes it evident that he did, indeed, intend that education be for all children, including girls.

THE REFORMED SCHOOL*

Secondly of the Education of Children

The Girles should all be lodged in the same house with the associated women; to be under the perpetuall inspection of the Governess, by whom, their severall tasks for all the dayes of the week and houres of the day, should be set unto them; and the tymes of taking an account of them concerning every thing, ordered and strictly observed.

The Boyes should be in a severall house, or part of the house so, that they should not be able at any time to have free communication with the Girles; but should be always under the inspection of their Tutors who should be men belonging to the association, for such Offices which women are not fit to be employed in: and these Tutors and Teachers should all be under one generall Overseer, who should give them their tasks, and see the

---

*Reprinted from Dury, John. *The Reformed School and the Reformed Library Keeper 1651.* Menston, England: The Scolar Press, Ltd., 1972, pp. 18-21. By permission of the publisher.

same performed according to settled Orders.

The main scope of the whole work of Education, both in the Boyes and Girles, should be none other but this; to train them up to know God in Christ, that they may walke worthy of him in the Gospell; and become profitable instruments of the Common-wealth in their Generations. And in order to this, two things are to bee taught them. First, the way of Godliness, wherein every day they are to be exercised, by prayers, reading of the word, Catecheticall Institutions, and other exercises subordinat unto the life of Christianity. Secondly, the way of Serviceableness towards the Society wherin they live, that they may be enabled each in their sex respectively, to follow lawfull calings for profitable uses; and not become a burden to their generation by living in Idleness and disorderlinesse, as most commonly those do which come from the Schools of this age.

The Rule then according to which their education is to be Reformed fundamentally, is this.

That no time of the day is to be lost without some teaching exercise; and that nothing is to bee taught but that which is usefull in itself to the Society of mankind, therin fitting them for employments approvable by the Gospel; and which will bring them to behave themselves so as it becometh those who are called to walke with the lamb upon mount Sion in the presence of God, that is, as Saints in his Church.

Upon this ground, all the matters of shew and appearance, which please the fancies of men in the world, whether they be in points of knowledge or practice; (wherin all the time of the youth is most commonly spent in ordinary Schools) are to be laid aside in the course of this Education.

Therefore as to the Girles, the ordinary vanity and curiosity of their dressing of hair and putting on of apparell; the customes and principles of wantonness and bold behaviours; which in their dancings are taught them; and whatsoever else doth tend onely to fomet pride and satisfie curiosity and imaginary delights, shall be changed, by this our course of Education, into plain, decent cleanliness and healthfull wayes of apparrelling themselves; and into such exercises of their hearts, heads and hands, which may habituat them through the fere of God, to become good and carefull housewives, loving towards their husbands and their children when God shall call them to be married; and understanding in all things belonging to the care of a Family, according to the Characters which Salomon doth give of a virtuous Godly woman. And such as may be found capable of Tongues and Sciences, (to perfect them in Graces and the knowledge of Christ for all is to be referred to him above the ordinary sort) are not to be neglected; but assisted towards the improvement of their intellectuall abilities.

As for the Boyes; the same Rule is to be observed in the way of their Education, both for Tongues, Sciences and Employments. So that all the preposterous Methods of teaching the same; by which, not only their time is lost, but their spirits and affections are inured to evill customes of Disorderliness, of Vanity, Pride and Self conceitedness, which is the root of all our contentions about matters of Learning and Science falsely so called: and all the unprofitable exercises of their mind and body in things which take them off from the aime of Christianity unto the customes of the world shall be altered into profitable employments which may fit them to be good Commonwealths men, by the knowledge of all things which are fundamentall for the settlement of a State in Husbandry, in necessary Trades, in Navigation, in Civill Offices for the Administration of Justice; in Peace and War; and in Oeconomicall Duties by which they may be serviceable to their own families, and to their neighbours.

And if these Generall Grounds be assented unto by those that have a mind to associat, and to help forward the Education of youth for a beginning of some Reall Reformation in our age; the particular Models both for Boyes and Girles Institution, Inspection and Employments may be soon added, and offered to their consideration.

ANNA VAN SCHÜRMAN (1607–1678)

Born in Cologne to a noble Protestant family, Anna attended a French school briefly when she was seven before her father assumed direct responsibility for her education. While she sat within hearing distance of the study group of her brothers, she prompted them in responses they were expected to give to their father's questions. Her answers clearly demonstrated that she was prepared for a learning experience; consequently, her father provided her with tutors in arithmetic, writing, vocal and instrumental music, painting, sculpture, engraving, geography, astronomy, philosophy, sciences, and theology. Her reading assignments were based upon the Bible and upon Greek and Latin literature. She was one of the first women to learn Oriental languages. In addition to Persian and Arabic, she was fluent in French, English, and Italian. She was known to have had inimitable handwriting in the various languages. Her mastery of the art of tapestry in three hours gave further evidence of her quick mind.

Frequently, their own letters have attested to the literary skills of women. Van Schürman exemplified this pattern, with Balzac among those who praised her writing style.

Many of her theories originated with Comenius, from whose *Great Didactic* she drew concepts.

It is probable that Anna van Schürman was the first "professional feminist"; surely, she was the first to refer to women's position as a "cause" and the first to seek the support of men to aid in the cause of women's rights. To continue this list of "firsts," she is the first female writer represented in this book of classics. In the following segment of *The Learned Maid* (1659), she poses the question of whether a maid should be a scholar, then justifies an affirmative answer.

THE LEARNED MAID, OR WHETHER A MAID MAY BE A SCHOLAR?*

"A Logick Exercise Written in Latine by That Incomparable Virgin Anna Marie A Schürman of Utrecht. With some Epistles to the famous Gaffendus and others."

The Learned Maid. A Logicall Exercise upon this Question. Whether A Maid may be a Scholar?

We hold the *Affirmative*, and will endeavor to make it good. These Pracognita we permit; First on the part of the *Subject*, and then of the *Predicate*. By a *Maid or a Woman*, I understand her that is a *Christian*, and that not in Profession onely, but really and indeed.

By a *Scholar*, I mean one that is given to the study of *Letters*, that is, the knowledge of Tongues and Histories, all kinds of Learning, both superior entitled *Faculties;* and inferior, call'd *Philosophy*. We accept onely *Scriptural Theology*, properly so named, as that which without Controversie belongs to all Christians.

When we enquire, *Whether she may be,* we mean whether it be *convenient,* that is, expedient, fit, decent.

The words being thus distinguished, the *Things* are to be distinguished also.

For some *Maids* are *ingenious*, others *not so:* some are *rich*, some *poor:* some engaged in Domestick cares, others *at liberty*.

The studies of a *Scholar* are either *universal*, when we give our selves to all sorts of Learning; or *particular*, when we learn some one Language or Science, or one distinct Faculty.

Wherefore we make use of these Limitations:

First of the *Subject;* and first, that our *Maid* be endued at least with an indifferent good *wit*, and not unapt for learning.

Secondly, that she be provided of necessaries and not oppressed with want: which exception I therefore put in, because few are so happy to have Parents to bread them up in studies, and Teachers are chargeable.

Thirdly, that the condition of the Times, and her quality be such, that she may have spare houres from her general and speciall

---

*From Schürman, Anna van. *The Learned Maid, or Whether a Maid May Be a Scholar?* London: Printed by John Redmayne, 1659, pp. 1-6.

Calling, that is, from the Exercises of Piety and household Affairs.
To which end will conduce, partly her immunity from cares and employment in her younger years, partly in her elder age either celibate, or the Ministry of handmaids, which are wont to free the richer sort of Matrons also from Domestick troubles.

Fourthly, let her end be, not vain glory and ostentation, or unprofitable curiosite: but beside the generall end, Gods Glory and the salvation of her own soul; that both her self may be the more vertuous and the more happy, and that she may (if that chargely upon her) instruct and direct her Family, and also be usefull, as much as may be to her whole Sex.

Next, *Limitations* of the *Predicate, Scholarship,* or the study of Letters I for limit, that I clearly affirm all honest Discipline, or the whole Circle and Crown of liberal Arts and Sciences (as the proper and universal Good and Ornament of Mankind) to be convenient for the *Head* of our *Christian Maid:* yet so, that according to the Dignity and Nature of every Art or Science, and according to the capacity and condition of the Maid herself, all in their order, place and time suceed each other in the learning of them, or be commodiously conjoyned. But especially let regard be had unto those Arts which have neerest alliance to *Theology* and the *Moral Virtues,* and are Principally subservient to them. In which number we reckon *Grammar, Logick, Rhetorick;* especially *Logick,* fitly called *The Key of all Sciences:* and then, *Physicks, Metaphysicks, History,* &c. and also the knowledge of Languages, chiefly of the *Hebrew* and the *Greek.* All which may advance to the more facile and full understanding of *Holy Scripture:* to say nothing now of other Books. The rest, i.e. *Mathematicks* (to which is also referred *Musick) Poesie, Picture,* and the like, not illiberal Arts, may obtain the place of pretty Ornaments and ingenious Recreations.

Lastly, those studies which pertain to the practice of the Law, Military Discipline, Oratory in the Church, Court, University, as less proper and less necessary, we do not very much urge. And yet we in no wise yield that our Maid should be excluded from the Scholastick knowledge or Theory of those; especially, not from understanding the most noble Doctrine of the *Politicks* or Civil Government.

And when we say a Maid may be a Scholar, it is plain we do not affirm Learning to be a property, or a thing requisite, and precisely needfull to eternall salvation: no, nor as such good thing which maketh to the very *Essence* of Happiness in this life: but as a mean and very usefull, conferring much to the integrity and

74 perfection thereof: and as that, which be the contemplation of excellent things which promote us to a higher degree in the love of God, and everlasting Felicity.

Therefore let our Thesis or Proposition be:

A MAID *may be a scholar.*

FRANÇOIS DE SALIGNAC DE LA MOTHE FÉNELON (1651–1715)

His noble French family was without wealth at the time of Fénelon's birth. Because of ill health, he was tutored at home during boyhood. A thorough background in Latin and Greek initiated an enduring love for the classics. At the age of twelve he entered the University of Cahors, where he studied humanities and philosophy. He attended the University of Paris before he became a student in the seminary of Saint-Suplice, from which he was ordained as priest in 1674 or 1675. This dignified, modest, kind, truly religious man became Archbishop of Cambrai in 1695.

Fénelon's experience as an educator began in 1689 when he tutored the eldest son of the Dauphin. He became a frequent visitor to Madame de Maintenon and her famous school at St. Cyr, near Versailles. A genuine supporter of education for women, he opposed the contention that women be regarded as members of an inferior sex. He cautioned, however, that females should be realistic in their perceptions of life, well read but not scholarly, good housewives and managers, and of a sound religious character. He maintained that a moral education is inseparable from an intellectual education.

His *The Education of Girls* (1687) is devoted to the education of both boys and girls who, he believed, should have an equal childhood education. Following two brief excerpts from this lengthy treatise is a letter Fénelon wrote to a mother, advising her on the education of her daughter. This letter, published in 1715, the year of the death of Fénelon, contains an examination of the importance of religion and of the dangers of worldliness.

THE EDUCATION OF GIRLS*

Chapter I

"The Importance of the Education of Girls"

Nothing is more neglected than the education of girls. Custom and maternal caprice often decide the matter entirely, and it is taken for granted that little instruction should be given to their sex. The education of boys is regarded as a most important affair with reference to the public welfare; and although almost as many mistakes are made in it as in the education of girls, at least the world is convinced that, there, much wisdom is necessary to success. On that subject, the most competent persons have undertaken to lay down rules. How many teachers and colleges for boys do we see! What vast expenditures in their behalf for editions of books, for scientific researches, for methods of teaching the languages, and for the choice of professors! All these great preparations are often more pretentious than effective, but at least they mark the lofty conception that the world has of the education of boys. As for girls, it is said, they should not be learned; inquisitiveness makes them vain and affected: it is enough for them to know how some day to manage their households and to obey their husbands without argument. Men do not fail to make use of the fact that they have known many women whom learning has made ridiculous, after which they think themselves justified in blindly abandoning their daughters to the guidance of ignorant and indiscreet mothers.

True, we must be on our guard against making them ridiculous bluestockings. Women, as a rule, have still weaker and more inquisitive minds than men; therefore it is not expedient to engage them in studies that may turn their heads: they are not destined to govern the state, to make war, or to minister in holy things; so they may pass by certain extended fields of knowledge that belong to politics, the art of war, jurisprudence, philosophy, and theology. Most of the mechanic arts, even, are not suited to women, who are fashioned for moderate exertions only. Their bodies as well as their minds are less strong and robust then those of men. As a compensa-

---

*From Lupton, Kate (trans.). *Fenelon's Education of Girls*. Boston: Ginn & Company, 1891, pp. 11-18.

tion, nature has given them for their portion neatness, industry, and
thrift, in order to keep them quietly occupied in their homes.

But what follows from this natural weakness of women? The weaker they are, the most important it is to strengthen them. Have they not duties to fulfil, and duties, too, that lie at foundation of all human life? Is it not the women, who ruin or uphold families, who regulate every detail of domestic life, and who consequently decide what touches the whole human race most nearly? In this way they exert a controlling influence on the good and bad morals of nearly all the world. A discreet, diligent, pious woman is the soul of an entire large household; she provides in it alike for temporal and spiritual welfare. Even men, who have exclusive authority in public, cannot, by their decisions, establish a real prosperity unless women aid them in its achievement.

The world is not an abstraction; it is the aggregate of all its families. And who can regulate these with nicer care than women, who, besides their natural authority and assiduity in their homes, have the additional advantage of being born careful, attentive to details, industrious, winning, and persuasive? Or can men hope for any happiness for themselves if their most intimate companionship —that of marriage—be turned to bitterness? And as to children, who will eventually constitute the entire human race,—what will become of them if their mothers spoil them in the early years?

Such, then, are the occupations of women, which are not less important to the public than those of men, since they involve the tasks of managing a household, making a husband happy, and training children well. Virtue, moreover, is no less incumbent on women than on men, and not to speak of the good or harm they may do to mankind, women constitute half of the human race redeemed by the blood of Christ and destined to eternal life.

In conclusion, we must consider, besides the good that women do if properly brought up, the evil they may cause in the world when they lack a training that inspires virtue. It is evident that a bad education is productive of more harm in the case of women than in that of men, since the excess of the latter often proceed both from the bad training received from their mothers and from the passions awakened in them at a later age by other women. What intrigues, what subversions of law and morality, what bloody wars, what innovations against religion, what revolutions in government caused by the profligacy of women, are presented to us in history! Such is the proof of the importance of training girls well: let us inquire into the means of accomplishing this object.

Chapter II

"Disadvantages of the Ordinary Methods of Education"

A girl becomes listless and is at a loss how to occupy herself innocently, because of her ignorance. When she has reached a certain age without giving her attention to things of real moment, she can neither have a taste for them nor appreciate their value; everything that is serious seems dreary to her, and everything that demands continued attention wearies her. The inclination to pleasure so strong in youth, the example of persons of the same age absorbed in amusement, everything tends to make her shrink from an orderly and industrious life. In these earlier years she lacks the experience and authority requisite for the oversight of anything in her parents' home. She does not even recognize the importance of applying herself to such matters unless her mother has taken the pains to call her attention to it in particular instances. If she be of the upper classes, she is exempt from manual labor. She is at work, therefore, for a few hours of the day only, because people say, without knowing why, that it is right for women to have something to do; but often this is a mere pretence, and she will not accustom herself to protracted effort.

Under these circumstances, what is a girl to do? The companionship of a mother who watches her, who scolds her, who thinks she is bringing her up well by pardoning nothing in her, who is stiff with her, who makes her the victim of her whims, and who appears to her always weighed down with all domestic cares, cramps and repels her; while she is surrounded by flattering maid-servants who, seeking to ingratiate themselves with her by servile and dangerous attentions, carry out all her fancies and talk to her of all that can give her a distaste for what is good. Piety appears to her an insipid occupation and its principles fatal to all pleasures. With what, then, shall she employ herself? With nothing useful. This lack of application even becomes an incurable habit.

Behold, then, a great void that we cannot hope to fill with substantial things; frivolous ones must, therefore, take their place. In this state of idleness, a girl gives herself up to indolence; and indolence, which is a languor of the soul, is an inexhaustible source of ennui. She forms the habit of sleeping a third longer than is necessary for perfect health. This long sleep only serves to enervate her, to make her more delicate, and more exposed to revolts of the

flesh. A moderate amount of sleep, on the contrary, accompanied
by regular exercise, makes one cheerful, vigorous, and robust; and
secures, without doubt, the true perfection of the body—not to
mention the advantages that accrue to the mind. This idleness and
self-indulgence, being united with ignorance, produce a hurtful
susceptibility to the charms of amusements and plays; it is these
also that excite an indiscreet and insatiable curiosity.

Well-informed persons, who are occupied with serious matters,
have usually only a moderate curiosity. What they know gives them
a contempt for much of which they are ignorant; they see the
uselessness and folly of most of the information that petty minds,
and know nothing and have nothing to do, are eager to acquire.

On the other hand, idle and badly taught girls have ever-
wandering imaginations. In the absence of solid food their curiosity
turns eagerly to foolish and dangerous objects. Those that have
talent often set themselves up for learned women, and read every
book that can feed their vanity. They delight in romances, in
comedies, and in tales of marvellous adventures in which un-
hallowed love is concerned. They acquire a fanciful turn of mind
from familiarity with the grandiloquent language of the heroes of
romance; thus they unfit themselves for real life; for all those airy
fine sentiments, all those generous emotions, all those adventures
invented by the authors of romances to gratify the fancy, have no
connection with the real motives that actuate mankind and decide
their affairs, nor with the disappointments that we meet with in
every undertaking.

The poor girl, full of the examples of the tender and the
marvellous that have charmed her in her reading, is astonished not
to meet in the world real persons that are like her heroes; she would
live like those imaginary princesses, who in the romances are ever
charming, ever adored, ever above all wants. How distasteful for
her to descend from such heroic heights to the lowest details of
housekeeping!

Some girls push their curiosity still further and aspire to decide
on religious questions to which they are not equal. Those that have
not ability enough for such investigations pursue others suited to
their capacity. They ardently desire to know everything that is said
and done; be it song, item of news, or intrigue; to receive letters and
to read those received by others. They are vain, and their vanity
makes them talkative; they are frivolous, and their frivolity prevents the reflections that would often keep them silent.

ADVICE FROM M. DE FENELON, ARCHBISHOP OF CAMBRAI, TO A LADY OF QUALITY, CONCERNING HER EDUCATION OF HER DAUGHTER*

In accordance with your wish, Madame, I will lay before you my ideas with regard to the education of your daughter.

If you had several daughters you might perhaps be excused this trouble in view of your many outside duties which are greater than you might desire. In that case you could choose a good convent where the boarders are carefully educated. But since you have only one girl to bring up and God has given you the opportunity of taking charge of her I think that you can give her a better education than any convent can. The eyes of a wise, loving and Christian mother can, no doubt, discern what other people cannot see. Because this gift is very rare the best course for mothers is to entrust convents with the task of educating their daughters, because they themselves often lack the knowledge necessary for this task. Or even if they do possess it they do not back it up by a serious, Christian way of life, without which the soundest instruction makes no impression; for everything which such a mother tells her daughter is counteracted by what the girl sees her do. That is not the case with you, Madame. Your only aim is to serve God. Religion is the first of your concerns, and you will inspire in your daughter that which she sees you practice. For this reason I exempt you from the general rule, and I prefer you to educate her rather than any convent. It is also a great advantage in the education which you give her to have her near you. If a convent is not well ordered she will see there vanity held in honour, and this is the subtlest of all poisons for a young person. There she will hear the world spoken of as a kind of enchanted place, and nothing makes a more pernicious impression than this false idea of the world which is regarded from afar with admiration, and the pleasures of which are exaggerated without showing its disappointments and sorrows. The world never dazzles so much as when one sees it from a distance and never close up, and without any warning against its deceits. For this reason I distrust a worldly convent even more than the world itself. If on the other hand a convent is full of religious zeal and keeps the rules of its Order faithfully, a girl of high birth

---

*Reprinted from Barnard, H.C. *Fenelon on Education.* Cambridge: University Press, 1966, pp. 97-107. By permission of the publisher.

grows up there in complete ignorance of the world outside. This is doubtless a happy ignorance if it is to go on for ever. But if this girl leaves the convent and at a certain age goes back to her father's house where the world confronts her, nothing is more to be feared than the resulting surprise and shock to a vivid imagination. A girl who has been shut off from the world simply by letting her know nothing about it, and in whom virtue is not as yet strongly rooted, is soon tempted to believe that whatever is most wonderful has hitherto been hidden from her. She leaves the convent like a person brought up in the darkness of a deep cavern who is suddenly taken out in the light of day. Nothing gives a greater shock than this unexpected transition and this glare to which one has not been accustomed. It would be much better to accustom a girl gradually to the world under the guidance of a wise and religious mother who will show her only so much of it as is fitting for her to see, who will point out its faults when they occur, and who will set her the example of making use of it only in moderation and so far as is necessary. I have a high opinion of the education given in good convents; but I count still more on that given by a good mother if she is free to take on this work. I conclude therefore, Madame, that your daughter is better with you than in the best convent that you could choose. But there are few mothers to whom one should give a piece of advice like this.

It is true that there are great risks in this kind of education if you are not careful to choose suitable women to be in your daughter's company. Your duties at home and your charitable works abroad do not allow you to have your child always under your eyes. It is desirable that she should leave you as little as possible, but you will not be able to take her with you everywhere. If you leave her to women of a frivolous, ill-regulated and indiscreet character they will do her more harm in a week than the good which you could do her in several years. These persons who themselves have as a rule received a bad education will gradually give her a similar one. They will talk too freely among themselves in the presence of the child who notices everything and wants to imitate it. They will express views which are false and dangerous. The child will hear them talk scandal, lie, suspect on inadequate grounds, criticise without justification. She will see jealousy and unfriendliness, whimsical and inconsistent behavior, sometimes devotions which are insincere or superstitious or irregular and her most serious faults will go uncorrected. Moreover, people of a servile disposition will not fail to try to please the child by humoring or flattering her in a most dangerous way. I admit that education in the most mediocre convent is better than this kind of home education. But I take it that you will never lose sight of your daughter except in case of absolute necessity, and that you will at least have a reliable person who will be responsible for her on the occasions when you are forced to leave her. It is essential that this person should have enough good sense and virtue to be able to exercise a kindly authority, which will keep the other women up to their duties, to call the child to order if need be without incurring her dislike, and to report to you whatever needs looking into. I confess that such a woman is not easy to find; but it is of the first importance to try to discover her and to spare no expense in making her position with you comfortable. I know that one may encounter many disappointments; but one has to be contented with the essential qualifications and put up with the faults which are mingled with them. Unless you have such a person ready to help you, you cannot hope to succeed.

Since your daughter shows considerable intelligence and has a quick, ready and acute mind I fear she may become affected and develop a vain and dangerous excess of curiosity. You will allow me, Madame, if you please, to add that this should not offend you because you are not in any way responsible. Women are usually even more keen on the adornments of the mind than on those of the body. Those who are capable of study and hope to distinguish themselves thereby, have even more enthusiasm for their books than for their clothes. They conceal their knowledge a little—but they only half conceal it so as to gain credit for modesty as well as ability. Other more crude forms of vanity are more easily corrected because they are noticed and censured and they are the mark of a frivolous character. But a woman of an inquiring mind, who sets up for knowing a great deal, prides herself on being an outstanding genius among her sex. She thinks it fine to despise the vain amusements of other women. She thinks she is always right and nothing will cure her of this obstinacy. As a rule she can never but half know anything. She is more dazzled than enlightened by what she knows. She flatters herself that she knows everything and can make the decisions. She becomes a passionate partisan of one party against another in all the disputes which take place, even in matters of religion. This is the reason why all these new-fangled sects have made so much headway owing to the women who have introduced and supported them. Women are eloquent in conversation and active in carrying on an intrigue. The gross vanity of women who are recognised as vain is less to be feared than the serious and refined vanity of those who aim at being highly intelligent in order to shine with a mere show of true merit. It is therefore of the first importance always to recall your daughter to a reasonable simplicity. It suffices if she knows enough about religion to believe it and to carry it out properly in practice, without ever arguing about it. She must listen only to the Church and not become a follower of some proscribed preacher or someone suspected of innovations. Her spiritual director must be a man who is openly opposed to anything which is called sect. She must avoid conversing with women who meddle with rash arguments concerning doctrine, and she must realise how unbecoming and dangerous this freedom is. She should have a horror of pernicious books, without wanting to find out what it is in them that makes them forbidden. She must learn to distrust herself and to beware of the snares of curiosity and presumption. She must learn to pray to God in all humility, to become poor in spirit, to meditate often, to obey without respite, to allow herself to be corrected even in her most fixed ideas by experienced persons who are fond of her, and to hold her peace and allow others to do the talking. I would rather she should know all about your major-domo's accounts than about the theologian's discussions on Grace. Keep her busy with a piece of needlework that will be useful in your house and which will accustom her to avoid dangerous relations with the outside world. But never let her argue about theology to the great danger of her faith. Everything is lost if she obstinately tries to be clever and gets a distaste for domestic duties. The virtuous woman spins, confines herself to her home, keeps quiet, believes and obeys; she does not argue against the Church.

I am quite sure, Madame, that you will know how to introduce, when occasion offers, some reflections on the immodesty and lack of principle which are found in some women of high intelligence, so that you may help your daugher to avoid this danger. But as the authority of a mother runs the risk of wearing out and as the wisest of lessons do not always convince a girl against her will, I hope that women of high reputation in society, who are among your friends, will talk with you in the presence of this young lady and without appearing to be concerned with her, in order to censure the vain and foolish behaviour of women who affect to be highly educated and who hanker after innovations in religion. These indirect lessons, it appears, make more impression than all that you can say to her directly when you are alone together.

As regards dress I hope that you will be able to give your

daughter a taste for true moderation. There is a type of woman who goes to extremes and who cannot endure the happy mean. They would prefer to have a plain austerity if this were the mark of some striking change of fashion, rather than to keep to the middle way which they despise as being characteristic of lack of taste and a dull disposition. It remains true that it is most praiseworthy, though very rare, to find a wise and moderate character which avoids these two extremes and which, while conceding to the proprieties that which one cannot refuse them, never oversteps the limit. True wisdom in the matter of furniture, household gear and clothes, is to have nothing that calls for comment, either good or bad. Let it be enough, you will say to your daughter, to avoid being criticised as a person lacking in taste or untidy or slovenly; but never show any kind of affectation or ostentation in your dress. In this way you will appear to possess a reason and a virtue which is in no way indicated by your furniture or your clothes. You will make use of these but you will not become their slave. This young person must be made to realise that it is luxury which breaks down class barriers and raises people of low birth, who have quickly grown rich by dishonourable means above persons of the highest distinction. It is this disorder that corupts the morals of a nation, which engenders greed, which makes us accustomed to intrigues and shameful actions, and which gradually undermines honesty. Your daughter must also understand that however great wealth a woman may have in her home, she will soon ruin it if she introduces luxury for which no resources can suffice. At the same time accustom her to think of the sufferings of the poor and to realise how unworthy of humanity it is that some men, who possess everything, set no bounds to their own superfluity while cruelly refusing bare necessities to others.

If you keep your daughter in a condition too inferior to that of other persons of her age and rank you run the risk of estranging her from you. She may ardently long for what she cannot have and covet it from afar in someone else. She may be tempted to consider you too severe and harsh. She may perhaps be longing to feel herself mistress of what she does, in order to give herself over to vanity without restraint. You will much more easily hold her in check if you suggest a middle course which will always meet with the approval of sensible and reputable people. She will realize that you want her to have whatever is seemly, that you are ready to make all possible allowances for her, and that you merely want to guard her against the excesses of persons whose vanity knows no bounds. What is really essential is never to sanction any immodesty which is unworthy of a Christian. You can have recourse to reasons of propriety and advantage to help and support religion in this matter. A young woman risks her happiness for the rest of her life if she marries a man who is vain, frivolous and dissolute. It is of the first importance therefore that she should fit herself for finding a wise, well-conducted husband who has a sound character and is likely to be successful in his occupations. To find such a man she must be modest and show no signs of frivolity or irresponsibility. Where is the sensible and discreet man who will be willing to marry a vain woman of whose character, to judge by her conduct, he cannot be sure?

But the best method is to win over the heart of your daughter to a Christian way of life. Do not scare her away from this by being unnecessarily severe. Leave her an honourable liberty and pleasures which are innocent. Accustom her to enjoy herself well out of the reach of sin and to get her pleasure far removed from dangerous amusements. Try to find for her companions who will do her no harm and at times entertainments which will not put her off serious occupations for the rest of the day. Try to make her enjoy God. Do not allow her to look upon Him as a powerful and stern judge who ceaselessly watches us in order to find fault with us and force us on every occasion. Make her see how kind He is, how He meets our needs and has pity on our shortcomings. Familiarise her with the idea of Him as a tender and merciful Father. Never let her regard prayer as an idle and boring performance or a mental exercise which one has to perform while letting one's imagination wander. Make her realise that one must often enter into oneself in order to find God, because 'the Kingdom of God is within you'. One has only to speak to God quite simply at any time, to confess our faults, to lay our needs before Him and with His help to take the measures necessary for correcting our failings. We must listen to God in the silence of our hearts, saying 'I will hear what the Lord says within me'. We must try to acquire the blessed habit of living in His presence and of doing everything, be it great or small, for love of Him. We must renew this contact whenever we find we have lost it. We must rid ourselves of the thoughts which distract us as soon as we realise what is happening, without distracting ourselves by dint of distractions, and without being disquieted if they return frequently. One must have patience with oneself and never be discouraged however weak one's efforts prove. Involuntary distractions do not separate us from God. Nothing is more pleasing to Him than the humble patience of a soul which is ready to try again to return to Him. Your daughter will soon find the road to prayer if you show her the true way thither. There is no need of great intellectual effort or flashes of imagination or over-refined feelings which God grants or takes away as He pleases. When the only prayer that one knows is that which consists of sentiments which are so apt to flatter one's mind, one is soon discouraged; for such a prayer dries up and then one feels that everything is lost. But tell her that prayer is like simple, familiar and tender fellowship with God—in fact, it is that fellowship. Accustom her to open her heart to God, to make use of whatever will keep her in touch with Him, and to speak to Him with confidence just as one speaks freely and without reserve to a person whom one loves and by whom one feels that one is sincerely loved. Most people who confine themselves to a fixed and formal type of prayer are with God as one is with persons whom one respects but sees only occasionally and in a ceremonial way, without loving them or being loved by them. Everything is a matter of etiquette and compliments. One becomes annoyed and bored and longs to get away. On the other hand, people who have God in their hearts are with Him as with their closest friends. One does not measure one's words because one knows to whom one is speaking. One speaks solely out of the abundance and simplicity of one's heart. We tell God of those everyday events which tend to His glory and our salvation. We mention our faults which we are trying to amend, our duties which we have to fulfil, our temptations which must be overcome, the fastidiousness and trickery of our self-love which must be repressed. One tells Him everything and listens to whatever He tells us. We repeat His Commandments and seek His guidance. This is no longer a formal conversation, it is free and friendly intercourse. Thus God becomes one's dearest friend, the Father in Whose bosom His children find consolation, the Spouse with Whom one's spirit is united through grace. One humbles oneself without losing courage. One has firm confidence in God and complete distrust of oneself. One never forgets oneself in order to listen to the flattering suggestions of self-love. If you instil into the heart of your daughter this simple and inward piety she will make great progress.

Believe me, Madame, etc.

DANIEL DEFOE (1660–1731)

Although he was from a fairly prosperous family, Defoe was refused admittance to Oxford and Cambridge universities because his father was a religious Nonconformist, i.e., not a member of the Church of England. This rejection led to his choice of Newington Green for his higher education.

Financial difficulties caused him to abandon his brief career in trade. He turned to a political career, which resulted in his imprisonment for publication of his pamphlet, "The Shortest Way with the Dissenters."

Defoe was the author of *Moll Flanders* and *Robinson Crusoe*. Two years prior to the publication of the latter, he wrote *An Essay upon Projects* (1697) which includes the chapter "An Academy for Women." He begins the chapter with the daring statement that it is barbarous to deny women an education, then goes on to outline details for the establishment of colleges for women.

*AN ESSAY UPON PROJECTS**

An Academy for Women

I have often thought of it as one of the most barbarous Customs in the world, considering us as a Civiliz'd and a Christian Countrey, that we deny the advantages of Learning to Women. We reproach the Sex every day with Folly and Impertinence, while I am confident, had they the advantages of Education equal to us, they wou'd be guilty of less than our selves.

One wou'd wonder indeed how it shou'd happen that Women are conversible at all, since they are only beholding to Natural Parts for all their Knowledge. Their Youth is spent to teach them to

---

*Defoe, Daniel. *An Essay upon Projects* (1697). Menston, England: The Scolar Press, Ltd., 1969, pp. 282–304. By permission of the publisher.

Stitch and Sow, or make Bawbles: They are taught to Read indeed, and perhaps to Write their Names, or so; and that is the heighth of a Woman's Education. And I wou'd but ask any who slight the Sex for their Understanding, What is a Man (a Gentleman, I mean) good for, that is taught no more?

I need not give Instances, or examine the Character of a Gentleman with a good Estate, and of a good Family, and with tolerable Parts, and examine what Figure he makes for want of Education.

The Soul is plac'd in the Body like a rough Diamond, and must be polish'd, or the Lustre of it will never appear: And 'tis manifest, that as the Rational Soul distinguishes us from Brutes, so Education carries on the distinction, and makes some less brutish than others: This is too evident to need any demonstration. But why then shou'd Women be deni'd the benefit of Instruction? If Knowledge and Understanding had been useless additions to the Sex, God Almighty wou'd never have given them Capacities; for he made nothing needless: Besides, I wou'd ask such, What they can see in Ignorance, that they shou'd think it a necessary Ornament to a Woman? Or how much worse is a Wise Woman than a Fool? Or what has the Woman done to forfeit the Privilege of being taught? Does she plague us with her Pride and Impertenence? Why did we not let her learn, that she might have had more Wit? Shall we upbraid Women with Folly, when 'tis only the Error of this inhuman Custom, that hindred them being made wiser?

The Capacities of Women are suppos'd to de greater, and their Senses quicker than those of the Men; and what they might be capable of being bred to, is plain from some Instances of Female-Wit, which this Age is not without; which upbraids us with Injustice, and looks as if we deni'd Women the advantages of Education, for fear they shou'd *vye* with the Men in their Improvements.

To remove this Objection, and that Women might have at least a needful Opportunity of Education in all sorts of Useful Learning, I propose the Draught of an Academy for that purpose.

I know 'tis dangerous to make Publick Appearances of the Sex; they are not either to be *confin'd* or *expos'd;* the first will disagree with their Inclinations, and the last with their Reputations; and therefore it is somewhat difficult; and I doubt a Method propos'd by an Ingenious Lady, in a little Book, call'd, *Advice to the Ladies,* would be found impracticable. For, saving my Respect to the Sex, the Levity, which perhaps is a little peculiar to them, at least in their

Youth, will not bear the Restraint; and I am satisfi'd, nothing but the heighth of Bigotry can keep up a Nunnery: Women are extravagantly desirous of going to Heaven, and will punish their *Pretty Bodies* to get thither; but nothing else will do it; and even in that case sometimes it falls out that *Nature will prevail.*

When I talk therefore of an Academy for Women, I mean both the Model, the Teaching, and the Government, different from what is propos'd by that Ingenious Lady, for whose Proposal I have a very great Esteem, and also a great Opinion of her Wit; different too from all sorts of Religious Confinement, and above all, from *Vows of Celibacy.*

Wherefore the Academy I propose should differ but little from Publick Schools, wherein such Ladies as were willing to study, shou'd have all the advantages of Learning suitable to their Genius.

But since some Severities of Discipline more than ordinary wou'd be absolutely necessary to preserve the Reputation of the House, that Persons of Quality and Fortune might not be afraid to venture their Children thither, I shall venture to make a small Scheme by way of Essay.

The House I wou'd have built in a Form by it self, as well as in a place by it self.

The Building shou'd be of Three plain Fronts, without any Jettings, or Bearing-Work, that the Eye might at a Glance see from one Coin to the other; the Gardens wall'd in the same Triangular Figure, with a large Moat, and but one Entrance.

When thus every part of the Scituation was contriv'd as well as might be for discovery, and to render *Intrieguing* dangerous, I wou'd have no Guards, no Eyes, no Spies set over the Ladies, but shall expect them to be try'd by the Principles of Honour and strict Virtue.

And if I am ask'd, *Why?* I must ask Pardon of my own Sex for giving this reason for it:

I am so much in Charity with Women, and so well acquainted with Men, that 'tis my opinion, There needs no other Care to prevent Intrieguing, than to keep the men effectually away: For tho *Inclination,* which we prettily call *Love,* does sometimes move a little too visibly in the Sex, and Frailty often follows; yet I think verily, *Custom,* which we miscall *Modesty,* has so far the Ascendant over the Sex, that *Solicitation* always goes before it.

> *Custom with Women 'Stead of Virtue rules;*
> *It leads the Wisest, and commands the Fools:*
> *For this alone, when Inclinations reign,*
> *Tho' Virtue's fled, will Acts of Vic restrain.*
> *Only by Custom 'tis that Virtue lives,*
> *And Love requires to be ask'd, before it gives.*
> *For that which we call* Modesty, *is* Pride:
> *They scorn to ask, and hate to be deni'd.*
> *'Tis Custom thus prevails upon their Want;*
> *They'll never beg, what askt they eas'ly grant.*
> *And when the needless Ceremony's over*
> *Themselves the Weakness of the Sex discover.*
> *If then Desires are Strong, and Nature free,*
> *Keep from her Men, and Opportunity.*
> *Else twill be vain to curb her by Restraint;*
> *But keep the Question off, you keep the Saint.*

In short, let a Woman have never such a Coming-Principle, she will let you ask before she complies, at least if she be a Woman of any Honour.

Upon this ground I am persuaded such Measures might be taken, that the Ladies might have all the Freedom in the world within their own Walls, and yet no Intrieguing, no Indecencies, nor Scandalous Affairs happen; and in order to this, the following Customs and Laws shou'd be observ'd in the Colleges; of which I wou'd propose One at least in every Country in *England,* and about Ten for the City of *London.*

After the Regulation of the Form of the Building as before;

(1.) All the Ladies who enter into the House, shou'd set their Hands to the Orders of the House, to signify their Consent to submit to them.

(2.) As no Woman shou'd be receiv'd, but who declar'd herself willing, and that it was the Act of her Choice to enter her self, so no Person shou'd be confin'd to continue there a moment longer than the same voluntary Choice inclin'd her.

(3.) The Charges of the House being to be paid by the Ladies, every one that entred shou'd have only this Incumbrance, That she shou'd pay for the whole Year, tho' her mind shou'd change as to her continuance.

(4.) An Act of Parliament shou'd make it Felony without Clergy, for any man to enter by Force or Fraud into the House, or to solicit any Woman, *tho' it were to Marry,* while she was in the House. And this Law wou'd by no means be severe; because any Woman who was willing to receive the Addresses of a Man, might discharge herself of the House when she pleas'd; and on the contrary, any Woman who had occasion, might discharge her self of the Impertinent Addresses of any Person she had an Aversion to, by entering into the House.

The Persons who Enter, shou'd be taught all sorts of Breeding suitable to both their Genius and their Quality; and in particular, *Musick* and *Dancing,* which it wou'd be cruelty to bar the Sex of, because they are their Darlings: But besides this, they shou'd be taught Languages, as particularly *French* and *Italian;* and I wou'd venture the Injury of giving a Woman more Tongues than one.

They shou'd, as a particular Study, be taught all the Graces of Speech, and all the necessary Air of Conversation; which our common Education is so defective in, that I need not expose it: They shou'd be brought to read Books, and especially History, and so to read as to make them understand the World, and be able to know and judge of things when they hear of them.

To such whose Genius wou'd lead them to it, I wou'd deny no sort of Learning; but the chief thing in general is to cultivate the Understandings of the Sex, that they may be capable of all sorts of Conversation; that their Parts and Judgments being improv'd, they may be as Profitable in their Conversation as they are Pleasant.

Women, in my observation, have little or no difference in them, but as they are, or are not distinguish'd by Education. Tempers indeed may in some degree influence them, but the main distinguishing part is their Breeding.

The whole Sex are generally Quick and Sharp: I believe I may be allow'd to say generally so; for you rarely see them lumpish and heavy when they are Children, as Boys will often be. If a Woman be well-bred, and taught the proper Management of her Natural Wit, she proves generally very sensible and retentive: And without partiality, a Woman of Sense and Manners is the Finest and most Delicate Part of God's Creation; the Glory of her Maker, and the great Instance of his singular regard to Man, his Darling Creature, to whom he gave the best Gift either God could bestow, or man receive: And 'tis the sordid'st Piece of Folly and Ingratitude in the world, to withhold from the Sex the due Lustre which the advantages of Education give to the Natural Beauty of their Minds.

A Woman well Bred and well Taught, furnish'd with the additional Accomplishments of Knowledge and Behaviour, *is a Creature without comparison;* her Society is the Emblem of sublimer Enjoyments; her Person is Angelick, and her Conversation heavenly; she is all Softness and Sweetness, Peace, Love, Wit, and Delight: She is every way suitable to the sublimest Wish; and the man that has such a one to his Portion, has nothing to do but to rejoice in her, and be thankful.

On the other hand, Suppose her to be the *very same* Woman, and rob her of the Benefit of Education, and it follows thus;

If her Temper be Good, want of Education makes her Soft and Easy.

Her Wit, for want to Teaching, makes her Impertinent and Talkative.

Her Knowledge, for want of Judgment and Experience, makes her Fanciful and Whimsical.

If her Temper be Bad, want of Breeding makes her worse, and she grows Haughty, Insolent, and Loud.

If she be Passionate, want of Manners makes her Termagant, and a Schold, *which is much at one with Lunatick.*

If she be Proud, want of Discretion (which still is Breeding) makes her Conceited, Fantastick, and Ridiculous.

And from these she degenerates to be Turbulent, Clamorous, Noisy, Nasty, *and the Devil.*

Methinks Mankind for their own sakes, since say what we will of the Women, we all think fit one time or other to be concern'd with 'em, shou'd take some care to breed them up to be *suitable* and *serviceable,* if they expected no such thing as *Delight* from 'em. Bless us! What Care do we take to Breed up a good Horse, and to Break him well! and what a Value do we put upon him when it is done, and all because he shou'd be fit for our use! and why not a Woman? Since all her Ornaments and Beauty, without suitable Behaviour, is a Cheat in Nature, like the false Tradesman, who puts the best of his Goods uppermost, that the Buyer may think the rest are of the same Goodness.

Beauty of the Body, which is the Womens Glory, seems to be now unequally bestow'd, and Nature, or rather Providence, to lye under some Scandal about it, as if 'twas given a Woman for a Snare to Men, and so make a kind of a *She-Devil* of her: Because they say Exquisite Beauty is *rarely* given with Wit; *more rarely* with Goodness of Temper, and *never at all* with Modesty. And some, pretending to justify the Equity of such a Distribution, will tell us 'tis the Effect of the Justice of Providence in dividing particular Excellencies among all his Creatures, *Share and Share alike, as it were,* that all might for something or other be acceptable to one another, else some wou'd be despis'd.

I think both these Notions false; and yet the last, which has the shew of Respect to Providence, is the worst; for it supposes

Providence to be Indigent and Empty; as if it had not wherewith to
furnish all the Creatures it had made, but was fain to be
parcimonious in its Gifts, and distribute them by *piece-meal,* for
fear of being exhausted.

If I might venture my Opinion against an almost universal
Notion, I wou'd say, Most men mistake the Proceedings of
Providence in this case, and all the world at this day are mistaken
in their Practice about it. And because the Assertion is very bold, I
desire to explain my self.

That Almighty First Cause which made us all, is certainly the
Fountain of Excellence, as it is of Being, and by an Invisible
Influence could have diffused Equal Qualities and Perfections to all
the Creatures it has made, as the Sun does its Light, without the
least Ebb or Diminution to himself; and has given indeed to every
individual sufficient to the Figure his Providence had design'd him
in the world.

I believe it might be defended, if I should say, That I do
suppose God has given to all Mankind equal Gifts and Capacities,
in that he has given them all *Souls* equally capable; and that the
whole difference in Mankind proceeds either from Accidental
Difference in the Make of their Bodies, or from the *foolish
Difference* of Education.

1. *From Accidental Difference in Bodies.* I wou'd avoid dis-
coursing here of the Philosophical Position of the Soul in the Body:
But if it be true as Philosophers do affirm, That the Understanding
and Memory is dilated or contracted according to the accidental
Dimensions of the Organ through which 'tis convey'd; then tho'
God has given a Soul as capable to me as another, yet if I have any
Natural Defect in those Parts of the Body by which the Soul shou'd
act, I may have the same Soul infus'd as another man, and yet he be
a Wife Man, and I a very Fool. *For example,* If a Child naturally
have a Defect in the Organ of Hearing, so that he cou'd never
distinguish any Sound, that Child shall never be able to speak or
read, tho' it have a Soul capable of all the Accomplishments in the
world. The Brain is the Centre of the Souls actings, where all the
distinguishing Faculties of it reside; and 'tis observable, A man who
has a narrow contracted Head, in which there is not room for the
due and necessary Operations of Nature by the Brain, is never a
man of very great Judgment; and that Proverb, *A Great Head and
Little Wit,* is not meant by Nature, but is a Reproof upon Sloth; as
if one shou'd, by way of wonder, say, *Fye, fye, you that have a Great
Head, have but Little Wit, that's strange! that must certainly be your*

94 *own fault,* From this Notion I do believe there is a great matter in the Breed of Men and Women; not that Wise Men shall always get Wise Children; but I believe Strong and Healthy Bodies have the Wisest Children; and Sickly Weakly Bodies affect the Wits as well as the Bodies of their Children. We are easily persuaded to believe this in the Breeds of Horses, Cocks, Dogs, and other Creatures; and I believe 'tis as visible in Men.

But to come closer to the business; the great distinguishing difference which is seen in the world between Men and Women, is in their Education; and this is manifested by comparing it with the difference between one Man or Woman, and another.

And herein it is that I take upon me to make such a bold Assertion, That all the World are mistaken in their Practice about Women: For I cannot think that God Almighty ever made them so delicate, so glorious Creatures, and furnish'd them with such Charms, so Agreeable and so Delightful to Mankind, with Souls capable of the same Accomplishments with Men, and all to be only Stewards of our Houses, *Cooks and Slaves.*

Not that I am for exalting the Female Government in the least: But, in short, *I wou'd have Men take Women for Companions, and Educate them to be fit for it.* A Woman of Sense and Breeding will scorn as much to encroach upon the Prerogative of the Man, as a Man of Sense will scorn to oppress the *Weakness* of the Woman. But if the Womens Souls were refin'd and improv'd by Teaching, that word wou'd be lost; to say, *The Weakness of the Sex,* as to Judgment, wou'd be Nonsense; for Ignorance and Folly wou'd be no more to be found among Women than Men. I remember a Passage which I heard from a very Fine Woman, she had Wit and Capacity enough, an Extraordinary Shape and Face, and a Great Fortune, but had been cloyster'd up all her time, and for fear of being stoll'n had not had the liberty of being taught the common necessary knowledge of Womens Affairs; and when she came to converse in the world, her Natural Wit made her so sensible of the want of Education, that she gave this short Reflection on her self:

I am a sham'd to talk with my very Maids, says she, *for I don't know when they do right or wrong: I had more need go to School, than be Married.*

I need not enlarge on the Loss the Defect of Education is to the Sex, nor argue the Benefit of the contrary Practice; 'tis a thing will be more easily granted than remedied: This Chapter is but an Essay at the thing, and I refer the Practice to those Happy Days, if ever they shall be, when men shall be wise enough to mend it.

PART V: ENLIGHTENMENT

The substantial number of eighteenth-century classics promoting the education of girls and women testifies to the impact of Enlightenment philosophy on female education. Academies and teacher education began in this century, but were destined to flourish in the next. The Great Awakening, a time of humanitarianism, demonstrated that the prevailing faith in the common man was, for many, a faith in the common woman, also.

The French Salon Movement was the most important eighteenth-century contribution of women. Each salonist was hostess to a daily gathering of prominent male intellectuals who engaged in scholarly discussions. Berlin also supported a Salon Movement. The corresponding English group was named the Bluestocking Movement because one gentleman accepted an invitation to attend an evening salon even though he was wearing unfashionable blue stockings.

Of the eleven selections chosen to represent the Enlightenment, six were written by women and five by men. The enlightened woman had become a reality.

MARY ASTELL (1668–1731)

It is fitting that the influential Mary Astell be the first of the Enlightenment authors. As the daughter of a merchant, she was not assured of an education; fortunately, an uncle who was a clergyman saw her intellectual promise, and tutored her in philosophy, mathematics, logic, French, and Italian. She fulfilled this promise by learning easily, by displaying wit, judgment, and an excellent memory, and by writing elegant, graceful letters. Plato, Xenophon, Tully, Seneca, and Epictetus were her favorite authors. After having devoted her early life to literature and study, Astell devoted her later life to religion.

Astell claimed, as did Plato, that women were inferior to men because of lack of education, not because of difference in nature. She emphasized the importance of training the mind rather than merely providing for acquisition of knowledge; recommended the establishment of women's colleges although most of her contemporaries regarded this as absurd; and favored a combination of religious and educational aims. Astell planned for her seminary students to teach after graduation, marry, and then teach their own children.

One limitation in her thinking was her confinement of education to ladies of noble families; another limitation was her insistence that women should not become lawyers or members of the clergy.

In writing her 1694 book, *A Serious Proposal to the Ladies,* she became the first author to suggest that women's schools should become comparable to existing men's schools. Her book represented the initial attempt to arouse the interest of Englishwomen in higher education. She wrote *A Serious Proposal* because she wanted to turn women's minds from frivolous, worldly thoughts to higher spiritual desires. Following the reprint of the opening section from this, her major work, is a precise commentary on education excerpted from her 1696 *Essay in Defence of the Female Sex.*

"For the Advancement of their true and greatest interest"
By a lover of her sex

LADIES,

Since the Profitable Adventures that have gone abroad in the World, have met with so great Encouragement, tho' the highest advantage they can propose, is an uncertain Lot for such matters as Opinion (not real worth) gives a value to; things which if obtain'd, are as flitting and fickle, as that Chance which is to dispose of them. I therefore persuade my self, you will not be less kind to a Proposition that comes attended with more certain and substantial Gain; whose only design is to improve your Charms and heighten your Value, by suffering you no longer to be cheap and contemptible. It's aim is to fix that Beauty, to make it lasting and permanent, which Nature with all the helps of Art, cannot secure: And to place it out of the reach of Sickness and Old Age, by transferring it from a corruptible Body to an immortal Mind. An obliging Design, which wou'd procure them *inward* Beauty, to whom Nature has unkindly denied the *outward;* and not permit those Ladies who have comely Bodies, to tarnish their Glory with deformed Souls. Wou'd have you all be wits, or what is better Wise. Raise you above the Vulgar by something more truely illustrious, than a founding Title, or a great Estate. Wou'd excite in you a generous Emulation to excel in the best things, and not in such Trifles as every mean person who has but Mony enough, may purchase as well as you. Not suffer you to take up with low thought of distinguishing your selves by anything that is not truly valuable; and procure you such Ornaments as all the Treasures of the *Indies* are not able to purchase. Wou'd help you to surpass the Men as much in Vertue and Ingenuity, as you do in Beauty; that you may not only be as lovely, but as wise as Angels. Exalt and Establish your Fame, more than the best wrought *Poems,* and loudest *Panegyricks,* by ennobling your Minds with such Graces as really deserve it. And instead of the Fustian Complements and Fulsome Flatteries of your Admirers, obtain for you the Plaudit of Good Men and Angels, and the approbation of him who cannot err. In a word, render you the Glory and Blessing of the present Age, and

---

*Astell, Mary, *A Serious Proposal to the Ladies.* London: R. Wilkin, 1694. At the King's Head in St. Paul's churchyard.

the Admiration and Pattern of the next.

And sure, I shall not need many words to persuade you to close with this Proposal. The very offer is a sufficient inducement; nor does it need the set-off's of *Rhetorick* to recommend it, were I capable, which yet I am not, of applying them with the greatest force. Since you cannot be so unkind to your selves, as to refuse your *real* Interest; I only entreat you to be so wise as to examine wherein it consists; for nothing is of worser consequence than to be deceiv'd in a matter of so great concern. 'Tis as little beneath your Grandeur as your Prudence, to examine curiously what is in this case offer'd you; and to take care that cheating Hucksters don't impose upon you with deceitful Ware. This is a matter infinitely more worthy your Debates, than what Colours are most agreeable, or whats the Dress becomes you best? Your *Glass* will not do you half so much service as a serious reflection on your own Minds; which will discover Irregularities more worthy your Correction, and keep you from being either too much elated or depress'd by the representations of the other. 'Twill not be near so advantagious to consult with your Dancing-master as with your own Thoughts, how you may with greatest exactness tread in the Paths of Vertue, which has certainly the most attractive *Air,* and Wisdom the most graceful and becoming *Meen:* Let these attend you, and your Carriage will be always well compos'd, and ev'ry thing you do will carry its Charm with it. No solicitude in the adornation of your selves is discommended, provided you employ your care about that which is really yourself; and do not neglect that particle of Divinity within you, which must survive, and may (if you please) be happy and perfect when it's unsuitable and much inferiour Companion is mouldring into Dust. Neither will any pleasure be denied you, who are only desir'd not to catch at the Shadow and let the Substance go. You may be as ambitious as you please, so you aspire to the best *things;* and contend with your Neighbours as much as you can, that they may not outdo you in any commendable Quality. Let it never be said, that they to whom preeminence is so very agreeable, can be tamely content that others shou'd surpass them in *this,* and precede them in a *better* World! Remember, I pray you, the famous Women of former Ages, the *Orinda's* of late, and the more Modern *D'acier* and others, and blush to think how much is now, and will hereafter be said of them, when you your selves (as great a Figure as you make) must be buried in silence and forgetfulness! Shall your Emulation fail *there only* where it is commendable? Why are you so preposterously humble, as not to contend for one of the highest

Mansions in the Court of Heav'n? Believe me Ladies, this is the only *Place* worth contending for; you are neither better nor worse in your selves for going before, or coming after *now;* but you are really so much the better, by how much the higher your station is in an Orb of Glory. How can you be content to be in the world like Tulips in a Garden, to make a fine *shew* and be good for nothing; have all your Glories set in the grave, or perhaps much sooner? What your own sentiments are, I know not, but I cannot without pity and resentment reflect, that those Glorious Temples on which your kind Creator has bestow'd such exquisite workmanship, shou'd enshrine no better than *Egyptian* Deities; be like a garnish'd Sepulchre, which for all it's glittering, has nothing within but Emptiness or Putrifaction! What a pity it is, that whilst your Beauty casts a lustre round about, your Souls which are infinitely more bright and radiant (of which if you had but a clear Idea, as lovely as it is, and as much as you now value it, you wou'd then despise and neglect the mean *Case* that encloses it) shou'd be suffer'd to overrun with Weeds, lye fallow and neglected, unadorn'd with any Grace! Altho the Beauty of the Mind is necessary to secure those Conquests which your Eyes have gain'd; and Time that mortal Enemy to handsome Faces, has no influence on a lovely Soul, but to better and improve it. For shame, let us abandon that *Old,* and therefore one wou'd think, unfashionable employment of pursuing Butterflies and Trifles! No longer drudge on in the dull beaten road of Vanity and Folly, which so many have gone, before us; but dare to break the enchanted Circle that custom has placed us in, and scorn the vulgar way of imitating all the Impertinencies of our Neighbours. Let us learn to pride our selves in something more excellent than the invention of a Fashion: And not entertain such a degrading thought of our own *worth,* as to imagine that our Souls were given us only for the service of our Bodies, and that the best improvement we can make of these, is to attract the eyes of men. We value *them* too much, and our *selves* too little, if we place any part of our worth in their Opinion; and do not think our selves capable of Nobler Things than the pitiful Conquest of some worthless heart. She who has opportunities of making an interest in Heav'n, of obtaining the love and admiration of GOD and Angels, is too prodigal of her Time, and injurious to her Charms, to throw them away on vain insignificant men. She need not make her self so cheap, as to descend to Court their Applauses; for at the greater distance she keeps, and the more she is above them, the more effectually she secures their esteem and wonder. Be so generous then Ladies, as to do nothing unworthy of you; so true to your Interest as not to lessen your Empire, and depreciate your Charms. Let not your Thoughts be wholly busied in observing what respect is paid you, but a part of them at least, in studying to deserve it. And after all, remember, that Goodness is the truest Greatness, to be wise for your selves, the greatest Wit, and *that* Beauty the most desirable, which will endure to Eternity.

Pardon me the seeming rudeness of this Proposal, which goes upon a supposition that there is something amiss in you, which it is intended to amend. My design is not to expose, but to recitfy your Failures. To be exempt from mistake, is a priviledge few can pretend to, the greatest is to be part Conviction, and too obstinate to reform. Even the *Men,* as exact as they wou'd seem, and as much as they divert themselves with our Miscarriages, are very often guilty of greater faults; and such as considering the advantages they enjoy, are much more inexcusable. But I will not pretend to correct their Errors, who either are or at least *think* themselves too wise to receive Instruction from a Womans Pen. My earnest desire is, that you Ladies, would be as perfect and happy as 'tis possible to be in this imperfect state; for I love you too well to endure a spot upon your Beauties, if I can by any means remove and wipe it off. I would have you live up to the dignity of your Nature, and express your thankfulness to GOD for the benefits you enjoy by a due improvement of them: As I know very many of you do, who countenance that Piety which the men decry, and are the brightest Patterns of Religion that the Age affords; 'tis my grief that all the rest of our Sex do not imitate such illustrious Patterns, and therefore I would have them encreas'd and render'd more conspicuous, that Vice being put out of countenance, (because Vertue is the only thing in fashion) may sneak out of the world, and it's darkness be dispell'd by the confluence of so many shining Graces. Some perhaps will cry out that I teach you false Doctrine; for because by their seductions, some amongst us are become very mean and contemptible, they would fain persuade the rest to be as despicable and forlorn as they. We are indeed oblig'd to them for their management, in endeavouring to make us so; who use all the artifice they can to spoil, and deny us the means of improvement. So that instead of inquiring why all Women are not wise and good, we have reason to wonder that there are any so. Were the men as much neglected, and as little care taken to cultivate and improve them, perhaps they wou'd be so far from surpassing those whom they now despise, that they themselves wou'd sink into the greatest stupidity and brutality. The preposterous returns that the most of them make, to all the care and pain that is bestow'd on them, renders this no uncharitable, nor improbable Conjecture. One wou'd therefore almost think, that the wise disposer of all things, foreseeing how unjustly Women are denied opportunities of improvement from *without*, has therefore by way of compensation endow'd them with greater propensions to Vertue, and a natural goodness of Temper *within*, which if duly manag'd, would raise them to the most eminent pitch of Heroick Vertue. Hither Ladies, I desire you wou'd aspire, 'tis a noble and becoming Ambition; and to remove such Obstacles as lye in your way, is the design of this Paper. We will therefore enquire what it is that stops your flight, that keeps you groveling here below, like *Domitian* catching Flies, when you should be busied in obtaining Empires?

Altho' it has been said by Men of more Wit than Wisdom, and perhaps of more malice than either, that Women are naturally Incapable of acting Prudently, or that they are necessarily determined to folly, I must by no means grant it; that Hypothesis would render my endeavours impertinent, for then it would be in vain to advise the one, or endeavour the Reformation of the other. Besides, there are Examples in all Ages, which sufficiently confute the Ignorance and Malice of this Assertion.

The Incapacity, if there be any, is acquired not natural; and none of their Follies are so necessary, but that they might avoid them if they pleased themselves. Some disadvantages indeed they labour under, & what these are we shall see by and by, and endeavour to surmount; but Women need not take up with mean things, since (if they are not wanting to themselves) they are capable of the best. Neither God nor Nature have excluded them from being Ornaments to their Families, and useful in their Generation; there is therefore no reason they should be content to be Cyphers in the World, useless at the best, and in a little time a burden and nuisance to all about them. And 'tis very great pity that they who are so apt to over-rate themselves in smaller matters, shou'd, where it most concerns them to know, and stand upon their Value, be so insensible of their own worth.

The cause therefore of the defects we labour under, is, if not wholly, yet at least in the first place, to be ascribed to the mistakes of our Education; which like an Error in the first Concoction, spreads its ill Influence thro' all our Lives.

The Soil is rich and would, if well cultivated, produce a noble Harvest, if then the Unskilful Managers not only permit, but incourage noxious Weeds, tho' we shall suffer by their Neglect, yet they ought not in justice to blame any but themselves, if they reap the Fruit of their own Folly. Women are from their very Infancy debar'd those Advantages, with the want of which, they are afterwards reproached, and nursed up in those Vices which will hereafter be upbraided to them. So partial are Men as to expect Brick where they afford no straw; and so abundantly civil as to take care we shou'd make good that obliging Epithet of *Ignorant,* which out of an excess of good Manners, they are pleas'd to bestow on us!

One wou'd be apt to think indeed, that Parents shou'd take all possible care of their Childrens Education, not only for *their* sakes, but even for their *own.* And tho the Son convey the Name to Posterity, yet certainly a great part of the Honour of their Families depends on their Daughters.

'Tis the kindness of Education that binds our duty fastest on us: For the being instrumental to the bringing us into the world, is no matter of choice, and therefore the less obliging. But to procure that we may live wisely and happily in it, and be capable of endless Joys hereafter, is a benefit we can never sufficiently acknowledge. To introduce poor Children into the world, and neglect to fence them against the temptations of it, and so leave them expos'd to temporal and eternal Miseries, is a wickedness, for which I want a Name; 'tis beneath Brutality, the Beasts are better natur'd, for they take care of their off-spring, till they are capable of caring for themselves. And, if Mothers had a due regard to their Posterity, how *Great* soever they are, they wou'd not think themselves too *Good* to perform what Nature requires, nor thro' Pride and Delicacy remit the poor little one to the care of a Foster Parent. Or, if necessity inforce them to depute another to perform their Duty, they wou'd be as choice at least in the Manners and Inclinations, as they are in the complections of their Nurses, least with their Milk they transfuse their Vices, and form in the Child such evil habits as will not easily be eradicated.

Nature as bad as it is, and as much as it is complain'd of, is so far improveable by the grace of GOD, upon our honest and hearty endeavours, that if we are not wanting to our selves, we may all in *some,* tho not in an *equal* measure, be instruments of his Glory, Blessings to this world, and capable of eternal Blessedness in that to come. But if our Nature is spoil'd, instead of being improv'd at first; if from our Infancy, we are nurs'd up in Ignorance and Vanity; are taught to be Proud and Petulent, Delicate and Fantastick, Humorous and Inconstant, 'tis not strange that the ill effects of this

Conduct appears in all the future Actions of our Lives. And seeing it is Ignorance, either habitual or actual, which is the cause of all sin, how are they like to escape *this*, who are bred up in *that?* That therefore women are unprofitable to most, and a plague and dishonour to some men is not much to be regretted on account of the *Men*, because 'tis the product of their own folly, in denying them the benefits of an ingenuous and liberal Education, the most effectual means to direct them into, and to secure their progress in the ways of Vertue.

For that Ignorance is the cause of most Feminine Vices may be instanc'd in that Pride and Vanity which is usually imputed to us, and which, I suppose, if throughly sifted, will appear to be some way or other, the rise and Original of all the rest. These, tho very bad Weeds, are the product of a good Soil; they are nothing else but Generosity degenerated and corrupted. A desire to advance and perfect its Being, is planted by GOD in all Rational Natures, to excite them hereby to every worthy and becoming Action; for certainly, next to the Grace of GOD, nothing does so powerfully restrain people from Evil, and stir them up to Good, as a generous Temper. And therefore to be ambitious of perfections is no fault; tho to assume the Glory of our Excellencies to our selves, or to Glory in such as we really have not, are. And were Womens haughtiness express'd in disdaining to do a mean and evil thing; wou'd they pride themselves in somewhat truly perfective of a Rational Nature, there were no hurt in it. But then they ought not to be denied the means of examining and judging what is so; they should not be impos'd on with tinsel ware. If by reason of a false Light, or undue Medium, they chuse amiss; theirs is the loss, but the Crime is the Deceivers. She who rightly understands wherein the perfection of her Nature consists, will lay out her Thoughts and Industry in the acquisition of such Perfections. But she who is kept ignorant of the matter, will take up with such Objects as first offer themselves, and bear any plausible resemblance to what she desires; a shew of advantage is sufficient to render them agreeable baits to her, who wants Judgment and skill to discern between reality and pretence. From whence it easily follows, that she who has nothing else to value her selfe upon, will be proud of her Beauty, or Money, and what that can purchase; and think her self mightily oblig'd to him, who tells her she has those Perfections which she naturally longs for. Her inbred self-esteem, and desire of good, which are degenerated into Pride, and mistaken self-love; will easily open her Ears to whatever goes about to nourish and delight them; and when a cunning designing Enemy from without, has drawn over to his Party these Traytors within, he has the Poor unhappy Person at his Mercy, who now very glibly swallows down his Poison, because 'tis presented in a Golden Cup, and credulously hearkens to the most disadvantageous Proposals, because they come attended with a seeming esteem. She whose Vanity makes her swallow praises by the whole sale, without examining whether she deserves them, or from what hand they come, will reckon it but gratitude to think well of him who values her so much, and think she must needs be merciful to the poor despairing Lover whom her Charms have reduc'd to die at her feet. Love and Honour are what every one of us naturally esteem, they are excellent things in themselves and very worthy our regard, and by how much the readier we are to embrace whatever resembles them, by so much the more dangerous it is that these venerable Names should be wretchedly abus'd and affixt to their direct contraries, yet this is the Custom of the World: And how can she possibly detect the fallacy, who has no better Notion of either than what she derives from Plays and Romances? How can she be furnished with any solid Principles whose very Instructors are Forth and emptiness? Whereas Women were they rightly Educated, had they obtain'd a well inform'd and discerning Mind, they would be proof against all these Batteries, see through and scorn those little silly Artifices which are us'd to ensnare and deceive them. Such an one would value her self only on her Vertue, and consequently be most chary of what she esteems so much. She would know, that not what others say, but what she herself does, is the true Commendation, and the only thing that exalts her; the loudest Encomiums being not half so satisfactory, as the calm and secret Plaudit of her own Mind; which moving on true Principles of Honour and Vertue, wou'd not fail on a review of itself to anticipate that delightful Eulogy she shall one day hear.

Whence is it but from ignorance, from a want of understanding to compare and judge of things, to chuse a right end, to proportion the means to the end, and to rate ev'ry thing according to its proper value; that we quit the substance for the Shadow, Reality for Appearance, and embrace those very things, which if we understood, we shou'd hate and fly, but now are reconcil'd to, merely because they usurp the Name, tho they have nothing of the Nature of those venerable Objects we desire and seek? Were it not for this delusion, is it probable a Lady who passionately desires to be admir'd, shou'd ever consent to such Actions as render her base and contemptible? Wou'd she be so absurd as to think either to get love,

or to keep it, by those methods which occasion loathing, and
consequently end in hatred? Wou'd she reckon it a piece of her
Grandeur, or hope to gain esteem by such excesses as really lessen
her in the eyes of all considerate and judicious persons? Wou'd she
be so silly as to look big, and think her self the better person,
because she has more Money to bestow profusely, or the good luck
to have a more ingenious Taylor or Milliner than her Neighbour?
Wou'd she who by the regard she pays to Wit, seems to make some
pretences to it, undervalue her Judgment so much as to admit the
Scurrility and profane noisy Nonsense of men, whose Foreheads
are better than their Brains to pass under that Character? Wou'd
she be so weak as to imagine that a few airy Fancies, joyn'd with a
great deal of Impudence (the right definition of modern Wit) can
bespeak him a Man of sense, who runs counter to all the sense and
reason that ever appear'd in the world? than which nothing can be
an Argument of greater shallowness, unless it be to regard and
esteem him for it. Wou'd a woman, if she truly understood her self,
be affected either with the praises or calumnies of those worthless
persons, whose Lives are a direct contradiction to Reason, a very
sink of corruption; by whom one wou'd blush to be commended,
lest they shou'd be mistaken for Partners or Connivers at their
Crimes? Will she who has a jot of discernment think to satisfy her
greedy desire of Pleasure, with those promising nothings that have
again & again deluded her? Or, will she to obtain such Bubbles, run
the risque of forfeiting Joys, infinitely satsifying and eternal? In
sum, did not ignorance impose on us, we would never lavish out the
greatest part of our Time and Care, on the decoration of a
Tenement, in which our Lease is so very short, and which for all our
industry, may lose its Beauty e're that Lease be out, and in the mean
while neglect a more glorious and durable Mansion! We wou'd
never be so curious of the House, and so careless of the Inhabitant,
whose beauty is capable of great improvement, and will endure for
ever without diminution or decay!

Thus Ignorance and a narrow Education, lay the Foundation
of Vice, and imitation and custom rear it up. Custom, that merciless
torrent that carries all before. And which indeed can be stem'd by
none but such as have a great deal of Prudence and a rooted Vertue.
For 'tis but Decorous that she who is not capable of giving better
Rules, shou'd follow those she sees before her, lest she only change
the instance, and retain the absurdity. 'Twou'd puzzle a considerate
Person to account for all that Sin and Folly that is in the World,
(which certainly has nothing in it self to recommend it,) did not

custom help to solve the difficulty. For Vertue without question has on all accounts the preeminence of Vice 'tis abundantly more pleasant in the *Act,* as well as more advantagious in the *Consequences,* as any one who will but rightly use her reason, in a serious reflection on her self, and the nature of things, may easily perceive. 'Tis custom therefore, that Tyrant Custom, which is the grand motive to all those irrational choices which we daily see made in the World, so very contrary to our *present* interest and pleasure, as well as to our Future. We think it an unpardonable mistake, not to do what others do round about us, and part with our Peace and Pleasure as well as our Innocence & Vertue, meerly in complyance with an unreasonable Fashion. And having inur'd ourselves to Folly, we know not how to quit it; we go on in Vice, not because we find satisfaction in it, but because we are unacquainted with the Joys of Vertue.

Add to this the hurry and noise of the world, which does generally so busy and preingage us, that we have little time, and less inclination to stand still and reflect on our own Minds. Those impertinent Amusements which have seiz'd us, keep their hold so well, and so constantly buz about our Ears, that we cannot attend to the Dictates of our Reason, nor to the soft whispers and winning persuasives of the divine Spirit, by whose assistance were we dispos'd to make use of it, we might shake off these Follies, and regain our Freedom. But alas! to complete our misfortunes, by a continual application to Vanity and Folly, we quite spoil the contexture and frame of our Minds; so loosen and dissipate, that nothing solid and substantial will stay in it. By an habitual inadvertency we render our selves incapable of any serious & improving thought, till our minds themselves become as light and frothy as those things they are conversant about. To all which, if we further add the great industry that bad people use to corrupt the good, and that unaccountable backwardness that appears in too many good persons, to stand up for, and propagate the Piety they profess; (so strangely are things transposed, that Vertue puts on the blushes, which belong to Vice, and Vice insults with the authority of Vertue!) and we have a pretty fair account of the Causes of our non-important improvement.

When a poor Young Lady is taught to value her self on nothing but her Cloaths, and to think she's very fine when well accoutred. When she hears say, that 'tis Wisdom enough for her to know how to dress her self, that she may become amiable in his eyes, to whom it appertains to be knowing and learned; who can blame her if she lay out her Industry and Money on such Accomplishments, and sometimes extends it farther than her misinformer desires she should? When she sees the vain and the gay, making Parade in the World, and attended with the Courtship and admiration of all about them, no wonder that her tender Eyes are dazled with the Pageantry; and wanting Judgment to pass a due Estimate on them and their Admirers, longs to be such a fine and celebrated red thing as they! What tho' she be sometimes told of another World, she has however a more lively perception of this, and may well think, that if her Instructors were in earnest, when they tell her of *hereafter,* they would not be so busied and concerned about what happens *here.* She is, it may be, taught the Principles and Duties of Religion, but not acquainted with the Reasons and Grounds of them; being told, 'tis enough for her to believe, to examin why, and wherefore belongs not to her. And therefore, though her Piety may be tall and spreading, yet because it wants foundation and Root, the first rude Temptation over-throws and blasts it; or perhaps the short liv'd Gourd decays and withers of its own accord. But why should she be blamed for letting no great value on her Soul, whose noblest Faculty, her Under-standing is render'd useless to her? Or censur'd for relinquishing a course of Life, whose Prerogatives she was never acquainted with, and tho highly reasonable in it self, was put upon the embracing it, with as little reason as she now forsakes it? For if her Religion it self, be taken up as the Mode of the Country, 'tis no strange thing that she lays it down again, in conformity to the Fashion. Whereas she whose Reason is suffer'd to display it self, to inquire into the grounds and Motives of Religion, to make a disquisition of its Graces, and search out its hidden Beauties; who is a Christian out of Choice, not in conformity to those about her, and cleaves to Piety, because 'tis her Wisdom, her Interest, her Joy, not because she has been accustom'd to it; she who is not only eminently and unmoveably good, but able to give a Reason *why* she is so; is too firm and stable to be mov'd by the pitiful Allurements of sin, too wise and too well bottom'd to be undermin'd and supplanted by the strongest Efforts of Temptation. Doubtless a truly Christian Life requires a clear Understanding, as well as regular Affections, that both together may move the Will to a direct choice of Good, and a stedfast adherence to it. For tho the heart may be honest, it is but by chance that the Will is right, if the Understanding be ignorant and Cloudy. And whats the reason that we sometimes unhappily see persons falling off from their Piety, but because 'twas their

Affections, not their Judgment, that inclin'd them to be Religious? Reason and Truth are firm and immutable, she who bottoms on them is on sure ground: Humour and Inclination are sandy Foundations; and she who is sway'd by her Affections more than by her Judgment, owes the happiness of her Soul in a great measure to the temper of her Body; her Piety may perhaps blaze higher, but will not last so long. For the Affections are various and changeable, mov'd by every Object, and the last comer easily undoes whatever its Predecessor had done before it. Such Persons are always in extreams; they are either violently good, or quite cold and indifferent, a perpetual trouble to themselves & others, by indecent Raptures, or unnecessary Scruples; there is no Beauty and order in their lives, all rapid and unaccountable; they are now very furious in such a course, but they cannot well tell why, & anon as violent in the other extream. Having more *Heat* than *Light,* their Zeal out runs their knowledge and instead of representing Piety as it is in it self, the most lovely and inviting thing imaginable, they expose it to the contempt and ridicule of the censorious World. Their Devotion being ricketed, starv'd and contracted in some of it's vital parts, and disproportioned and over grown in less material instances; whilst one Duty is *over done,* to commute for the neglect of another, and the mistaken Person thinks the being often on her knees, attones for all the miscarriages of her Conversation: Not considering that 'tis in vain to Petition for those Graces which we take no care to Practice, and a mockery to adore those Perfections we run counter to: and that the true end of all our Prayers and external Observances, is to work our minds into a truly Christian temper, to obtain for us the Empire of our Passions, and to reduce all irregular Inclinations, that so we may be as like GOD in Purity, Charity, and all his imitable excellencies, as is consistent with the imperfection of a Creature.

And now having discovered the Disease and its cause, 'tis proper to apply a Remedy; single Medicines are too weak to cure such complicated Distempers, they require a full Dispensatory; and what wou'd a good woman refuse to do, could she hope by that to advantage the greatest part of the world, and improve her Sex in Knowledge and true Religion? I doubt not Ladies, but that the Age, as bad as it is, affords very many of you who will readily embrace whatever has a true tendency to the Glory of GOD, and your mutual Edification, to revive the antient Spirit of Piety in the World, and to transmit it to succeeding Generations. I know there are many of you who so ardently love GOD, as to think no time too

much to spend in his service, nor any thing too difficult to do for his
sake; and bear such a hearty good-will to your Neighbours, as to
grudge no Prayers or Paints to reclaim and improve them. I have
therefore no more to do, but to make the Proposal, to prove that it
will answer these great and good Ends, and then 'twill be easy to
obviate the Objections that Persons of more Wit than Vertue may
happen to raise against it.

Now as to the Proposal, it is to erect a *Monastery,* or if you will
(to avoid giving offence to the scrupulous and injudicious, by
names which tho innocent in themselves, have been abus'd by
superstitious Practices.) we will call it a *Religious Retirement,* and
such as shall have a double aspect, being not only a Retreat from
the World for those who desire that advantage; but likewise, an
institution and previous discipline, to fit us to do the greatest good
in it; such an institution as this (if I do not mightily deceive my self,)
would be the most probable method to amend the present, and
improve the future Age. For here, those who are convinc'd of the
emptiness of earthly Enjoyments, who are sick of the vanity of the
world, and its impertinencies, may find more substantial and
satisfying entertainments, and need not be confin'd to what they
justly loath. Those who are desirous to know and fortify their weak
side, first do good to themselves, that hereafter they may be capable
of doing more good to others; or for their greater security are
willing to avoid *temptation,* may get out of that danger which a
continual stay in view of the Enemy, and the familiarity and
unwearied application of the Temptation may expose them to; and
gain an opportunity to look into themselves, to be acquainted at
home, and no longer the greatest strangers to their own hearts.
Such as are willing in a more peculiar and undisturb'd manner, to
attend the great business they came into the world about, the
service of GOD, and improvement of their own Minds, may find a
convenient and blissful recess from the noise and hurry of the
world. A world so cumbersom, so infectious, that altho' thro' the
grace of GOD, and their own strict watchfulness, they are kept
from sinking down into its corruptions, 'twill however damp their
flight to heav'n, hinder them from attaining any eminent pitch of
Vertue.

You are therefore Ladies, invited into a place, where you shall
suffer no other confinement, but to be kept out of the road of sin:
You shall not be depriv'd of your grandeur, but only exchange the
vain Pomps and Pageantry of the world, empty Titles and Forms of
State, for the true and solid Greatness of being able to dispise *them.*

110   You will only quit the Chat of insignificant people, for an ingenious Conversation; the froth of flashy wit for real wisdom; idle tales for instructive discourses. The deceitful Flatteries of those who under pretence of loving and admiring you, really served their *own* base ends, for the seasonable Reproofs and wholsom Counsels of your hearty well-wishers and affectionate Friends; which will procure you those perfections your feigned lovers pretended you had, and kept you from obtaining. No uneasy task will be enjoyn'd you, all your labour being only to prepare for the highest degrees of that Glory, the very lowest of which, is more than at present you are able to conceive, and the prospect of it sufficient to outweigh all the Pains of Religion, were there any in it, as really there is none. All that is requir'd of you, is only to be as happy as possibly you can, and to make sure of a Felicity that will fill all the capacities of your Souls! A happiness, which when once you have tasted, you'l be fully convinc'd, you could never do too much to obtain it; nor be too solicitous to adorn your Souls, with such tempers and dispositions, as will at present make you in some measure such holy and Heavenly Creatures, as you one day hope to be in a more perfect manner; without which Qualifications you can neither reasonably *expect,* nor are *capable* of enjoying the Happiness of the Life to come. Happy Retreat! which will be the introducing you into such a *Paradise* as your Mother *Eve* forfeited, where you shall feast on Pleasures, that do not, like those of the World, disappoint your expectations, pall your Appetites, and by the disgust they give you, put you on the fruitless search after new Delights, which when obtain'd are as empty as the former; but such as will make you truly happy *now,* and prepare you to be *perfectly* so hereafter. Here are no Serpents to deceive you, whilst you entertain your selves in these delicious Gardens. No Provocations are given in this Amicable Society, but to Love and to good Works, which will afford such an entertaining employment, that you'l have as little inclination as leisure to pursue those Follies which in the time of your ignorance pass'd with you under the name of love; altho' there is not in nature two more different things, than *true Love,* and that *brutish Passion* which pretends to ape it. Here will be no Rivalling but for the love of GOD, no ambition but to procure his Favour, to which nothing will more effectually recommend you, than a great and dear affection to each other. Envy, that Canker, will not here disturb your Breasts; for how can she repine at anothers wel-fare, who reckons it the greatest part of her own? No Covetousness will gain admittance in this blest abode, but to amass huge Treasure of good

Works, and to procure one of the brightest Crowns of Glory. You
will not be solicitous to encrease your Fortunes, but enlarge your
Minds; esteeming no Grandeur like being conformable to the meek
and humble JESUS. So that you only withdraw from the noise and
trouble, the folly and temptation of the world, that you may more
peaceably enjoy your selves, and all the innocent Pleasures it is able
to afford you, and particularly that which is worth all the rest, a
noble, Vertuous and Disinteress'd Friendship. And to compleat all
that *acme* of delight which the devout Seraphic Soul enjoys, when
dead to the World, she devotes her self entirely to the contemplation and fruition of her Beloved; when having disengag'd her self
from all those Lets which hindred her from without, she moves in
a direct and vigorous motion towards her true and only Good,
whom now she embraces and acquiesces in, with such an unspeakable pleasure, as is only intelligible to them who have tried
and felt it, which we can no more describe to the dark and sensual
part of Mankind, than we can the beauty of Colours, and harmony
of Sounds, to the Blind and Deaf. In fine, the place to which you are
invited will be a Type and Antipast of Heav'n, where your
Employment will be as there, to magnify GOD, and to love one
another, and to communicate that useful *knowledge,* which by the
due improvement of your time in Study and Contemplation you
will obtain; and which when obtain'd, will afford you a much
sweeter and durable delight, than all those pitiful diversions, those
revellings and amusements, which now thro your ignorance of
better, appear the only grateful and relishing Entertainments.

But because we were not made for our selves, nor can by any
means so effectually glorify GOD, and do good to our own Souls,
as by doing Offices of Charity and Beneficence to others; and to the
intent, that every Vertue, and the highest degrees of every Vertue,
may be exercis'd & promoted the most that may be; your Retreat
shall be so manag'd as not to exclude the good Works of an *Active,*
from the pleasure and serenity of a *contemplative* Life, but by a due
mixture of both, retain all the advantages, and avoid the inconve-
niences that attend either. It shall not so cut you off from the world,
as to hinder you from bettering and improving it; but rather qualify
you to do it the greatest Good, and be a Seminary to stock the
Kingdom with pious and prudent Ladies; whose good Example it is
to be hop'd, will so influence the rest of their Sex, that Women may
no longer pass for those little useless and impertinent Animals,
which the ill conduct of too many, has caus'd them to be mistaken
for.

We have hitherto consider'd our Retirement only in relation to Religion, which is indeed its *main,* I may say, its *only* design; nor can this be thought too contracting a word, since Religion is the adequate business of our lives, and largely consider'd, takes in all we have to do; nothing being a fit employment for a rational Creature, which has not either a *direct* or *remote* tendency to this great and *only* end. But because, as we have all along observ'd, Religion never appears in it's true Beauty, but when it is accompanied with Wisdom and Discretion; and that without a good Understanding, we can fearce be *truly,* but never *eminently* Good; being liable to a thousand seductions and mistakes, for even the men themselves, if they have not a competent degree of Knowledge, they are carried about with every wind of Doctrine. Therefore, one great end of this institution, shall be to expel that cloud of Ignorance, which custom has involv'd us in, to furnish our minds with a stock of solid and useful Knowledge, that the Souls of women may no longer be the only unadorn'd and neglected things. It is not intended that our Religious shou'd waste their time, and trouble their heads about such unconcerning matters, as the vogue of the world has turn'd up for Learning; the impertinency of which has been excellently expos'd by an ingenious Pen, but busy themselves in a serious enquiry after *necessary* and *perfective* truths; something which it *concerns* them to know, and which tends to their real interest and perfection, and what this is, the excellent Author just now mention'd, will sufficiently inform them, such a course of Study will neither be too troublesome nor out of the reach of a Female Virtuoso; for it is not intended she shou'd spend her hours in learning *words* but *things,* and therefore no more Languages than are necessary to acquaint her with useful Authors nor need she trouble her self in turning over a huge number of Books, but take care to understand and digest a few well-chosen and good ones. Let her but obtain right Ideas, and be truly acquainted with the nature of those Objects that present themselves to her mind, and then no matter whether or no she be able to tell what fanciful people have said about them: And thoroughly to understand Christianity as profess'd by the *Church of England,* will be sufficient to confirm her in the truth, tho she have not a Catalogue of those particular errors which oppose it. Indeed a Learner of Education of the Women will appear so unfashionable, that I began to startle at the singularity of the proposition, but was extreamly pleas'd when I found a late ingenious Author (whose Book I met with since the writing of this) agree with me in my Opinion. For speaking of the Repute that

Learning was in about 150 years ago: *It was so very modish* (says he)
that the fair Sex seem'd to believe that Greek *and* Latin *added to their Charms; and* Plato *and* Aristotle *untranslated, were frequent Ornaments of their Closets. One wou'd think by the effects, that it was a proper way of Educating them, since there are no accounts in History of so many great Women in any one Age, as are to be found between the years* 15 *and* 1600.

For, since GOD has given Women as well as Men intelligent Souls, why should they be forbidden to improve them? Since he has not denied us the faculty of Thinking, why shou'd we not (at least in gratitude to him) employ our Thoughts on himself, their noblest Object, and not unworthily bestow them on Trifles and Gaities and Secular Affairs? Being the Soul was created for the contemplation of Truth, as well as for the fruition of Good, is it not as cruel and unjust to preclude Women from the knowledge of the one, as well as from the enjoyment of the other? Especially since the Will is blind, and cannot chuse but by the direction of the Understanding; or to speak more properly, since the Soul always *Wills* according as she *Understands,* so that, if she *Understands* amiss she *Wills* amiss: And as Exercise enlarges and exalts any Faculty, so thro' want of using, it becomes crampt and lessened; if we make little or no use of our Understandings we shall shortly have none to use; and the more contracted, and unemploy'd the deliberating and directive Power is, the more liable is the elective to unworthy and mischievous options. What is it but the want of an ingenious Education that renders the generality of Feminine Conversations so insipid and foolish, and their solitude so *insupportable?* Learning is therefore necessary to render them more agreeable and useful in company, and to furnish them with becoming entertainments when alone, that so they may not be driven to those miserable shifts, which too many make use of to put off their time, that precious Talent that never lies on the hands of a judicious Person. And since our Happiness in the next world depends so far on those dispositions which we carry along with us out of this, that without a right habitude and temper of mind, we are not capable of Felicity; and seeing our Beatitude consists in the contemplation of the divine Truth and Beauty, as well as in the fruition of his Goodness, can Ignorance be a fit preparative for Heaven? Is't likely that she whose Understanding has been busied about nothing but froth and trifles, shou'd be capable of delighting her self in noble and sublime Truths? Let such therefore as deny us the improvement of our Intellectuals, either take up *his* Paradox, who said, *That Women have no Souls;* which at

114   this time a day, when they are allow'd to Brutes, wou'd be as unphilosophical as it is unmannerly; or else let them permit us to cultivate and improve them. There is a sort of Learning indeed which is worse than the greatest Ignorance: A woman may study Plays and Romances all her days, & be a great deal more knowing, but never a jot the wiser. Such a Knowledge as this serves only to instruct and put her forward in the practice of the greatest Follies; yet how can they justly blame her, who forbid, or at least, won't afford opportunity of better? A rational mind *will* be employ'd, it will never be satisfy'd in doing nothing; and if you neglect to furnish it with good materials, 'tis like to take up with such as come to hand.

We pretend not that Women shou'd teach in the Church, or usurp Authority where it is not allow'd them; permit us only to understand our *own* duty, and not be forc'd to take it upon trust from others; to be at least so far learned, as to be able to form in our minds a true Idea of Christianity, it being so very necessary to fence us against the danger of these last and *perilous days,* in which Deceivers, a part of whose Character is, to *lead captive silly Women,* need not *creep into Houses,* since they have Authority to proclaim their Errors on the *House top.* And let us also acquire a true Practical Knowledge, such as will convince us of the absolute necessity of *Holy Living,* as well as of *Right Believing,* and that no Heresy is more dangerous, than that of an ungodly and wicked Life. And since the *French Tongue* is understood by most Ladies, methinks they may much better improve it by the study of Philosophy (as I hear the *French Ladies* do,) *Des Cartes, Malebranch,* and others, than by reading idle *Novels* and *Romances.* 'Tis strange we shou'd be so forward to imitate their Fashions and Fopperies, and have no regard to what is truly imitable in them! And why shall it not be thought as genteel, to understand *French Philosophy,* as to be accoutred in a *French Mode?* Let therefore the famous Madam *D'acier, &c.* and our own incomparable *Orinda,* excite the Emulation of the English Ladies.

The Ladies, I'm sure, have no reason to dislike this Proposal, but I know not how the Men will resent it, to have their enclosure broke down, and Women invited to tast of that Tree of Knowledge they have so long unjustly *monopoliz'd.* But they must excuse me, if I be as partial to my own Sex as they are to theirs, and think Women as capable of Learning as Men are, and that it becomes them as well. For I cannot imagine wherein the hurt lyes, if instead of doing mischief to one another, by an uncharitable and vain

Conversation, women be enabled to inform and instruct those of their own Sex at least; the Holy Ghost having left it on record, that *Priscilla* as well as her Husband catechis'd the eloquent *Apollos,* and the great Apostle found no fault with her. It will therefore be very proper for our Ladies to spend part of their time in this Retirement, in adorning their minds with useful Knowledge.

To enter into the detail of the particulars concerning the Government of the *Religious,* their Offices of Devotion, Employments, Work, &c. is not now necessary. Suffice it at present to signify, that they will be more than ordinarily careful to redeem their time, spending no more of it on the Body than the necessities of Nature require, but by a judicious choice of their Employment, and a constant industry about it, so improve this invaluable Treasure, that it may neither be buried in Idleness, nor lavish'd out in unprofitable concerns. For a stated portion of it being daily paid to GOD in Prayers and Praises, the rest shall be employ'd in innocent, charitable, and useful Business; either in study (in learning themselves, or instructing others; for it is design'd that part of their Employment be the Education of those of their own Sex) or else in spiritual and corporal Works of Mercy, relieving the Poor, healing the Sick, mingling Charity to the Soul with that they express to the Body, instructing the Ignorant, counselling the Doubtful, comforting the Afflicted, and correcting those that err and do amiss.

AN ESSAY IN DEFENCE OF THE FEMALE SEX*

Let us look into the manner of our Education, and see wherein it falls short of the Mens, and how the defects of it may be, and are generally supply'd. In our tender years they are the same, for after Children can Talk, they are promiscuously taught to Read and Write by the same Persons, and at the same time both Boys and Girls. When these are acquir'd, which is generally about the Age of Six or Seven Years, they begin to be separated, and the Boys are sent to the *Grammer School,* and the Girls to *Boarding Schools*, or other places, to learn Needle Work, Dancing, Singing, Musick, Drawing, Painting, and other Accomplishments according to the Humour and Ability of the Parents, or Inclination of the Children. Of all

*Astell, Mary. *An Essay in Defence of the Female Sex.* London: A. Roper and E. Wilkinson, 1696.

116   these, Reading and Writing are the main Instruments of Conversation; though Musick and Painting may be allow'd to contribute something towards it, as they give us an insight into two Arts, that makes up a great Part of the Pleasures and Diversions of Mankind. Here then lies the main Defect, that we are taught only our Mother Tongue, or perhaps *French*, which is now very fashionable and almost as Familiar amongst Women of Quality as Men; whereas the other Sex by means of a more extensive Education to the knowledge of the *Roman* and *Greek* Languages, have a vaster Field for their Imaginations to rove in, and their Capacities thereby enlarg'd. To see whether this be strictly true or not, I mean in what relates to our debate, I will for once suppose, that we are instructed only in our own Tongue, and then enquire whether the disadvantage be so great as it is commonly imagin'd. You know very well, *Madam*, that for Conversation, it is not requisite we should be Philologers, Rhetoricians, Philosophers, Historians or Poets; but only that we should think pertinently and express our thoughts properly, on such matters as are the proper Subjects for a mixt Conversation.

MARY WRAY

Richard Steele (1672–1729) and a friend, Joseph Addison, founded two widely read periodicals: *The Tatler* and *The Spectator*. Steele, who consistently encouraged improvement of girls' education, in 1714 printed a series titled, "The Ladies Library." Presumably, a Mary Wray, about whom no information is readily available, assembled this data to be published by Steele. The following excerpt relates directly to curriculum.

THE LADIES LIBRARY*

The Ladies are apt to think that the Softness of their Sex excuses their Idleness, and a Woman who can do nothing, imagines therefore that she has nothing to do.

It is not shameful to see how Women of *Wit* and *Politeness* neglect the common Rudiments of Education? 'Tis enough for them to understand what they *read*, if they do not know how to *pronounce* it, and *read* with a Grace. The more trivial these Faults appear, the greater Shame for such as cannot correct them; and how can they without blushing be in Company guilty of Errors, which they ought not to have brought out of their Nursery? They should not read with a *Tone*, nor hesitate in reading; they should go on smoothly, and with a plain, natural, and uniform Pronunciation. Their Deficiencies in Spelling are become so fashionable, that to spell well, is, among the fair Sex, reckon'd a sort of Pedantry; they are taught a little more care in Writing a good Hand, but that care goes no farther than the making their Letters; the connexing them, and an orderly placing their Words in streight Lines, is what they are, for the most Part, utterly Strangers to.

They will find no manner of Inconvenience in acquainting themselves a little with the Grammar of their native Language; not

*Wray, Mrs. Mary. "The Ladies Library." Vol. I. Written by a lady. Published by Mr. Steele. London: Jacob Tonfon, at Shakespear's Head over-against Catherine-Street in the Strand, 1714, pp. 16-29.

118   to learn it tediously by Rule, as Boys do *Latin*, but so as that they may be able to express themselves properly, and to explain their Thoughts with Clearness and Brevity. 'Tis well known, that in old *Rome, Sempronia,* the Mother of the *Gracchi*, contributed very much to the forming of the Eloquence of her Sons, who became afterwards so great Men.

    If the Ladies understood *Arithmetick* better, perhaps the keeping Family Accounts would not be such a Piece of ill Breeding. The Convenience and Advantage of having the *Mistress* of the House the *Steward*, shou'd, methinks, make their Learning the four first great Rules of Arithmetick be thought more necessary than it is at present. Let none think themselves above such *Business*. An illustrious Lady, now a *Dowager,* did not only help her Lord in examining Bills, and stating Accounts, but even in writing his Letters and drawing his Covenants, tho' his Fortune was so large, that it might well have excus'd the keeping more Stewards than one. Such an Employment as this may at first seem too troublesome; but if Ladies were by their Education prepar'd for it, and us'd to it from their Childhood, the trouble of it wou'd be little, the most intricate Accounts being made familiar to them, wou'd lose the Terror which their seeming Difficulty raises in the Ignorant; and the Pleasure of reducing things from Confusion to Order by the Power of Numbers, would be the greater for the Advantage which would accrue to them by their Exactness.

    The very Name of the *Law* is frightful to the most of the *weaker* Sex, who are us'd to depend entirely on the Protection of the *Stronger*. It would be well however if they knew something of the common Rules of *Right*, the Difference between a *Will* and a *Deed of Gift*, what a *Contract* is, what a *Partition of Coheirs*, what a *Legacy*, a *Bond*, or the like, and by what *Laws* they are in force; what *Property* is, what a *personal* and what a *real* Estate; for tho' they may not trust to their own Judgment in Matters of such weight, yet it will direct them in the Use of that of others, either in a single or a married Life. Those of them, who out of a vexatious Humour are for flying to the *Law* upon all Occasions, or rather upon no Occasion at all, are not by this encourag'd to indulge themselves in so expensive a Folly, which a great Comick Poet has so happily expos'd in the Character of the Widow *Blackacre*. But because that litigious Widow knew too much Law, it does not follow that the rest of the Sex should know none at all. What Knowledge is there that may not be, that is not abus'd? And when the Ladies are advis'd to acquaint themselves with so much of the

Law as may help 'em to demand or defend their Right, it is not meant that they should think it is to be got no where but in a Court of Justice; that they should fly all Terms of *Peace* and *Arbitrament,* and put themselves immediately into the Hands of Attorneys and Solicitors: They should only so far inform themselves in these Matters, that they may know what is their due, and not lose it for want of claiming; which may very well happen by the profound Ignorance that Women are bred in of things of this Nature.

'Tis very necessary that Women of Quality, and of Estates, should know exactly what those Estates are; what part in Land, what in Houses, what in Mony, where and in whose Hands: They should be as well acquainted with the *Rentals* of their Lands, the Draughts of them, the Situation, Leases, and Condition of their Houses, as their Husbands; what Debts they owe, as well as what are owing to them. By this they regulate their domestick and other Expences, provided for the future Settlement of their Children, and answer the Ends of Marriage, to be Helps to their Husbands in the Discharge of paternal Duties. How far it is convenient for them to understand well the Business of the Kitchen, to be the Physicians and Surgeons of the Village, I shall not meddle with, reckoning such Accomplishments as casual only, and not of absolute Necessity to the forming a compleat Gentlewoman, which the other Qualities are, and none more so than a good Taste of Books.

In order to which, young Ladies should be encourag'd to read the *Greek* and *Roman* Histories in the best Translations; they will find in them wonderful Instances of Courage, Faithfulness, Generosity, and a great Contempt of their own *private* Advantage when the *publick* Good was in question. Neither should they be ignorant of the History of *Britain*, which furnishes them with many Examples of brave Actions, hardly exceeded by any thing in Antiquity. Among their own Sex too, they will in both meet with illustrious Patterns of Virtue, which will make the stronger Impressions on their Minds. The *Histories* of other *Nations*, Accounts of *Voyages* and *Travels,* the Lives of *Heroes* and *Philosophers,* will be both a pleasant and instructive Entertainment. The reading the best Authors on these Subjects, will enlarge and elevate their Souls, and give them a Contempt for the common Amusements of the Sex. Let them in their reading avoid Vanity and Affectation; but let them not have so mean an Opinion of themselves as to think they are incapable of improving by it; nor of Books, as to think they are incapable of improving them; there's no Lady, let the Measure of her Understanding be what it will, but may benefit by them; it will add a Lustre to her other shining Qualities, and help to supply the place of 'em where such Qualities are wanting. The Fair may be supportable without them, but with them they are admirable. Naked Reason could never discover many things, which we acquire the Knowledge of by Reading. It gives Solidity to our Thoughts, Sweetness to our Discourse, and finishes what Nature began. Good Wit, without Study, is like a good Face without Ornament. The brighter the Genius, the more worthy is it of Improvement, as well as the more capable.

To Reading must be added Conversation, which are together absolutely necessary to form a sound Understanding and an agreeable Temper. No Reading better qualifies a Person to converse well in the World than that of *History*, which is here especially recommended, because most of the other Parts of Learning are clogg'd with Terms that are not easily intelligible. Reason speaks all Languages, and there is no part of Learning but may be exprest in *English*, as well as in *Greek* and *Latin*. 'Tis an affected piece of Pendantry in Men of certain learned Professions to hide their Arts with a peculiar *Jargon*, as if Clearness rendered them less venerable, and Darkness added to their Lustre and Ornament. While Custom makes this Practice common to them, let the Ladies despise those Arts which have no Complacency for the Deficiencies of their Education, and take Pleasure and Profit in such as freely lay open all their Stores to them, as do History, Poetry and Eloquence. The Ladies may be also enlighten'd by *moral Philosophy,* which is said to give Hands to *Reason* as well as a *Mouth.* Are not they equally concern'd with the other Sex in the Divine Lectures we are taught by it, upon the *Chief Good,* upon the *Principle of human Actions,* upon the *Nature and Springs of Virtue and Vice,* and upon the *Passions?* which in the best Authors are not wrapt up in mystical Phrases, as were the *Oracles* of old, but deliver'd in plain and easie Language, in our own Tongue, either Original or Translations.

Languages are an Accomplishment, without which it is hardly possible for a Lady to be well bred. I do not see the Necessity of a Woman's learning the *ancient* Tongues, but there are so many polite Authors in *French* and *Italian*, that it is pity the Ladies should not have the *Profit* and *Pleasure* of them. To learn enough only of a Language, as enables 'em to carry on a trifling Conversation, will rather teach them Impertinence than Politeness; but to be able to read *Voiture, Racine* and *Boileau*, or rather *Paschal,* among the *French; Tasso* and *Guarimi* among the *Italians*, will certainly refine their *Taste,* and add that *Variety* to their Studies, which will very

much contribute to *the Delight* of them. If a Lady knew a little 121
Latin, she would find no manner of Inconvenience in it, not so
much to improve her self in that *Language* as to help her in her own.
The main thing is to put good Books into her Hands, wherein she
may find so much Benefit as compensates for the Loss of that Time,
which otherwise will be wasted in the Study of her own Tongue as
well as others. It is not so strange as some may imagine it, that
Improvement in *English* should be recommended. Our Native
Language will not come to us by Inspiration, and we shall write and
speak with Rudeness or Affectation, if we know no more of it than
we are bred with. 'Twas a Saying of a great Father of our Church,
eminent above any in the learned World, to a Gentleman who had
made him a Compliment on his general Knowledge of Tongues,
*That indeed he knew enough of other Languages, and would spend his
time in learning English,* which he wrote with as much Force and
Eloquence as any one. Let not the Ladies then despise the Study of
a Tongue which Nature has given 'em, and with it a Talent of
speaking and writing it, with more Grace than even the Men
themselves. *La Bruyere* observes, that their Conversation is one of
the best Methods to make Men *polite,* and that, methinks, should
incline them to give it as many Advantages as they can; of which, to
speak politely is not the least. Tho' this is often acquir'd by those
Ladies that know no Tongue but their Native, yet those surely will
have it in greater Perfection, who know the Beauties of other
Languages, and how to make use of them in their natural one. The
gallant Writers have distinguish'd themselves as much as any by
their Politeness. The Poyson in them is conceal'd as much as
possible, and 'tis insensibly that they would lead the Heart to Love:
Let them therefore be avoided with Care; for there are elegant
Writers enough on Moral and Divine Subjects, and the Danger of
reading soft and wanton Writings, which warm and corrupt the
Imagination, is so great, that one cannot be too careful in the
Choice of our Authors. Too much of this will be found among the
Works of *Poetry* and *Eloquence,* with which none but Ladies of
good *Taste* and solid Judgment should be trusted.

The like Cautions are necessary with respect to *Musick* and
Painting; the Fancy is often too quick in them, and the Soul too
much affected by the Senses. Musick especially so softens that it
enervates it, and exposes it to be conquer'd by the first Temptation
which invades it. The Antients were so well convinc'd of its
Perniciousness, that they would never suffer it in a well-regulated
State. Why are languishing Airs pleasant, but because the Soul

gives it self to the Charms of the Senses? What is it you mean by transporting or moving in Musick, but the Fury or the Softness of Desire? If the wife Magistrates of *Sparta* broke all the musical Instruments, whose Harmony was too delicious and melting, and *Plato* rejected all the softer Airs of the *Asiatick* Musick; what should we Christians do with the *Italian,* as moving as any that ever were known to Antiquity? How can chaste Minds delight in the Languishments of wanton Poetry, made yet more languishing by the Graces of Musick? What great or noble is there in the dying Notes of foreign Strumpets and Eunuchs? The Power of Musick never appear'd more in *England* than it has done of late; we have seen it draw after it numerous Audiences of both Sexes at a very extravagant Expence, who knowing nothing of the Language were bewitched only with the Magick of the Sounds. Was it either Vanity or Pleasure? or if either, was it not alike criminal? Should Christians squander away so many precious Hours in *Vanity*, or take *Pleasure* in gratifying a *Sense* that has so often been a *Traytor* to *Virtue*?

Not that all *Poetry* and *Musick* is of the same dangerous nature. Retrench from them whatever tends not to the true End, and they may be very usefully employ'd to excite in the Soul lively and sublime Notions of God and Religion. As for Poetry, many parts of the Holy Scriptures are Poems, and were sung by the *Hebrews*. The first Precepts of Morality were deliver'd in Verse, and the singing the Praise of God was the most ancient Worship among Men. Our Church has carefully provided for the Refreshment of the Souls of her Children; the Musick of our Choirs give us a ravishing, tho' a faint Idea, of the happy Choirs in Heaven. For this Reason ought not these Arts, consecrated by the Spirit of God, to be condemn'd. If a Christian *Turn* was given to *Musick* and *Poetry,* it would be the greatest of all Helps to disrelish prophane Pleasures. Those Ladies that are sensible of the Impressions made by these two Arts, should early be directed to put them to Divine Uses. And such as have Genius's and Voices may innocently and usefully indulge themselves in them, if they find their Souls rais'd by it in Devotion, and their Passions are free from those irregular Emotions which are the Effects of all Pleasures that owe their Birth to the Senses. If young Gentlewomen are forbidden Poetry and Musick, it will only encrease their Curiosity, and make 'em fancy there's more in them than they will find upon the Experiment. If they have no *Taste* nor *Genius*, which are Blessings that every one is not endown'd with, without Genius and Taste they will soon be weary of them: wherefore the best way is to humour their Inclinations, and take Care that what Talents they have, may rather serve to improve than to injure their Virtue. The less is to be said of *Painting*, for that few have a Genius for it, and those that have none, would reckon it ridiculous to have Advice given them about a thing they despise. All these Arts, Poetry, Musick and Painting, are proper Entertainments only for Women of Quality; not for such as the Duties of their Families, and what they owe to Heaven, would wholly employ.

The common Education of young Gentlewomen at Boarding-Schools is render'd useless, and indeed pernicious. Whole Years are spent in teaching a tasteless Girl to paint on *Glass*, and such sort of useless Knowledge, which should be employed in forming their Minds to Virtue, and the moral Duties of Life. To *draw* or to know something of *Design* will be useful in several Works that pass thro' the Hands of those Ladies, who do not take *Idleness* to be the greatest Privilege of their *Sex* and *Quality*. For want of knowing the Rules of *Drawing* do we meet with so many extravagant Figures in Laces, Linnen, Stuffs and Embroideries. Every thing is ill design'd and confus'd; without Art, without Proportion. These pass for *fine,* because they cost a great deal of Labour; their Lustre dazles those that see them afar off, or do not understand them. However the Ladies have their Rules which they will not depart from, and as irregular as they are, Custom has so habituated them to 'em, that they reckon nothing more fantastical than to dispute them. The Principles of Painting, if known to them, would make them look with Contempt on things they otherwise set the highest Value upon. This Knowledge would lessen the Labour and the Expence of their Works, and given them that Variety and Beauty, that Regularity and Grace, which can only set a Price upon them.

In whatever innocent Employments they spend their time, certain it is, that 'tis their Duty to employ it about something, and that *Idleness* is a Vice as well in Women as in Men.

SARAH FIELDING (1710–1768)

After the death of her mother when Sarah was seven years old, and after the subsequent re-marriage of her father, Sarah lived with her maternal grandmother. She attended a boarding school where she learned reading, writing, French, dancing, and how to be a Gentlewoman. She was fortunate to have access to the library of her deceased grandfather, a judge. Her favorite reading was Shakespeare, Milton, Horace, Virgil, Pope, Montaigne, the Bible, and books written by her brother, Henry, whose love of classical literature inspired her to learn Greek. The writing of Fenelon also influenced her thinking.

Sarah Fielding wrote five or six novels of which the best known was *The Adventures of David Simple.* She translated Xenophon's *Memoirs of Socrates* from Greek into English.

Advanced thought was evident in her perception that a child needs love, good health, and natural ease in carriage and dress. Fielding maintained that one must never require the impossible of a child. Her concerns extended beyond children to an active opposition of cruelty to animals.

Her largely autobiographical *The Governess* was an enormously popular children's book, imitated in many stories, e.g., *Little Goody Two-Shoes,* and printed in Ireland, Germany, Sweden, and the United States. This 1749 book set many precedents. It is said to have been the first known full length original story book written for children, the first moral tale, the first educational novel, the first story set in a school, the first children's book in which events are located in a detailed time and place, and the first to apply child psychology in a book for children. The book is divided into nine sections with each section representing one day. There are dialogues among Mistress Teachum and her nine scholars, descriptions of the lives of the students, and stories about children, animals, giants, queens, and princesses. The following selection is the introductory chapter of this important book.

"The History of Mistress Teachum, and Her Nine Scholars"

There lived in the Northern Parts of *England,* a Gentlewoman who undertook the Education of young Ladies; and this Trust she endeavor'd faithfully to discharge, by instructing those committed to her Care in Reading, Writing, Working, and in all proper Forms of Behaviour. And tho' her principal Aim was to improve their Minds in all useful Knowlege; to render them obedient to their Superiors, and gentle, kind, and affectionate to each other; yet did she not omit teaching them an exact Neatness in their Persons and Dress, and a perfect Gentility in their whole Carriage.

This Gentlewoman, whose Name was *Teachum,* was the Widow of a Clergyman, with whom she had lived nine Years in all the Harmony and Concord which forms the only satisfactory Happiness in the married State. Two little Girls (the youngest of which was born before the second Year of their Marriage was expired) took up a great Part of their Thoughts; and it was their mutual Design to spare no Pains or Trouble in their Education.

Mr. *Teachum,* was a very sensible Man, and took great Delight in improving his Wife; as she also placed her chief Pleasure in receiving his Instructions. One of his constant Subjects of Discourse to her was concerning the Education of Children: So that, when in his last Illness his Physicians pronounced him beyond the Power of their Art to relieve, he expressed great Satisfaction in the Thought of leaving his Children to the Care of so prudent a Mother.

Mrs. *Teachum,* tho' exceedingly afflicted by such a Loss, yet thought it her Duty to call forth all her Resolution to conquer her Grief, in order to apply herself to the Care of these her dear Husband's Children. But her Misfortunes were not here to end: For within a Twelvemonth after the Death of her Husband, she was deprived of both her Children by a violent Fever that then raged in the Country; and about the same time, by the unforeseen Breaking of a Banker, in whose Hands almost all her Fortune was just then placed, she was bereft of the Means of her future Support.

The Christian Fortitude with which (thro' her Husband's Instructions) she had armed her Mind, had not left it in the Power

---

*Reprinted from Grey, Jill E. (ed.). *The Governess.* London: Oxford University Press, 1968, pp. 99-108. By permission of Oxford University Press.© Oxford University Press 1968.

of any outward Accident to bereave her of her Understanding, or to make her incapable of doing what was proper on all Occasions. Therefore, by the Advice of all her Friends, she undertook what she was so well qualified for; namely, the Education of Children. But as she was moderate in her Desires, and did not seek to raise a great Fortune, she was resolved to take no more Scholars than she could have an Eye to herself, without the Help of other Teachers; and, instead of making Interest to fill her School, it was looked upon as a great Favour when she would take any Girl: And as her Number was fixed to Nine, which she on no Account would be prevailed on to increase, great Application was made, when any Scholar went away, to have her Place supplied; and happy were they who could get a Promise for the next Vacancy.

Mrs. *Teachum* was about Forty Years old, tall and genteel in her Person, tho' somewhat inclined to Fat. She had a lively and commanding Eye, insomuch that she naturally created an Awe in all her little Scholars; except when she condescended to smile, and talk familiarly to them; and then she had something perfectly kind and tender in her Manner. Her Temper was so extremely calm and good, that tho' she never omitted reprehending, and that pretty severely, any Girl that was guilty of the smallest Fault proceeding from an evil Disposition; yet for no Cause whatsoever was she provoked to be in a Passion: But she kept up such a Dignity and Authority by her steady Behaviour, that the Girls greatly feared to incur her Displeasure by disobeying her Commands; and were equally pleased with her Approbation, when they had done anything worthy her Commendation.

At the Time of the ensuing History, the School (being full) consisted of the Nine following young Ladies:

Miss *Jenny Peace,*

Miss *Sukey Jennett,*	Miss *Nanny Spruce,*
Miss *Dolly Friendly,*	Miss *Betty Ford,*
Miss *Lucy Sly,*	Miss *Henny Fret,*
Miss *Patty Lockit,*	Miss *Polly Suckling.*

The eldest of these was but fourteen Years old, and none of the rest had yet attained their twelfth Year.

An Account of a Fray, begun and carried on for the Sake of an Apple: In which are Shewn the Sad Effects of Rage and Anger.

It was on a fine summer's Evening, when the School-hours

were at an End, and the young Ladies were admitted to divert
themselves for some time as they thought proper, in a pleasant
Garden adjoining to the House, that their Governess, who delighted in pleasing them, brought out a little Basket of Apples,
which were intended to be divided equally amongst them: But Mrs.
Teachum being hastily called away (one of her poor Neighbours
having had an Accident which wanted her Assistance), she left the
Fruit in the Hands of Miss *Jenny Peace,* the eldest of her Scholars,
with a strict Charge to see that every one had an equal Share of her
Gift.

But here a perverse Accident turned good Mrs. *Teachum's*
Design of giving them Pleasure into their Sorrow, and raised in
their little Hearts nothing but Strife and Anger; For, alas! there
happened to be one Apple something larger than the rest, on which
the whole Company immediately placed their desiring Eyes, and all
at once cried out, 'Pray, Miss *Jenny,* give me that Apple.' Each gave
her Reasons why she had the best Title to it: The youngest pleaded
her Youth, and the eldest her Age; one insisted on her Goodness,
another from her Meekness claimed a Title to Preference; and one,
in confidence of her Strength, said positively, she would have it; but
all speaking together, it was difficult to distinguish who said this, or
who said that.

Miss *Jenny* begged them all to be quiet: But in vain: For she
could not be heard: They had all set their Hearts on that fine Apple,
looking upon those she had given them as nothing. She told them,
they had better be contented with what they had, than be thus
seeking what it was impossible for her to give to them all. She
offered to divide it into Eight Parts, or to do anything to satisfy
them: But she might as well have been silent; for they were all
talking, and had no Time to hear. At last, as a Means to quiet the
Disturbance, she threw this Apple, the Cause of her Contention,
with her utmost Force, over a Hedge into another Garden, where
they could not come at it.

At first they were all silent, as if they were struck dumb with
Astonishment with the Loss of this one poor Apple, tho' at the
same time they had Plenty before them.

But this did not bring to pass Miss *Jenny's* Design: For now
they all began again to quarrel which had the most Right to it, and
which *ought* to have had it, with as much Vehemence as they had
before contended for the Possession of it: And their Anger by
degrees became so high, that Words could not vent half their Rage;
and they fell to pulling of Caps, tearing of Hair, and dragging the

Cloaths off one another's Backs. Tho' they did not so much strike, as endeavour to scratch and pinch their Enemies.

Miss *Dolly Friendly* as yet was not engaged in the Battle: But on hearing her Friend Miss *Nanny Spruce* scream out, that she was hurt by a sly Pinch from one of the Girls, she flew on this sly Pincher, as she called her, like an enraged Lion on its Prey; and not content only to return the Harm her Friend had received, she struck with such Force, as felled her Enemy to the Ground. And now they could not distinguish between Friend and Enemy; but fought, scratch'd, and tore, like so many Cats, when they extend their Claws to fix them in their Rival's Heart.

Miss *Jenny* was employed in endeavouring to part them.

In the Midst of this Confusion, Mrs. *Teachum*, who was returning in Hopes to see them happy with the Fruit she had given them, appeared: But she was some time there before either her Voice or Presence could awaken them from their Attention to the Fight; when on a sudden they all faced her, and Fear of Punishment began now a little to abate their Rage. Each of the Misses held in her Right-hand, fast clenched, some Marks of Victory; for they were beat and beaten by Turns. One of them held a little Lock of Hair, torn from the Head of her Enemy: Another grasped a Piece of a Cap, which, in aiming at her Rival's Hair, had deceived her Hand, and was all the Spoils she could gain: A third clenched a Piece of an Apron; a fourth, of a Frock. In short, every one unfortunately held in her Hand a Proof of having been engaged in the Battle. And the Ground was spread with Rags and Tatters, torn from the Backs of the little inveterate Combatants.

Mrs. *Teachum* stood for some time astonished at the Sight: But at last she required Miss *Jenny Peace,* who was the only Person disengaged, to tell her the whole Truth, and to inform her of the Cause of all this Confusion.

Miss *Jenny* was obliged to obey the Commands of her Governess; tho' she was so good-natured, that she did it in the mildest Terms; and endeavoured all she could to lessen, rather than increase, Mrs. *Teachum's* Anger. The guilty Persons now began all to excuse themselves as fast as Tears and Sobs would permit them.

One said, "Indeed, Madam, it was none of my Fault; for I did not begin; for Miss *Sukey Jennett,* without any Cause in the World (for I did nothing to provoke her), hit me a great Slap in the Face, and made my Tooth ach: The Pain *did* make me angry; and then, indeed, I hit her a little Tap. But it was on her Back; and I am sure it was the smallest Tap in the World; and could not possibly hurt her half so much as her great Blow did me."

"Law, Miss!" replied Miss *Jennett,* "How can you say so? When you know that you struck me first, and that yours was the great Blow, and mind the little Tap; for I only went to defend myself from your monstrous Blows."

Such like Defences they would all have made for themselves, each insisting on not being in Fault, and throwing the Blame on her Companion: But Mrs. *Teachum* silenced them by a positive Command; and told them, that she saw they were all equally guilty, and as such would treat them.

Mrs. *Teachum's* Method of punishing I never could find out. But this is certain, the most severe Punishment she had ever inflicted on any Misses, since she had kept a School, was now laid on these wicked Girls, who had been thus fighting, and pulling one another to Pieces, for a sorry Apple.

The first thing she did, was to take away all the Apples; telling them, that before they had any more Instances of like Kindness from her, they should give her Proofs of better deserving them. And when she had punished them as much as she thought proper, she made them all embrace one another, and promise to be Friends for the future; which, in Obedience to her Commands, they were forced to comply with, tho' there remained a Grudge and Ill-will in their Bosoms; every one thinking she was punished most, altho' she would have it, that she deserved to be punished least; and they contrived all the sly Tricks they could think on to vex and teaze each other.

JEAN JACQUES ROUSSEAU (1712–1778)

Few persons have equalled Rousseau in the extent to which he influenced future educational philosophers. Although this famous French writer saw social evolution and progress as being dependent upon education, he stressed the need for free, natural learning.

In 1762 Rousseau wrote the novel *Emile* in which he described the life-style and education of a boy who was educated by a tutor. Emile was not forced to learn, but was taught when he expressed a readiness and desire to learn. This book had the following influences upon eighteenth-century French life: (1) women nursed their babies; (2) fathers emulated the tutor of Emile; (3) noble families prepared their children for revolution; (4) a new children's literature developed.

Believing that men and women differ psychologically, Rousseau presumed that men and women require dissimilar educations. To provide Emile with an ideal wife, Rousseau created the character of Sophie, who was to become subservient to the needs of her husband. The following excerpt from *Emile* is representative of Rousseau's outlook on the nature and education of women.

EMILE*

The women, on the other hand, are apt to complain, that we bring them up to be vain and coquettish, that we continually amuse them with childish toys, the more easily to master their minds; in short, they blame us for the imperfections, of which we accuse them. But how foolish the charge! and how long is it since men have concerned themselves about female education? Who debars their mothers from bringing them up in what manner they please? You

*From Mr. Nugent (trans.). *Emilius.* London: Printed for J. Nourse and P. Valliant, in the Strand, 1763, pp. 186–223.

will say, they have no colleges: a great misfortune indeed. Would to
God there were none for boys; they would be educated in a more
judicious and more virtuous manner. Are your daughters com-
pelled to spend their time in trifles and nonsense? Are they obliged
to follow your example, in passing one half of the day at the
toilette? Who hinders you from instructing, and employing others
to instruct, them in what manner you think proper? Is it our fault
if we are pleased when they are handsome, if we are seduced by
their affected airs, if we are attracted and flattered by those
wheedling arts they have learnt of you, if we like to see them richer
decorated, if we allow them to whet those weapons, by which they
subdue our deluded sex? Well, then, henceforward determine to
bring them up as men; the latter will consent to it with all their
hearts! The more the fair-sex endeavour to resemble ours, the less
power and influence they will have over us; and then it is that we
shall be really masters.

The abilities common to the two sexes, are not equally divided
between them; but upon the whole, the difference is compensated:
the woman has a much greater weight by the qualities of her own
sex, than by those of ours; wherever she asserts her own rights, she
has the advantage of us; wherever she attempts to usurp ours, the
advantage then is on our side. It is impossible to answer this general
truth any other way than by exceptions; a manner of arguing
constantly used by the gallant admirers of the fair-sex.

Were women to cultivate the manly qualities, and to neglect
those which belong to their sex, they would evidently act contrary
to their own interest: of this they are perfectly sensible, and they
have too much art to be caught in such a snare. While they
endeavour to usurp our rights, they do not relinquish their own.
But from thence it follows, that not being able to manage them
both, because they are incompatible, they remain below their own
standard, without coming up to ours, and decrease in one half of
their value. Ye mothers that have judgment, follow my advice; do
not, in defiance of nature, bring up your daughters to be gentlemen,
give them the education of ladies, and assure yourselves, it will be
much better both for them and for us.

But does it follow from thence, that a woman ought to be
educated in absolute ignorance, and confined to the interior
management of a family? Shall man make a servant of his help-
mate, and deprive himself in her company of the greatest endear-
ment of society? The better to keep her under subjection, shall he
debar her from all sensation and knowledge? Shall he make a mere

machine of her? No, surely; this was never the intent of nature, who endowed the sex with so much wit, and sprightly fancy; on the contrary, nature requires they shold think, they shold judge, they shold learn, and improve their understandings as well as their persons: these are the arms with which she has supplied them, to compensate for their want of that strength, with which our sex has been invested. They ought not to learn a great many things, but only such as it is proper for them to know.

Whether I consider the particular destination of the sex, with their inclinations and duties, all concur in pointing out that form of education, which suits them best. Man and woman are formed for one another, but their mutual dependance is not equal: the men depend on the women by their desires; the women on us, both by their desires and their wants; we could subsist much better without them, than they without us. It is impossible for them to have necessaries, or to live agreeably to their condition, unless they are supplied by our sex, and we think them worthy of our assistance. They are dependent on our opinions, on the price we set upon their merit, and on the estimation we make of their charms and virtues. Even the law of nature has subjected both the women, and their offspring, to the jurisdiction of the male sex. It is not sufficient for them to be worthy of esteem, they must be actually esteemed; it is not enough for them to be beautiful, it is necessary they should give pleasure; it is not sufficient that they are endued with wisdom and virtue, they must be acknowledged to be wise and virtuous: their honour does not solely depend on their conduct, but on their reputation; and it is impossible that she who consents to part with her good name, should ever be a honest woman. The good actions of a man depend solely of himself; he may bid defiance to the public judgment: but those of a woman depend also upon others, since her reputation, which is nothing but opinion, is as dear to her as life. The consequence is, that their system of education ought to be different from ours. Opinion is the grave of virtue among men, but its throne with women.

The good habit and disposition of children, is derived from that of their mothers; the early education of the males, is connected with the care taken of us by females; and on them also depend our manners, our passions, our tastes, our pleasures, and even happiness itself. Thus the education of the fair-sex should be intirely relative to ours. To oblige us, to do us service, to gain our love and esteem, to rear us when young, to attend us when grown up, to advise, to console us, to soothe our pains, and to soften life with every kind of blandishment; these are the duties of the sex at all times, and what they ought to learn from their infancy. Unless they are guided by this principle, they will miss their aim, and all the instructions bestowed on them, will neither contribute to their happiness nor to ours.

But although every woman should be willing, both by inclination and duty, to please our sex, yet there is a wide difference between desiring to oblige a man of worth, who is really deserving of love, and endeavouring to be agreeable to those little effeminate fops, who are the disgrace of their own sex, and of that which they foolishly attempt to rival. Neither nature nor reason can induce a woman to love a man for those qualities, in which he resembles herself; neither is it by imitating our manner, that she is to endeavour to conciliate our affection.

Whenever therefore the women lay aside the modesty and decorums of their own sex, to affect the airs of those fribbles, instead of acting according to nature, they greatly deviate from it, and forfeit the very rights, which they would fain usurp. Were we to behave otherwise, say they, we should not be agreeable to the men: but they are mistaken. They must be fools, to be in love with fools; the desire of gaining the affection of such men, shews the taste of those women. If we had no silly fellows among our sex, the women would soon make us such, and our weaknesses would be much more owing to them, than theirs to us. The women who love real men, and desire to please them, pitch upon such means as are agreeable to their design. Woman is by nature a coquette, but her coquettry changes its form and its object, according to her different views; let us regulate these by nature, and then she will have the education suitable to her sex.

Girls, almost from their cradle, are fond of dress: not content with being pretty, they would be thought so; by their airs we perceive, that this is already an object of their attention; and scarce are they capable of understanding us, when they are governed by what is said concerning their person and behaviour. But no such consideration has an influence on boys. Provided they can have their pleasure, and be independent, they give themselves but very little trouble about what the world may think of their conduct. It requires time, and a good deal of trouble, to subject them to the same law, as that by which the girls are intirely directed.

From whatever quarter the women receive this first lesson, it is a very good one. Since the body is born, in some measure, before the mind, it requires the first culture: the above order is common to both sexes, but the object is different; in one, this object is improving its strength; in the other, its charms. Not that these ought to be exclusive qualities in each sex, but only the order is inverted: women must have a sufficient power to perform all their actions with a graceful air; men must have sufficient dexterity to do theirs with ease.

From the too great delicacy of women, that of men is derived. The former ought not to be robust for themselves, but for our sake, to the end that their male offspring may be strong and vigorous. On this account, it is preferable by far to educate young ladies in nunneries, where they have a very simple diet, but are permitted to play, to jump, and run about in the open air, and in the garden; than to bring them up at home, where they are fed with dainties; where they are constantly flattered or reprimanded; where seated under their mother's eye, in a close apartment, they neither dare to rise, nor to speak, nor hardly to draw their breath; where of course they have not a moment's liberty to play, to run about, to make a noise, and fall into the little levities so natural to their age: they are either indulged in such liberties as are dangerous, or checked by an injudicious severity. In this manner are young people ruined, both in body and mind.

In Sparta the girls, as well as the boys, were exercised in military games, not with a view of being trained to war, but of bearing such children, as should be stout and robust, and able to sustain every kind of fatigue. Not that I approve this method: to provide the government with troops, it is not at all necessary that their mothers should have carried a musket, and be expert at the Prussian discipline; but I find, that in this part the Greek education was extremely judicious. The young girls appeared often in public, not intermixed with the boys, but assembled by themselves. There was scarce a feast, a sacrifice, or any public ceremony, in which the daughters of the principal citizens were not seen to walk in bands, crowned with garlands, chanting of hymns, dancing in chorusses, with baskets, vases, and other offerings, whereby the sensual Greeks were entertained with a spectacle capable of counteracting the pernicious effect of that indecency practised in their gymnastic exercises. Whatever might be the impression, which this custom made in the hearts of men, it was highly commendable to confirm the bodily health of young girls, by such exercises as were moderate and agreeable; to excite and form their taste, by a constant desire of pleasing our sex, without ever endangering their manners.

As soon as these young maidens were married, they ceased to

appear in public: they shut themselves up, and confined their whole care to domestic economy. Such is the form of living, which nature, as well as reason, prescribes to the fair-sex; and from those mothers came a hardy offspring, the soundest, and the best-made men in the world. And notwithstanding the disrepute of some islands, it is impossible to produce an instance of any nation upon earth, not even excepting the Romans, where the women were more modest and more agreeable, by a happy union of virtue and beauty, than in ancient Greece.

It is well known, that the easy dress of both sexes contributed greatly to those beautiful proportions, which we still admire in their statues, and which serve as a model to the artists, when nature has degenerated in her real productions. They had none of those Gothic fetters, none of those numerous ligatures, which check the circulation, and confine the different limbs. Their women were strangers to the use of those stays and bodices, by which ours rather counterfeit, than express their true shape. In England, where this abuse has been carried to a very great excess, I wonder it has not caused the species to degenerate; besides I take upon me to affirm, that the pleasure proposed to the eye by that practice, is founded in a vicious taste. It is not at all agreeable to see a woman cut in two like a wasp; it offends the eye, and it gives pain to the imagination. A fine shape, like every thing else, has its proportions and measure, beyond which it is certainly a blemish: a defect of this kind would be very disagreeable in a naked object; and why then should it be reckoned a beauty, when under a garment?

I am almost ashamed to mention the arguments, by which the women so obstinately maintain this custom of cloathing their bodies in armour: a breast hanging down, a prominent belly, etc. are, I grant you, disagreeable in a girl of twenty, but cease to be disgustful in a woman at thirty; and since at all times, what is agreeable to nature, must be pleasing to the eye, and in that respect we are never mistaken, these sorts of blemishes are less disgustful at any age, than the foolish affectation of a maid at forty.

Whatever restrains or confines nature, is founded in a vicious taste; this is true in regard to the decorations of the body, as well as to the accomplishments of the mind. Life, health, reason, and real welfare, ought to take the lead in every thing; there is no such thing as grace without ease; nor is there any delicacy in being languid; to be agreeable, it is not requisite to be in bad health. Compassion may arise from sufferings; but pleasure and desire are excited by the bloom of health.

The children of both sexes have a great many amusements in common, and this must ever be the case; but is it not the seam, when they grow up to maturity? They have likewise their peculiar tastes by which the sex is distinguished. The boys like whatever is productive of motion and noise, as drums, tops, and hobby-horses; the girls are fonder of decorations that please the eye, such as looking glasses, toys, and baby-cloathes. Dolls are the favourite amusement of the sex, which plainly indicates the design for which they were formed. The natural part of the art of pleasing consists in dress, and this is all that children are capable of learning.

It is curious to see how a little girl will spend whole days about her baby, continually changing its attire, dressing and undressing it a hundred times, ever contriving modes of ornament, whether well or ill chosen, it does not signify. Her fingers are not supple, her taste is not formed, and yet her turn of mind begins to shew itself: amidst this incessant occupation, the time insensibly glides away, the hours pass unknown to her; she even forgets her repast, and has a greater appetite for fine cloaths, than for nourishment. But you will tell me, that her care is about dressing her doll, and not her own person; no doubt, because she sees her doll, and does not view herself; she is incapable of entering upon any action on her own account; her taste is not yet formed; she has neither power nor abilities; in short, she herself is nothing, she is intirely absorbed in her child, on that she places all her coquettry; but it will not abide there for ever; she waits for the happy minute, when she herself is to be the baby.

Here we have therefore an original taste, of which there can be no sort of doubt. Your business is only to trace it, and bring it under a proper regulation. It is very certain, that the little innocent would be glad with all her heart to know how to decorate her baby herself, to make its top-knots, its handkerchief, its furbelow, its lace: in all these articles, she is under so strict a necessity of depending on the good pleasure of others, that it would be much more convenient to her, were she indebted for the whole to her own industry. Thus do we account for the first lessons that are given to little girls, they are not ordered to perform a hard task under heavy penalties, but indulged with particular favours. And indeed most girls shew a vast aversion to reading and writing; but it is with the greatest pleasure they learn their needle-work. They imagine them-selves grown women, and are delighted with the notion, that these abilities will one day contribute to render their persons more agreeable by the decorations of dress.

When once this road is open, it is very easy to follow: needlework, embroidery, lace, come of themselves; but they are not so fond of tapestry. The taste of furniture is too much out of their way; nor is it connected with their person, being a mere matter of opinion. Tapestry is the amusement of grown women; young girls will never take any great pleasure in it.

These voluntary improvements may extend as far as designing, an art some-how connected with that of dressing in taste. But I would not have them apply themselves to landskips, much less to portrait painting. It is sufficient for them to design foliages, fruits, flowers, drapery, and whatever is capable of giving an embellishment to dress; and to draw a pattern of embroidery after their own fancy, when they cannot meet with one to their liking. If it be incumbent on men in general, to confine their studies to practical knowledge, this is a point of still greater importance to women: for the latter, from their manner of life, which, though less laborious, either is, or ought to be, filled up with more different cares, cannot possibly indulge their inclination for any particular amusement, to the prejudice of their domestic duties. Let those who delight in pleasantry say what they will, good sense falls equally to the share of both sexes. The girls in general are more docile than boys; and we ought even to exert more authority over them, as I shall presently observe: but it does not follow, that we should exact any thing at their hands, without convincing them of its utility. It is the business, it is the art of mothers to point utility out to them, in every action they perform; and to effect this is so much the easier, as the understanding ripens much earlier in girls, than in boys. By this rule their sex, as well as ours, is excused, not only from all studies that are productive of no real advantage, or do not render them more agreeable in company, but even from those in which the prospect of utility is very distant, consequently not adapted to a child's capacity, and is sometimes unperceived even by those who are more advanced in life. If I am not willing that a boy should be obliged to learn to read, by a much stronger reason am I against using this compulsion with girls, before I shew to what use this reading is conducive; but in the manner this utility is commonly pointed out to them, we rather follow our own, than their ideas. Where is the necessity, after all a girl should learn so early to read and write? Will she have a family so soon to conduct? There are very few of the sex, who do not rather abuse, than make a good use of this dangerous invention; and they are all too curious not to learn it of their own accord, when they have a proper time and opportunity. Perhaps the first thing a girl should endeavour to be mistress of, is cyphering; for no one article can be of greater and more constant use, nor guard her against more errors of consequence, than the knowledge of accompts. Were the little creature under a necessity of performing a sum in arithmetic, in order to gain her afternoon's nunchion, I engage she would soon learn to cast up accounts.

I remember an instance of a young girl, who learned to write before she could read, and began to make letters with her needle, when she knew not how to handle a pen. Out of the whole alphabet, she would write at first no other letter but O. She was continually making great O's and little O's, O's of every shape, but always drawn the wrong way. One day however that she was extremely busy in this useful employ, she happened unfortunately to see herself in the glass; and finding that the constraint of this attitude did not at all become her, like a second Minerva, she threw away her pen, and would write no more O's. Her brother was no more fond of writing then herself; but what gave him the most disgust, was the restraint, and not the disagreeableness of the attitude. Yet another method was found out to bring the girl back to her writing; the little creature was so vain and delicate, that she would not suffer her sisters to make use of her linnen; for this reason it had been marked, but now they would mark her shifts no longer; she was therefore reduced to the necessity of marking them herself; the consequence is obvious.

Always assign your reasons for the employ you give to young girls, but be sure you keep them constantly busy. Idleness and indocility are two vices of the most dangerous tendency, and from which it is most difficult for girls ever to recover. They ought to be vigilant and laborious; but this is not all: they should be inured betimes to bear the abridgment of their liberty. This misfortune, if it be one in regard to them, is inseparable from their state; and if ever they escape it, it is only to expose themselves to severer hardships. They will be slaves during their whole lives to continual and most rigid restraint, namely, that of decency and good manners: they should be therefore accustomed betimes to a restriction of their will, to the end that habit may render it easy to them; and the caprices of fancy be brought into subjection to the will of others. Should they shew themselves desirous to be always at work, it will be sometimes proper to oblige them to do nothing. Dissipation, trifling and levity, are defects that easily flow from the corruption and constant indulgence of their first inclinations. To prevent this abuse, teach them more particularly to conquer themselves. Under our ridiculous institutions, the life of a virtuous woman is a perpetual struggle with herself; and it is but just, that this sex should give us a share in the pain of those evils, of which we are the cause.

Use all the art you can to prevent young girls from growing tired of their work, or from being passionately fond of their amusements; as it generally happens in the common method of education, where, as Fenelon expresses it, the disgust lies all on one side, and pleasure on the other. The first of these inconveniencies cannot happen, if the preceding rules be observed, except they should conceive a dislike to those with whom they live and converse. A girl that loves her mother or her aunt, will work with them all day, without being tired; the chat alone makes amends for the article of restraint. But if she has taken a disgust to her governante, she will be displeased with whatever she does under her eye. Those who are not better satisfied to be with their own mothers, than with any body else upon earth, scarce ever turn out good for any thing. But to judge of their real sentiments, it is necessary to study their disposition, and not to rely on what they say; for they are full of flattery and dissimulation, and learn how to disguise themselves betimes. Neither should we lay any injunction on them to love their mothers; affection never flows from duty, and therefore it is of no use, on this occasion, to have recourse to constraint. Inclination, tenderness, and even habit alone, will make a girl fond of her mother, if the latter has done nothing to incur her aversion. Even the very restraint in which she is kept, if properly directed, instead of weakening, will strengthen this inclination; for dependance being a state natural to women, girls will soon perceive they were formed to obey.

As they ought to be allowed but very little liberty, hence that little they enjoy, they carry to excess; in every thing they are upon the extreme, which is the reason of their being more passionate and eager after their diversons, than boys generally are; and this is the second inconveniency I have just been mentioning. This eagerness ought to be checked; for it is the cause of several vices peculiar to women, and among the rest, of that capricious fondness, through which a woman is to-day infatuated with what tomorrow she will look upon with an eye of indifference. Fickleness in taste is as fatal to them as excess; and both are derived from the same source. Do not debar them from gaiety and laughter, from their loud chat, and noisy romp; but see that they be not so surfeited of the one diversion, as to run to the other; do not suffer them to be free from all restraint a single minute in their lives. Accustom them to be called away in the very middle of their play, and to return to their work without the least murmur or regret. Habit alone is sufficient also for this, because it only seconds the operations of nature.

From this habitual constraint arises a docility which women stand in need of all their lives, since they never cease to be subject either to the persons, or opinions of men, and they are never permitted to render themselves independent of those opinions. The first and most important qualification of a woman, is good temper: formed to obey so imperfect a being as man, a being oftentimes so deformed with vice, and always abounding with imperfections, she ought to learn betimes to submit even to injustice, and to bear oppression from a husband, without complaining. It is for her own sake, not for his, that a woman ought to be good-tempered: sourness and obstinacy do but add to their misfortunes; they irritate their husbands, who are conscious that these are not the arms by which our sex is to be subdued. Women were not endowed by heaven with those soft persuasive arts, to shew themselves humoursome and peevish; they were not formed of so delicate a mould, to behave like tyrants; they were not blessed with so tuneful a voice, to pour out torrents of abuse; their countenance was not embellished with such sweet features, to disfigure them by passion. When they fret and vex, they forget themselves; they have oftentimes reason to complain, but never to grumble. Every one ought to act up to their own sex; too mild a husband might render a wife impertinent; but unless a man be a very monster indeed, the mildness and good temper of a wife will sooner or later bring him back to himself, and triumph over his anger.

Let daughters by submissive, but let not mothers be inexorable. To make a young person docile, you must not render her unhappy; to make her modest and diffident, you must not render her stupid. On the contrary, I should be glad she were permitted to use a little artifice, not in order to elude the punishment due for her disobedience, but to excuse herself from the obligation of obeying. The point in view is not to render her dependance painful, it is sufficient she be made to feel it. Artifice is natural to the fair-sex; and as I am in my own mind convinced, that all natural inclinations are in themselves upright and good, I would be fore cultivating them as well as the rest: we must only take care to prevent their being abused.

For the truth of this remark, I refer to every sincere observer. I am not for examining the women themselves, in regard to this article; the restraint of our institutions may oblige them to sharpen

their wits. Examine the girls, those little things who are but just
come into the world; compare them to boys of the same age; and if
the latter do not appear heavy and stupid, in comparison to the
former, I shall acknowledge myself to be in the wrong. May I be
permitted to make use of a single example, taken from childish
simplicity?

It is usual to forbid children to ask any thing at table; for we
imagine, that the best education is that which is most encumbered
with useless precepts: as if a bit of this or that were not soon refused
or granted,* without killing a poor child, by tantalizing his appetite.
Every body must have heard of the artifice of a little boy, subject to
this law, who having been forgot at table, bethought himself of the
expedient of asking salt, &c. I do not pretend to say that he might
be found fault with for calling directly for salt, and indirectly for
meat; the omission was so cruel, that had he even infringed the law,
and told them without ceremony that he was hungry, I do not
believe he would have been punished. But I shall mention the
artifice used in my presence, by a little girl of six years old, in a case
of much greater difficulty; for besides that there was a strict
injunction for her to ask for nothing either directly or indirectly, her
disobedience would have admitted of no excuse, since she had eaten
of every dish but one, which was her favourite, and they had forgot
to give her any of it.

Now the way she took to repair the injury done by this
forgetfulness, without incurring the crime of disobedience, was to
put out her finger, and to point to every plate, saying, with a loud
voice, *I have eaten of this, I have eaten of that:* but she so visibly
affected to pass over that, of which she had not tasted, without
speaking a word, that somebody taking notice of it, asked her,
whether she had eat any of that? O *no,* answered the little glutton,
very softly; and fixing her eyes on the ground. I shall make no
further comment; compare these two stories: one is the artifice of a
girl, the other that of a boy.

Whatever is, is right; and there is no such thing as a general law
of a bad tendency. This ingenuity of the sex, is a very just indemnity
for their unequal share of strength; otherwise woman would not be
man's help-mate, but his slave; it is by this superior ability that she
maintains an equality with man, and keeps him in subjection, at the
same time that she pays him obeisance. The woman has many
disadvantages on her side; our vices, her own timidity and

---

*A child grows importunate, when he finds his account in it; but he will
never ask twice for the same thing, if the first answer be always irrevocable.

weakness: in her favour she has nothing more than wit and beauty. And is it not just she should cultivate both? But beauty is not a general accomplishment; it is destroyed by a thousand accidents, it fades in time, and loses its effect by habit. Wit alone is the true resource of the fair-sex; not that foolish wit so greatly esteemed in the world, though it does not in the least contribute to the happiness of society; but the wit and ingenuity belonging to her state and condition, the art of improving by our sex, and of benefiting by our advantages. You cannot imagine how useful this ingenuity is to the fair; what a charm it adds to the union of the two sexes, how fastly it contributes to restrain the petulance of children and the brutality of husbands, and to maintain that good harmoney in families, which would otherwise be greatly interrupted. You will say, that bad women make an illuse of it; I know it very well: but what is there that vice does not abuse? Let us not destroy the means of happiness, because the wicked sometimes make use of them to our prejudice.

It is possible to make a figure by dress, but it is the person only that can render one agreeable; our attire, and we, are different; finery often displeases, by being too curious and elegant; and often times the dress that renders the person who wears it most con-spicuous, is itself the least observed. The education of young women is in this respect altogether contrary to good sense. They are given to understand, they shall have decorations for their reward, and they are taught to love the most costly attire. They are told, *what a beauty!* when they are set off in the most gorgeous apparel. But quite the contrary, they should be made to think, that so much decoration is designed only to conceal their blemishes; and that to shine with its own lustre, is the real triumph of beauty. The love of fashions is a vicious taste, because our countenances do not change with the caprice of custom; and as our figure continues the same, what became it once, is always becoming.

Were I to behold a young girl, strutting in her pompous array, I should express my uneasiness at this disfiguring of her person, and at the impression it may possibly make in the eye of the public: I should say; these ornaments are too fine, it is a great pity; do you think she would become a plainer dress? Is she handsome enough to do without this or that? Very likely she would then be the first to desire you to strip her of that ornament, and try how she would look: in that case you may praise her figure, if there be room for it. I should never commend her so much, as when her apparel was plain and modest. Were she to consider the embellishment of dress, only as a supplement to the graces of her person, and as a tacit confession, that she stands in need of something to set herself off, she would not be so proud of her finery; nay it would rather be a cause of humiliation to her; and should she happen to be in a richer dress than ordinary, and to hear a person say, How lovely she now appears! her blushes would shew her resentment.

There are however some forms, that have need of ornaments, but none that require a magnificent dress. Expensive apparel may distinguish your fortune, but cannot embellish your person; it is the effect of pride, and intirely founded in prejudice. Real coquettry is sometimes curious and nice, but never sumptuous: Juno would affect to dress finer than Venus. *Since you cannot make her handsome, you have made her rich,* said Apelles to a bad painter, who had drawn a picture of Helena most splendidly dressed. And indeed I have observed, that the most ordinary women generally wear the richest attire: but there cannot be a more ridiculous vanity. Let a young damsel, that has a right taste for dress, without regard to fashions, be provided with ribbands, gauze, muslins, and artificial flowers; though she has no diamonds or Brussels lace,* she will deck herself in a much more agreeable manner, than if she were loaded with jewels.

Since what is once becoming is always so, and it is right for a woman to adorn herself in the best manner possible, those women, who understand any thing of dress, chuse and suit in the best taste, and stick to it; and as they do not change every day, they are less employed, than those who never know where to fix. The true taste, in point of dress, requires but very little time at the toilette; young ladies have rarely a dressing-table in form; their time is filled up with needle-work and reading; yet in general they are as well adorned, though not painted, as the grown ladies, and frequently in a much better taste. We have a wrong notion of the abuse of the toilette; it arises less from vanity, than from want of employment. A woman that spends six hours at her dressing-table, knows very well that she is not better equipped, than another who dispatched the important business in half an hour; but she has killed so much time; and it is much better to amuse herself about her own person, than to be tired of every thing else. Were it not for the toilette, what would the ladies do with themselves from noon till nine at night?

---

*The women who have so fair a skin, as not to stand in need of lace, would greatly mortify the others of the darker hue, if they wore none. It is generally the ordinary women who introduce the fashions, to which those who are handsome are so foolish as to submit.

They collect their own sex together, and take a delight in vexing them; that is something: then they avoid any tete a tete explanations with their husbands, whom they see only at that hour; this is rather an advantage: then there is the amusement of the milliners, the brokers, the petit-maitres, the scribblers, with their verses, their songs, and pamphlets: without the toilette it would be impossible to make this heterogeneous mixture. The only real advantage founded in the thing itself, is the pretence of displaying their abilities a little more, than when they are dressed; but this advantage is not so considerable as some imagine, and the ladies do not make any improvement at the toilette worth mentioning. Be not afraid to give a female education to women, let them love the employments of their sex, let them be modest, let them know how to look after a family, and to busy themselves in domestic concerns, then the toilette will drop of itself, and of course their taste in dress will be much more elegant.

The first thing that young women observe, upon quitting the state of infancy, is that all their external ornaments are insufficient, unless they have some that are personal. Beauty is a perfection they cannot bestow on themselves; coquettry is an accomplishment which requires some time to attain; but they strive to give an agreeable turn to their gesture, to express themselves in a soft tone of voice, to compose their countenance, to trip lightly, to throw themselves into graceful attitudes, and to chuse every advantage to set off their person. The voice becomes more sonorous and settles; the arms unfold themselves more easily; the tread grows firmer; and whatever decorations they may use, they are convinced there is an art in attracting admiration. From thenceforward they have something more to think of, than being employed at their needle: new talents present themselves; and they perceive the use of new accomplishments.

I am not ignorant, that rigid preceptors are against learning young girls to sing, or to dance, or any of the agreeable arts. This is very pleasant indeed! And who then are to learn them? Are those accomplishments only for boys? Are they most proper to adorn the female sex, or ours? You will say, they are proper for neither. To sing profane songs is a crime; dancing is an invention of Satan; a young woman ought to have no other way of employing her time, but in needle-work and prayer. Strange employments for a child only ten years old! For my part, I am very much afraid, that all those little saints who are obliged to pass their infancy in prayer, will spend their youth in a different manner, and when they come to be married, will indemnify themselves in the best manner they can, for the time they imagine themselves to have lost, when they were maidens. I am of opinion there ought to be some regard paid to the age as well as the sex; that a young girl ought not to live like her grandmother, that she ought to be lively, and chearful, to play about, to dance, and to sing as much as she pleases, and to taste all the innocent pleasures of her stage of life; the time will soon, too soon, come for her to be more sedate, and to put on a more serious countenance.

But is there a real necessity for this change? Does it not in all probability proceed from our prejudices? By subjecting modest women to none but dismal observances, the marriage-state has been stripped of every thing that could render it agreeable to husbands. Are we then to be surprized, if observing so great a taciturnity at home, they are driven abroad; or if those who are single, should be so little inclined to enter into so disagreeable a state. Christian teachers, by straining our respective duties, defeat their end, and render them impracticable; by forbidding the women to sing or dance, and to partake of the other diversions in life, they render them sluts and scolds, and quite intolerable in their families. In no religion is matrimony subject to such severe laws as in ours; and in no other is this sacred engagement so greatly abused. Such endeavours have been used to hinder the wives from being amiable, and the husbands are grown indifferent about them. I am told, it ought not to be so; but for my part I think it cannot be otherwise, since, after all, Christians are flesh and blood. I confess I would have the prettiest young woman in England take as much pains to render herself, by every accomplishment, agreeable to her husband, as a Circassian girl would to improve herself in the Harem of Ispahan. Husbands, you will say, do not trouble their heads about those fine accomplishments: truly I believe you, when instead of being exerted to give them pleasure, they only serve as a bait to draw a parcel of impudent young fellows into their house, to the dishonour of the master of the family. But do you imagine, that a prudent woman, with a good agreeable person, and possessed of the like perfections, which she employed intirely to please her husband, would not make a considerable addition to his happiness, and hinder him, after he had almost exhausted himself with study, from going abroad in search of diversion? Whoever saw a family thus happily united, where every one contributes his share to the common amusement; let him say, whether the chearful innocent mirth, in which the company indulges themselves on those occasions, does not more than compensate for the empty shew, or tumultuous joy of public entertainments?

The agreeable accomplishments are taught of late with too much formality; they have been rendered too systematical; every thing has been reduced to maxim and precept, and young people are tired to death with what was intended only for their amusement. Nothing can be imagined more ridiculous, than an old dancing-master, or teacher of music, addressing himself with a grim sour face to young people, who desire only to laugh; and assuming a more pedantic and more magisterial air, to instruct them in his trifling science, than if they were to be taught their catechism. To know how to sing, for instance, is it necessary to learn music? Might not a girl know how to tune her voice, so as to sing in state, and even to accompany an instrument, without being acquainted with a single note? Is the same sort of music suited to all voices? Is the same method agreeable to every genius? I can never be made to believe that the same attitudes, the same steps, the same movements, gestures and dances, are proper for a young lively brunet, as for a fair beauty with large languishing eyes. Whenever therefore I see a master giving exactly the same lessons to both, I affirm, this man goes by rote, but understands nothing of his art.

It is a question with some, whether girls should be taught by their own sex, or by ours? For my part, I know not which to determine, I should be glad they wanted neither masters nor mistresses; that they were at full liberty to learn what they have so strong an inclination to; and that such a number of laced dancing-masters were not seen strolling about the country. I can hardly believe, but the conversation of those fellows must be more pernicious to young girls, then their lessons can be of use; and that from the strangeness of their jargon, from their tone of voice, and ridiculous airs, their female scholars imbibe that turn for trifles, so important to their masters, which, taught by their example, the young misses will soon learn to make their sole employment.

In regard to those arts that having nothing but pleasure for their object, young people may take their instructions from whom they please. They may consult their father, their mother, their brother, their sister, their friends, their governantes, their looking-glass, but especially their own taste. Let us not offer to teach them, it is they should desire of us to be instructed; we ought not to turn a reward into a task; and it is chiefly on these kinds of study that we should first endeavour to succeed. However, if we must have lessons in form, I will not take upon me to determine the sex that

is to give them. I know not whether it be necessary, for a dancing-
master to take his pretty scholar by her softe delicate hand, to make
her extend her pettycoats, raise her eyes, stretch out her arms, and
project her panting breast: but I am very certain that I would not be
in that station for all the world.

By industry and abilities our taste is formed; by taste the mind
soon acquires the ideas of the beautiful in every kind, and at length
the moral notions, to which the others are related. This perhaps is
one reason, why the sense of decency and shame is sooner imbibed
by girls than by boys; for to imagine this forward sensation to be
the work of governantes, one must be very ill acquainted with the
tendency of their lessons, and the progress of the human understanding. Elocution holds the first rank in the art of pleasing; by
this alone can we enhance those charms, to which the senses are
already accustomed. This is the spirit which not only quickens, but
in some measure renews the body; by the succession of sensations
and ideas, it animates the countenance, and gives it an agreeable
variety; by supplying the tongue with a constant flow of words, it
keeps up the attention, and interests the hearer in the same object.
Hence, I apprehend, it is, that girls so soon acquire a pretty manner
of prattling, that they lay a due emphasis on their words, before
they feel the weight of the expression; and that we take so much
pleasure in hearing them, even before they are capable of understanding what they say; we watch the moment when their understanding begins to dawn, in order to judge of their sensibility.

The women have a voluble tongue; their speech comes on
earlier, is more fluent, and more agreeable than ours; and they are
also charged with being more loquacious. It cannot be otherwise;
this is an accusation which, I think, redounds to their honour. Their
organs of seeing and speaking have the same activity, and for the
same reason. Man says what he knows, woman what she pleases;
the one, in order to speak, stands in need of knowledge, the other
of taste; the principal object of the one ought to be the useful, of the
other the agreeable. Their discourse should have no common forms
but those of truth.

We ought not therefore to restrain the prattling of young girls,
like that of boys, by this harsh interrogation, *Of what use is that?*
but by the following, which is not at all easier to answer, *What
effect will that produce?* At this early period of life, when they are as
yet incapable of discerning good from evil, and therefore are no
judges of any person's conduct, they ought to lay it down as an
invariable rule, never to say any thing disagreeable to those they

converse with; and what renders this rule more difficult to practise, is its being always subordinate to the former, which is never to tell an untruth.

I am sensible of a great many other difficulties, but they belong to a riper age. For the present, young girls can have no other obstacle in telling the truth, but that of being sometimes rude, and this is a quality to which they have a natural repugnance; education teaches them to avoid it. In regard to human intercourse, I observe in general, that politeness in men is more officious, in women more affectionate. This difference is not owing to education, it is founded in nature. The man seems to take more pains to serve you, the woman to give you pleasure. From thence it follows, that let the character of the women be what it will, their politeness is more sincere than ours, as it only extends their natural instinct; but when a man pretends to prefer my interest to his own, whatever colour he may give to this declaration, I am sure it is a falsity. There is no great difficulty, therefore, for women to be polite, nor of course for girls to learn that behavior. The first lesson proceeds from nature; this is improved by art, which determines according to our customs, in what form it ought to display itself. With regard to their politeness among themselves, it is quite a different thing. In their behavior there is such an air of affectation, and such indifference in their grimaces, that they take very little trouble to conceal the restraint they give to one another; they seem to be sincere in their deception, by scarce endeavouring to disguise it. Yet there are some young women that have a real friendship for each other. At their time of life, chearfulness supplies the place of good-nature; and being content in their own mind, they are content with all the world. It is very certain that they kiss one another more heartily, and exchange caresses with a much better grace, in the presence of men, than when by themselves; the reason is, they are proud to tantalize us with impunity, by the representation of favours, which they know to be envied by our sex.

If boys are not allowed to ask indiscreet questions, much less ought that to be permitted young girls, since, considering their quickness of apprehension, and their curiosity in diving into things, which should be mysteriously concealed from their knowledge, the resolving their questions is a matter of much greater consequence. But without permitting them to interrogate, I should be glad they were questioned a good deal themselves, and that care were taken to make them prattle and talk with freedom and ease, in order to give them a quickness of repartee, and to set both their understanding and their tongue at full liberty, while it can be effected without danger. These conversations, enlivened with mirth and gaiety, but managed at the same time with art, and under proper direction, would be a most delightful amusement to girls at this period of life, and might imprint in their innocent minds the first and perhaps the most useful, instructions of morality and vanity, they will learn, to what qualities men really annex their esteem, and what constitutes the glory and happiness of a virtuous woman.

If boys are incapable of forming a true idea of religion, by a much stronger reason, that idea is above the comprehension of young girls; and for this very reason I should talk to the latter much sooner upon this subject. For were we to wait till they were capable of entering into a methodical discussion of these profound questions, we should be in danger of never hitting our mark. The reason of women is a practical faculty, which renders them very dexterous at finding out the means of arriving at a known end, but does not enable them to discover the end itself. The social relation of the sexes is admirable. From this society there results a moral person; this person's eye is the woman, and man is the arm; but with so strict a dependance on each other, that from man, the woman learns what is proper to be seen, and from woman, the man acquires his knowledge of what is fit to be done. Could the female sex ascend to the first principles, as well as ours, and could we have the same spirit of detail as they, ever independent of each other, we should live in perpetual discord, and human society could not possibly subsist. But in the present state of harmoney and union, between the two sexes, every thing tends to one common end; they know not which contributes most towards it; each follows the other's impulse; each obeys; and they both command.

Since a woman's conduct is subject to public opinion, for this very reason her belief depends on authority. Every girl ought to follow the religion of her mother; and every married woman, that of her husband. Were this to be a false persuasion, yet the subjection in which the mother and daughter are held, by the order of nature, justifies their docility, and cancels the sin of ignorance. Incapable of judging for themselves, they ought to receive the decision of their fathers and husbands, like that of the church.

The women having no possibility of deriving the rule of their faith from their own inquiry, cannot confine its bounds to those of evidence and reason, but suffer themselves to be drawn away by a thousand impulses of a different nature; they are always either beyond or on this side the truth. Ever in extremes, they are either libertines or devotees; they know not how to unite piety and discretion. This evil has its source, not only in the extravagance of their sex, but in the ill-regulated authority of our immorality is the cause of despising this authority; repentance arms it with too much terror; and thus it is always either too much, or too little respected.

Since the religion of females is to be regulated by authority, the business is not so much to acquaint them with the reasons of our belief, as clearly to explain to them what we do believe: for to give faith to obscure ideas, is the source of fanaticism; and to require it for absurdities, leads to folly or incredulity. I know not whether our catechisms, have a greater tendency to impiety, than to enthusiasm; but I am very well satisfied, they are necessarily productive of one or the other.

In the first place, when you initiate young girls into religion, do not represent it as an object of gloom and restraint, nor as a talk or duty; of course never let them learn any thing by heart, that has a tendency that way, not even their prayers. Be content with saying yours in their presence, yet without obliging them to join with you. Let them be short, pursuant to Christ's instructions. Let them always be uttered with due reverence; remember that when you ask the supreme Being to attend to your prayers, it becomes you to attend to what you say.

It is not of so much consequence, that young girls should learn their religion betimes, as that they should know it perfectly well, and even love it. When you render it a burden to their minds, by representing the Deity as always angry with them; when you subject them, in his name, to a thousand painful duties, which they never see you perform; what can they possibly think, but that their catechism, and their prayers, are imposed only upon little girls? consequently they must desire to grow up, in order to be exempted, like you, from this subjection. Be sure you set them an example, otherwise you will never to able to do any thing with children.

When you explain the articles of faith to them, do it by the way of a direct instruction, and not by questions and answers. They ought never to make any other answer, than what is framed by themselves, and not dictated by others. All the answers in the catechism are absurd; they give you the disciple instructing the master; they are even so many falsities in the mouths of children, since they explain what they do not understand, and affirm what they are incapable of believing. Even among people of the best understanding, shew me one who does not lie in saying his catechism.

The first question I observe in ours,* is this: *Who created you, and brought you into the world?* The little girl, without least hesitation, answers *God*, though at the same time she believes it was her mother. The only thing she perceives, is, that she is asked a question, of which she apprehends but very little, and that she makes an answer without understanding any thing at all about the matter.

I should be glad, if some person who knew something of the intellectual progress of children, would undertake a catechism for their use. It would be perhaps the most useful book that ever was penned; and, in my opinion, it would do not small honour to the author. This however is very certain, that if the book were good for any thing, it would bear very little resemblance to ours.

A catechism of that kind would be of use only, when, from the nature of the questions, the child would be able to frame his answers himself; provided, however, it be his turn sometimes to interrogate. In order to convey my meaning, it would be necessary to sketch some sort of a model, and I am very sensible of my own inequality for the task. I shall attempt nevertheless to give a faint idea of it.

The Mistress.	Do you remember the time when your mother was a maid?
Little Girl.	No, madam.
The Mistress.	Why so! you have a very good memory?
Little Girl.	Because I was not born.
The Mistress.	Then you have not been always living?
Little Girl.	No.
The Mistress.	Will you live for ever?
Little Girl.	Yes.
The Mistress.	Are you young or old?
Little Girl.	I am young.
The Mistress.	And your grand-mamma, is she young or old?
Little Girl.	She is old.
The Mistress.	Has she been young?
Little Girl.	Yes.
The Mistress.	And why is not she so still?
Little Girl.	Because she is grown old.
The Mistress.	And will you grow old, like her?

---

*That of the French Protestants.

152	
Little Girl.	I cannot tell.*
The Mistress.	Where are the clothes you wore last year?
Little Girl.	They have been taken to pieces.
The Mistress.	And why have they been taken to pieces?
Little Girl.	Because they were too little for me.
The Mistress.	And how came they to be too little for you?
Little Girl.	Because I am grown.
The Mistress.	Will you grow any bigger?
Little Girl.	Yes! to be sure.
The Mistress.	And what becomes of grown girls?
Little Girl.	They become women.
The Mistress.	And what becomes of the women?
Little Girl.	They become mothers.
The Mistress.	And what becomes of them, after they are mothers?
Little Girl.	They grow old.
The Mistress.	Will you grow old?
Little Girl.	When I have been a mother.
The Mistress.	And what becomes of old people?
Little Girl.	I cannot tell.
The Mistress.	Where is your grand-papa gone to?
Little Girl.	He is dead.†
The Mistress.	And how came he to die?
Little Girl.	Because he was old?
The Mistress.	What then becomes of old people?
Little Girl.	They die.
The Mistress.	And you, when you grow old, what—
Little Girl interrupting her.	O, madam, I do not chuse to die.
The Mistress.	My dear, no body chuses to die, and yet we are all mortal.
Little Girl.	How so! will my mamma die to?
The Mistress.	Every body must die. The women grow

---

*If wherever I have put, *I cannot tell,* the little girl makes a different answer, you should distrust what she says, and oblige her to explain it.

†The little girl will say so, because she heard it said: but it will be proper to try whether she has a right idea of death for this idea is not so simple, nor so obvious to the capacity of children, as some imagine. In the little poem of Abel, there is an instance of the manner in which they ought to be made acquainted with it. This is a most charming composition; it breathes a delightful simplicity, in which you cannot familiarize yourself too much, to converse with children.

Little Girl.	What must I do, to grow old a great while hence?
The Mistress.	Be good while you are young.
Little Girl.	Madam, I will always be good.
The Mistress.	So much the better for you. But after all, do you expect to live for ever?
Little Girl.	When I come to be old, very old . . .
The Mistress.	Well then?
Little Girl.	In short, when we grow old, you say we must die.
The Mistress.	Then you must die once?
Little Girl.	Ah! yes.
The Mistress.	Who was living before you?
Little Girl.	My father and mother.
The Mistress.	Who was living before them?
Little Girl.	Their father and mother.
The Mistress.	Who will live after you are gone?
Little Girl.	My children.
The Mistress.	Who will live after they are gone?
Little Girl.	Their children, &c.

Pursuing this track we shall find, by sensible inductions, that the human race, like every thing else, has had a beginning and an end; that is, a father and a mother, who had neither father nor mother; and children who will have no children, &c.* Thus the first question in the catechism should not be introduced, till after a long series of the like questions then, and not till then, can it be made with propriety or the child be capable of understanding you. But from thence to the second question, which is in some measure a definition of the divine essence, how immense the distance! When will this space be filled up? God is a spirit! And what is a spirit? Shall I go and engage a child in this dark maze of metaphysics, from which even grown-up persons find it so difficult to extricate themselves? It does not belong to a little girl to resolve such questions; it is at the most her business to propose them. Then I should give her a plain simple answer: you ask me what God is; it is not an easy matter to tell you. God can neither be heard, seen nor touched; he is known only by his works. In order to judge what he

---

*The idea of eternity is unapplicable, with any propriety, to human generations. Every numerical succession reduced to act, is incompatible with that idea.

154   is, stay till you know what he has done.

If the articles of our religion are all equally true, yet they are not all of equal importance. It is very indifferent to the divine glory, whether it be manifested to us in every particular; but it is of the utmost consequence to human society, and to each of its members, that every man should know and fulfill the several duties towards his neighbour, and toward himself, which are injoined him by the divine law. This is what we ought constantly to teach one another; and in this particularly are parents obliged to instruct their children. Whether a virgin be the mother of her Creator, whether she brought forth the Deity, or only a man to whom the divine nature was conjoined; whether the substance of the Father and the Son be the same, or only similar; whether the Holy Ghost proceeds from one of the two, who are both the same, or from both jointly; I do not perceive that the determination of these questions, in appearance so essential, is of more importance to the human species, than to know on which day of the month we ought to solemnize Easter; whether it be proper to say our beads, to fast, to abstain from flesh, to use the Latin or French language in church, to bedeck the wall with images, to celebrate or to assist at mass, and to live in a state of celibacy. Let every one think of these matters as he pleases; I know not how far they may be important to others, for my part they are not at all interesting to me. But the matter of consequence to me and my fellow-creatures is, that every man should know, that there is an arbiter of the fate of human beings, on whom we all depend as his children; that he commands us all to be just, to love each other, to be beneficent and merciful, to keep our engagements with all the world, even with our enemies and his; that the apparent felicity of this life is nothing; that there is another to come, in which the supreme Being will distribute rewards to the good, and punishments to the wicked. These, and the like doctrines, are proper to be inculcated to children, and instilled into the minds of all mankind. Whosoever opposes them, is incontestibly deserving of punishment, because he is a common disturber, and an enemy to society. Whosoever overlooks them, and wants to subject us to his private opinions, drives towards the same point by an opposite road; to establish order after his manner, he disturbs the public tranquillity; in the pride and rashness of his heart, he sets himself up for an interpreter of the Deity; he demands the homage and praise of men in the divine name; he erects himself, to the best of his power, in the place of God; he ought to be punished for sacrilege, if not for the guilt of persecution.

Take no notice therefore of all those mysterious articles, which in regard to use are only bare words that convey no ideas, and of all those extravagant and whimsical doctrines, the idel study of which supplies the place of virtue among formal professors, and contributes to render them fools instead of good men. Keep your children within the narrow circle of the doctrine of morality. Make them fully sensible, that there is no other knowledge useful to man, but that which teaches him to do good. Do not make your daughters philosophers and divines; learn them no thing, in regard to celestial things, but what contributes to human wisdom: let them be accustomed to feel themselves always in the presence of the Deity, to have him for a witness to their actions, to their thoughts, to their virtues, and their pleasures; to do good without ostentation, because he loves it; to suffer evil without repining because he will make them amends; in short, to be every day of their lives the same as they would desire to have been, when they are to appear in his presence. This is the true system of religion, the only one unsusceptible of abuse, impiety, or fanaticism. Let others preach sublimer systems as long as they please, for my part I acknowledge none but this.

It is proper, however, to observe, that till they attain the use of reason, and begin to hear the internal voice of conscience, young persons have no notion of good or evil, but from the declaration of the people about them. What they are commanded to do is good, what they are forbid to do is bad; that is all they ought to know; whereby it appears how much more important it is to girls than to boys, that the persons who approach them be judiciously chosen, and invested with some authority. At length the moment is arrived, when they will begin to judge things by themselves, and then it is time to change the plan of their education.

Hitherto, perhaps, I have said too much upon this subject. To what a situation should we reduce the women, were we to allow them no other law than public prejudice? Let us not so far debase the sex by which we are governed, and which treats us with respect unless we degrade it. There exists a rule for the whole human species antecedent to opinion. To the invariable direction of this rule, all others ought to be reduced; it pronounces judgement even on prejudice itself; and human esteem ought to be of authority with us, only so far as it agrees with it.

This rule is the moral sense. I shall not repeat in this place, what has been elsewhere mentioned; it is sufficient for me to observe, that unless these two rules concur in the education of women, it will certainly be defective. The moral sense, independent of opinion, will not give them that delicacy of mind, which adorns good actions with reputation and honour; and opinion, without it, will only render the sex false and dishonest, so as to substitute appearance in the place of virtue.

It therefore behoves them greatly to cultivate a faculty, which serves for an umpire between the two guides, hinders the conscience from being misled, and rectifies the errors of prejudice. This faculty is reason: but at the bare mentioning of this word, what a number of questions arise! Are women capable of solid reasoning? Is it of consequence for them to cultivate this faculty? Will the pains they take in the cultivation be attended with success? Is this cultivation any way serviceable in the duties assigned them; or is it consistent with the simplicity that becomes their state?

From the different ways of considering and solving these questions, people have given into contrary extremes: some are for confining a woman to the needle and distaff, in company with her maids, and thus only make her the upper servant to the master: others, not content with ascertaining her rights, make her usurp ours; for to leave her superior to us in the qualities peculiar to her sex, and to render her our equal in those which are common to both, is depriving the husband of the superiority he received from nature, and transferring it to the woman.

The reasons which lead man to the knowledge of his duty, are not very complex; those which confine a woman to hers, are still more simple. The obedience and fidelity which she owes to her husband, the care and tenderness she ought to have for her children, are consequences so naturally and so sensibly derived from her condition, that she cannot sincerely refuse her consent to the interior sensations which are her guide, nor mistake her duty, unless her inclinations are corrupted.

I should not absolutely condemn the institution of confining women to domestic concerns, and suffering them to remain in a profound ignorance of every thing else; but such an institution I own would require, that the morals of the people were very simple and incorrupt, or that the women led a very retired life. In great cities, and among debauched men, such a woman would be too easily seduced; her chastity oftentimes would be exposed to great danger; and this delicate age requires of the sex a virtue capable of standing the severest trial. She should previously know what proposals may be made to her, and what answers it is proper for her to give.

Besides, as she is subject to the judgment of men, she should endeavour to deserve their esteem; above all things she ought to obtain that of her husband, she not only should study to make him love her person, but likewise approve her conduct; she ought to justify his choice in the eye of the public, and to contrive so, that the respect which is paid the wife, shall redound to the husband's honour. Now is it possible for her to effect any thing of this, if she be ignorant of our constitutions, our customs, and laws of decorum; if she knows not the source of human opinions, nor of the passions, by which they are determined? As she is dependent at one and the same time on her own conscience, and on the sentiments of others, she must learn to compare, and to reconcile those two rules, and never to prefer the former, but when it clashes with the latter. She becomes the umpire of her own judges, by determining when she ought to obey, and when to oppose their commands. Before she admits or rejects their prejudices, she weighs them with great care, she traces them to that source, she anticipates them in some measure, and renders them propitious to her cause; she studies, particularly, never to incur any censure, when her duty permits her to avoid it. Nothing of all this can be done, without attending to the cultivation of her reason and understanding.

JOHANN HEINRICH PESTALOZZI (1746–1827)

A giant among educators, Pestalozzi altered educational theory and practice in many countries of the world. His two major contributions were to introduce the concept of object lessons and to encourage teachers to love their students.

Perhaps because his own mother devotedly educated him and his two siblings, Pestalozzi was convinced that the home is the ideal educational institution. He believed that mothers should accept the responsibility to generate the virtues of love, trust, gratitude, patience, and obedience which, in turn, develop higher aspects of moral, social, and religious life. As a child grows, dependence upon the mother decreases and finally vanishes. Although he thought mothers should be teachers of housework, social arts, manners, morals and piety, Pestalozzi deemed formal schools to be essential because most mothers are not ideally suited to assume all these responsibilities. His teaching career was limited, primarily, to the operation of boarding schools for boys at Yverdun and Neuhof.

In 1781 Pestalozzi wrote *Leonard and Gertrude* in which, apparently, he patterned the pious Gertrude after his own mother. In early sections of this novel, Gertrude was the only teacher in the town. There was no formal school; all instruction was oral and was combined with children's work and play at Gertrude's home. There appears to have been no consistent attempt to teach reading and writing early, but the ability to speak was taught early and with great care. During meals, work, worship, and play, Gertrude taught without seeming to teach. The children sang morning and evening hymns and repeated Bible verses; a special teacher came to teach the girls to sew and spin. The following excerpt is a charming account of the educational environment created by Gertrude.

Chapter XXV

"Gertrude's Method of Instruction"

It was quite early in the morning when Arner, Glulphi and the pastor went to the mason's cottage. The room was not in order when they entered, for the family had just finished breakfast, and the dirty plates and spoons still lay upon the table. Gertrude was at first somewhat disconcerted, but the visitors reassured her, saying kindly: "This is as it should be; it is impossible to clear the table before breakfast is eaten!"

The children all helped wash the dishes, and then seated themselves in their customary places before their work. The gentlemen begged Gertrude to let everything go on as usual, and after the first half hour, during which she was a little embarrassed, all proceeded as if no stranger were present. First the children sang their morning hymns, and then Gertrude read a chapter of the Bible aloud, which they repeated after her while they were spinning, rehearsing the most instructive passages until they knew them by heart. In the mean time, the oldest girl had been making the children's beds in the adjoining room, and the visitors noticed through the open door that she silently repeated what the others were reciting. When this task was completed, she went into the garden and returned with vegetables for dinner, which she cleaned while repeating Bible-verses with the rest.

It was something new for the children to see three gentlemen in the room, and they often looked up from their spinning toward the corner where the strangers sat. Gertrude noticed this, and said to them: "Seems to me you look more at these gentlemen than at your yarn." But Harry answered; "No, indeed! We are working hard, and you'll have finer yarn to-day than usual."

Whenever Gertrude saw that anything was amiss with the wheels or cotton, she rose from her work, and put it in order. The smallest children, who were not old enough to spin, picked over the cotton for carding, with a skill which excited the admiration of the visitors.

Although Gertrude thus exerted herself to develop very early

*From Channing, Eva (trans.). *Pestalozzi's Leonard and Gertrude*. Boston: D. C. Heath & Co., 1885, pp. 129–131.

the manual dexterity of her children, she was in no haste for them to learn to read and write. But she took pains to teach them early how to speak; for, as she said, "of what use is it for a person to be able to read and write, if he cannot speak?—since reading and writing are only an artificial sort of speech." To this end she used to make the children pronounce syllables after her in regular succession, taking them from an old A-B-C book she had. This exercise in correct and distinct articulation was, however, only a subordinate object in her whole scheme of education, which embraced a true comprehension of life itself. Yet she never adopted the tone of instructor toward her children; she did not say to them: "Child, this is your head, your nose, your hand, your finger;" or: "Where is your eye, your ear?"—but instead, she would say: "Come here, child, I will wash your little hands," "I will comb your hair," or: "I will cut your fingernails." Her verbal instruction seemed to vanish in the spirit of her real activity, in which it always had its source. The result of her system was that each child was skilful, intelligent and active to the full extent that its age and development allowed.

The instruction she gave them in the rudiments of arithmetic was intimately connected with the realities of life. She taught them to count the number of steps from one end of the room to the other, and two of the rows of five panes each, in one of the windows, gave her an opportunity to unfold the decimal relations of numbers. She also made them count their threads while spinning, and the number of turns on the reel, when they wound the yarn into skeins. Above all, in every occupation of life she taught them an accurate and intelligent observation of common objects and the forces of nature.

All that Gertrude's children knew, they knew so thoroughly that they were able to teach it to the younger ones; and this they often begged permission to do. On this day, while the visitors were present, Jonas sat with each arm around the neck of a smaller child, and made the little ones pronounce the syllables of the A-B-C book after him; while Lizzie placed herself with her wheel between two of the others, and while all three spun, taught them the words of a hymn with the utmost patience.

When the guests took their departure, they told Gertrude they would come again on the morrow. "Why?" she returned; "You will only see the same thing over again." But Glulphi said: "That is the best praise you could possibly give yourself." Gertrude blushed at this compliment, and stood confused when the gentlemen kindly pressed her hand in taking leave.

The three could not sufficiently admire what they had seen at the mason's house, and Glulphi was so overcome by the powerful impression made upon him, that he longed to be alone and seek counsel of his own thoughts. He hastened to his room, and as he crossed the threshold, the words broke from his lips: "I must be school master in Bonnal!" All night visions of Gertrude's schoolroom floated through his mind, and he only fell asleep toward morning. Before his eyes were fairly open, he murmured: "I will be schoolmaster!"—and hastened to Arner to acquaint him with his resolution.

MARY WOLLSTONECRAFT (1759–1797)

Mary Wollstonecraft acquired a basic education in a small school in Enfield. Her family moved to rural Wales where she continued her education by reading her father's books on philosophy, poetry, and divinity. She founded a school which soon failed, then tutored for a brief time but disliked it. Aside from these experiences, she limited her educational contributions to her highly esteemed writing.

Wollstonecraft viewed education as a means to develop character and to produce strength of mind and body, regardless of one's sex. She advocated a national system of coeducation. She reasoned that women needed economic training in order to become independent and, further, to manage an estate if she were widowed. Although she claimed that nature is opposed to all inequality, she commented on the importance of having women perform domestic duties.

In light of what John Dewey was to say over a century later, it is interesting to read Wollstonecraft's similar comment in which she stated that she considered it a waste to spend one's life in preparation to live.

Women's rights movements are indebted to her for pioneering efforts. In *A Vindication of the Rights of Woman* she claimed for women the right to be representatives in Parliament; this was in 1792, one hundred twenty-seven years before Lady Nancy Astor became the first woman admitted to the House of Commons. Wollstonecraft argued, formidably, for women's educational advancement, economic independence, political enfranchisement, and social equality. In the preface to *Vindication,* she explained that she wanted women to be in a position where they would advance, instead of retard, progress of the human race. She was aware that formal education would be essential to accomplish this goal. Furthermore, she supported the idea that women should be companions to men; this, too, pointed to a need for female education, Chapter XII, "On National Education," from *Vindication,* is recommended

162

reading related to the topic of female education.

The name Wollstonecraft became a symbol for the un-womanly woman. American clergymen opposed her views. Although her proposals were considered radical in her lifetime, by the end of the eighteenth century American theorists were affected by her writing.

Wollstonecraft's premature death resulted from the birth of her daughter, Mary, who would gain fame as the wife of Percy Shelley and the author of *Frankenstein.*

Her essays "Exterior Accomplishments," "The Fine Arts," "Reading," and "Boarding Schools" from *Thoughts on the Education of Daughters* (1787) are reprinted here. Other essays which reveal her thoughts on such topics as temper, love, matrimony, benevolence, and the theatre are not reprinted here.

THOUGHTS ON THE EDUCATION OF DAUGHTERS*

"Exterior Accomplishments"

Under this head may be ranked all those accomplishments which merely render the person attractive; and those half-learnt ones which do not improve the mind. "A little learning of any kind is a dangerous thing;" and so far from making a person pleasing, it has the contrary effect.

Parents have mostly some weighty business in hand, which they make a pretext to themselves for neglecting the arduous task of educating their children; they are therefore sent to school, and the allowance for them is so low, that the person who undertakes the charge must have more than she can possibly attend to; of course, the mechanical parts of education can only be observed. I have known children who could repeat things in the order they learnt them, that were quite at a loss when put out of the beaten track. If the understanding is not exercised, the memory will be employed to little purpose.

---

*Wollstonecraft, Mary. *Thoughts on the Education of Daughters with Reflections on Female Conduct, in the More Important Duties of Life.* London: J. Johnson, 1787; New York & London: Garland Publishing, Inc., 1974, pp. 24–29, 42–60.

Girls learn something of music, drawing, and geography; but they do not know enough to engage their attention, and render it an employment of the mind. If they can play over a few tunes to their acquaintance, and have a drawing or two (half done by the master) to hang up in their rooms, they imagine themselves artists for the rest of their lives. It is not the being able to execute a trifling landscape, or any thing of the kind, that is of consequence—These are at best but trifles, and the foolish, indiscriminate praises which are bestowed on them only produce vanity. But what is really of no importance, when considered in this light, becomes of the utmost, when a girl has a fondness for the art, and a desire of excellence. Whatever tends to make a person in some measure independent of the senses, is a prop to virtue. Amusing employments must first occupy the mind; and as an attention to moral duties leads to piety, so whoever weighs one subject will turn to others, and new ideas will rush into the mind. The faculties will be exercised, and not suffered to sleep, which will give a variety to the character.

Dancing and elegance of manners are very pleasing, if too great a stress is not laid on them. These acquirements catch the senses, and open the way to the heart; but unsupported by solid good qualities, their reign is short.

The lively thoughtlessness of youth makes every young creature agreeable for the time; but when those years are flown, and sense is not substituted in the stead of vivacity, the follies of youth are acted over, and they never consider, that the things which please in their proper season, disgust out of it. It is very absurd to see a woman, whose brow time has marked with wrinkles, aping the manners of a girl in her teens.

I do not think it foreign to the present subject to mention the trifling conversations women are mostly fond of. In general, they are prone to ridicule. As they lay the greatest stress on manners, the most respectable characters will not escape its lash, if deficient in this article. Ridicule has been, with some people, the boasted test of truth—if so, our sex ought to make wonderful improvements; but I am apt to think, they often exert this talent till they lose all perception of it themselves. Affectation, and not ignorance, is the fair game for ridicule; and even affectation some good-natured persons will spare. We should never give pain without a design to amend.

Exterior accomplishments are not to be despised, if the acquiring of them does not satisfy the possessors, and prevent their cultivating the more important ones.

Music and painting, and many other ingenious arts, are now brought to great perfection, and afford the most rational and delicate pleasure.

It is easy to find out if a young person has a taste for them. If they have, do not suffer it to lie dormant. Heaven kindly bestowed it, and a great blessing it is; but, like all other blessings, may be perverted: yet the intrinsic value is not lessened by the perversion. Should nature have been a niggard to them in this respect, persuade them to be silent, and not seigh raptures they do not feel; for nothing can be more ridiculous.

In music I prefer expression to execution. The simple melody of some artless airs has often soothed my mind, when it has been harassed by care; and I have been raised from the very depths of sorrow, by the sublime harmony of some of Handel's compositions. I have been lifted above this little scene of grief and care, and mused on Him, from whom all bounty flows.

A person must have sense, taste, and sensibility, to render their music interesting. The nimble dance of the fingers may raise wonder, but not delight.

As to drawing, those cannot be really charmed by it, who do not observe the beauties of nature, and even admire them.

If a person is fond of tracing the effects of the passions, and marking the appearances they give to the countenance, they will be glad to see characters displayed on canvass, and enter into the spirit of them; but if by them the book of nature has not been read, their admiration is childish.

Works of fancy are very amusing, if a girl has a lively fancy; but if she makes others do the greatest part of them, and only wishes for the credit of doing them, do not encourage her.

Writing may be termed a fine art; and, I am sure, it is a very useful one. The style in particular deserves attention. Young people are very apt to substitute words for sentiments, and clothe mean thoughts in pompous diction. Industry and time are necessary to cure this, and will often do it. Children should be led into correspondences, and methods adopted to make them write down their sentiments, and they should be prevailed on to relate the stories they have read in their own words. Writing well is of great consequence in life as to our temporal interest, and of still more to the mind; as it teaches a person to arrange their thoughts, and digest them. Besides, it forms the only true basis of rational and elegant conversation.

Reading, and such arts as have been already mentioned, would fill up the time, and prevent a young person's being lost in dissipation, which enervates the mind, and often leads to improper connections. When habits are fixed, and a character in some measure formed, the entering into the busy world, so far from being dangerous, is useful. Knowledge will imperceptibly be acquired, and the taste improved, if admiration is not more fought for than improvement. For those seldom make observation who are full of themselves.

"Reading"

It is an old, but a very true observation, that the human mind must ever be employed. A relish for reading, or any of the fine arts, should be cultivated very early in life; and those who reflect can tell, of what importance it is for the mind to have some resource in itself, and not be entirely dependant on the senses for employment and amusement. If it unfortunately is so, it must submit to meanness, and often to vice, in order to gratify them. The wisest and best are too much under their influence; and the endeavouring to conquer them, when reason and virtue will not give their sanction, constitutes great part of the warfare of life. What support, then, have they who are all senses, and who are full of schemes, which terminate in temporal objects?

Reading is the most rational employment, if people seek food for the understanding, and do not read merely to remember words; or with a view to quote celebrated authors, and retail sentiments they do not understand or feel. Judicious books enlarge the mind and improve the heart, though some, by them, "are made coxcombs whom nature meant for fools."

Those productions which give a wrong account of the human passions, and the various accidents of life, ought not to be read before the judgment is formed, or at least exercised. Such accounts are one great cause of the affectation of young women. Sensibility is described and praised, and the effects of it represented in a way so different from nature, that those who imitate it must make themselves very ridiculous. A false taste is acquired, and sensible books appear dull and insipid after those superficial performances, which obtain their full end if they can keep the mind in a continual ferment. Gallantry is made the only interesting subject with the novelist; reading, therefore, will often co-operate to make his fair admirers insignificant.

I do not mean to recommend books of an abstracted or grave cast. There are in our language many, in which instruction and amusement are blended; the Adventurer is of this kind. I mention this book on account of its beautiful allegories and affecting tales, and similar ones may easily be selected. Reason strikes most forcibly when illustrated by the brilliancy of fancy. The sentiments which are scattered may be observed, and when they are relished, and the mind set to work, it may be allowed to chuse books for itself, for every thing will then instruct.

I would have every one try to form an opinion of an author themselves, though modesty may restrain them from mentioning it. Many are so anxious to have the reputation of taste, that they only praise the authors whose merit is indisputable. I am sick of hearing of the sublimity of Milton, the elegance and harmony of Pope, and the original, untaught genius of Shakespear. These cursory remarks are made by some who know nothing of nature, and could not enter into the spirit of those authors, or understand them.

A florid style mostly passes with the ignorant for fine writing; many sentences are admired that have no meaning in them, though they contain "words of thundering sound," and others that have nothing to recommend them but sweet and musical terminations.

Books of theology are not calculated for young persons; religion is best taught by example. The Bible should be read with particular respect, and they should not be taught reading by so sacred a book; lest they might consider that as a task, which ought to be a source of the most exalted satisfaction.

It may be observed, that I recommend the mind's being put into a proper train, and then left to itself. Fixed rules cannot be given, it must depend on the nature and strength of the understanding; and those who observe it can best tell what kind of cultivation will improve it. The mind is not, cannot be created by the teacher, though it may be cultivated, and its real powers found out.

The active spirits of youth may make time glide away without intellectual enjoyments; but when the novelty of the scene is worn off, the want of them will be felt, and nothing else can fill up the void. The mind is confined to the body, and must sink into sensuality; for it has nothing to do but to provide for it, "how it shall eat and drink, and wherewithal it shall be clothed."

All kinds of refinement have been found fault with for increasing our cares and sorrows; yet surely the contrary effect also arises from them. Taste and thought open many sources of pleasure, which do not depend on fortune.

No employment of the mind is a sufficient excuse for neglecting domestic duties, and I cannot conceive that they are incompatible. A woman may fit herself to be the companion and friend of a man of sense, and yet know how to take care of his family.

"Boarding Schools"

If a mother has leisure and good sense, and more than one daughter, I think she could best educate them herself; but as many family reasons render it necessary sometimes to send them from home, boarding-schools are fixed on. I must own it is my opinion, that the manners are too much attended to in all schools; and in the nature of things it cannot be otherwise, as the reputation of the house depends upon it, and most people can judge of them. The temper is neglected, the same lessons are taught to all, and some get a smattering of things they have not capacity ever to understand; few things are learnt thoroughly, but many follies contracted, and an immoderate fondness for dress among the rest.

To prepare a woman to fulfil the important duties of a wife and mother, are certainly the objects that should be in view during the early period of life; yet accomplishments are most thought of, and they, and all-powerful beauty, generally gain the heart; and as the keeping of it is not considered of until it is lost, they are deemed of the most consequence. A sensible governess cannot attend to the minds of the number she is obliged to have. She may have been many years struggling to get established, and when fortune smiles, does not chuse to lose the opportunity of providing for old age; therefore continues to enlarge her school, with a view to accumulate a competency for that purpose. Domestic concerns cannot possibly be made a part of their employment, or proper conversations often entered on. Improper books will by stealth be introduced, and the bad example of one or two vicious children, in the play-hours, infect a number. Their gratitude and tenderness are not called forth in the way they might be by maternal affection. Many miseries does a girl of a mild disposition suffer, which a tender parent could guard her from. I shall not contest about the graces, but the virtues are best learnt at home, if a mother will give up her time and thoughts to the task; but if she cannot, they should be sent to school; for people who do not manage their children well, and have not large fortunes, must leave them often with servants, where they are in danger of still greater corruptions.

BENJAMIN RUSH (1745–1813)

Benjamin Rush, one of Philadelphia's leading citizens, is the first American writer represented in this book of classics. Rush was a physician, member of the Continental Congress, signer of the Declaration of Independence, and member of the American Philosophical Society. Moreover, he was regarded as an authority on the theories of Fenelon, whose ideas paralleled his own rather closely.

Rush was the best known Colonial American advocate of women's capacity for education. He preferred that women read travel stories, moral essays, and poetry instead of novels. He recommended that American schools exclude instrumental music and French because of the short study time available to American girls. Predictably, he condemned the common American practice of copying English education and fashions.

Rush was a member of the original Board of Directors at Andrew Brown's Philadelphia Academy for Young Ladies where, in 1787, he presented a series of twelve lectures. His "Thoughts Upon Female Education," delivered at Brown's School, became the most widely quoted United States paper on female education prior to 1790. This well-organized essay is reprinted here in its entirety.

*THOUGHTS UPON FEMALE EDUCATION**

THOUGHTS UPON FEMALE EDUCATION, ACCOM-
 MODATED TO THE PRESENT STATE OF SOCIETY,
 MANNERS, AND GOVERNMENT, IN THE UNITED
 STATES OF AMERICA. ADDRESSED TO THE VIS-
 ITORS OF THE YOUNG LADIES' ACADEMY IN PHIL-

---

*Rush, Benjamin. *Essays, Literary, Moral and Philosophical.* Philadelphia: Printed by Thomas and William Bradford, No. 8, South Front Street, 1806, pp. 75–92.

ADELPHIA, 28TH JULY, 1787, AT THE CLOSE OF THE QUARTERLY EXAMINATION, AND AFTERWARDS PUBLISHED AT THE REQUEST OF THE VISITORS.

GENTLEMEN,

I have yielded with diffidence to the solicitations of the Principal of the Academy, in undertaking to express my regard for the prosperity of this seminary of learning, by submitting to your candor, a few Thoughts upon Female Education.

The first remark that I shall make upon this subject, is, that female education should be accommodated to the state of society, manners, and government of the country, in which it is conducted.

This remark leads me at once to add, that the education of young ladies, in this country, should be conducted upon principles very different from what it is in Great Britain, and in some respects, different from what it was when we were part of a monarchical empire.

There are several circumstances in the situation, employments, and duties of women in America, which require a peculiar mode of education.

I. The early marriages of our women, by contracting the time allowed for education, renders it necessary to contract its plan, and to confine it chiefly to the more useful branches of literature.

II. The state of property in America, renders it necessary for the greatest part of our citizens to employ themselves, in different occupations, for the advancement of their fortunes. This cannot be done without the assistance of the female members of the community. They must be the stewards, and guardians of their husbands' property. That education, therefore, will be most proper for our women, which teaches them to discharge the duties of those offices with the most success and reputation.

III. From the numerous avocations from their families, to which professional life exposes gentlemen in America, a principal share of the instruction of children naturally devolves upon the women. It becomes us therefore to prepare them by a suitable education, for the discharge of this most important duty of mothers.

IV. The equal share that every citizen has in the liberty, and the possible share he may have in the government of our country, make it necessary that our ladies should be qualified to a certain degree by a peculiar and suitable education, to concur in instructing their sons in the principles of liberty and government.

V. In Great Britain the business of servants is a regular
occupation; but in America this humble station is the usual retreat of unexpected indigence; hence the servants in this country possess less knowledge and subordination than are required from them; and hence, our ladies are obliged to attend more to the private affairs of their families, than ladies generally do, of the same rank in Great Britain. "They are good servants," said an American lady of distinguished merit, in a letter to a favorite daughter, "who will do well with good looking after." This circumstance should have great influence upon the nature and extent of female education in America.

The branches of literature most essential for a young lady in this country, appear to be,

I. A knowledge of the English language. She should not only read, but speak and spell it correctly. And to enable her to do this, she should be taught the English grammar, and be frequently examined in applying its rules in common conversation.

II. Pleasure and interest conspire to make the writing of a fair and legible hand, a necessary branch of a lady's education. For this purpose she should be taught not only to shape every letter properly, but to pay the strictest regard to points and capitals.*

I once heard of a man who professed to discover the temper and disposition of persons by looking at their hand writing. Without enquiring into the probability of this story; I shall only remark, that there is one thing in which all mankind agree upon this subject, and that is, in considering writing that is blotted, crooked, or illegible, as a mark of vulgar education. I know of few things more rude or illiberal, than to obtrude a letter upon a person of rank or business, which cannot be easily read. Peculiar care should be taken to avoid every kind of ambiguity and affectation in writing *names.* I have now a letter in my possession upon business, from a gentleman of a liberal profession in a neighbouring state, which I am unable to answer, because I cannot discover the name which is subscribed to it.† For obvious reasons I would recommend the

*The present mode of writing among persons of taste is to use a capital letter only for the first word of a sentence, and for names of persons, places and months, and for the first word of every line in poetry. The words should be so shaped that a straight line may be drawn between two lines, without touching the extremities of the words in either of them.

†Dr. Franklin received many letters while he was in France during the American war, from persons who wished to migrate to America, and who appeared to possess knowledge and talents that would have been useful to his country, but their names were subscribed to their letters in so artificial and affected a manner, that he was unable to decypher them, and of course, did not answer them.

writing of the first or christian name at full length, where it does not consist of more than two syllables. Abbreviations of all kind in letter writing, which always denote either haste or carlessness, should likewise be avoided. I have only to add under this head that the Italian and inverted hands which are read with difficulty, are by no means accommodated to the active state of business in America, or to the simplicity of the citizens of a republic.

III. Some knowledge of figures and book-keeping is absolutely necessary to qualify a young lady for the duties which await her in this country. There are certain occupations in which she may assist her husband with this knowledge; and should she survive him, and agreeably to the custom of our country be the executrix of his will, she cannot fail of deriving immense advantages from it.

IV. An acquaintance with geography and some instruction in chronology will enable a young lady to read history, biography, and travels, with advantage; and thereby qualify her not only for a general intercourse with the world, but to be an agreeable companion for a sensible man. To these branches of knowledge may be added, in some instances, a general acquaintance with the first principles of astronomy, natural philosophy and chemistry, particularly, with such parts of them as are calculated to prevent superstition, by explaining the causes, or obviating the effects of natural evil, and such, as are capable of being applied to domestic, and culinary purposes.

V. Vocal music should never be neglected, in the education of a young lady, in this country. Besides preparing her to join in that part in public worship which consists in psalmody, it will enable her to soothe the cares of domestic life. The distress and vexation of a husband—the noise of a nursey, and, even, the sorrows that will sometimes intrude into her own bosom, may all be relieved by a song, where sound and sentiment unite to act upon the mind. I hope it will be thought foreign to this part of our subject to introduce a fact here which has been suggested to me by my profession, and that is, that the exercise of the organs of the breast, by singing, contributes very much to defend them from those diseases to which our climate; and other causes, have of late exposed them.—Our German fellow citizens are seldom afflicted with consumptions, nor have I ever known but one instance of spitting of blood among them. This, I believe, is in part occasioned by the strength which their lungs acquire, by exercising them frequently in vocal music, for this constitutes an essential branch of their education. The music-master of our academy has furnished me with an observation still more in favour of this opinion. He informed me that he had known several instances of persons who were strongly disposed to the consumption, who were restored to health, by the moderate exercise of their lungs in singing.

VI. Dancing is by no means an improper branch of education for an American lady. It promotes health, and renders the figure and motions of the body easy and agreeable. I anticipate the time when the resources of conversation shall be so far mutiplied, that the amusement of dancing shall be wholly confined to children. But in our present state of society and knowledge, I conceive it to be an agreeable substitute for the ignoble pleasures of drinking, and gaming, in our assemblies of grown people.

VII. The attention of our young ladies should be directed, as soon as they are prepared for it, to the reading of history—travels —poetry—and moral essays. These studies are accommodated, in a peculiar manner, to the present state of society in America, and when a relish is excited for them, in early life, they subdue that passion for reading novels, which so generally prevails among the fair sex. I cannot dismiss this species of writing and reading without observing, that the subjects of novels are by no means accommodated to our present manners. They hold up *life*, it is true, but it is not as yet *life* in America. Our passions have not as yet "overstepped the modesty of nature," nor are they "torn to tatters," to use the expressions of the poet, by extravagant love, jealousy, amibition, or revenge. As yet the intrigues of a British novel, are as foreign to our manners, as the refinements of Asiatic vice. Let it not be said, that the tales of distress, which fill modern novels, have a tendency to soften the female heart into acts of humanity. The fact is the reverse of this. The abortive sympathy which is excited by a recital of imaginary distress, blunts the heart to that which is real; and, hence, we sometimes see instances of young ladies, who weep away a whole forenoon over the criminal sorrows of a fictitious Charlotte or Werter, turning with disdain at three o'clock from the sight of a beggar, who solicits in feeble accents or signs, a small portion only of the crumbs which fall from their fathers' tables.

VIII. It will be necessary to connect all these branches of education with regular instruction in the christian religion. For this purpose the principles of the different sects of christians should be taught and explained, and our pupils should early be furnished with some of the most simple arguments in favour of the truth of christianity.* A portion of the bible (of late improperly banished from our schools) should be read by them every day, and such questions should be asked, after reading it as are calculated to imprint upon their minds the interesting stories contained in it.

Rousseau has asserted that the great secret of education consists in "wasting the time of children profitably." There is some truth in this observation. I believe that we often impair their health, and weaken their capacities, by imposing studies upon them, which are not proportioned to their years. But his objection does not apply to religious instruction. There are certain simple propositions in the christian religion, which are suited in a peculiar manner, to the infant state of reason and moral sensibility. A clergyman of long experience in the instruction of youth informed me, that he always found children acquired religious knowledge more easily than knowledge upon other subjects; and that young girls acquired this kind of knowledge more readily than boys. The female breast is the natural soil of christianity; and while our women are taught to believe its doctrines, and obey its precepts, the wit of Voltaire, and the stile of Bolingbroke, will never be able to destroy its influence upon our citizens.

I cannot help remarking in this place, that christianity exerts the most friendly influence upon science, as well as upon the morals and manners of mankind. Whether this be occasioned by the unity of truth, and the mutual assistance which truths upon different subjects afford each other, or whether the faculties of the mind be sharpened and corrected by embracing the truths of revelation, and thereby prepared to investigate and perceive truths upon other subjects, I will not determine, but I believe that the greatest discoveries in science have been made by christian philosophers, and that there is the most knowledge in those countries where there is the most christianity.† If this remark be well founded, then those

---

*Baron Haller's letters to his daughter on the truths of the christian religion, and Dr. Beatie's "evidence of the christian religion briefly and plainly stated" are excellent little tracts, and well adapted for this purpose.
†This is true in a peculiar manner in the science of medecine. A young Scotch physician of enterprizing talents, who conceived a high idea of the state of medecine in the eastern countries, spent two years in enquiries after medical knowledge in Constantinople, and Grand Cairo. On his return to Britain he confessed to an American physician whom he met at Naples, that after all his researches and travels, he "had discovered nothing except a single fact relative to the plague, that he thought worth remembering or communicating." The science of medecine in China according to the accounts of De Halde is in as imperfect a state as among the Indians of North America.

philosophers who reject christianity, and those christians, whether parents or school-masters, who neglect the religious instruction of their children and pupils, *reject* and *neglect* the most effectual means of promoting knowledge in our country.

IX. If the measures that have been recommended for inspiring our pupils with a sense of religious and moral obligation be adopted, the government of them will be easy and agreeable. I shall only remark under this head, that *strictness* of discipline will always render *severity* unnecessary, and that there will be the most instruction in that school, where there is the most order.

I have said nothing in favour of instrumental music as a branch of female education, because I conceive it is by no means accommodated to the present state of society and manners in America. The price of musical instruments, and the extravagant fees demanded by the teachers of instrumental music, form but a small part of my objections to it.

To perform well, upon a musical instrument, requires much time and long practice. From two to four hours in a day, for three or four years appropriated to music, are an immense deduction from that short period of time which is allowed by the peculiar circumstances of our country for the acquisition of the useful branches of literature that have been mentioned. How many useful ideas might be picked up in these hours from history, philosophy, poetry, and the numerous moral essays with which our language abounds, and how much more would the knowledge acquired upon these subjects add to the consequence of a lady, with her husband and with society, than the best performed pieces of music upon a harpsichord or a guittar! Of the many ladies whom we have known, who have spent the most important years of their lives, in learning to play upon instruments of music, how few of them do we see amuse themselves or their friends with them, after they become mistresses of families! Their harpsichords serve only as side-boards for their parlours, and prove by their silence, that necessity and circumstances, will always prevail over fashion, and false maxims of education.

Let it not be supposed from these observations that I am insensible of the charms of instrumental music, or that I wish to exclude it from the education of a lady where a musical ear irresistably disposes to it, and affluence at the same time affords a prospect of such an exemption from the usual cares and duties of the mistress of a family, as will enable her to practice it. These circumstances form an exception to the general conduct that should arise upon this subject, from the present state of society and manners in America.

It is agreeable to observe how differently modern writers, and the inspired author of the Proverbs, describe a fine woman. The former confine their praises chiefly to personal charms, and ornamental accomplishments, while the latter celebrates only the virtues of a valuable mistress of a family, and a useful member of society. The one is perfectly acquainted with all the fashionable languages of Europe; the other, "opens her mouth with wisdom" and is perfectly acquainted with all the uses of the needle, the distaff, and the loom. The business of the one, is pleasure; the pleasure of the other, is business. The one is admired abroad; the other is honoured and beloved at home. "Her children arise up and call her blessed, her husband also, and he praiseth her." There is no fame in the world equal to this; nor is there a note in music half so delightful, as the respectful language with which a grateful son or daughter perpetuates the memory of a sensible and affectionate mother.

It should not surprise us that British customs, with respect to female education, have been transplanted into our American schools and families. We see marks of the same incongruity, of time and place, in many other things. We behold our houses accommodated to the climate of Great Britain, by eastern and western directions. We behold our ladies panting in a heat of ninety degrees, under a hat and cushion, which were calculated for the temperature of a British summer. We behold our citizens condemned and punished by a criminal law, which was copied from a country, where maturity in corruption renders public executions a part of the amusements of the nation. It is high time to awake from this servility—to study our own character—to examine the age of our country—and to adopt manners in every thing, that shall be accommodated to our state of society, and to the forms of our government. In particular it is incumbent upon us to make ornamental accomplishments yield to principles and knowledge, in the education of our women.

A philosopher once said "let me make all the ballads of a country and I care not who makes its laws." He might with more propriety have said, let the ladies of a country be educated properly, and they will not only make and administer its laws, but form its manners and character. It would require a lively imagination to describe, or even to comprehend, the happiness of a country, where knowledge and virtue, were generally diffused among the female

sex. Our young men would then be restrained from vice by the
terror of being banished from their company. The loud laugh, and
the malignant smile, at the expence of innocence, or of personal
infirmities—the feats of successful mimickry—and the low priced
wit, which is borrowed from a misapplication of scripture phrases,
would no more be considered as recommendations to the society of
the ladies. A double entendre in their presence, would then exclude
a gentleman forever from the company of both sexes, and probably
oblige him to seek an asylum from contempt, in a foreign country.
The influence of female education would be still more extensive and
useful in domestic life. The obligations of gentlemen to qualify
themselves by knowledge and industry to discharge the duties of
benevolence, would be encreased by marriage; and the patriot—the
hero—and the legislator, would find the sweetest reward of their
toils, in the approbation and applause of their wives. Children
would discover the marks of maternal prudence and wisdom in
every station of life; for it has been remarked that there have been
few great or good men who have not been blessed with wife and
prudent mothers. Cyrus was taught to revere the gods, by his
mother. Mandane—Samuel was devoted to his prophetic office
before he was born, by his mother Hannah—Constantine was
rescued from paganism by his mother Constantia—and Edward the
sixth inherited those great and excellent qualities which made him
the delight of the age in which he lived, from his mother, lady Jane
Seymour. Many other instances might be mentioned, if necessary,
from ancient and modern history, to establish the truth of this
proposition.

I am not enthusiastical upon the subject of education. In the
ordinary course of human affairs, we shall probably too soon
follow the footsteps of the nations of Europe in manners and vices.
The first marks we shall perceive of our declension, will appear
among our women. Their idleness, ignorance, and profligacy will be
the harbingers of our ruin. Then will the character and performance
of a buffoon on the theatre, be the subject of more conversation and
praise, than the patriot or the minister of the gospel;—then will our
language and pronunciation be enfeebled and corrupted by a flood
of French and Italian words;—then will the history of romantic
amours, be preferred to the pure and immortal writing of Addison,
Hawkesworth and Johnson;—then will our churches be neglected,
and the name of supreme being never be called upon, but in profane
exclamations;—then will our Sundays be appropriated, only to
feasts and concerts?—and then will begin all that train of domestic

and political calamities—But, I forbear. The prospect is so painful, that I cannot help, silently, imploring the great arbiter of human, affairs, to interpose his almighty goodness, and to deliver us from these evils, that, at least one spot of the earth may be reserved as a monument of the effects of good education, in order to shew in some degree, what our species was, before the fall, and what it shall be, after its restoration.

Thus, gentlemen, have I briefly finished what I proposed. If I am wrong in those opinions in which I have taken the liberty of departing from general and fashonable habits of thinking, I am sure you will discover, and pardon my mistakes. But if I am right, I am equally sure you will adopt my opinions; for to enlightened minds truth is alike acceptable, whether it comes from the lips of age, or the hand of antiquity, or whether it be obtruded by a person, who has no other claim to attention, than a desire of adding to the stock of human happiness.

I cannot dismiss the subject of female education without remarking, that the city of Philadelphia first saw a number of gentlemen associated for the purpose of directing the education of young ladies. By means of this plan, the power of teachers is regulated and restrained, and the objects of education are extended. By the separation of the sexes in the unformed state of their manners, female delicacy is cherished and preserved. Here the young ladies may enjoy all the literary advantages of a boarding-school, and at the same time live under the protection of their parents.* Here emulation may be excited without jealousy,— ambition without envy,—and competition without strife. The attempt to establish this new mode of education for young ladies, was an experiment, and the success of it hath answered our expectations. Too much praise cannot be given to our principal and his assistants, for the abilities and fidelity with which they have carried the plan into execution. The proficiency which the young ladies have discovered in reading—writing—spelling—arithmetic—grammar—geography—music—and their different catechisms, since the last examination, is a less equivocal mark of the merit of our teachers, than any thing I am able to express in their favour.

But the reputation of the academy must be suspended, till the public are convinced, by the future conduct and character of our

---

*"Unnatural confinement makes a young woman embrace with avidity every pleasure when she is set free. To relish domestic life, one must be acquainted with it; for it is in the house of her parents a young woman acquires the relish." Lord Kaim's thoughts upon education, and the culture of the heart.

pupils, of the advantages of the institution. To you, therefore, Young Ladies, an important problem is committed for solution; and that is, whether our present plan of education be a wise one, and whether it be calculated to prepare you for the duties of social and domestic life. I know that the elevation of the female mind, by means of moral, physical and religious truth, is considered by some men as unfriendly to the domestic character of a woman. But this is the prejudice of little minds, and springs from the same spirit which opposes the general diffusion of knowledge among the citizens of our republics. If men believe that ignorance is favourable to the government of the female sex, they are certainly deceived; for a weak and ignorant woman will always be governed with the greatest difficulty. I have sometimes been led to ascribe the invention of ridiculous and expensive fashions in female dress, entirely to the gentlemen*, in order to divert the ladies from improving their minds, and thereby to secure a more arbitrary and unlimited authority over them. It will be in your power, Ladies, to correct the mistakes and practice of our sex upon these subjects, by demonstrating, that the female temper can only be governed by reason, and that the cultivation of reason in women, is alike friendly to the order of nature, and to private as well as public happiness.

---

*The very expensive prints of female dresses which are published annually in France, are invented and executed wholly by GENTLEMEN.

CLARA REEVE (1729–1807)

Reeve's father, a minister, tutored her when she was a child. Eventually, his prescribed reading for her included parliamentary debates, Rapin's *History of England,* Cato's *Letters,* Greek and Roman history, and Plutarch. She became an author of mediocre rank with one successful novel, *The Old English Baron.*

Clara Reeve shared an interest in women's rights with a number of English contemporary authors; in fact, Wollstonecraft's *A Vindication of the Rights of Woman* was published in the same year, 1792, as was Reeve's *Plans of Education, with Remarks on the Systems of Other Writers.* The following selection from her book on education contains a detailed description of a female boarding school in Middlesex.

THE PLAN OF
A SEMINARY
OF FEMALE EDUCATION
Which was opened at Tottenham, Middlesex,
By Mrs. M. Scriven
in the year 1788*

The defects of the present system of Female Education are generally acknowledged by all who think seriously upon this important subject: they are too apparent in the manners of the women of these times.

English Ladies have been celebrated, above any in Europe, for the modesty of their dress;—the purity, and even sanctity, of their manners. There are many individuals who sustain the national reputation; but yet it is evident, that the manners of our country-

---

*Reeve, Clara. *Plans of Education with Remarks on the Systems of Other Writers.* London: T. Hookham and J. Carpenter, 1792; New York & London: Garland Publishing, Inc., 1974, pp. 178-188.

women, in general, exhibit a great and alarming alteration within 181 the present century. The most common observer cannot but see and lament the public victims of pride, vanity, and folly; to say nothing of the train of more destructive vices which have disgraced the annals of female character within the last fifty years—these are too notorious to leave any room to doubt the truth of the present declension of manners in this country.

Those honourable and worthy examples who support and assert the national character, perceive and lament this alarming alteration, are solicitous to investigate the causes of it, and to seek for a remedy: they ardently seek to stop the progress of vice and folly: to preserve the rising generation from the contagion of bad example; the absurdities arising from a false education; and to restore the national character of virtue, modesty, and discretion. Under the patronage of these most respectable Ladies we presume to offer to the public an attempt to rectify some of those errors which have been sanctified by custom; and have, therefore, long passed unnoticed.

The first cause of this national decline of manners, arises from a bad method of education: the second, from bad examples after this education is finished.—Leaving the latter to those whose province it is to correct the morals of the age, we confine ourselves to the first article.—

People of condition give up their children very early to the care of servants and nurses: persons generally ignorant and uninformed, frequently unprincipled, who prevent the seeds of future virtues from germinating, and bring forward the weeds of pride, self-will, artifice, and every bad passion and propensity. From the nursery they are sent to school, where they are supposed to learn the rudiments of morals, manners, every useful virtue, and every ornamental accomplishment: but all must depend upon the persons to whose care they are entrusted. When we consider how very few are duly qualified for this sacred trust, we need not wonder at the mischiefs that arise from the misconduct, or abuses in the discharge of it. They ate such as have often been remarked upon by those who have been sufferers by them; or by those who have seen and felt the effects of them upon any in whose fate they were interested. It is not in this little essay that we mean to enumerate them; none who think seriously, can be ignorant of them; we shall only just point out the causes, and then seek for a remedy for those evils.

When we consider the great increase of common boarding schools, we shall not be surprised at the numerous mischiefs arising from them. In every town, village, and even hamlet, there is one or more persons who take upon themselves the great and important charge of female education: over their doors may be seen in letters of gold, A Boarding School for Young Ladies.

Adventurers of all kinds have found resources in the profession. Needy foreigners, without friends and recommendation,—ladies' upper servants,—broken traders,—ladies of lost reputation,—nay, even menial servants, have succeeded in raising schools of this kind: what must we think of the negligence and credulity of such parents, who intrust their most precious treasures, their children, the sacred deposits of heaven and their country, to the care of an unknown, ignorant, and, too frequently, unprincipled people; who return them back in a state that often obliges them to wish them ignorant of all that they have learned?—We do not, however, mean to include all boarding-schools under this description. We know that there are some that answer every purpose of ingenuous and virtuous education; such as we wish to promote and recommend; but we still insist, that there are far more that are either pernicious, or fall very short of the advantages expected from them.

Among those of the better kinds, the attention is chiefly, if not entirely, directed to external accomplishments; while the moral duties and social virtues are neglected.—We daily see young people come from these schools, filled with pride, vanity, and self-consequence;—ignorant of every necessary duty, and every useful quality in domestic life;—insolent to their equals and inferiors; rejecting every kind of restraint; and void of that modesty, humility, and delicacy of mind, which are the surest guards of female virtue, and the best pledges of their future conduct in life, as wives, mothers, and worthy members of society.

Having traced these evils to their sources, we shall offer to the public our best endeavours towards a remedy for them.

We conceive that it is practicable to inculcate the highest principles of religion and virtue, and to blend them with the most elegant and most useful female accomplishments; and this is our aim in offering to the public our plan of female education.

With these important objects constantly in view (under the sanction of many ladies the most respectable; of rank, fortune, and character) several ladies of unblemished characters and unquestionable abilities, some of whom have had the honour of educating young ladies of the first distinction, and can produce credentials of indisputable authority, have determined to open a Seminary of

Education, upon a plan different from any boarding-school, in many respects, in a pleasant and healthy situation; within such a distance from London, as will ensure the attendance of the best masters of all kinds.

The Terms

For boarding, washing &c. learning grammatically the French, English, and Italian languages; the belles-lettres; the use of the globes; history, music, dancing, singing, drawing, and painting; every useful and fashionable kind of needle-work; books, threads, tapes, needles, and every other necessary, Fifty Pounds a year.— Holidays twice a year, Christmas and Midsummer:—at the latter there will be a public examination of the young pupils, by persons of approved judgment and ability, and rewards given to distinguished merit in every department.

Each child shall have a separate bed; and in case of sickness, proper apartments in a part of the house, unconnected, with the rest of it; every medical assistance, and proper attendance.

In order to extend the benefits of this Seminary, it is proposed to admit young ladies, who, either from want of opportunity, or neglect of the means of instruction, are under the necessity of applying for it at a later season of life, and who have objections to mixing with pupils younger than themselves. Upon these considerations, the Ladies are determined to receive such boarders, if they can conform to the rules of the house.

Such persons shall receive all the advantages, without being obliged to attend the classes; and persons, duly qualified, will be appointed to attend them in their own apartments, to give them private lessons, and every instruction they can require.

They shall pay Fifty Pounds a year, finding their own wine, fire, candles, and washing.

N.B. No Money to teachers or servants.

JOHN BURTON (1696–1771)

An Oxford classical scholar and clergyman, Burton wrote tracts, sermons, Latin verses, and Greek textbooks. He presented fourteen Sunday evening lectures to pupils attending a female boarding school. These lectures cover a wide range of topics which include the following opinions: (1) vacations are essential in order for children and parents to see one another, and for children to demonstrate to their parents what they have learned; (2) early religious education is desirable; (3) even wealthy girls must be taught domestic arts; (4) schools are responsible for introducing moral principles to students; (5) mothers have a great responsibility for the early education of their children; (6) female education should be different from male education because of the differing roles of the sexes; (7) girls should avoid the use of cosmetics and should be neat and clean in their dress; (8) manners and placid tempers should be advanced at schools. Burton described ornamental accomplishments in the following lecture.

LECTURES ON FEMALE EDUCATION AND MANNERS*

Lecture IX

That Works of Ingenuity and Elegance are particulary becoming in your Sex, and that the Study of them ought to enter into Female Education as much as possible, all, I think, are agreed.

DR. FORDYCE

---

*Burton, J. *Lectures on Female Education and Manners.* Vol. I. London: Printed for J. Johnson, St. Paul's Church-yard; J. Murray, Fleet-street; and J. Evans, Pater-noster-row, 1793. 2nd Edition.

184

I have already explained to you, what are the proper offices and employments of the Female Sex. I shall now proceed to recommend to you those accomplishments, which will be either necessary or agreeable.

The first I shall mention is Needle Work; the knowledge of which, as applying chiefly to domestic affairs, is absolutely requisite. This art may be divided into the useful and the ornamental.

The useful part is attended with so many advantages, and is at the same time so comprehensive, that it is needles for me to enlarge upon the subject. Whether you confine it to your own dress; or whether you extend it to that of a family, over which you may possibly preside, an acquaintance with it forms a very essential part of female education: Because you will not only be able to render great assistance, by your own application, but you will also be skilful Judges of the performance of others.

The knowledge of this branch of Needle Work is also requisite on the principle of frugality; for if your circumstances should be too confined, to employ either the Semstress or the Milliner, you will then have it in your power to appear with decency, at a small expence, by your own labour.

Ornamental Needle Work will furnish you with the means of employing your vacant hours innocently and perhaps profitably. Your Ancestors have left behind them lasting monuments of their skill and industry in this art. But works of Tapestry will be regarded, by our modern Ladies, as tasks which require too much time and attention; or as fit only for those, who, in Catholic Countries, have retreated from the World. Though the manners of the present age are so much changed from those of the last, yet the exercise of the needle, at proper intervals, is graceful in the Female Sex; and is well adapted to their constitutions and sedentary life.

The Spectator, who devoted several of his Papers to the use and instruction of the Female Sex, has, in one of his Numbers, made some observations on this accomplishment. The subject is introduced by a Letter, addressed to him from an elderly Lady, who complains, that her two Nieces spent much of their time in gadding abroad; that dress, play and visits were their chief employment; and that they retired to rest at night, fatigued with doing nothing. She remarks, that those hours, which in this age, are dissipated in the manner already mentioned, were engaged in her time, in working Beds and Chairs for the family. She informs him, that she had plied her Needle for fifty years, with equal pleasure and satisfaction; and that she is grieved to see her young flighty relations sipping their tea for a whole afternoon, in a room hung round by the industry of their Progenitors. She concludes by desiring him to recommend the laudable art of embroidery. —The arguments offered in it's favour, by the Spectator, are these:

"It must," says he, "be a delightful entertainment to the fair Sex, to pass their time in imitating fruits and flowers; and transplanting all the Beauties of Nature into their own dress; or raising a new creation in their closets and apartments. How pleasing is the amusement of walking among the shades and groves planted by themselves; or in surveying Heroes slain by their needle! Here they may indulge their fancy in rural Landscapes, and in pourtraying the innocence and felicity of the pastoral age."

He also recommends this female art from another motive, which, indeed, may be called a moral one—that it relieves the fair Practitioners of it from the horrid custom of scandal; and from other inactive scenes of life. A Lady, who exercises her Genius, in these works of fancy, has neither leisure nor inclination to concern herself with the affairs of others.

A third reason is, the advantage arising to a family, where these ingenious arts are encouraged. This way of life, if adopted by our modern females, would not only prevent them from running into expences, but would afford them, at the same time, an actual improvement.

To what has been observed I would add, that Embroidery serves likewise to exercise the imagination, and correct the taste. It is connected with drawing and design; therefore, those who would excel in it, must not be ignorant of the principles of the fine arts. To shad with skill, and to imitate nature, require som knowledge of colours; the blending and disposing of which, so as to produce an exact resemblance, and to please the eye, by those nice gradations, which may be exhibited from various dies, is no small effort of female Genius.

It may also be observed, in recommendation of this art, that there are a great many of your Sex, who live by the needle; so that here is a resource to those, who are acquainted with the use of it, if the misfortunes and vicissitudes of life should reduce them to distress. But supposing, that your situation should be such as not to require much application to Needle Work, yet by being acquainted with it's several branches, you will be more competent to direct others, who may be employed under you. But abstracted from every other consideration, the exercise of the needle will serve to fill up many of the vacant hours of life.

It may be further remarked, that this qualification is neither mean nor degrading. It is an ornament to Women, even of the highest rank. You surely will not think it an humiliating employment, when I inform you, that the first Lady in this Kingdom, not only amuses herself with this art, but has also instituted a kind of Academy for it's further progress and improvement.

Amongst the Ancients it was considered as an accomplishment, by no means to be dispensed with in the female sex. With them the loom and the distaff were also in great repute; and, as the Women were much confined at home, they had great leisure and opportunity for this kind of work.

Solomon gives the following description of a prudent and industrious wife: *She seeketh wool and flax, and worketh willingly with her hands;* that is, if the ordering and inspecting of household matters should not be sufficient to employ all her time, yet she will not suffer herself to be idle. *She layeth her hands to the spindle, and her hands hold the distaff.* She thinks it no disparagement to her to employ her fingers in the art of weaving and spinning; for by her own diligence and skill, *she maketh herself coverings of tapestry, and her clothing is silk and purple.* She prepares the elegant and ornamental, as well as the useful parts of dress. These being the works of her own hands are less costly; and she can appear with more splendour than others of the same fortune, who are at the expence, not only of purchasing all the materials, but also of having them wrought, and made into garments. Your Sex should be rather ambitious of preparing, as much as possible, the articles of your dress. You would certainly wear them with more pleasure, and, out of respect to your own labour, would be careful in preserving them. They would, at the same time, recommend your ingenuity and application.

The Grecian Ladies of antiquity, even those in elevated situations, employed their leisure hours in embroidery and other works. Penelope, the wife of Ulysses, passed her time, during the long absence of her husband, in weaving. Homer describes her as mixing the variegated thread, and forming the animated figures. There was a custom, which prevailed in Greece, of honouring the funerals of the dead with the finest pieces of weaving and embroidery. Thus Penelope employed herself in preparing a winding sheet for Laertes, her husband's father.

Homer, in describing the robe of Ulysses, takes notice of the figures with which it was embroidered.

In the rich woof, a hound Mosaic drawn,
Bore in full stretch, and seized a dappled fawn:
Deep in the neck, his fangs indent their hold,
They pant and struggle in the moving gold.

Whence it appears, that this art was known in the early ages of the world; and perhaps was in greater perfection than at present. Homer frequently extols the Grecian embroidery. Antinous, says he, presented Penelope with a mantle most beautifully embroidered; the colours being shaded with great skill, and most admirably blended.

A late Traveller into Greece observes, that the Ladies of that Country are as industrious as in the time of the Ancients. He remarks, that there are large rooms appropriated to the Mistress of the House, for the conveniency of carrying on works of embroidery with her attendants. This corresponds with the description given by Terence, a Latin Poet, in one of his Comedies, which are a faithful copy of Grecian Manners. A Valet, being sent by his Master with a message to a Lady, thus represents the situation, in which he found her. "At my arrival," says her, "I discovered the fair one engaged with the most studious application; finishing a piece of embroidery; and dressed in mournful attire, on account of a recent death in the family."

Embroidery, he also remarks, is the constant employment of the Greek Women; and it is to them we are indebted for this art. It was, likewise, considered by the Men, as a female accomplishment. Thus, Agamemnon, contending with Achilles for the possession of the beautiful Bryseis, cries out, in the warmth of their disputes—"I would prefer her even to Clytemnestra my Queen; neither is she inferior to her in beauty, or fine works."

That this art was practised by the Orientals, and that it was very ancient, appear also from the Scriptures. Thus in Judges, it is said—"Have they not sped? Have they not divided the prey? To Sisera a prey of divers colours—of divers colours of Needle Work on both sides, meet for the necks of them, that take the spoil."

The Psalmist, in describing the celebration of the marriage of Solomon with the daughter of Pharaoh King of Egypt, gives this account of her dress and appearance:

"The king's daughter is all glorious within; her clothing is of wrought gold."

"She shall be brought unto the King, in raiment of needle work."

The productions of the needle were in high esteem, in the reign of Elizabeth. The Ladies of her Court employed their time in exercising their fingers in this art, or in spinning silk. Though they were the attendants of a Queen, yet they did not neglect domestic qualifications; these had their due weight in forming what was then considered an accomplished Woman. They understood, say the Writers of that age, the cookery and distillation; and were very expert in whatever relates to the conveniencies and ornaments of Dress, or the furniture of the House. Our modern Ladies may, probably, ridicule these antiquated practices, as fit only for such as are destined to act in the humble character of Housewives. But to convince them, that their judgments are wrong in this instance, I shall only observe, that the Ladies of Rank and Fortune, in the period already mentioned, paid much attention to the cultivation of their minds; and were better acquainted with ancient Learning, than the Women are at present.

From what has been said on the antiquity and usefulness of Needle Work, it cannot be denied, that it is a domestic accomplishment, absolutely necessary in the female sex. But in praising it's excellency, I would not have it inferred, that this branch of Education is so important, as, in a manner, to supersede every other; an opinion, however, which is entertained by some; who, if their daughters can use the needle with dexterity, are very indifferent respecting every other attainment. And in regard to works of embroidery, they should be considered as ornamental more than useful; but principally as expedient in filling up those leisure hours, which some may probably enjoy. The great art, then, consists in blending what is necessary with what is agreeable. There cannot, I confess, be a more pleasing sight, than to see a circle of young Ladies, busily employed in ingenious works, whilst one of them is reading aloud to the rest.

And here I cannot help remarking what appears to be a defect in female education; and that is, the instructing of Girls in those trifling arts, where the needle is not employed; and in others, no less superficial ones, where it is; because they are, in general, the whim of a moment, soon become unfashionable, and are laid aside; so that, when they leave School, it is but seldom that they employ themselves in those works, which they have spent much time to learn. But admitting the ingenuity of them, some regard should be had to the circumstances of the Parents, and probable future destination of their daughters. If their situation in point of fortune, should be such, as to afford them frequent opportunities of exercising their Genius in works of fancy, they may then with propriety be instructed in them; but if the contrary should be the case, it must surely be more prudent to have them taught useful arts, such as may qualify them for those household employments, which they will hereafter be engaged in.

Having thus considered the domestic duties of the female sex, and the instruction which is necessary to qualify them for the discharge of those duties, I shall conclude this Lecture with a few slight remarks on those branches of Education, which may be called ornamental.

The first I shall take notice of is the art of drawing. This, as I have already observed, may be useful in improving the female taste with respect to dress; some parts of which depend upon those outlines or patterns which are sketched by the Pencil. These are the originals which are afterwards to be imitated by the needle; and the more perfect they are, the more beautiful will be the Copies. Drawing is also an elegant accomplishment; and, where there is a natural inclination for designing, you will have recourse to it with pleasure, and it may prevent you from misemploying your leisure hours. This part of Education, therefore, is not unworthy the attention of the female sex: But Rousseau, with respect to them, has prescribed limits to the practice of this art: "I would not have them," says he, "apply themselves to Landscapes, much less to Portrait Painting.

It is sufficient for them to design foliages, fruits, flowers, drapery, and whatever is capable of giving an embellishment to Dress; and to draw a Pattern after their own fancy, when they cannot meet with one to their liking."

Music is also polite accomplishment; and may be considered as one of the most agreeable arts of pleasing practised by the fair sex. When the Spinnet or Harpsicord is touched by those, who have a mind and ear formed for harmony, the most delightful sounds may be produced, and correspondent emotions excited. But without the predispositions already mentioned, it will be toil and labour; it will be a mechanical exertion, tasteless and insipid in its effects. As the acquisition of musical skill requires much time and application, those females will make but little proficiency, who have not sufficient leisure to practise the Lessons which are taught them. But it often happens, that when the Master is gone, the Lessons are forgotten; and when they leave school, the instrument is rejected. But a good ear is so necessary for improvement in this science, that without it, it is a manifest absurdity to impose on children a task, which they can neither perform with pleasure to themselves, nor

credit to their Teachers. It is a waste of time, and useless expen-
diture of money.

The last ornamental accomplishment I shall mention is Dancing. This may be called a personal one, as it respects the figure, and has no connection with the mind. In the present age, whatever relates to the exterior manners is considered as important; though perhaps this opinion is carried to an excess: It is necessary, however, that the improvement of the Person should have it's due share of attention; and, indeed, this part of Education is now become so general, as not to be dispensed with. Dancing, under proper regulations, may be innocent and useful. But let me remind you, my young Audience, of it's principal design; which is, to improve the attitudes of the Body, and render the gait easy and graceful. Without this outward polish, your deportment would be awkward; in company a silly bashfulness might confuse you; and an address or appearance inelegant might expose you to a more than general observation, with no other design, perhaps, than to ridicule the rusticity of your manners. You would be liable also to the mortification of being excluded from the Dance, if that amusement should be the object of the meeting, because you were not qualified to join in it.

But having said this, I would also remark, that you are not instructed in this art, that it might be an inducement to you to run to all public places, wheresoever there be an assembly of Persons met for the sake of Dancing. In this respect prudence and moderation are necessary. The characters and manners of the Company are to be previously considered. If these are irreproachable, the utmost decency and politeness may be expected; the greatest decorum and regularity will be observed; and the time of departure will not be unreasonably delayed. All midnight routs are to be avoided, as well as those Parties, where you are not under the eye of your Friends; and where the professed design of the meeting is to enjoy a kind of unrestrained festivity. At such Assemblies danger is to be apprehended; as improper freedoms may be taken.

Dancing should likewise be considered as affording you that kind of exercise, which you seem to require more than the other sex; because your employments are more sedentary, and your amusements less athletic.

ERASMUS DARWIN (1731–1802)

Erasmus Darwin, grandfather of Charles Darwin, was judged one of the most important intellectuals of the eighteenth century. He was a physician, botanist, and poet.

A Plan for the Conduct of Female Education in Boarding Schools was written as the direct result of a 1766 correspondence between Darwin and Rousseau. It was intended to assist persons who were managing English boarding schools, which had risen in popularity after the closing of nunneries during the Reformation. Valuable sections on Musick [sic] and Dancing, Languages, Arithmetic, Geography, History, Drawing and Embroider, The Heathen Mythology, Polite Literature, Arts and Sciences are not included here because of space limitations, but are recommended reading. The Female Character, The Rudiments of Taste, and Morals are subjects of the following excerpts.

A PLAN FOR THE CONDUCT OF
FEMALE EDUCATION
IN BOARDING SCHOOLS*

Section I

"The Female Character"

The parents and guardians of young ladies of the last half century were less solicitous about procuring for them so extensive an education, as modern refinement requires. Hence it happens, that female education has not yet been reduced to a perfect system; but is frequently directed by those, who have not themselves had a

*Darwin, Erasmus. *A Plan for the Conduct of Female Education in Boarding Schools.* Derby: J. Dewry for J. Johnson, 1797, pp. 9-11, 15, 16, 25-27, 45, 46.

good education, or who have not studied the subject with sufficient attention. And tho' many ingenious remarks are to be found in the works of Locke, Rousseau, Genlis, and other writers still more modern; yet few of them are exactly applicable to the management of boarding schools; the improvement of which is the intent of the present treatise.

The advantages of a good education consist in uniting health and agility of body with chearfulness and activity of mind; in superadding graceful movements to the former, and agreeable tastes to the latter; and in the acquirement of the rudiments of such arts and sciences, as may amuse ourselves, or gain us the esteem of others; with a strict attention to the culture of morality and religion.

The female character should possess the mild and retiring virtues rather than the bold and dazzling ones; great eminence in almost any thing is sometimes injurious to a young lady; whose temper and disposition should appear to be pliant rather than robust; to be ready to take impressions rather than to be decidedly mark'd; as great apparent strength of character, however excellent, is liable to alarm both her own and the other sex; and to create admiration rather than affection.

There are however situations in single life; in which, after the completion of their school-education, ladies may cultivate to any extent the fine arts or the sciences for their amusement or instruction. And there are situations in a married state; which may call forth all the energies of the mind in the care, education, or provision, for a family; which the inactivity, folly, or death of a husband may render necessary. Hence if to softness of manners, complacency of countenance, gentle unhurried motion, with a voice clear and yet tender, the charms which enchant all hearts! can be superadded internal strength and activity of mind, capable to transact the business or combat the evils of life; with a due sense of moral and religious obligation; all is obtain'd, which education can supply; the female character becomes compleat, excites our love, and commands our admiration.

Education should draw the outline, and teach the use of the pencil; but the exertions of the individual must afterwards introduce the various gradations of shade and colour, must illuminate the landscape, and fill it with the beautiful figures of the Graces and the Virtues.

Section IV

"Writing"

Writing, as it keeps the body in a fix'd posture, as well as drawing, and needlework, should not be too long applied to at a time; since the body, and even the countenance, may thus get a certain tendency to one attitude; as is seen in children, who are brought up to some mechanic art, as in polishing buttons or precious stones on a lathe. A proper manner of holding the pen, or pencil, or needle, with an easy but graceful attitude of the person, and an agreeable moderate attention of the countenance, should first be taught; for which purposes an inclined desk has many advantages over an horizontal table for the books, or working frames; as the body is thence less bent forwards; and the light in general situations more vividly reflected to the eye.

If the desk be sixteen inches broad, the furthermost edge of it should rise about three inches and half from the horizontal line; which produces the most convenient inclination, and the table or frame, which supports it, for the use of the taller children, should rise about two feet eight inches from the ground.

Section XI

"The Rudiments of Taste"

Are too much neglected in most boarding schools; these should be taught with some care, as perhaps peculiarly belonging to Ladies; since taste enters into their dress, their motions, their manners, as well as into all the fine arts, which they have leisure to cultivate; as drawing, painting, modelling, making artificial flowers, embroidery; writing letters, reading, speaking, and into almost every circumstance of life.

The general rudiments of taste are to be acquired first by reading books, which treat professedly on the subject; as the ten papers by Mr. Addison on the power of imagination in the Spectator, vol. 6, No. 411; Akinside's pleasures of imagination; Burke on the sublime and beautiful; Hogarth's analysis of beauty; Mason's English garden; Wheatley's ornamental gardening; and Gilpin's picturesque views. Secondly by selecting and explaining admired passages from classical authors, as the Beauties of Shakespear, of Johnson, and of Stern. And lastly by exhibiting and explaining the prints of beautiful objects, or casts of the best antique gems and medallions.

The authors above mentioned have divided the objects of Taste into the sublime, the beautiful, and the new; but a new sect of inquirers into this subject have lately added the Picturesque; which is supported to differ from the beautiful by it's want of smoothness, and from the sublime from it's want of size, but this circumstance has not yet perhaps undergone sufficient examination.—See essay on Picturesque, by U. Price.

Others have endeavoured to make a distinction between beauty and grace; and have esteem'd them, as it were, rivals for the possession of the human heart. But Grace may be defined Beauty in action; for a sleeping beauty can not be called graceful, in whatever attitude she may recline; the muscles must be in action to produce a graceful attitude, and the limbs to produce a graceful motion. The supposed origin of our ideas of beauty acquired in our early infancy from the curved lines, which form the female bosom, is deliver'd in Zoonomia, vol. I. sect, xvi, 6; but is too metaphysical an investigation for young ladies.

Section XVI

"Morals"

The criterion of moral duties has been variously delivered by different writers: Expediency, by which is meant whatever increases the sum of public happiness, is by some called the criterion of virtue; and whatever diminishes that sum is term'd vice. By others the happiness or misery of the individual, if rightly understood, is said to be the bond of moral obligation. And lastly, by others the will of God is said to constitute the sole criterion of virtue and vice.

But besides systematic books of morality, which are generally too abstruse for young minds, morals may be divided into five departments for the greater conveniency of the manner of instruction.

1. A sympathy with the pains and pleasures of others, or compassion.
2. A strict regard to veracity.
3. Prudence, justice, and chastity.
4. Fortitude.
5. Temperance.

HESTER CHAPONE (1727–1801)

The precocious Hester Chapone became an avid reader of current literature. Her skill in the art of conversation led to her membership in the English Bluestocking Movement (see introduction to Enlightenment). Thackeray valued her highly enough to mention her in both *Vanity Fair* and *The Virginians.*

Many eminent persons persuaded Chapone to educate their children. She viewed English, French, and Italian translations as adequate, so she saw no need for women to read Greek and Latin. She promoted the study of French because she believed that there were more acceptable books of female literature in French than in any other language.

Chapone cautioned that too high a degree of intellectualism might provoke envy and jealousy; although she and her Bluestocking friends were well educated, she thought the average woman did not need as extensive an education as did most men. She specified that women must not learn sciences; instead, she encouraged them to read Shakespeare, Milton, Homer, Virgil, and the Bible. Chapone prescribed minimal female education because she claimed that the primary responsibility of women was to become companions and homemakers.

In 1787 she wrote a series of letters about the education of girls. The following letter to a niece exemplifies Chapone's possession of detailed knowledge of the field of education.

*LETTER IX**

On Geography and Chronology

---

*Chapone, Hester. *Letters on The Improvement of the Mind, Addressed to a Young Lady.* London: Printed for J. Walter, at Homer's Head, Charing-Cross; and C. Dilly, in the Poultry, 1797, pp. 195-221.

I have told you that you will not be able to read history, with much pleasure or advantage, without some little knowledge of *Geography* and *Chronology*. They are both very easily attained—I mean in the degree that will be necessary for you. You must be sensible that you can know but little of a country, whose situation with respect to the rest of the world you are entirely ignorant of—and that, it is to little purpose that you are able to mention a fact, if you cannot nearly ascertain the *time* in which it happened, which alone, in many cases, gives importance to the fact itself.

In Geography—the easiest of all sciences and the best adapted to the capacity of children—I suppose you to have made some beginning; to know at least the figure of the earth—the supposed lines—the degrees—how to measure distances—and a few of the common terms: If you do not already know these, two or three lessons will be sufficient to attain them: the rest is the work of memory, and is easily gained by reading with maps; for I do not wish your knowledge to be exact and masterly—but such only as is necessary for the purpose of understanding history, and, without which, even a news-paper would be unintelligible. It may be sufficient for this end, if, with respect to *ancient* Geography, you have a general idea of the situation of all the great states, without being able precisely to ascertain their limits. But, in the *modern*, you ought to know the bounds and extent of every state in Europe, and its situation with respect to the rest. The other parts of the world will require less accurate knowledge, except with regard to the European settlements.

It may be an useful and agreeable method, when you learn the situation of any important country, to join with that knowledge some one or two leading facts or cirumstances concerning it, so that its particular property may always put you in mind of the situation, and the situation, in like manner, recall the particular property. When, for instance, you learn in what part of the globe to find Ethiopia, to be told at the same time that, in that vast unknown tract of country, the Christian religion was once the religion of the state, would be of service—because the geographical and historical knowledge would assist each other. Thus, to join with Egypt, *The nurse and parent of arts and of superstition*—with Persia, *Shocking despotism and perpetual revolutions*—with ancient Greece, *freedom and genius*—with Scythia, *hardiness and conquest,* are hints which you may make use of as you please. Perhaps annexing to any country the idea of some familiar form which it most resembles may at first assist you to retain a general notion of it; thus Italy has been called a *boot*—Europe compared to a *woman sitting*.

The difference of the ancient and modern names of places is somewhat perplexing; the most important should be known by both names at the same time, and you must endeavour to fix a few of those which are of most consequence so strongly in your mind, by thinking of them, and being often told of them, that the ancient name should always call up the modern one to your memory, and the modern the ancient: Such as the AEgean Sea, now *The Archipelage*—The Peloponnesus, now *The Morea*—Crete, *Candia* —Gaul, *Franc*—Babylon, *Bagdat*—Byzantium—to which the Romans transplanted their feat of empire—*Constantinople, &c.*

There have been so many ingenious contrivances to make Geography easy and amusing, that I cannot hope to add any thing of much service; I would only prevail with you not to neglect acquiring, by whatever method pleases you best, that share of knowledge in it, which you will find necessary, and which is so easily attained; and I entreat that you would learn it in such a manner as to fix it in your mind, so that it may not be lost and forgotten among other childish acquisitions, but that it may remain ready for use through the rest of your life.

Chronology indeed has more of difficulty, but if you do not bewilder yourself by attempting to learn too much and too minutely at first, you need not despair of gaining enough for the purpose of reading history with pleasure and utility.

Chronology may be naturally divided into three parts, *the Ancient—the Middle—*and *the Modern.*—With respect to all these, the best direction that can be given is to fix on some periods or epochas, which, by being often mentioned and thought of, explained and referred to, will at last be so deeply engraven on the memory, that they will be ready to present themselves whenever you call for them: these indeed should be few, and ought to be well chosen for their importance, since they are to serve as elevated stations to the mind, from which it may look backwards and forwards upon a great variety of facts.

Till your more learned friends shall supply you with better, I will take the liberty to recommend the following, which I have found of service to myself.

In the ancient chronology, you will find there were four thousand years from the creation to the redemption of man—and that Noah and his family were miraculously preserved in the ark 1650 years after Adam's creation.

As there is no history, except that in the Bible, of any thing before the flood, we may set out from the great event, which happened, as I have said above, in the year of the world 1650.

The 2350 years, which passed from the deluge to our Saviour's birth may be thus divided.—There have been four successive *Empires* called *Universal*, because they extended over a great part of the then known world—these are usually distinguished by the name of *The Four Great Monarchies:* the three first of them are included in ancient Chronology, and begun and ended in the following manner:

1st, THE ASSYRIAN EMPIRE, founded by Nimrod in the year of the world 1800, ended under Sardanapalus in 3250, endured 1450 years.

The Median—though not accounted one of the four great monarchies, being conquests of rebels on the Assyrian empire —comes in here for about 200 years.

2d, THE PERSIAN EMPIRE, which began under Cyrus, in the year of the world 3450, ended in Darius in 3670, before Christ 330, lasted a little more than 200 years.

3d, THE GRECIAN EMPIRE, begun under Alexander the Great in 3670, was soon after his death dismembered by his successors, but the different parcels into which they divided it were possessed by their respective families, till the famous Cleopatra, the last of the race of Ptolemy, one of Alexander's captains who reigned in Egypt, was conquered by Julius Caesar, about half a century before our Lord's birth, which is a term of about 300 years.

Thus you see that from the deluge to the establishment of the first great monarchy—the Assyrian—is

....	150 years.
The Assyrian empire continued.................	1450 years.
The Median..	200
The Persian..	200
The Grecian...	300
From Julius Ceasar, with whom began the fourth great monarchy —viz. the Roman—to Christ....................	50
In all..	2350 years;

the term from the deluge to Christ.

I do not give you these dates and periods as correctly true, for I have taken only round numbers, as more easily retained by the memory; so that when you come to consult chronological books or tables, you will find variances of some years between them and the above accounts; but precise exactness is not material to a beginner.

I offer this short table as a little specimen of what you may easily do for yourself, but even this sketch, slight as it is, will give you a general notion of the ancient history of the world, from the deluge to the birth of Christ.

Within this period flourished the Grecian and Roman republics, with the history and chronology of which it will be expected you should be tolerably well acquainted; and indeed you will find nothing in the records of mankind so entertaining. Greece was divided into many petty states, whose various revolutions and annals you can never hope distinctly to remember; you are therefore to consider them as forming together one great kingdom—like the Germanic body, or the united provinces—composed separately of different governments, but sometimes acting with united force for their common interest. The *Lacedemonian* government, formed by Lycurgus in the year of the world 3100—and the *Athenian,* regulated by Solon about the year 3440—will chiefly engage your attention.

In pursuing the *Grecian* chronology, you need only perhaps make one stand or Epocha—at the time of *Socrates*, that wisest of philosophers, whom you must have heard of—who lived about 3570 years from the creation, and about 430 before Christ: for within the term of 150 years *before* Socrates, and 200 *after* him, will fall in most of the great events and illustrious characters of the Grecian history.

I must inform you that the Grecian method of dating time was by *Olympiads*—that is four complete years—so call'd from the celebration, every fifth year, of the Olympic Games, which were contests in all the manly exercises, such as wrestling—boxing—running—chariot-racing, &c.—They were instituted in honour of Jupiter, and took their name from Olympia, a city of Elis, near which they were performed: they were attended by all ranks of people, from every state in Greece; the noblest youths were eager to obtain the prize of victory, which was no other than an olive crown, but esteem'd the most distinguishing ornament. These games continued all the time that Greece retain'd any spark of liberty; and with them begins the authentic history of that country—all before being considered as fabulous. You must therefore endeavour to remember that they began in the year of the world 3228—after the flood, 1570 years after the destruction of Troy 400—before the building of Rome 23—before Cyrus about 200—and 770 before Christ. If you cannot retain *all* these dates, at least you must not fail to remember the near coincidence of the first *Olympiad* with the *building of Rome,* which is of great consequence, because, as the Grecians reckoned time by Olympiads, the Romans dated from the

building of their city: and as these two Eras are within 23 years of
each other, you may, for the ease of memory, suppose them to begin together, in the year of the world 3228.

In reading the history of the *Roman Republic*—which continued in that form of government to the time of Julius Caesar's dictatorship, about the year of the world 3960, and about 48 years before Christ—you will make as many epochas as you shall find convenient: I will mention only two—the sacking of Rome by the Gauls, which happened in the year of the world 3620—in the 365th year of the city—in the 97th Olympiad before Christ 385—and about 30 years before the birth of Alexander. The second epocha may be the 608th year of the city—when, after three obstinate wars, Carthage was destroyed, and Rome was left without a rival.

Perhaps the following bad verses, which were given me when I was young, may help to fix in your mind the important Eras of the Roman and Grecian dates:—You must not laugh at them, for chronologers do not pique themselves on their Poetry, but they make use of numbers and rhymes merely as assistants to memory, being so easily learned by heart.

> "Rome and Olympiads bear the same date,
> Three thousand two hundred and twenty-eight.
> In* three hundred and sixty was Rome sack'd
> and torn,
> Thirty summers before Alexander was born."

You will allow that what I have said in these few pages is very easily learn'd—yet, little as it is, I will venture to say that, was you as perfectly mistress of it as of your alphabet, you might answer several questions relating to ancient chronology more readily than many who pretend to know something of this science. One is not so much required to tell the precise year, in which a great man lived, as to know with whom he was contemporary in other parts of the world.—I would know then, from the slight sketch above given, about what year of the Roman republic Alexander the Great lived. —You would quickly run over in your mind, "Alexander lived in the 3670th year of the world—330 before Christ—consequently he must have flourished about the *400th of Rome*, which had endured 750 years when Christ was born." Or, suppose it was asked, what was the condition of Greece, at the time of the sacking of Rome by the Gauls; had any particular state, or the united body, chosen then to take advantage of the misfortunes of the Romans?—You

---

*That is, in the 365th year of the city.

consider that the 365th year of the city—the date of that event—is 385 before Christ; consequently this must have happened about the time of Philip of Macedon, father of Alexander, when the Grecians under such a leader, might have extirpated the Roman nation from the earth, had they ever heard of them, or thought the conquest of them an object worthy their ambition.

Numberless questions might be answered in like manner, even on this very narrow circumscribed plan, if it was completely mastered. I might require that other periods or epochas should be learned with the same exactness—but these may serve to explain my meaning, and to shew you how practicable and easy it is. One thing, however, I must observe—though perhaps it is sufficiently obvious —which is, that you can make no use of this sketch of ancient Chronology, nor even hope to retain it, till you have read the ancient *history*. When you have gone through Rollin's Histoire Ancienne *once*, then will be the time to fix the ancient Chronology deep in your mind, which will very much enhance the pleasure and use of reading it a *second* time; for you must remember that nobody reads a history to much purpose, who does not go over it more than once.

When you have got through your course of ancient history, and are come to the more modern, you must then have recourse to the second of the three divisions—viz. *middle Chronology*; containing about 800 years, from the birth of our Lord, and from within 50 years of the rise of the Roman empire, to Charlemagne, who died in 814.

This period, except in the earliest part of it, is too much involved in obscurity to require a very minute knowledge of its history—it may be sufficient to fix two or three of the most singular circumstances by their proper dates.

The first epocha to be observed is the year of our Lord 330— when Constantine, the first Christian emperor, who restored peace to the oppressed and persecuted church, removed the seat of empire from Rome to Byzantium, called afterwards from him Constantinople. After this time—about the year 400—began those irruptions of the Goths and Vandals, and other northern nations, who settled themselves all over the western parts of the Roman empire, and laid the foundation of the several states which now subsist in Europe.

The next epocha is the year 622—for the ease of memory say 600—when Mahomet, by his successful imposture, became the founder of the Saracen empire, which his followers extended over a great part of Asia and Africa, and over some provinces of Europe.

—At the same time, St. Gregory, bishop of Rome, began to assume a spiritual power, which grew by degrees into that absolute and enormous dominion, so long maintained by the popes over the greatest part of Christendom. St. Augustine—a missionary from St. Gregory—about this time, began the conversion of Great Britain to Christianity.

The third and concluding epocha in this division is the year 800; when Charlemagne, king of France—after having subdued the Saxons, repressed the Saracens, and established the temporal dominion of the pope by a grant of considerable territories—was elected emperor of the west and protector of the church. The date of this event corresponds with that remarkable period of our English history—the union of the Heptarchy—or Seven kingdoms —under Egbert.

As to the *third* part of Chronology—namely the *Modern,* I shall spare you and myself all trouble about it at present; for if you follow the course of reading which I shall recommend, it will be some years before you reach modern history—and when you do, you will easily make periods for yourself, if you do but remember carefully to examine the dates as you read, and to impress on your memory those of very remarkable reigns or events.

I fear you are my sole intention in what I have said is to convince you that it is a science not out of your reach, in the moderate degree that is requisite for you: *the last volume of the Ancient Universal History* is the best English Chronological Work I know; if that does not come in your way there is an excellent French one called Tablettes Chronologiques de l'Histoire Universelle, Du Fresnoy, 3 tomes, Paris: there is also a *chart* of universal history, including Chronology—and a *Biographical* chart—both by Priestly —which you may find of service to you.

Indeed, my dear, a woman makes a poor figure who affects, as I have heard some ladies do, to disclaim all knowledge of times and dates: the strange confusion they make of events, which happened in different periods, and the stare of ignorance when such are referred to as are commonly known, are sufficiently pitiable: but the highest mark of folly is to be proud of such ignorance—a resource, in which some of our sex find great consolation.

Adieu, my dear child!—I am, with the tenderest affection,

ever Yours.

HANNAH MORE (1745–1833)

Hannah More's mother began to teach her daughter to read at the age of three; by the age of four, Hannah repeated the catechism in church. When she was eight years old, her father, the master of a grammar school, read to her stories of Greek and Roman heroes, first in the original, then translated into English. He grew alarmed at the extent of her intellectual capacity, so he discontinued her study of Latin and mathematics. This alarm is a clear expression of society's failure to accept the concept of a female intellectual.

More wrote essays on education, dramas, ballads, and poems. She organized weekend Bible readings for adults. In 1789 she and her sisters opened the first Sunday School in Cheddar, where they taught the children of the poor to read and memorize scripture. They encouraged parents to come on Sunday evenings to study what the children were learning during the day. Eventually, the school became a Normal School.

Between 1790 and 1798, More opened eight schools with practical curricula including French, reading, writing, arithmetic, and needlework. Her effective educational philosophy combined moderate demands with advanced views. She held that the average girls should be taught in such a way as to inculcate principles, polish taste, regulate temper, subdue passion, direct feelings, habituate reflection, train self-denial, and instill a love and a fear of God. During her later years she and her sisters donated their services to teach spinning, knitting, and catechism to needy children.

Certain critics rated her as too severe in her condemnation of the frivolity of her day. She decried what she termed an excessive struggle for accomplishment, because she viewed home management as the primary role of women. She believed that the female mind is not capable of attaining as high a degree of perfection as the male—this concept from a woman of extraordinary intellectual ability and achievement! Not sur-

204

prisingly, American clergymen were allied with this writer,
reformer, and philanthropist, who was read and quoted as
frequently in the United States as in England.

Dozens of letters written by her contemporaries praise
Hannah More's *Strictures on Female Education* (1799). The
chapter "On Female Study," is reproduced as the last of the
classics demonstrating Enlightenment thought.

STRICTURES ON FEMALE EDUCATION*

Chapter VIII

ON FEMALE STUDY, AND INITIATION INTO KNOWL-
EDGE.—ERROR OF CULTIVATING THE IMAGINA-
TION TO THE NEGLECT OF THE JUDGMENT.—
BOOKS OF REASONING RECOMMENDED.

As this little work by no means assumes the character of a
general scheme of education, the author has purposely avoided
expatiating largely on any kind of instruction, but as it happens to
be connected, either immediately or remotely, with objects of a
moral or religious nature. Of course she has been so far from
thinking it necessary to enter into the enumeration of those popular
books which are used in general instruction, that she has purposely
forborne to mention any. With such books the rising generation is
far more copiously and ably furnished than any that has preceded
it: and out of an excellent variety the judicious instructor can hardly
fail to make such a selection as shall be beneficial to the pupil.

But while due praise ought not to be withheld from the
improved methods of communicating the elements of general
knowledge; yet is there not some danger that our very advantages
may lead us into error, by causing us to repose so confidently on the
multiplied helps which facilitate the entrance into learning, as to
render our pupils superficial through the very facility of acquirement? Where so much is done for them, may they not be led to do
too little for themselves? and besides that exertion may slacken for
want of a spur, may there not be a moral disadvantage in possessing

---

*More, Hannah. *Strictures on Female Education*. Vol. VII of her Works.
London: Printed for T. Cadell and W. Davies, in the Strand, 1818, pp.
196–221.

young persons with the notion that learning may be acquired without diligence, and knowlege be attained without labour? Sound education never *can* be made a "primrose path of dalliance." Do what we will we cannot *cheat* children into learning, or *play* them into knowledge, according to the conciliating smoothness of the modern creed, and the selfish indolence of modern habits. There is no idle way to any acquisitions which really deserve the name. And as Euclid, in order to repress the impetuous vanity of greatness, told his Sovereign that there was no royal way to geometry; so the fond mother may be assured that there is no short cut to any other kind of learning; no privileged bye-path cleared from the thorns and briars of repulse and difficulty, for the accommodation of opulent inactivity or feminine weakness. The tree of knowledge, as a punishment, perhaps, for its having been at first unfairly untasted, cannot now be climbed without difficulty; and this very circumstance serves afterwards to furnish not only literary pleasures, but moral advantages. For the knowledge which is acquired by unwearied assiduity is lasting in the possession, and sweet to the possessor; both perhaps in proportion to the cost and labour of the acquisition. And though an able teacher ought to endeavour, by improving the communicating faculty in himself, (for many know what they cannot teach), to soften every difficulty; yet in spite of the kindness and ability with which he will smooth every obstruction, it is probably among the wise institutions of Providence that great difficulties should still remain. For education is but an initiation into that life of trial to which we are introduced on our entrance into this world. It is the first breaking-in to that state of toil and labour to which we are born, and to which sin has made us liable; and in this view of the subject the pains taken in the acquisition of learning may be converted to higher uses than such as are purely literary.

Will it not be ascribed to a captious singularity, if I venture to remark that real knowledge and real piety, though they may have gained in many instances, have suffered in others from the profusion of little, amusing, sentimental books with which the youthful library overflows? Abundance has its dangers as well as scarcity. In the first place may not the multiplicity of these alluring little works increase the natural reluctance to those more dry and uninteresting studies, of which, after all, the rudiments of every part of learning *must* consist? And secondly, is there not some danger (though there are many honourable exceptions) that some of those engaging narratives may serve to infuse into the youthful heart a sort of spurious goodness, a confidence of virtue, a parade of charity? And that the benevolent actions with the recital of which they abound, when they are not made to flow from any source but *feeling,* may tend to inspire a self-complacency, a self-gratulation, a "stand by, for I am holier than thou?" May not the success with which the good deeds of the little heroes are uniformly crowned; the invariable reward which is made the instant concomitant of well-doing, furnish the young reader with false views of the condition of life, and the nature of the divine dealings with men? May they not help to suggest a false standard of morals, to infuse a love of popularity and an anxiety for praise, in the place of that simple and unostentatious rule of doing whatever good we do, *because it is the will of God?* The universal substitution of this principle would tend to purify the worldly morality of many a popular little story. And there are few dangers which good parents will more carefully guard against than that of giving their children a mere political piety; that sort of religion which just goes to make people more respectable, and to stand well with the world; a religion which is to save appearances without inculcating realities; a religion which affects to "preach peace and goodwill to men," but which forgets to give "glory to God in the highest."*

There is a certain precocity of mind which is much helped on by these superficial modes of instruction; for frivolous reading will produce its correspondent effect, in much less time than books of solid instruction; the imagination being liable to be worked upon, and the feelings to be set a-going, much faster than the understanding can be opened and the judgment enlightened. A talent for conversation should be the result of instruction, not its precursor; it is a golden fruit when suffered to ripen gradually on the tree of knowledge; but if forced in the hot-bed of a circulating library, it will turn out worthless and vapid in proportion as it was artificial and premature. Girls who have been accustomed to devour a multitude of frivolous books, will converse and write with a far greater appearance of skill as to style and sentiment at twelve or fourteen years old, than those of a more advanced age who are under the discipline of severer studies; but the former having early attained to that low standard which had been held out to them,

---

*An ingenious (and in many respects useful) French Treatise on Education has too much encouraged this political piety; by considering religion as a thing of human convention, rather than of divine institution; as a thing creditable, rather than commanded; by erecting the doctrine of expediency in the room of Christian simplicity; and wearing away the spirit of truth, by the substitution of occasional deceit, equivocation, subterfuge, and mental reservation.

become stationary; while the latter, quietly progressive, are passing through just gradations to a higher strain of mind; and those who early begin with talking and writing like women, commonly end with thinking and acting like children.

I would not however prohibit such works of imagination as suit this early period. When moderately used they serve to stretch the faculties and expand the mind; but I should prefer works of vigorous genius and pure unmixed fable to many of those tame and more affected moral stories, which are not grounded on Christian principle. I should suggest the use on the one hand of original and acknowledged fictions; and on the other, of accurate and simple facts; so that truth and fable may ever be kept separate and distinct in the mind. There is something that kindles fancy, awakens genius, and excites new ideas in many of the bold fictions of the East. And there is one peculiar merit in the Arabian and some other oriental tales, which is, that they exhibit striking, and in many respects faithful views of the manners, habits, customs, and religion of their respective countries; so that some tincture of real local information is acquired by the perusal of the wildest fable, which will not be without its uses in aiding the future associations of the mind in all that relates to Eastern history and literature.

The irregular fancy of women is not sufficiently subdued by early application, nor tamed by labour, and the kind of knowledge they commonly do acquire is easily attained; and being chiefly some slight acquisition of the memory, something which is given them to get off by themselves, and not grounded in their minds by comment and conversation, it is easily lost. The superficial *question*-and-*answer*-way, for instance, in which they often learn history, furnishes the mind with little to lean on: the events being detached and separated, the actions having no links to unite them with each other; the characters not being interwoven by mutual relation; the chronology being reduced to disconnected dates, instead of presenting an unbroken series; of course, neither events, actions, characters, nor chronology, fasten themselves on the understanding, but rather float in the memory as so many detached episodes, than contribute to form the mind and to enrich the judgment of the reader, in the important science of men and manners.

The swarms of *Abridgments, Beauties,* and *Compendiums,* which form too considerable a part of a young lady's library, may be considered in many instances as an infallible receipt for making a superficial mind. The *names* of the renowned characters in history thus become familiar in the mouths of those who can neither attach

to the ideas of the person, the series of his actions, nor the
peculiarities of his character. A few line passages from the poets
(passages perhaps which derived their chief beauty from their
position and connection) are huddled together by some extract-
maker, whose brief and disconnected patches of broken and
discordant materials, while they inflame young readers with the
vanity of reciting, neither fill the mind nor form the taste: and it is
not difficult to trace back to their shallow sources the hackney'd
quotations of certain *accomplished* young ladies, who will be
frequently found not to have come legitimately by any thing they
know. I mean not to have drawn it from its true spring, the original
works of the author from which some *beauty-monger* has severed it.
Human inconsistency in this, as in other cases, wants to combine
two irreconcileable things; it strives to unite the reputation with the
pleasures of idleness, forgetting that nothing that is valuable can be
obtained without sacrifices, and that if we would purchase knowledge, we must pay for it the fair and lawful price of time and
industry. For this *extract-reading,* while it accommodates itself to
the convenience, illustrates the character, of the age in which we
live. The appetite for pleasure, and that love of ease and indolence
which is generated by it, leave little time or taste for sound
improvement; while the vanity, which is equally a characteristic of
the existing period, puts in its claim also for indulgence, and
contrives to figure away by these little snatches of ornamental
reading, caught in the short intervals of successive amusements.

Besides, the taste, thus pampered with delicious morsels, is
early vitiated. The young reader of these *clustered beauties* con-
ceives a disrelish for every thing which is plain, and grows
impatient, if obliged to get through those equally necessary though
less showy parts of a work, in which perhaps the author gives the
best proof of his judgment by keeping under that occasional
brilliancy and incidental ornament, of which these superficial
students are in constant pursuit. In all well-written books, there is
much that is good which is not dazzling; and these shallow critics
should be taught, that it is for the embellishment of the more tame
and uninteresting parts of his work, that the judicious poet
commonly reserves those flowers, whose beauty is defaced when
they are plucked from the garland into which he had so skilfully
woven them.

The remark, however, as it relates to abridgments, is by no
means of general application; there are many valuable works which
from their bulk would be almost inaccessible to a great number of
readers, and a considerable part of which may not be generally

useful. Even in the best written books there is often superfluous matter; authors are apt to get enamoured of their subject, and to dwell too long on it: every person cannot find time to read a longer work on any subject, and yet it may be well for them to know something on almost every subject; those, therefore, who abridge voluminous works judiciously, render service to the community. But there seems, if I may venture the remark, to be a mistake in the *use* of abridgments. They are put systematically into the hands of *youth,* who have, or ought to have, leisure for the works at large; while abridgments seem more immediately calculated for persons in more advanced life, who wish to recall something they had forgotten; who want to restore old ideas rather than acquire new ones; or they are useful for persons immersed in the business of the world, who have little leisure for voluminous reading: they are excellent to refresh the mind, but not competent to form it: they serve to bring back what had been formerly known, but do not supply a fund of knowledge.

Perhaps there is some analogy between the mental and bodily conformation of women. The instructor therefore should imitate the physician. If the latter prescribe bracing medicines for a body of which delicacy is the disease, the former would do well to prohibit relaxing reading for a mind which is already of too soft a texture, and should strengthen its feeble tone by invigorating reading.

By softness, I cannot be supposed to mean imbecility of understanding, but natural softness of heart, and pliancy of temper, together with that indolence of spirit which is fostered by indulging in seducing books, and in the general habits of fashionable life.

I mean not *here* to recommend books which are immediately religious, but such as exercise the reasoning faculties, teach the mind to get acquainted with its own nature, and to stir up its own powers. Let not a timid young lady start if I should venture to recommend to her, after a proper course of preparatory reading, to swallow and digest such strong meat as Watt's or Duncan's little book of Logic, some part of Mr. Locke's Essay on the Human Understanding, and Bishop Butler's Analogy. Where there is leisure, and capacity, and an able friend to comment and to counsel, works of this nature might be profitably substituted in the place of so much English Sentiment, French Philosophy, Italian Love-Songs, and fantastic German imagery and magic wonders. While such enervating or absurd books sadly disqualify the reader for solid pursuit or vigorous thinking, the studies here recommended would act upon the constitution of the mind as a kind of alternative, and, if I may be allowed the expression, would help to brace the intellectual stamina.

This suggestion is, however, by no means intended to exclude works of taste and imagination, which must always make the ornamental part, and of course a very considerable part of female studies. It is only intimated, that they should not form them entirely and exclusively. For what is called dry tough reading, independent of the knowledge it conveys, is useful as a habit, and wholesome as an exercise. Serious study serves to harden the mind for more trying conflicts; it lifts the reader from sensation to intellect; it abstracts her from the world and its vanities; it fixes a wandering spirit, and fortifies a weak one; it divorces her from matter; it corrects that spirit of trifling which she naturally contracts from the frivolous turn of female conversation and the petty nature of female employments; it concentrates her attention, assists her in a habit of excluding trivial thoughts, and thus even helps to qualify her for religious pursuits. Yes, I repeat it, there is to woman a Christian use to be made of sober studies; while books of an opposite cast, however unexceptionable they may be sometimes found in point of expression, however free from evil in its more gross and palpable shapes, yet from their very nature and constitution they excite a spirit of relaxation, by exhibiting scenes and suggesting ideas which soften the mind and set the fancy at work; they take off wholesome restraints, diminish sober-mindedness, impair the general powers of resistance, and at best feed habits of improper indulgence, and nourish a vain and visionary indolence, which lays the mind open to error and the heart to seduction.

Women are less accustomed to close reasoning on any subject; still less do they inure their minds to consider particular parts of a subject; they are not habituated to turn a truth round, and view it in all its varied aspects and positions; and this perhaps is one cause of the too great confidence they are disposed to place in their own opinions. Though their imagination is already too lively, and their judgment naturally incorrect; in educating them we go on to stimulate the imagination, while we neglect the regulation of the judgment. They already want ballast, and we make their education consist in continually crowding more sail than they can carry. Their intellectual powers being so little strengthened by exercise, makes every petty business appear a hardship to them: whereas serious study would be useful, were it only that it leads the mind to the habit of conquering difficulties. But it is peculiarly hard to turn at once from the indolent repose of light reading, from the concerns of mere animal life, the objects of sense, or the frivolousness of female chit chat; it is peculiarly hard, I say, to a mind so softened, to rescue itself from the dominion of self-indulgence, to resume its powers, to call home its scattered strength, to shut out every foreign intrusion, to force back a spring so unnaturally bent, and to devote itself to religious reading, to active business, to sober reflection, to self-examination. Whereas to an intellect accustomed to think at all, the difficulty of thinking seriously is obviously lessened.

Far be it from me to desire to make scholastic ladies or female dialecticians; but there is little fear that the kind of books here recommended, if thoroughly studied, and not superficially skimmed, will make them pendants or induce conceit; for by showing them the possible powers of the human mind, you will bring them to see the littleness of their own: and surely to get acquainted with the mind, to regulate, to inform it; to show it its own ignorance and its own weakness, does not seem the way to puff it up. But let her who is disposed to be elated with her literary acquisitions, check the rising vanity by calling to mind the just remark of Swift, "that after all her boasted acquirements, a woman will, generally speaking, be found to possess less of what is called learning than a common school-boy."

Neither is there any fear that this sort of reading will convert ladies into authors. The direct contrary effect will be likely to be produced by the perusal of writers who throw the generality of readers at such an unapproachable distance as to check presumption, instead of exciting it. Who are those ever multiplying authors, that with unparalleled fecundity are overstocking the world with their quick-succeeding progeny? They are NOVELWRITERS; the easiness of whose productions is at once the cause of their own fruitfulness, and of the almost infinitely numerous race of imitators to whom they give birth. Such is the frightful facility of this species of composition, that every raw girl, while she reads, is tempted to fancy that she can also write. And as Alexander, on perusing the Iliad, found by congenial sympathy the image of Achilles stamped on his own ardent soul, and felt himself the hero he was studying; and as Corregio, on first beholding a picture which exhibited the perfection of the graphic art, prophetically felt all his own future greatness, and cried out in rapture, "And I too am a painter!" so a thorough-paced novel-reading Miss, at the close of every tissue of hackney'd adventures, feels within herself the stirring impulse of corresponding genius, and triumphantly exclaims, "And I too am an author!" The glutted imagination soon overflows with the redundance of cheap sentiment and plentiful incident, and by a sort

of arithmetical proportion, is enabled by the perusal of any three
novels, to produce a fourth; till every fresh production, like the
prolific progeny of Banquo, is followed by

Another, and another, and another!

Is a lady, however destitute of talents, education, or knowledge of
the world, whose studies have been completed by a circulating
library, in any distress of mind? the writing a novel suggests itself as
the best soother of her sorrows! Does she labour under any
depression of circumstances? writing a novel occurs as the readiest
receipt for mending them! And she solaces her imagination with the
conviction that the subscription which has been extorted by her
importunity, or given to her necessities, has been offered as a
homage to her genius. And this confidence instantly levies a fresh
contribution for a succeeding work. Capacity and cultivation are so
little taken into the account, that writing a book seems to be now
considered as the only sure resource which the idle and the illiterate
have always in their power.

May the Author be indulged in a short digression while she
remarks, though rather out of its place, that the corruption
occasioned by these books has spread so wide, and descended so
low, as to have become one of the most universal, as well as most
pernicious, sources of corruption among us. Not only among
milliners, mantua-makers, and other trades where numbers work
together, the labour of one girl is frequently sacrificed that she may
be spared to read those mischievous books to the others; but she
has been assured by clergymen who have witnessed the fact, that
they are procured and greedily read in the wards of our hospitals!
an awful hint, that those who teach the poor to read, should not
only take care to furnish them with principles which will lead them
to abhor corrupt books, but that they should also furnish them with
such books as shall strengthen and confirm their principles.* And

---

*The above facts furnish no argument on the side of those who would keep
the poor in ignorance. Those who cannot *read* can *hear,* and are likely to
hear to worse purpose than those who have been better taught. And that
ignorance furnishes no security for integrity either in morals or politics, the
late revolts more than one country, remarkable for the ignorance of the
poor, fully illustrate. It is earnestly hoped that the above facts may tend to
impress ladies with the importance of superintending the instruction of the
poor, and of making it an indispensable part of their charity to give them
moral and religious books.

The late celebrated Henry Fielding (a man not likely to be suspected
of overstrictness) assured a particular friend of the Author that during his

214   let every Christian remember, that there is no other way of entering truly into the spirit of that divine prayer, which petitions that the name of God may be "hallowed," that "his kingdom (of grace) may come," and that "his will may be done on earth as it is in heaven," than by each individual contributing according to his measure to accomplish the work for which he prays; for to pray that these great objects may be promoted, without contributing to their promotion by our exertions, our money, and our influence, is a palpable inconsistency.

---

long administration of justice in Bow-Street, only *six* Scotchmen were brought before him. The remark did not proceed from any national partiality in the magistrate, but was produced by him in proof of the effect of a sober and religious education among the lower ranks, on their morals and conduct.

See farther the sentiments of a still more celebrated contemporary on the duty of instructing the poor.—"We have been taught that the circumstance of the Gospel's being preached to the poor was one of the surest tests of its mission. We think, therefore, that those do not believe it who do not care it should be preached to the poor" *(Burke on the French Revolution)*.

PART VI: NINETEENTH CENTURY

The nineteenth century was one of progress in female education, especially at secondary and higher levels. Private female seminaries and public coeducational high schools in the United States provided expanding opportunity for many young women. In both the United States and Europe, higher education became available to women, who finally were granted college and university degrees enabling them to enter professions formerly limited to men.

Normal Schools were responsible for improvement in the preparation of the increasing numbers of women who became teachers. The presence of qualified teachers moved many people to regard teaching as a profession.

Nineteenth-century selections are divided according to the nationality of authors who represent English, French, German, and American educational theory. Writings included in this section are witness to the increasing acceptance and influence of educated women.

ENGLAND

SYDNEY SMITH (1771–1845)

Smith is the first of three nineteenth-century English authors whose work is included in this volume. Although he had been a Canon of St. Paul's, Smith's enduring fame is not based upon his having filled that position. Instead, recognition is the result of his having been named the most famous wit of his generation.

His description of the ecclesiastical career of a baker's son is an example of his casual, clever, irreverent writing style.

> Young Crumpet is sent to school—takes to his books—spends the best years of his life, as all eminent Englishmen do, in making Latin verses—knows that the *crum* in crum-pet is long, and the *pet* is short—goes to the University—gets a prize for an Essay on the Dispersion of the Jews—takes orders—becomes a Bishop's chaplain—has a young nobleman for his pupil—publishes a useless classic, and a serious call to the unconverted—and then goes through the Elysian transitions of Prebendary, Dean, Prelate, and the long train of purple, profit and power.*

At an unknown date, but surely after 1808, Smith wrote an essay on "Female Education," an artful argument for equal educational advantages for girls.

FEMALE EDUCATION†

A great deal has been said of the original difference of capacity

---

*W.H. Auden, *Selected Writings of Sydney Smith* (New York: Farrar, Straus, and Cudahy, 1957), p. ix.

†From *The Works of the Rev. Sydney Smith,* 2nd ed., Vol. I. London: Printed for Longman, Orme, Brown, Green, and Longmans, Paternoster-Row, 1840, pp. 200-220.

between men and women; as if women were more quick and men more judicious—as if women were more remarkable for delicacy of association, and men for stronger powers of attention. All this, we confess, appears to us very fanciful. That there is a difference in the understandings of the men and the women we every day meet with, everybody, we suppose, must perceive; but there is none surely which may not be accounted for by the difference of circumstances in which they have been placed, without referring to any conjectural difference of original conformation of mind. As long as boys and girls run about in the dirt, and trundle hoops together, they are both precisely alike. If you catch up one half of these creatures, and train them to a particular set of actions and opinions, and the other half to a perfectly opposite set, of course their understandings will differ, as one or the other sort of occupations has called this or that talent into action. There is surely no occasion to go into any deeper or more abstruse reasoning, in order to explain so very simple a phenomenon. Taking it, then, for granted, that nature has been as bountiful of understanding to one sex as the other, it is incumbent on us to consider what are the principal objections commonly made against the communication of a greater share of knowledge to women than commonly falls to their lot at present: for though it may be doubted whether women should learn all that men learn, the immense disparity which now exists between their knowledge we should hardly think could admit of any rational defence. It is not easy to imagine that there can be any just cause why a woman of forty should be more ignorant than a boy of twelve years of age. If there be any good at all in female ignorance, this (to use a very colloquial phrase) is surely too much of a good thing.

Something in this question must depend, no doubt, upon the leisure which either sex enjoys for the cultivation of their under-standings:—and we cannot help thinking, that women have fully as much, if not more, idle time upon their hands than men. Women are excluded from all the serious business of the world; men are lawyers, physicians, clergymen, apothecaries, and justices of the peace—sources of exertion which consume a great deal more time than producing and suckling children; so that if the thing is a thing that ought to be done—if the attainments of literature are objects really worthy the attention of females, they cannot plead the want of leisure as an excuse for indolence and neglect. The lawyer who passes his day in exasperating the bickerings of Roe and Doe, is certainly as much engaged as his lady, who has the whole of her morning before her to correct the children and pay the bills. The apothecary, who rushes from an act of phlebotomy in the western parts of the town to insinuate a bolus in the east, is surely as completely absorbed as the fortunate female who is darning the garment or preparing the repast of her AEsculapius at home; and in every degree and situation of life, it seems that men must necessarily be exposed to more serious demands upon their time and attention, than can possibly be the case with respect to the other sex. We are speaking always of the fair demands which ought to be made upon the time and attention of women; for, as the matter now stands, the time of women is considered as worth nothing at all. Daughters are kept to occupations in sewing, patching, mantua-making, and mending, by which it is impossible they can earn ten pence a day. The intellectual improvement of women is considered to be of such subordinate importance, that twenty pounds paid for needle-work would give to a whole family leisure to acquire a fund of real knowledge. They are kept with nimble fingers and vacant understandings, till the season for improvement is utterly past away, and all chance of forming more important habits completely lost. We do not therefore say that women have more leisure than men, if it be necessary they should lead the life of artisans; but we make this assertion only upon the supposition that it is of some importance women should be instructed; and that many ordinary occupations, for which a little money will find a better substitute should be sacrificed to this consideration.

We bar, in this discussion, any objection which proceeds from the mere novelty of teaching women more than they are already taught. It may be useless that their education should be improved, or it may be pernicious; and these are the fair grounds on which the question may be argued. But those who cannot bring their minds to consider such an unusual extension of knowledge, without connecting with it some sensation of the ludicrous, should remember, that, in the progress from absolute ignorance, there is a period when cultivation of the mind is new to every rank and description of persons. A century ago, who would have believed that country gentlemen could be brought to read and spell with the ease and accuracy which we now so frequently remark,—or supposed that they could be carried up even to the elements of ancient and modern history? Nothing is more common, or more stupid, than to take the actual for the possible—to believe that all which is, is all which can be; first to laugh at every proposed deviation from practice as impossible—then, when it is carried into effect, to be astonished that it did not take place before.

It is said, that the effect of knowledge is to make women pedantic and affected; and that nothing can be more offensive, than to see a woman stepping out of the natural modesty of her sex, to make an ostentatious display of her literary attainments. This may be true enough; but the answer is so trite and obvious, that we are almost ashamed to make it. All affectation and display proceed from the supposition of possessing something better than the rest of the world possesses. Nobody is vain of possessing two legs and two arms;—because that is the precise quantity of either sort of limb which every body possesses. Who ever heard a lady boast that she understood French?—for no other reason, that we know of, but because everybody in these days does understand French; and though there may be some disgrace in being ignorant of that language, there is little or no merit in its acquisition. Diffuse knowledge generally among women, and you will at once cure the conceit which knowledge occasions while it is rare. Vanity and conceit we shall of course witness in men and women as long as the world endures:—but by multiplying the attainments upon which these feelings are founded, you increase the difficulty of indulging them, and render them much more tolerable, by making them the proofs of a much higher merit. When learning ceases to be uncommon among women, learned women will cease to be affected.

A great many of the lesser and more obscure duties of life necessarily devolve upon the female sex. The arrangement of all household matters, and the care of children in their early infancy, must of course depend upon them. Now, there is a very general notion, that the moment you put the education of women upon a better footing than it is at present, at that moment there will be an end of all domestic economy: and that, if you once suffer women to eat of the tree of knowledge, the rest of the family will very soon be reduced to the same kind of aerial and unsatisfactory diet. These, and all such opinions are referable to one great and common cause of error;—that man does everything, and that nature does nothing; and that everything we see, is referable to positive institution, rather than to original feeling. Can anything, for example, be more perfectly absurd than to suppose, that the care and perpetual solicitude which a mother feels for her children depends upon her ignorance of Greek and Mathematics; and that she would desert an infant for a quadratic equation? We seem to imagine, that we can break in pieces the solemn institutions of nature by the little laws of a boarding-school; and that the existence of the human race depends upon teaching women a little more or a little less;—that Cimmerian ignorance can aid parental affection, or the circle of arts and sciences produce its destruction. In the same manner, we forget the principles upon which the love of order, arrangement, and all the arts of economy depend. They depend not upon ignorance or idleness; but upon the poverty, confusion, and ruin which would ensue from neglecting them. Add to these principles the love of what is beautiful and magnificent, and the vanity of display;—and there can surely be no reasonable doubt but that the order and economy of private life is amply secured from the perilous inroads of knowledge.

We would fain know, too, if knowledge is to produce such baneful effects upon the material and the household virtues, why this influence has not already been felt? Women are much better educated now than they were a century ago; but they are by no means less remarkable for attention to the arrangements of their household, or less inclined to discharge the offices of parental affection. It would be very easy to show, that the same objection has been made at all times to every improvement in the education of both sexes, and all ranks—and been as uniformly and completely refuted by experience. A great part of the objections made to the education of women are rather objections made to the female sex: for it is surely true, that knowledge, where it produces any bad effects at all, does as much mischief to one sex as to the other,—and gives birth to fully as much arrogance, inattention to common affairs, and eccentricity among men, as it does among women. But it by no means follows, that you get rid of vanity and self-conceit, because you get rid of learning. Self-complacency can never want an excuse; and the best way to make it more tolerable, and more useful, is to give to it as high and as dignified an object as possible. But, at all events, it is unfair to bring forward against a part of the world an objection which is equally powerful against the whole. When foolish women think they have any distinction, they are apt to be proud of it; so are foolish men. But we appeal to any one who has lived with cultivated persons of either sex, whether he has not witnessed as much pedantry, as much wrongheadedness, as much arrogance, and certainly a great deal more rudeness, produced by learning in men than in women: therefore, we should make the accusation general—or dismiss it altogether; though, with respect to pedantry, the learned are certainly a little unfortunate, that so very emphatic a word, which is occasionally applicable to all men embarked eagerly in any pursuit, should be reserved exclusively for them: for, as pedantry is an ostentatious obtrusion of knowledge, in which those who hear us cannot sympathise, it is a fault of which soldiers, sailors, sportsmen, gamesters, cultivators, and all men engaged in a particular occupation, are quite as guilty as scholars;

but they have the good fortune to have the vice only of pedantry,—
while scholars have both the vice and the name for it too.

Some persons are apt to contrast the acquisition of important knowledge with what they call simple pleasures; and deem it more becoming that a woman should educate flowers, make friendships with birds, and pick up plants, than enter into more difficult and fatiguing studies. If a woman have no taste and genius for higher occupations, let her engage in these, rather than remain destitute of any pursuit. But why are we necessarily to doom a girl, whatever be her taste or her capacity, to one unvaried line of petty and frivolous occupation? If she be full of strong sense and elevated curiosity, can there be any reason why she should be diluted and enfeebled down to a mere culler of simples, and fancier of birds?—why books of history and reasoning are to be torn out of her hand, and why she is to be sent, like a butterfly, to hover over the idle flowers of the field? Such amusements are innocent to those whom they can occupy; but they are not innocent to those who have too powerful understandings to be occupied by them. Light broths and fruits are innocent food only to weak or to infant stomachs; but they are poison to that organ in its perfect and mature state. But the great charm appears to be in the word *simplicity*—simple pleasure! If by a simple pleasure is meant an innocent pleasure, the observation is best answered by showing, that the pleasure which results from the acquisition of important knowledge is quite as innocent as any pleasure whatever: but if by a simple pleasure is meant one, the cause of which can be easily analysed, or which does not last long, or which in itself is very faint; then simple pleasures seem to be very nearly synonymous with small pleasures; and if the simplicity were to be a little increased, the pleasure would vanish altogether.

As it is impossible that every man should have industry or activity sufficient to avail himself of the advantages of education, it is natural that men who are ignorant themselves, should view, with some degree of jealousy and alarm, any proposal for improving the education of women. But such men may depend upon it, however the system of female education may be exalted, that there will never be wanting a due proportion of failures; and that after parents, guardians, and preceptors have done all in their power to make everybody wise, there will still be a plentiful supply of women who have taken special care to remain otherwise; and they may rest assured, if the utter extinction of ignorance and folly be the evil they dread, that their interests will always be effectually protected, in spite of every exertion to the contrary.

We must in candour allow, that those women who begin, will

have something more to overcome than may probably hereafter be the case. We cannot deny the jealousy which exists among pompous and foolish men, respecting the education of women. There is a class of pedants, who would be cut short in the estimation of the world a whole cubit, if it were generally known that a young lady of eighteen could be taught to decline the tenses of the middle voice, or acquaint herself with the Aeolic varieties of that celebrated language. Then women have, of course, all ignorant men for enemies to their instruction, who being bound (as they think), in point of sex to know more, are not well pleased, in point of fact, to know less. But, among men of sense and liberal politeness, a woman who has successfully cultivated her mind, without diminishing the gentleness and propriety of her manners, is always sure to meet with a respect and attention bordering upon enthusiasm.

There is in either sex a strong and permanent disposition to appear agreeable to the other: and this is the fair answer to those who are fond of supposing, that a higher degree of knowledge would make women rather the rivals than the companions of men. Presupposing such a desire to please, it seems much more probable, that a common pursuit should be a fresh source of interest than a cause of contention. Indeed, to suppose that any mode of education can create a general jealousy and rivalry between the sexes, is so very ridiculous, that it requires only to be stated in order to be refuted. The same desire of pleasing secures all that delicacy and reserve which are of such inestimable value to women. We are quite astonished, in hearing men converse on such subjects, to find them attributing such beautiful effects to ignorance. It would appear, from the tenor of such objections, that ignorance had been the great civiliser of the world. Women are delicate and refined only because they are ignorant;—they manage their household, only because they are ignorant;—they attend to their children, only because they know no better. Now, we must really confess, we have all our lives been so ignorant, as not to know the value of ignorance. We have always attributed the modesty and the refined manners of women, to their being well taught in moral and religous duty,—to the hazardous situation in which they are placed,—to that perpetual vigilance which it is their duty to exercise over thought, word, and action,—and to that cultivation of the mild virtues, which those who cultivate the stern and magnanimous virtues expect at their hands. After all, let it be remembered, we are not saying there are no objections to the diffusion of knowledge among the female sex. We would not hazard such a proposition respecting anything; but we are saying, that, upon the whole, it is the best method of employing time; and that there are fewer objections to it than to any other method. There are, perhaps, 50,000 females in Great Britain, who are exempted by circumstances from all necessary labour: but every human being must do something with their existence; and the pursuit of knowledge is, upon the whole, the most innocent, the most dignified, and the most useful method of filling up that idleness, of which there is always so large a portion in nations far advanced in civilization. Let any man reflect, too, upon the solitary situation in which women are placed,—the ill treatment to which they are sometimes exposed, and which they must endure in silence, and without the power of complaining,—and he must feel convinced that the happiness of a woman will be materially increased in proportion as education has given to her the habit and the means of drawing her resources from herself.

There are a few common phrases in circulation, respecting the duties of women, to which we wish to pay some degree of attention, because they are rather inimical to those opinions which we have advanced on this subject. Indeed, independently of this, there is nothing which requires more vigilance than the current phrases of the day, of which there are always some resorted to in every dispute, and from the sovereign authority of which it is often vain to make any appeal. "The true theatre for a woman is the sick chamber,"— "Nothing so honourable to a woman as not to be spoken of at all." These two phrases, the delight of *Noodledom,* are grown into commonplaces upon the subject; and are not unfrequently employed to extinguish that love of knowledge in women, which, in our humble opinion, it is of so much importance to cherish. Nothing, certainly, is so ornamental and delightful in women as the benevolent affections; but time cannot be filled up, and life employed, with high and impassioned virtues. Some of these feelings are of rare occurrence—all of short duration—or nature would sink under them. A scene of distress and anguish is an occasion where the finest qualities of the female mind may be displayed; but it is a monstrous exaggeration to tell women that they are born only for scenes of distress and anguish. Nurse father, mother, sister, and brother, if they want it;—it would be a violation of the plainest duties to neglect them. But, when we are talking of the common occupations of life, do not let us mistake the accidents for the occupation;—when we are arguing how the twenty-three hours of the day are to be filled up, it is idle to tell us of those feelings and agitations above the level of common existence, which may employ the remaining hour. Compassion, and every other virtue, are the great objects we all ought to have in view; but no man (and no woman) can fill up the twenty-four hours by acts of virtue. But one is a lawyer, and the other a ploughman, and the third a merchant; and then, acts of goodness, and intervals of compassion and fine feeling, are scattered up and down the common occupations of life. We know women are to be compassionate; but they cannot be compassionate from eight o'clock in the morning till twelve at night:—and what are they to do in the interval? This is the only question we have been putting all along, and is all that can be meant by literary education.

Then, again, as to the notoriety which is incurred by literature. —The cultivation of knowledge is a very distinct thing from its publication; nor does it follow that a woman is to become an author, merely because she has talent enough for it. We do not wish a lady to write books,—to defend and reply,—to squabble about the tomb of Achilles, or the plain of Troy,—any more than we wish her to dance at the opera, to play at a public concert, or to put pictures in the Exhibition, because she has learned music, dancing, and drawing. The great use of her knowledge will be that it contributes to her private happiness. She may make it public: but it is not the principal object which the friends of female education have in view. Among men, the few who write bear no comparison to the many who read. We hear most of the former, indeed, because they are, in general, the most ostentatious part of literary men; but there are innumerable persons who, without ever laying themselves before the public, have made use of literature to add to the strength of their understandings, and to improve the happiness of their lives. After all, it may be an evil for ladies to be talked of: but we really think those ladies who are talked of only as Mrs. Marcet, Mrs. Somerville, and Miss Martineau are talked of, may bear their misfortunes with a very great degree of Christian patience.

Their exemption from all the necessary business of life is one of the most powerful motives for the improvement of education in women. Lawyers and physicians have in their professions a constant motive to exertion; if you neglect their education, they must in a certain degree educate themselves by their commerce with the world; they must learn caution, accuracy, and judgment, because they must incur responsibility. But if you neglect to educate the mind of a woman, by the speculative difficulties which occur in literature, it can never be educated at all: if you do not effectually rouse it by education, it must remain for ever languid. Uneducated men may escape intellectual degradation; uneducated women cannot. They have nothing to do; and if they come untaught from the events.

Women have not their livelihood to gain by knowledge; and that is one motive for relaxing all those efforts which are made in the education of men. They certainly have not; but they have happiness to gain, to which knowledge leads as probably as it does to profit; and that is a reason against mistaken indulgence. Besides, we conceive the labour and fatigue of accomplishments to be quite equal to the labour and fatigue of knowledge; and that it takes quite as many years to be charming as it does to be learned.

Another difference of the sexes is, that women are attended to, and men attend. All acts of courtesy and politeness originate from the one sex, and are received by the other. We can see no sort of reason, in this diversity of condition, for giving to women a trifling and insignificant education; but we see in it a very powerful reason for strengthening their judgment, and inspiring them with the habit of employing time usefully. We admit many striking differences in the situation of the two sexes, and many striking differences of understanding, proceeding from the different circumstances in which they are placed; but there is not a single difference of this kind which does not afford a new argument for making the education of women better than it is. They have nothing serious to do;—is that a reason why they should be brought up to do nothing but what is trifling? They are exposed to greater dangers;—is that a reason why their faculties are to be purposely and industriously weakened? They are to form the characters of future men;—is that a cause why their own characters are to be broken and frittered down as they now are? In short, there is not a single trait in that diversity of circumstances, in which the two sexes are placed that does not decidedly prove the magnitude of the error we commit in neglecting (as we do neglect) the education of women.

If the objections against the better education of women could be overruled, one of the great advantages that would ensue would be the extinction of innumerable follies. A decided and prevailing taste for one or another mode of education there must be. A century past, it was for housewifery—now it is for accomplishments. The object now is, to make women artists,—to give them an excellence in drawing, music, painting, and dancing,—of which, persons who make these pursuits the occupation of their lives, and derive from them their subsistence, need not be ashamed. Now, one great evil of all this is, that it does not last. If the whole of life were an Olympic game,—if we could go on feasting and dancing to the end,—this might do; but it is in truth merely provision for the little interval between coming into life and settling in it; while it leaves a long and dreary expanse behind, devoid both of dignity and cheerfulness. No mother, no woman who has passed over the few first years of life, sings, or dances, or draws, or plays upon musical instruments. These are merely means for displaying the grace and vivacity of youth, which every woman gives up, as she gives up the dress and the manners of eighteen: she has no wish to retain them; or, if she has, she is driven out of them by diameter and derision. The system of female education, as it now stands, aims only at embellishing a few years of life, which are in themselves so full of grace and happiness, that they hardly want it; and then leaves the rest of existence a miserable prey to idle insignificance. No woman of understanding and reflection can possibly conceive she is doing justice to her children by such kind of education. The object is, to give to children resources that will endure as long as life endures—habits that time will ameliorate, not destroy,—occupations that will render sickness tolerable, solitude pleasant, age venerable, life more dignified and useful, and therefore death less terrible: and the compensation which is offered for the omission of all this, is a short-lived blaze,—a little temporary effect, which has not other consequence than to deprive the remainder of life of all taste and relish. There may be women who have a taste for the fine arts, and who evince a decided talent for drawing, or for music. In that case, there can be no objection to the cultivation of these arts; but the error is, to make such things the grand and universal object,—to insist upon it that every woman is to sing, and draw, and dance,—with nature, or against nature,—to bind her apprentice to some accomplishment, and if she cannot succeed in oil or water colours, to prefer gilding, varnishing, burnishing, box-making, to real and solid improvement in taste, knowledge, and understanding.

A great deal is said in favour of the social nature of the fine arts. Music gives pleasure to others. Drawing is an art, the amusement of which does not centre in him who exercises it, but is diffused among the rest of the world. This is true; but there is nothing, after all, so social as a cultivated mind. We do not mean to speak slightingly of the fine arts, or to depreciate the good humour with which they are sometimes exhibited; but we appeal to any man, whether a little spirited and sensible conversation—displaying, modestly, useful acquirements—and evincing rational curiosity, is not well worth the highest exertions of musical or graphical skill. A woman of accomplishments may entertain those who have the pleasure of knowing her for half an hour with great brilliancy; but a mind full of ideas, and with that elastic spring which the love

of knowledge only can convey, is a perpetual source of exhilaration
and amusement to all that come within its reach;—not collecting its
force into single and insulated achievements, like the efforts made
in the fine arts—but diffusing, equally over the whole of existence
a calm pleasure—better loved as it is longer felt—and suitable to
every variety and every period of life. Therefore, instead of hanging
the understanding of a woman upon walls, or hearing it vibrate
upon strings,—instead of seeing it in clouds, or hearing it in the
wind, we would make it the first spring and ornament of society, by
enriching it with attainments upon which alone such power depends.

If the education of women were improved, the education of
men would be improved also. Let any one consider (in order to
bring the matter more home by an individual instance) of what
immense importance to society it is, whether a nobleman of first-
rate fortune and distinction is well or ill brought up; —what a taste
and fashion he may inspire for private and for political vice!—and
what misery and mischief he may produce to the thousand human
beings who are dependent on him! A country contains no such
curse within its bosom. Youth, wealth, high rank, and vice, form a
combination which baffles all remonstrance and beats down all
opposition. A man of high rank who combines these qualifications
for corruption, is almost the master of the manners of the age, and
has the public happiness within his grasp. But the most beautiful
possession which a country can have is a noble and rich man who
loves virtue and knowledge;—who without being feeble or fanatical
is pious—and who without being factious is firm and independent;
—who, in his political life, is an equitable mediator between king
and people; and, in his civil life, a firm promoter of all which can
shed a lustre upon his country, or promote the peace and order of
the world. But if these objects are of the importance which we
attribute to them, the education of women must be important, as
the formation of character for the first seven or eight years of life
seems to depend almost entirely upon them. It is certainly in the
power of a sensible and well educated mother to inspire, within that
period, such tastes and propensities as shall nearly decide the
destiny of the future man; and this is done, not only by the inten-
tional exertions of the mother, but by the gradual and insensible
imitation of the child; for there is something extremely contagious
in greatness and rectitude of thinking, even at that age; and the
character of the mother with whom he passes his early infancy is
always an event of the utmost importance to the child. A merely
accomplished woman cannot infuse her tastes into the minds of her

sons; and, if she could, nothing could be more unfortunate than her success. Besides, when her accomplishments are given up, she has nothing left for it but to amuse herself in the best way she can; and, becoming entirely frivolous, either declines altogether the fatigue of attending to her children, or, attending to them, has neither talents nor knowledge to succeed; and, therefore, here is a plain and fair answer to those who ask so triumphantly, Why should a woman dedicate herself to this branch of knowledge? or, why should she be attached to such science?—Because, by having gained information on these points, she may inspire her son with valuable tastes, which may abide by him through life, and carry him up to all the sublimities of knowledge;—because she cannot lay the foundation of a great character if she is absorbed in frivolous amusements, nor inspire her child with noble desires when a long course of trifling has destroyed the little talents which were left by a bad education.

It is of great importance to a country that there should be as many understandings as possible actively employed within it. Mankind are much happier for the discovery of barometers, thermometers, steam-engines, and all the innumerable inventions in the arts and sciences. We are every day and every hour reaping the benefit of such talent and ingenuity. The same observation is true of such works as those of Dryden, Pope, Milton, and Shakespeare. Mankind are much happier that such individuals have lived and written; they add every day to the stock of public enjoyment—and perpetually gladden and embellish life. Now, the number of those who exercise their understandings to any good purpose is exactly in proportion to those who exercise it at all; but as the matter stands at present, half the talent in the universe runs to waste, and is totally unprofitable. It would have been almost as well for the world, hitherto, that women, instead of possessing the capacities they do at present, should have been born wholly destitute of wit, genius, and every other attribute of mind of which men make so eminent an use: and the ideas of use and possession are so united together, that, because it has been the custom in almost all countries to give to women a different and a worse education than to men, the notion has obtained, that they do not possess faculties which they do not cultivate. Just as, in breaking up a common, it is sometimes very difficult to make the poor believe it will carry corn, merely because they have been hitherto accustomed to see it produce nothing but weeds and grass—they very naturally mistake present condition for general nature. So completely have the talents of women been kept down, that there is scarcely a single work, either of reason or imagination, written by a woman, which is in general circulation,

either in the English, French, or Italian literature;—scarcely one
that has crept even into the ranks of our minor poets.

If the possession of excellent talents is not a conclusive reason why they should be improved, it at least amounts to a very strong presumption; and, if it can be shown that women may be trained to reason and imagine as well as men, the strongest reasons are certainly necessary to show us why we should not avail ourselves of such rich gifts of nature; and we have a right to call for a clear statement of those perils which make it necessary that such talent should be totally extinguished, or, at most, very partially drawn out. The burthen of proof does not lie with those who say, Increase the quantity of talent in any country as much as possible—for such a proposition is in conformity with every man's feelings: but it lies with those who say, Take care to keep that understanding weak and trifling which nature has made capable of becoming strong and powerful. The paradox is with them, not with us. In all human reasoning, knowledge must be taken for a good, till it can be shown to be an evil. But now, Nature makes to us rich and magnificent presents; and we say to her—You are too luxuriant and munificent —we must keep you under, and prune you;—we have talents enough in the other half of the creation; and, if you will not stupify and enfeeble the minds of women to our hands, we ourselves must expose them to a narcotic process, and educate away that fatal redundance with which the world is afflicted, and the order of sublunary things deranged.

One of the greatest pleasures of life is conversation:—and the pleasures of conversation are of course enhanced by every increase of knowledge: not that we should meet together to talk of alkalis and angels, or to add to our stock of history and philology,— though a little of these things is no bad ingredient in conversation; but let the subject be what it may, there is always a prodigious difference between the conversation of those who have been well educated and those who have not enjoyed this advantage. Education gives fecundity of thought, copiousness of illustration, quickness, vigour, fancy, words, images, and illustration;—it decorates every common thing, and gives the power of trifling without being undignified and absurd. The subjects themselves may not be wanted upon which the talents of an educated man have been exercised; but there is always a demand for those talents which his education has rendered strong and quick. Now, really, nothing can be further from our intention than to say anything rude and unpleasant; but we must be excused for observing, that it is now a very common thing to be interested by the variety and extent of female knowledge, but it is a very common thing to lament that the finest faculties in the world have been confined to trifles utterly unworthy of their richness and their strength.

The pursuit of knowledge is the most innocent and interesting occupation which can be given to the female sex; nor can there be a better method of checking a spirit of dissipation, than by diffusing a taste for literature. The true way to attack vice, is by setting up something else against it. Give to women, in early youth, something to acquire, of sufficient interest and importance to command the application of the mature facilities, and to excite their perseverance in future life;—teach them, that happiness is to be derived from the acquisition of knowledge, as well as the gratification of vanity; and you will raise up a much more formidable barrier against dissipation, than an host of invectives and exhortations can supply.

It sometimes happens that an unfortunate man gets drunk with very bad wine—not to gratify his palate but to forget his cares: he does not set any value on what he receives, but on account of what it excludes;—it keeps out something worse than itself. Now, though it were denied that the acquisition of serious knowledge is of itself important to a woman, still it prevents a taste for silly and pernicious works of imagination; it keeps away the horrid trash of novels; and, in lieu of that eagerness for emotion and adventure which books of that sort inspire, promotes a clam and steady temperament of mind.

A man who deserves such a piece of good fortune, may generally find an excellent companion for all the vicissitudes of his life; but it is not so easy to find a companion for his understanding, who has similar pursuits with himself, or who can comprehend the pleasure he derives from them. We really can see no reason why it should not be otherwise; nor comprehend how the pleasures of domestic life can be promoted by diminishing the number of subjects in which persons who are to spend their lives together take a common interest.

One of the most agreeable consequences of knowledge, is the respect and importance which it communicates to old age. Men rise in character often as they increase in years;—they are venerable from what they have acquired, and pleasing from what they can impart. If they outlive their faculties, the mere frame itself is respected for what it once contained; but women (such is their unfortunate style of education) hazard everything upon one cast of the die;—when youth is gone, all is gone. No human creature gives his admiration for nothing; either the eye must be charmed, or the understanding gratified. A woman must talk wisely or look well.

Every human being must put up with the coldest civility, who has neither the charms of youth nor the wisdom of age. Neither is there the slightest commiseration for decayed accomplishments;—no man mourns over the fragments of a dancer, or drops a tear on the relics of musical skill. They are flowers destined to perish; but the decay of great talents is always the subject of solemn pity; and, even when their last memorial is over, their ruins and vestiges are regarded with pious affection.

There is no connection between the ignorance in which women are kept, and the preservation of moral and religious principle; and yet certainly there is, in the minds of some timid and respectable persons, a vague, indefinite dread of knowledge, as if it were capable of producing these effects. It might almost be supposed, from the dread which the propagation of knowledge has excited, that there was some great secret which was to be kept in impenetrable obscurity, that all moral rules were a species of delusion and imposture, the detection of which, by the improvement of the understanding, would be attended with the most fatal consequences to all, and particularly to women. If we could possibly understand what these great secrets were, we might perhaps be disposed to concur in their preservation; but believing that all the salutary rules which are imposed on women are the result of true wisdom, and productive of the greatest happiness, we cannot understand how they are to become less sensible of this truth in proportion as their power of discovering truth in general is increased, and the habit of viewing questions with accuracy and comprehension established by education. There are men, indeed, who are always exclaiming against every species of power, because it is connected with danger: their dread of abuses is so much stronger than their admiration of uses, that they would cheerfully give up the use of fire, gunpowder, and printing, to be freed from robbers, incendiaries, and libels. It is true, that every increase of knowledge may possibly render depravity more depraved, as well as it may increase the strength of virtue. It is in itself only power; and its value depends on its application. But, trust to the natural love of good where there is no temptation to be bad—it operates nowhere more forcibly than in education. No man, whether he be tutor, guardian, or friend, ever contents himself with infusing the mere ability to acquire; but giving the power, he gives with it a taste for the wise and rational exercise of that power; so that an educated person is not only one with stronger and better faculties than others, but with a more useful propensity —a disposition better cultivated—and associations of a higher and more important class.

In short, and to recapitulate the main points upon which we have insisted,—Why the disproportion in knowledge between the two sexes should be so great, when the inequality in natural talents is so small; or why the understanding of women should be lavished upon trifles, when nature has made it capable of higher and better things, we profess ourselves not able to understand. The affectation charged upon female knowledge is best cured by making that knowledge more general: and the economy devolved upon woman is best secured by the ruin, disgrace, and inconvenience which proceeds from neglecting it. For the care of children, nature has made a direct and powerful provision; and the gentleness and elegance of women is the natural consequence of that desire to please which is productive of the greatest part of civilisation and refinement, and which rests upon a foundation too deep to be shaken by any such modifications in education as we have proposed. If you educate women to attend to dignified and important subjects, you are multiplying, beyond measure, the chances of human improvement, by preparing and *medicating* those early impressions, which always come from the mother; and which, in a great majority of instances, are quite decisive of character and genius. Nor is it only in the business of education that women would influence the destiny of men.—If women knew more, men must learn more—for ignorance would then be shameful—and it would become the fashion to be instructed. The instruction of women improves the stock of national talents, and employs more minds for the instruction and amusement of the world;—it increases the pleasures of society, by multiplying the topics upon which the two sexes take a common interest,—and makes marriage an intercourse of understanding as well as of affection, by giving dignity and importance to the female character. The education of women favours public morals; it provides for every season of life, as well as for the brightest and the best; and leaves a women when she is stricken by the hand of time, not as she now is, destitute of everything, and neglected by all; but with the full power and the splendid attractions of knowledge,—diffusing the elegant pleasures of polite literature, and receiving the just homage of learned and accomplished men.

EMILY DAVIES (1830–1921)

Davies did not contemplate the question of whether to educate girls, but rather what to teach them. She argued for a more comprehensive goal than to prepare women to be wives and mothers, but felt that existing education failed to accomplish even that. She claimed that formal education was not providing women with adequate knowledge of government and administration to manage servants and a household. She commented that there was a limited need for needlework, and that even reading can be excessive if aimless. She emphasized that, if financially able, an eighteen-year-old girl should be permitted to pursue higher education.

The demand for female access to examinations occupied a considerable share of Davies' time in her crusade for educational advancement. As the founder and secretary of an examination committee, she accomplished her objective that girls be allowed to write university entrance examinations. She campaigned successfully for equal rather than preferential treatment; she insisted that women be given more demanding university examinations than they had been given in the past. She was instrumental in the 1865 opening of university local examinations to girls, the 1878 admission of women to degree granting programs at the University of London, and the 1881 accessibility of Cambridge degree examinations for women.

In 1869 in Hitchin, Davies opened New College for Women, which was transferred to Girton in 1873, then was made a part of Cambridge University in 1880.

Her 1868 essay, "Special Systems of Education for Women," is representative of the detail, determination, and strength that was characteristic of this woman who achieved prodigious success in expanding educational opportunity for her sex.

Among the controversies to which the movement for improving the education of women has given rise, there is one which
presses for settlement. The question has arisen and must be
answered—Is the improved education which, it is hoped, is about to
be brought within reach of women, to be identical with that of men,
or is it to be as good as possible, but in some way or other
specifically feminine? The form in which the question practically
first presents itself is—What shall be the standards of examination?
For though there are still a not inconsiderable number of places of
so-called education, into which no examiners from without are
allowed to penetrate, the persons by whom these establishments are
kept up are pretty certain to disapprove of any change in the
existing practice, and are not likely to be troubled with perplexing
questions as to the direction in which the reforming tendency
should work. The controversy may therefore be assumed to be
between two parties, each equally accepting examinations as "valuable and indispensible things" alike for women and for men—each
equally admitting that "their use is limited," and that they may be
abused.

Of these two parties, one regards it as essential that the
standards of examination for both sexes should be the same; the
other holds that they may without harm—perhaps with advantage
be different. The controversy does not lie between those on the one
hand who, believing men and women to be exactly alike, logically
hold that all the conditions to which they may be subjected ought
to be precisely similar, and those on the other who, regarding them
as completely unlike, cannot believe that anything which is good for
one sex can be anything but bad for the other. No rational person
takes either of these clearly-defined views; but between the two
there is a kind of cloudland in whose dimness it is not always easy
to see the way to wise action. It may do something towards clearing
away the haze to endeavour to give some answer to the question—
Why do you ask for a common standard? Do you want to prove the
intellectual equality of the sexes? or their identity? If you desire to
improve female education, why not strive after what is ideally best,
instead of trying to get things for women which have produced
results far short of perfection in men?

The abstract questions as to equality and identity may be

*Davies, Emily. "Special Systems of Education for Women." *The London
Student,* 1868. Reprinted in *Thoughts on Some Questions Relating to
Women 1860–1908.* New York: Kraus Reprint Co., 1971.

quickly dismissed. The advocates of the "common" principle—
those who hold what may be called the humane theory—altogether
disclaim any ambition to assert either. As to what may be expected
as the statistical result of comparison by a common standard, there
may be much difference of opinion. If it should be to show a general
average of somewhat inferior mental strength in women, a fact will
have been discovered of some scientific interest perhaps, but surely
of no very good importance. That complete similarity should be
proved seems in the nature of things impossible, even if there could
be any reason for attempting it; for supposing it to be a fact, it is not
the sort of fact which could be brought to light by the test of an
examination. A comparision between male and female novelists, or
male and female poets—if one may venture to apply such epithets
to "the double-natured"—would be a better criterion, for those
who are curious in such matters, than any which could be devised
by examiners. In a discussion of practical policy, these considerations may be set aside as matters of chiefly speculative interest.

We come down, therefore, to the narrower and more hopeful
inquiry—Which is best, to extend methods of education admitted
to be imperfect, or to invent new ones presumably better?

The latter course is urged on the ground that there are
differences between men and women which educational systems
ought to recognise; or supposing this to be disputed, that at any rate
the conditions of women's lives are special, and ought to be
specially prepared for; or there is a latent feeling of repugnance to
what may appear like an ungraceful, perhaps childish, attempt to
grasp at masculine privileges—an idea which jars upon a refined
taste. Considerations of this sort, resting mainly upon sentiment or
prejudice, can scarcely be met by argument. It is usually admitted
that we are as yet in the dark as to the specific differences between
men and women—that we do not know how far they are native, and
to what extent those which strike the eye may have been produced
by artificial influences—that even if we knew much more than we
do about the nature of the material to be dealt with, we should still
have much to learn as to the kind of intellectual discipline which
might be most suitable. Nor have we as yet any trustworthy
evidence—scarcely so much as a plausible suggestion—as to the
manner in which the differences of the work in life to which men
and women respectively are said to be called, could be met by
corresponding differences in mental training. The arbitrary differences established by fashion seem to have been directed by the
rule of contraries rather than by any intelligent judgment. Practically, what we come to is something like this—People who want to

impose a special system have some theories as to the comparative merits of certain studies, which they feel a friendly impulse to press upon others at every convenient opportunity; or they have a vague impression that as certain subjects and methods have been in a manner set apart for women ever since they can remember, there is most likely something in them which distinguishes them either as suitable to the female mind, or as specially useful to women in practical life. To discover how much of truth there may be behind this opinion would be a tedious and difficult task. It may be enough to remark that experience seems to be against it. It is precisely because the special system, as hitherto tried, has proved a signal failure, that reform is called for.

There are other advocates, however, of independent schemes, who take up a totally different ground. They only half believe, or perhaps altogether repudiate, the female mind theory; and they are prepared to go great lengths in assimilating the education of the sexes. But they say—1. Male education is in a very bad state—therefore it is not worth while to spread it. 2. Rightly or wrongly, it *is* different from that of women. It would be useless to examine people in things they have not learnt; and women do not as a rule learn Latin and Greek and Mathematics. We must recognize facts.

By all means let us recognize facts. But let us remember also that facts are created things, and mortal. There are old facts, of a bad sort, which want to be put an end to, and there are new and better facts, which may by wise measures be called into being. And speaking of facts, let this be considered—that however bad the education of men may be, that of women is undoubtedly worse. On this point the Report of the Schools Inquiry Commission speaks very distinctly. After adverting to the general deficiency in girls' education, which "is stated with the utmost confidence and with entire agreement, with whatever difference of words, by many witnesses of authority," the Commissioners observe that "the same complaints apply to a great extent to boys' education. But on the whole, the evidence is clear that, not as they might be but as they are, the girls' schools are inferior in this view to the boys' schools." And if this is the evidence as regards the school period, during which girls are receiving more or less regular and systematic instruction, it is likely to be still more unanimous and emphatic as to the later stage, during which men are, in however antiquated and foolish a manner, as the reformers tell us, at any rate in some sort taken in hand by the universities, while women are for the most part left altogether to their own resources. It will probably be admitted, without further argument, that to make the education of average

women only as good as that of men, would be a step in advance of
what it is now.

But is this intermediate step an indispensable one? Are we obliged to go through a course of wandering along paths which have been found to lead away from the desired end? Cannot we use the light of experience, and, avoiding exploded errors, march straight on to perfection by the nearest road? To a great extent, Yes. There is no reason, for example, to imitate boys' schools in their excessive devotion to physical sports; or in the exclusion of music from the ordinary school routine; or to take up methods of teaching of which the defects have been discovered. Again, looking to the higher stage, no one would wish to reproduce among women either the luxurious idleness of the lower average of university men, or the excessive strain of the competition for honours which is said to act so injuriously on the studious class. But these are evils from which women are pretty securely guarded by existing social conditions. There is at present not much fear that girls will take too much out-of-door exercise, that they will give too little time to music, or that governesses will blindly model their teaching on the plans in vogue in boys' schools. Fashionable young ladies are not in danger of idling away their time at college, and the studious are not tempted by valuable rewards attached to academical distinction. It is not in its weak points that male education is likely to be imitated by women.

The immediate controversy turns, as has been said, upon examinations—examinations regarded as a controlling force, directing the course of instruction into certain channels; pronouncing upon the comparative value of subjects, fixing the amount of time and attention bestowed upon each, and to some extent guiding the method of teaching; wholesomely stimulating; and aptly fulfilling its great function of plucking. What are the conditions required to produce the right kind of controlling force? We want authority—that no one disputes. We want the best subjects encouraged. What they are, the most competent judges have not yet settled; but most people, perhaps not all, will agree that when they have made up their minds their verdict ought to be acted upon. We want an examination which can be worked beneficially. To adopt an examination so radically bad that it could not in itself be made an improving exercise, might be defensible, perhaps even justifiable, taking a very enlarged view of contingent moral influences. But it would be a difficult case to defend, and no one has taken it in hand. We want an examination for which candidates will be forthcoming. Finally, we want an examination which will sift. We do not want to

238   have certificates of proficiency given to half-educated women. There are examinations which will do this already within reach.

Authority; wise choice of subjects; so much skill in the construction of questions that at any rate they do not invite shallow and unthorough preparation; practicability; and due severity— these are requisites which most people will agree in regarding as essential. But the agreement does not go much farther. As to authority, what constitutes it? Is it the personal reputation of the examiners, or is it their official position? Or is it the prestige acquired by prescription? Or has the quality of the candidates anything to do with it? It is as to the two last points that opinions differ. We can agree so far as this, that an examination by men of high repute will carry more weight than one of men unknown, and that an examination by an official body such as a university, will be more readily believed in than one by any self-constituted board, however respectable. But supposing these two points secured, is a new examination conducted by competent examiners appointed by a university all that is to be desired? Will an unknown standard, having expressly in view candidates drawn from a limited and notoriously illiterate class, be worth much as regards authority? Mr. Matthew Arnold remarks that "High pitched examinations are the result, not the cause, of a high condition of general culture, and examinations tend, in fact, to adjust themselves to studies." There is much reason to expect that such a scheme as has been supposed would from the outset be, whether justly or unjustly, regarded as in some way accommodated to the inferior attainments of the class, and that starting with small repute, it would have to contend with the natural tendency of all things to justify their character. The most highly cultivated women would not care to submit themselves to an ordeal in which to fail might be disgrace, but to pass would be no distinction. The mere fact of its special character would in itself repel them. That the greatest of female novelists should have taken the precaution to assume a masculine *nom de plume* for the express purpose of securing their work against being measured by a class standard, is significant of the feeling entertained by women. Right or wrong, wise or foolish, here is at any rate a fact to be recognised, and a fact having a manifest bearing on the question in hand. An examination limited to a class, and with which the *elite* of that class will have nothing to do, is not likely to command very high respect.

As regards the choice of subjects and the practical manipulation, so to speak, it appears that if we are to have an examination stamped by official authority, we must go to the old authorities for it, and these authorities may be supposed to have already done their

best, according to their light, in devising the existing examinations.
University examiners are human, and no doubt make mistakes, but if they are incompetent to direct the education with which they are familiar, why should they become suddenly wise when they enter upon a field unknown to them by experience, but as regards which they are but too well supplied with theories? It may be said that the new work would probably fall into the hands of new men, who would start with more advanced ideas, and that they might be able to carry through for women what they cannot get for men. But the counsels of inexperience are not always the wisest, and supposing the case to be as represented, it seems to be merely a question of a very short time. At the Universities the generations succeed each other much more rapidly than anywhere else. The young men of to-day will be the governing body a few years hence, and will then be able to carry out their ideas for both men and women. If the new thing proposed is better than what men have already, women do not wish to monopolise it.

The questions of practicability and severity may be taken together. A medium is required between a test so far out of reach that no one will go in for it, and one so loose that it fails to discriminate. And here we must not forget that, though without any fault of their own, the great majority of women *are* very imperfectly educated, and it is therefore impossible, in the nature of things, to devise any test which can at once embrace the great mass and yet be sufficiently exclusive. There are a few educated women. We want to find them. We may be very sorry that other women, perhaps equally intelligent and willing, have not had the chance of being educated too. We are bound to do all we can to bring education within their reach. But we are not bound to perpetuate the evils with which we are struggling, by certifying competent knowledge where it does not exist.

And it is not, except perhaps to some small extent, that the education of women has taken a different line, and that they do know some things thoroughly well, if only they had the opportunity of showing it. The defectiveness of female education tells all the way through. The schools are indeed improving, but then it is to be observed that the best girls' schools are precisely those in which the "masculine" subjects have been introduced, and by which therefore the imposition of a feminine test is least likely to be desired. The real question of practicability therefore seems to be, not what would exactly fit female education as it is, but what it may be made to fit itself to, within a reasonable time and without great inconvenience and difficulty.

On this question much valuable evidence is to be found in the Reports of the Schools Inquiry Assistant Commissioners. Mr. Giffard says, "If I were to sum up the impressions I derived from my visits to girls' schools, I should say (1) that the mental training of the best girls' schools is unmistakeably inferior to that of the best boys' schools; (2) that there is no natural inaptitude in girls to deal with any of the subjects which form the staple of a boy's education; (3) that there is no disinclination on the part of the majority of teachers to assimilate the studies of girls to those of boys; (4) that the present inferiority of girls' training is due to the despotism of fashion, or, in other words, the despotism of parents and guardians." Other evidence to the same effect abounds. Any one who knows well the better class of teachers of girls will endorse Mr. Giffard's statement as to their willingness to adopt innovations. There is no insuperable difficulty in getting teaching of any subject where there is sufficient demand for it. It would probably be easier to get first-rate teaching in classics and mathematics than in, say modern languages, because they are the subjects which have hitherto been chiefly cultivated by highly educated men. And though a test which would at first exclude the great majority of ordinary women may have an appearance of rigour almost amounting to cruelty, it is consoling to know that there are already open to women many opportunities of bringing to the test such elementary or fragmentary knowledge as circumstances may have enabled them to pick up. The Society of Arts gives examinations not to be despised, in a great variety of subjects, and the machinery for conducting them brings them within easy reach. The Government Department of Science and Art gives certificates of competency to teach in various branches of science and art. The Royal Academy of Music gives examinations and a diploma. The Home and Colonial School Society holds examinations for governesses, which include, besides the ordinary subjects of instruction, such as modern languages, music and drawing, the special qualifications required by governesses in schools, namely, teaching power, and governing power. It cannot be truly said that female teachers have no means of showing competency, and that those who are willing rather to work gradually for radical reform than to catch hastily at half measures, are sacrificing the present generation for the sake of shadowy advantages in a distant future.

The kind of result which is likely to follow from an adaptation of a female examination to the *examinees,* may be conjectured from the advice given by a schoolmistress in reference to the Cambridge Local Examinations. Complaining of the vexatious demands for a degree of attainment in arithmetic not commonly reached in girls' schools, she remarked briefly, "I would have all that expunged." The suggestion that one advantage of these examinations might consist in the pressure brought to bear in favour of unpopular subjects, was met by the rejoinder, "But why press an unpopular subject which is of no use in after-life?"

The tendency of examinations to adjust themselves to studies is a consideration of great importance. At present the weak points in the education of men are the comparatively strong points in that of women, and therefore less need attention. It is where men are strong that women want stimulus and encouragement—and it may be added, they need this only in order to produce satisfactory results. The Cambridge Local Examinations furnish a case in point. In the first examination to which girls were admitted, 90 per cent of the senior candidates failed in the preliminary arithmetic. Fortunately, the standard was fixed by reference to an immense preponderance of boy candidates, and it was understood that the girls must be brought up to it. Extra time, and probably better teaching, aided by greater willingness on the part of the pupils, who had been made aware of their deficiency, were devoted to the unpopular and "useless" subject. In the next examination, out of the whole number of girls only three failed in it.

Other reasons for desiring a common standard, of a more subtle character can scarcely be apprehended perhaps in their full force without personal experience. Probably only women who have laboured under it can understand the weight of discouragement produced by being perpetually told that, as women, nothing much is ever to be expected of them, and it is not worth their while to exert themselves—that they can write lively letters, full of graphic description and homely touches, but that anything like original research or profound learning is not for them to think of—that whatever they do they must not interest themselves, except in a second-hand and shallow way, in the pursuits of men, for in such pursuits they must always expect to fail. Women who have lived in the atmosphere produced by such teaching know how it stifles and chills; how hard it is to work courageously through it. Every effort to improve the education of women which assumes that they may, without reprehensible ambition, study the same subjects as their brothers and be measured by the same standards, does something towards lifting them out of the state of listless despair of themselves into which so many fall. Supposing that the percentage of success attained by women should be considerably less than that of men, the sense of discouragement thus engendered would be as nothing compared with the general self-distrust produced by having it taken for granted that they are by nature disqualified to stand the ordinary tests. To make the discovery of individual incompetence may be wholesomely humbling or stimulating, as the case may be, but no one is the better for being told, on mere arbitrary authority, that he belongs to a weak and incapable class. And this, whatever may be the intention, is said in effect by the offer of any test of an exclusively female character. No doubt there are university men whose opinion of their own education is so low that they can honestly propose a special standard for women with the intention and expectation of its being better than anything that has been known before, and an example to be imitated in male examinations. But this idea is so new and so bewildering to the outside world that it is simply incomprehensible. The statement of it is regarded as irony.

If it were otherwise—supposing that in the future the relative positions of men and women as regards Learning should be reversed—the arguments in favour of common standards would be changed in their application, but would remain substantially the same. There would still be the same reasons for desiring that in all department of study boys and girls, men and women, should walk together in the same paths. Why should they be separated? And the whole specializing system has a tendency, so far as its influence goes, to separate—to divide where union is most to be desired. The easy way in which it is often taken for granted that, as a matter of course, men care for men and women for women—that a certain *esprit de corps* is natural, if not positively commendable—must surely arise from a most inhuman way of looking at things. Conceive a family in which the brothers and sisters form rival *corps,* headed by the father and mother respectively! If on the small scale, the spectacle is revolting, surely it ought to be no less so in the great human family. In the rebellion of the best instincts of human nature against such a theory, we have a security that it will never prevail. But sympathy may be checked even where it cannot be destroyed; and to put barriers in the way of companionship in the highest kinds of work and pleasure, is to carry out in the most effectual way the devices of the dividing spirit.

But when all has been said that can be, or that need be, said in favour of common standards, it may still be urged—All this is very well, but can you get them? What university is likely to open its degree-examinations to women? Would it not be well to try some judicious compromise?

To those who are aware that women have at this moment free

access to the degrees of several foreign universities, to say nothing of historic precedent, the idea of extending those of our own country is not so very startling. We see in the papers from time to time notices of ladies who have taken the degree of Bacheliere-es-Sciences, or Bacheliere-es-Lettres, at Paris, Lyons, or elsewhere; and three English ladies are now studying for the medical degree at the University of Zurich, without the hindrance or restriction of any sort. In England the only university which could at present be reasonably asked to open its examinations of women is that of London. The condition of residence imposed by the old universities must exclude women until they are able, by means of a college of their own, to offer guarantees as to instruction and discipline similar to those which are required at Oxford and Cambridge. It is probable that within no very distant period the opportunity of complying with this essential condition will be within reach of women, and there is no reason to hope that the examinations of the University of Cambridge may then be substantially, if not in name —and this last is a secondary consideration—as accessible to women as they are to men. But when this shall arrive, the wants of non-resident students will remain to be supplied; and here it is manifestly reasonable to look to the one English university which undertakes this particular work. The question has been before the University of London for some years, and a supplemental charter has been obtained, empowering the university to institute special examinations for women. The first step taken under this charter has been to draw up a scheme for a general or testing examination for women parallel with the matriculation examination for men; and by a curious coincidence, the subjects found specially appropriate to women are, with a few exceptions, precisely those which had already been laid down as specially proper for men. Greater option is given in the section for languages; for some inscrutable reason, one book of Euclid instead of four is considered enough for women, and by way of compensation physical geography is thrown in; English *Literature* is added to English language; and a choice is permitted between chemistry and botany. It will be observed that, except three books of Euclid, nothing which is considered good for men is *omitted,* the only substantial difference being that women are allowed greater freedom in selection. Whether this gift of liberty is better than guidance need not here be discussed. As to the level of attainment to be exacted, no official announcement has been made. It is confidently asserted that it will be in no way inferior, as regards difficulty, to the parallel matriculation examination; and as the subjects prescribed will, for a time at any rate, exclude ordinary half-educated women, it seems likely that the assertion will be justified.

Here then seems to be a fair case for compromise. To begin with, we have the authority of a university which is growing in public estimation and importance, which is recognised as the great examining board for all students whose circumstances preclude college life, and which year by year is acquiring more of that dignity which belongs only to age. Then, looking at the examination itself, and especially at the programme of subjects prescribed, it cannot be denied that it is admirably suited to the education of women in its present state of transition. Modern languages and English literature have their place by the side of classics, mathematics, and physical science. Taking the Schools Inquiry Commissioners as a guide—and there could scarcely be a better—we find that in their chapter on "Kinds of education desirable," their recommendations show a remarkable correspondence with the course laid down in the London programme. Some provision will no doubt be required to bring the requisite instruction within reach of women; but here we come upon one of the advantages of community of subjects. It is certain that as young men all over England are continually preparing for this examination, there must be people employed in teaching them, and by a little arrangement, the same teachers may be made available for their sisters. One of the benefits contingent on the use of such an examination is, that it may lead to the extension of good teaching. It is, of course, also possible that women may become the prey of the crammers, but probably not at all to the same extent as their brothers—the inducement to an unstudious woman to go through an examination merely for the sake of a pass being comparatively small. The matriculation examination is taken up by a large proportion of male students as their one and final test, and as such it will no doubt be made immediate use of by women.* If it should be found that the machinery works well, that the demand which has been alleged on the part of women is real, and if the students, by passing creditably this first stage, establish their claim to the complete university course, there is little doubt that it will ultimately be acknowledged. The step which has already been taken may be regarded as a tentative effort in the right direction, and public opinion is not likely to permit backsliding.

*It is estimated that nearly one-half of the undergraduates go no farther than matriculation. Taking the year 1865 as a specimen, it appears there were 616 candidates for matriculation and only 309 for the degree of Bachelor in the various faculties. The average age of candidates for matriculation has varied from seventeen years and eleven months to twenty years and ten months. In the years 1863–64–65 it was over twenty years.

CHARLOTTE MARY YONGE (1823–1901)

Committed to conveying moral ideals and religious concepts, Yonge, an English author of historical romances and books for young people, wrote in excess of one hundred sixty works. Among her books is a biography of Hannah More, her brilliant compatriot, whose *Strictures on Female Education* is reprinted in this classics collection.

Yonge, the epitome of Victorian propriety, wrote *Womankind,* in which she recommended alternatives for educating girls. She named options in the following descending order of desirability: (1) learning from the father at home, (2) learning from the mother at home, (3) learning from a good governess, (4) learning in a good school. Specific recommendations for female education are stated in the chapter on "Lessons," chosen from *Womankind* (1876).

*WOMANKIND**

Chapter VI

"Lessons"

During the schoolroom years there is a necessity of being taught. The old verb, *to learn* was transitive, and I will take leave so to use it. In childhood we are learnt—afterwards we learn.

"When will Miss Rosamond have finished her education?" says one of Miss Edgeworth's foolish ladies. "Never," is the answer.

The difference is, or ought to be, that during the time of tutelage, much must be acquired irrespective of natural taste and ability, while afterwards there is freedom to pursue whatever line is most obvious and agreeable.

---

*Yonge, Charlotte Mary. *Womankind.* London: Mozley and Smith, 6, Pasternoster Row, 1876, pp. 38-49.

In comes the question, Why do girls learn a little of everything? a smattering, as it is contemptuously called. Let it not be a smattering, but a foundation. The philosophy of the matter seems to be this: woman is the helpmeet, and it is impossible to predict in what line her aid and sympathy may be needed: Therefore it is well to give her the germs of many varieties of acquirement in readiness to be developed on occasion.

Of course there are certain demands of the present level of culture to which every girl has to be worked up alike, if she would be spared disgrace and mortification, and be on equal terms with those about her.

I suppose the *lowest* standard for a lady must include, besides reading aloud, tolerable composition of a letter, and arithmetic enough for accounts, respectably grammatical language, and correct pronunciation; command of the limbs and figure, facility in understanding French, history enough not to confound Romans with Greeks, and some fuller knowledge of that of England, with so much geography as to avoid preposterous blunders, dexterity in needlework, and general information and literature sufficient to know what people are talking about.

This is indeed a minimum. Some knowledge of music is almost always added, and less invariably the power of using a pencil; but without one or either of these, a person may pass in the crowd without being remarked for falling beneath ordinary mediocrity. The most frivolous mother knows that the most frivolous girl must learn thus much, and be up to a kind of Mangnall's Questions perception of things in general.

Of course this shallow surface ought to mean such grammatical instruction in English as to make slip-slop impossible and disgusting, and render the language and its construction real matter of interest. This is perhaps best learnt, not by the old-fashioned theme, but by accounts of something that has been read, or by translations, very carefully revised, and made into good English. N.B.—Nobody would imagine how very few people there are capable of making a good prose translation, even when the original language is perfectly understood; and early pains to make a translation good readable current English, and yet give the spirit of the original tend to teach a great deal of the idiom and anatomy of both languages. Correct English, neither careless, stilted, nor slangy, is becoming more and more rare; but it is a mark of real refinement of mind and cultivation. If simple in the choice of words and turn of phrases, it need never give the idea of formal precision: *e. g.* "I shall begin to write to my mother," is infinitely better than

"I shall commence to write home," which is not grammatical, since
commence ought to be followed by a noun instead of an infinitive,
and *home* is not an adverb. "I shall commence my letter to my
mother," is grammatical, but has a sound of affectation. To learn
grammar thoroughly, and then use it, should be the training of
every lady in the land; and it is rather hard to find that story-books
unanimously represent insistance on it as a governess's way of
making herself tiresome. Is it owing to this that the poor verbs *to
lie* and *to lay* are so cruelly misused, and that there is a general
misapprehension about the verb *to dare?*

People generally say that grammar is better learnt through
another language than our own; and this is true to a certain extent,
provided they do not mean colloquial French through a *bonne,* and
German by the Ollendorf method. I say only to a certain extent,
even when the second language has been really and grammatically
learnt, because, though a general knowledge of grammar in the
abstract is thus acquired, the idioms and peculiarities of the
acquired tongue are the study, while our own are left to the light of
nature, practice, and observation. It seems to me that after the first
baby foundations of the parts of speech are laid, and ordinary
speech and writing made correct, that one foreign grammar, no
matter what, should be thoroughly taught, and then that the
construction of any additional language will be easily acquired,
while in the latter year or two of education, some very thorough
book on English grammar should be well got up. Those provided
for training-schools are generally excellent of their kind; and the
practice of thorough analyzing a sentence is a very useful one. It is
a good thing when grammar passes into logic; and though even the
rudiments of logic are a little beyond the schoolroom grasp of
mind, a girl who has the capacity would do well to cultivate them,
not so much for their own sake, as because the power of reasoning
is a most important element in having a right judgment in all things.

As to other languages, French is a necessity. To speak it with
perfect ease and a Parisian accent is a useful and graceful accomplishment, only to be acquired by intercourse with natives early
enough in life for the organs to be flexible; but this is only
exceptionally an entire matter of necessity. French after "the school
of Stratford-le-Bowe" has been prevalent among educated Englishwomen ever since Chaucer's time; and a thorough grammatical
knowledge, with such pronunciation as can be obtained through
good lessons, is to stay-at-home people more valuable than mere
ease of speech, which they only rarely have to exercise.

But if it be needful, a German *bonne* is generally kind, true, and faithful, and not likely to do harm to little children. It is the further advantage in making this pronunciation a nursery, not a schoolroom matter, that no girl reading ancient history with a foreigner has a chance of hearing the usual English pronunciation of the classical names. To me it seems that the fashion of teaching German as a matter of course is rather a pity. I had rather make Latin the schoolroom lesson, and leave German to be volunteered afterwards. German is so difficult, as to require a great deal of time; and it is so irregular, as not to be the key to nearly so much as Latin —in learning which it is quite possible to learn the great outlines of both French and Italian—at any rate, the study of both, alike in construction and words, is much simplified, since both are Latin broken in different ways. German leads to nothing (except in the case of philology) but reading its own literature; whereas Latin is needful for clear knowledge of our own tongue, and moreover gives much greater facility of comprehension and power of exactness in the terminology of every other science, from Theology downwards. Latin, and at least enough Greek to read the words and find them in the lexicon, are real powers. With the knowledge of grammar thus acquired, German might be one of the studies taken up in the later young-lady days, though it is a pity it should now always have the preference to Italian, the language of Dante, Tasso, and Manzoni.

A woman's practical arithmetic is said to consist in keeping her accounts. But if she undertakes the care of any charity, she often needs to know book-keeping; and for useful training of the mind, apart from utilitarianism, I have great faith in arithmetic. Heads are very different; and in some few cases there would seem to be almost an incapacity for it, certainly a great aversion. Often this dislike arises from bad teaching at first, never entirely surmounted, or from being dragged on beyond the power of following. In mental arithmetic, the child of slow calculation should not be put in contact with the quick one, or it never understands at all.

It seems to me that intelligent arithmetic is sometimes attempted too soon. Some processes are really better done mechanically and by the memory than by intellectual force; and most people are capable of working a sum long before they can comprehend it. Few of us but could *do* a long-multiplication or long-division sum on occasion, but I suspect that only persons employed in teaching could instantly explain why the one becomes a flight of steps, and the other "a long ladder of figures." I doubt if the brain can take in the full idea before eleven or twelve years old, though the mechanical operation may be performed with perfect ease, "a sort of

conjuring," as some inspector contemptuously says of girls'
arithmetic.

Let it be conjuring then at first, only do not give very long difficult sums to be done without assistance. The strain of attention is too great and too long, and the toil caused by a blunder disheartening. Shorter "problems," *always proved,* teach a great deal more, with much less disgust. Proof should be required, for establishing that the correctness of the answer does not depend upon the caprice of the key, but is really a fact and cannot be otherwise. It shows how and why a blunder in the working affects the result, and assists in understanding the principle; moreover, it assists in preventing one rule from being forgotten while another is being mastered. I believe we do not really know anything till it becomes the means of learning something else. Our last acquisition may always fly away till it has been rammed down with something above it; and thus the past rule is best secured by becoming the means of learning the new one.

Mechanical arithmetic extends, we should say, as far as Practice, and ought to be worked well through by eleven or twelve years old. It is best to go through all the varieties of weights and measures, not for the sake of learning how to work them, but of fixing them in the memory, and using them does this far better than learning them by heart. There are exceptional beings, who like Mrs. Mozley's Bessie Gray, learn arithmetic with their understanding, and cannot get on without appreciating the reason why; but these are not common. Nature makes the childish brain willing to take an immense deal of rote work rather than use one effort to think; and we believe she is right. It is thinking, not learning nor working, that damages; and the memory may be stored, and facility of working can be obtained, without that dangerous feat of comprehension and deduction which is what "pressing a child too much" really means.

Between ten and thirteen, according to their powers, girls should *begin at the beginning* of some easy book of scientific arithmetic. De Morgan's is a very good one. They should read it aloud with a thorough-going person, who will not let them leap over the self-evident foundations that they will view as insults to their understanding. The real meaning of the working of the first four rules, there mastered, leads on the vulgar fractions, proportion, and decimals; and only the minds which are more than commonly blind to calculation can help comprehending and being interested.

Somewhere about this time a beginning of mathematics should be made. Long previously the primary terms should have been accurately understood. Reading, or geography, in fact, must lead to the learning the difference between an angle and a triangle, about parallels, rectangles, and the like. N.B.—If the teacher happens to find her own head in confusion on the subject, she had better look the definitions up at the beginning of the books of Euclid. Nobody can teach properly or understand accurately, who alternately talks of a hexagon and a sexagon, or who does not perceive that an angle of ninety degrees must be a right angle. There are things which a person of moderate capacity can gather while reading, but that cannot be *taught* without being learnt instead of picked up. It is absolute amusement to children to be taught to use a case of instruments, and the names and something of the natures of the simpler mathematical figures; and the manner of drawing them can be taught them as part of that rational occupation which is the next thing to play. Even girls' patchwork can be the foundation of a good deal of real experimental information, if it be drawn on a symmetrical design, requiring as it does perfect exactness.

But it is well towards the end of the schoolroom course to study the earlier books of Euclid, more perhaps for the sake of the reasoning than of the knowledge. Observe, this is not to be enforced upon beings devoid of all mathematical capacity, of whom both sexes possess some specimens of average intellect in other respects. These, if hard driven, will learn the propositions by a feat of memory, but never comprehend a word of them. They must be given up, just as the earless are given up as to music.

The discipline of mathematics is, however, very valuable to the feminine creature in itself, and it is the key to a great deal more, above all when the point is reached where the properties of plane figures begin to meet and explain the operations of arithmetic. I remember to this hour the delight of finding the meaning of the working of a square-root sum. It is an immense stage in life to rise, even for a moment, above the rule of thumb.

Algebra and the further study of geometry are very good to be carried on beyond the schoolroom. Indeed, those who have capacity and opportunity, and who have gone through arithmetic, perhaps as far as the cube root, by the last year of their schoolroom life, had better be then initiated into algebra, for the sake of simplifying the operations they are learning to understand, and for the benefit that the comprehension of the symbols will be in every other study.

But we may hardly repeat too often, the schoolroom is the place for learning beginnings. Afterwards the pursuit of the study depends upon taste and circumstance. Nobody is obliged to know more arithmetic than enough to keep the accounts, but those who have the capacity will do well by themselves if they carry on the study; and not only by themselves, for who can tell what opportunities of assisting brother, father, husband, or son, this cultivated power may not given them; nay, in the lowest and most utilitarian view, the same instruction that enables them to appreciate the vast theories of astronomy serves to reckon the quantity of carpeting needed for a room.

So again, a moderate knowledge of history is *de rigueur;* but there are persons so constituted that they can take no interest in the past. Neither the great changes which deal with the welfare of nations, the striking characters, nor the romantic incidents, have power to touch them; they cannot project their imagination into bygone days, nor care about that which is not in immediate action. These must go through historical study enough not to be liable to absurd blunders; and intelligent teaching would probably make it much more interesting to them, by showing the bearing upon the present.

History should be taught from the first moment that reading has become not so much an art as a stepping-stone. The names and dates of English kings are, to the rest of history, much what the multiplication table is to arithmetic, and so the succession and some idea connected with each name should be got into the head as soon as possible; and many of the old traditions are just as necessary to be known as if they were arithmetic. Kind Alfred and the cakes, Knut and the tide, the Conqueror and the curfew, Rufus and the arrow—are all connections that *can* be established in the first lustre, and serve as foundations for life. Some wise man recommended teaching history backwards, beginning with the Reform Bill. I wonder whether he ever tried it upon children, or reasoned only from men, to whom elections are realities, and who may need to be shown the why and wherefore.

The childish mind can take in small personal details, but nothing of large interests; and the best way to give the framework upon which the structure of real knowledge is to be built, is to connect the name with an idea that can be grasped, and that gives a sense of amusement. If *Little Arthur's History* were not so flagrantly incorrect, it would answer the purpose; but I have felt the need of another so much as to write *Aunt Charlotte's Stories of the History of England.* (Marcus Ward.) On this the names and dates can be grafted, and should be rehearsed often enough to make them always within call by the memory in after life. There is generally connection enough with France to make the name of the king of one country recall that of his contemporary, and almost all the other continental powers were in like manner connected with France, so that a certain knowledge of English dates enables those of the rest of modern history to be perceived with sufficient accuracy for common purposes, though not for an examination.

This course of easy English history should begin as soon as the art of reading has been attained with facility enough to allow of story-books being laid aside as lessons—a time varying from five to eight, according to the mechanical reading powers of the child or the abilities of the teacher in imparting what is really the most difficult though the earliest acquisition of our lives, the linking sounds to signs. If the child cannot read well enough, the names and stories should be told or read to it in association with pictures. Anyway this alphabet should be acquired by seven or eight years old, and kept up by rehearsals of dates or writing out when another book is taken in hand.

This book had better be some outline of ancient history. There is sufficient analogy between the childhood of individuals and the childhood of nations, to make early history, when motives are simple, and passions on the surface, much more easy to enter into then the later complications of politics. Moreover, at seven, eight, or nine, the mind is developed enough to acquire that which is perhaps one of the great distinctions between the cultivated and uncultivated—some sense of the perspective of history. And there is, or ought to be, sufficient knowledge of Scripture events to serve as some amount of scaffolding. If the child comes to this point *young,* Maria Hack's *True Stories from Ancient History* or *Aunt Charlotte's Grecian and Roman History* serve very well to give a warm interest in individuals; or for a somewhat more advanced child, *Landmarks of Ancient History* connect the "five empires" with the Bible narrative.

This will last about a year, by which time the mind will be grown enough for a somewhat more detailed English history, either the "Kings of England" or the "New School History of England" (Parker)—the ancient history being meantime kept up, as the English before, by repetition of dates. That admirable chart, Stork's "Stream of Time," ought to be in every school-room, if only it were adapted to modern discoveries and brought down to the present time. It teaches by the eye

"How changing empires wane and wax,
Are founded, flourish and decay,"

more plainly than almost any amount of study or of oral instruction, and it is preferable to Le Sage's tables (which also need renewing and modernizing), inasmuch as they are shut up in a book, and this hangs, or should hang, on the wall. Who that has loitered near it can forget the streams of ancient realms falling into the Macedonian Empire, and in one generation, breaking forth from it again only to fatten the Roman Empire, which soon after its plethora begins to wax lean and emit the more modern nations? Who can forget this, who has seen it with their eyes, and referred to it with their reading? N.B.—Historical reading should always be accompanied by maps.

Looking out the places is one of the works most wearying to human indolence, but which best rewards itself in the clearness and interest it gives; and as children like anything that breaks the continuity of a lesson, they are sure to be pleased by it. Maps are so cheap now that they can be had in sufficient numbers to provide each child with one, and if intelligently used, *i.e.,* pointing to the shape of the harbour, the proximity of a mountain, or the river whose passage caused the battle, they obtain life and animation.

After the more detailed English history course, it may be well to go back to ancient history with Miss Sewell's admirable "Greece" and "Rome." Mythology is so entertaining, that it can be pretty well imparted by a discreet use of Kingsley's and Cox's tales, which are just what might be read aloud to little girls at needlework, and then might follow a translation of Homer, which hardly ever fails to interest and delight much younger than some would suppose. Translations of the Greek tragedians can carry on the course. The Aeneid, if girls learn Latin, should be reserved to be read in the original.

After this ancient course, I believe my own *Landmarks of the Middle Ages and of Modern History* will answer best for sketching European history. And good historical novels and poetry had better be used to illustrate them, being either read aloud while the girls work or draw, or put into their hands as a favour. Many of G. P. R. James's novels may be very well applied to this purpose. They by no means deserve the contempt that has been bestowed on them; their romance is always pure and high-minded, and the characters and manners are carefully studied. The faults—namely, want of variety, and lack of power to rise to the highest class of portraiture —do not *tell* in this kind of reading; and where there is a hiatus in the course of Scott, the "two travellers" will be found very valuable.

Shakespeare's historical plays should of course be read in their places, ancient and modern; and Scott's poems in the same manner.

The course of history described above will probably last till the girl is thirteen or fourteen years old; and then, if she be intelligent and capable, I would entreat that her further historical reading should be of some *real* book, not an abridgment or compilation. *Tales of a Grandfather* I should reckon as real reading; and if the child be not advanced or studious enough to read them for herself, it would be better to make them the reading lesson. There are historical errors here and there, but these can be corrected; and the contact with a really powerful thinking mind is so important a part of education, that it ought not to be sacrificed to the mere fact-cramming. The skeleton of chronology once learnt, and the power of easy writing attained, the facts can be kept up and put in by other means; but after twelve years old, history should be read aloud from authors of real force and style.

If French be by this time familiar, French history had better be read through that medium, and stories be dropped into reading for amusement, or only used occasionally as a treat on semi-holidays after the language is once mastered. Historical reading ought to be the habit of many years, so that there is much more advantage in giving the impulse to read a long book without alarm, than in galloping through any form of history made easy. The custom of hunting down a subject by its date in as full or as original a history as lies within reach, should also be taught about this time; and this can often be done by proposing a subject—say the account of some battle, or siege, or some biography, and awarding the meed of honour to the fullest and most accurate composition.

FRANCE

LOUIS AIMÉ-MARTIN (1786–1847)

Aimé-Martin, the only nineteenth-century French writer represented in this volume, studied at the Polytechnique School where Louis XVIII subsequently appointed him professor of history.

Aimé-Martin believed that fathers lack the inclination and time to teach, while mothers have innate teaching ability. Because he urged mothers to impart inspiration and direction as well as knowledge, he advised that female education should have a moral component in addition to an intellectual emphasis.

His book, *The Education of Mothers: or the Civilization of Mankind by Women,* won the 1837 French Academy Award. The chapter "Of Present Education and Its Insufficiency" is a description of the status of women's education in early nineteenth-century France.

*THE EDUCATION OF MOTHERS**

Chapter VI

"Of Present Education and Its Insufficiency"

Since the periods of Fénelon and Rousseau there has been progress among men, and the education of women has consequently improved. We now no longer discuss the question, whether they should be instructed, or the amount of the instruction which should

*From Lee, Edwin (trans.). *The Education of Mothers: or the Civilization of Mankind by Women.* Philadelphia: Lea and Blanchard, 1843, pp. 56-61.

be allowed them. We consent to develope their intelligence. We go further, and give them the talents of artists, and of doctors of sciences; they skim, if we may so speak, encyclopaedial studies, but in these studies there is nothing which leads them to think with their own thoughts. When, therefore, the passions arrive, to which it is not too much to oppose habits of virtue, the powers of the soul, and the principles of religion, they find hands skilful upon the piano, a memory which recites, and a soul which sleeps. Such is, with a few rare exceptions, the woman which the age gives us, with her petty devotional practices, her school morality, her mechanical talents, her love of pleasure, the ignorance of the affairs of life, and the want of loving and of being beloved.

It is not that this education has not also its bright side. It introduces into society artistical taste and manners, more grace, more originality. The duchess and the *bourgeoise* may compete in our salons with first-rate talents; some compose *poems,* which are sold for the benefit of the Greeks and Poles; others paint *pictures,* the price of which is appropriated to charitable purposes; all write with gracefulness, and the style of Sevigné and of Lafayette is become almost common. Thus education gradually levels society; its uniformity is the most powerful democracy, and I do not think that I advance a paradox in saying that the talents of women have done more towards the equality of ranks, than all the decrees of our national assemblies. Enter our most fashionable *salons,* observe that group of men, of all ages, standing in the centre, and who all appear as if dressed from the same piece of cloth; one of them is a banker, another a marquis; this a magistrate, that a virtuoso. Well, notwithstanding the monotony of their black coats, there is in their language—in their gait—a something which distinguishes and classifies them. It is not the same with respect to women. From their graceful attitudes, the elegance of their manners, you would think them all equal in point of birth and rank. There is the same instruction, the same charm, the same taste for the arts. No means of distinguishing the daughters of a notary from those of a courtier; those of a capitalist from those of a general. Look at that charming group assembled around the piano, executing together one of Rossini's best productions, with as much self-possession as Italian singers—they are the wife of a peer of France, and of a physician; a marchioness, a young *artiste,* and the daughter of a man of business; nothing distinguishes one from another except talent.

Now cast your eyes on that lady whose toilet is so simple and yet so elegant; she is one of our prettiest duchesses. See what an amiable smile she exchanges with the young person seated near her.

Both are remarkable women. The duchess teaches her sons Latin, and writes novels; the other composes verses. She is a poetess; she is beautiful! the Corinna of the age: her glory is her nobility. Thus in this elegant assembly in which all is confounded, birth, fortune, titles, conditions, there is no blemish; beauty attracts the eyes, talent marks the places, and education passes the level.

Certainly, if the life of women were to be restricted to exhibitions and *fetes,* if their business were only to dazzle and to please, the great problem would be resolved by this education of *soirees:* but the hours of pleasure are short, and in their train follow the hours of reflection. The life of home, moral life, the duties of mother and wife, all this comes, and all has been forgotten. Then they find themselves as in a void in the bosoms of their families, with romantic passions, an unbridled exaltation, and *ennui,* that great destroyer of female virtue. The lamentations of the fatal consequences of this state of matters assail our ears on all sides; it is the cry of all mothers, the complaint of all husbands; and in these painful straits, wherein each one is agitated and desponding, the worst effect is, that carelessness terminates all.

What is requisite in order to obtain a correct idea of the want of foresight in our education? If we ask ourselves what is the end to be attained: is it religion? But religion, improperly understood, it is true, condemns almost all that is taught. Is it domestic happiness? But the talents acquired with so much pains, those talents which prevent thought, disappear in the routine of household affairs. Is it the prosperity, the glory of the country? Ridiculous! what mother thinks of such matters now-a-days? Thus, in proportion as we seek the end, every thing disappears; nothing for private happiness, nothing for the general prosperity. The world remains, and it is to that point, in fact, towards which all our previsions are directed. The object is more to please the world than to resist it; to shine, to reign. Vanity; such is the object which the tenderest mothers do not cease to show their daughters, and upon which rock the world, which cheers them on, sees them wreck themselves with indifference. Vanity in dress, vanity in agreeable talents, vanity in instruction. Be handsome, be polite, people see you; be gentle, be submissive, people hear you, says a mother to her daughter; that is to say, let appearance always take the place of reality. The soul, like the body, has its light dresses, to which we are accustomed from the cradle. The evil is not cured, it is concealed; the character is not changed, it is disguised; thus vanity covers all; to *seem* not to *be,* constitutes the aim of education.

Let music, painting, and dancing charm the leisure hours of a young girl, nothing can be better. But wherefore should we turn delightful recreations into heavy and painful tasks? why satiate her with occupations which ought only to be pleasurable? What a question! You wish that she should possess talents which amuse her, and we wish talents that shall cause her to be applauded; an artist's hand and foot. Once more vanity!

Here are books; good taste has presided over their selection. Racine, La Fontaine, Fenelon, Bossuet, Pascal, Lamartine: very well; enlarge the young soul, furnish it with rich thoughts, strengthen it with wise maxims, cause to spring up the appreciation of the *beautiful*—a sentiment which God himself has implanted in it. But, say you, our lessons are not intended to make learned women! Ah! I understand; the object should be to fill the memory. She has remembered some verses, she can repeat certain portions of geography, of chronology, of history, a few dates, a few events: it is an affair of *covenance;* the varnish which causes a piece of furniture to shine, the gilding which gives the appearance of gold to the vilest metal; the covering is a little thin; no matter, provided the copper do not appear. Still vanity!

It is true one seeks to check the excess by the exercise of some religious practices; but this teaching, at all times somewhat monastic, is but another impediment in our education. You give to a young girl a taste for worldly toilettes, a dancing and a singing master, and at the same time you prohibit balls and brilliant assemblies. On the one hand, you inculcate a contempt for worldly pleasures; on the other, you give her lessons which excite her love for these pleasures. You enrich her memory with the *chefs d'oeuvre* of the stage, and you prohibit theatrical entertainments. You praise before her the destiny of virgins, and you give her a husband. Always a step forwards and backwards; temptation and a moral discourse; a preparation for sin, and a scruple of conscience. Pitiful admixture of the fifteenth and the nineteenth centuries, which tends to make the same person a penitent and a coquette: the delight of a salon, and the angel of a convent. These contrasts, so violently united, jostle with each other at the outset, and the war of the passions and of prejudices begins amidst the seductions of the world, and in the absence of all moral strength and reason. Such are our foresight and our wisdom; such is the way in which education places us under the necessity of offending either the law or nature. The point of setting out is always a stumble, and a stumble on the brink of an abyss.

Thus our belief and our sciences only meet to confront each other; the war is within us, it is ourselves which it destroys; and our educations have no other result than to propagate its fury. All these elements of discord, all these opposing principles, which should be amalgamated into one universal reason, are case at our intelligence in their sharp and crude forms, without modifying them, without even seeking to render their union possible; their union, which alone could constitute a reasonable education. It would appear as if a religious and a worldly life were the two champions in a deadly conflict. Whichever be the conqueror, the man who adopts it is no more than a mutilated incomplete being; the deplorable remains of passions or of superstitions.

The perfect man is he who at the same time leads a social and a religious life; with a powerful hand he puts an end to the strife of the two adversaries, and giving to each his place, he advances with a firm step in the ways of God, and in the light of reason. But in order that this light, so rare in the present day, should be diffused in the world, it must shine in our educations; it can only arrive at the multitude mixed with the first emotions of our lives, and beneath the irresistible influence of a mother. It is the sacred lamp which the laborious wife of Virgil lighted in the night for her work near the cradle of her child.

Mention is made in the Paradise Lost of a lion, the creation of which is not yet terminated; one sees him half emerging from the earth, his eye sparkles, his mane is agitated, but his body is an inert immovable mass, which still adheres to the earth, while impatiently waiting for the last spark to leap out.

Sublime image of the human race, it has only the head living; the rest has not even motion. Cause the light to penetrate into it, snatch the lion from nothingness, and let him take possession of his empire.

GERMANY

JEAN PAUL RICHTER (1763–1825)

Richter, a prominent novelist, is the first of two German representatives of nineteenth-century educational theory. He used education as the theme for a novel titled *Life of the Complacent Little Schoolmaster Maria Wuz* (1790).

Combining his experiences as a tutor with his considerable strengths in theology and philosophy, he wrote *Levana; or, the Doctrine of Education* (ca. 1804). In Greek mythology Levana was the goddess who watched over newborn infants. In *Levana,* Richter devoted the majority of one chapter to the education of girls. A portion of that chapter is reprinted here.

*LEVANA; OR, THE DOCTRINE OF EDUCATION**

Let everything be taught a girl which forms and exercises the habit of attention, and the power of judging things by the eye. Consequently botany,—this inexhaustible, tranquil, ever-interesting science attaching the mind to nature with bonds of flowers. Then astronomy, not the properly mathematical, but the Lichtenbergian and religious, which with the expansion of the universe expands the mind; along with which it does no harm if a girl experiences why a longest night is advantageous to sleep, a full moon to love. I should also even recommend mathematics; but here, unfortunately, women who have a Fontenelle for astronomy have not one for mathematics; for, with regard to girls, I only mean those simplest principles of pure and mixed mathematics which boys can understand. And geometry itself, as a second eye, or

---

*Richter, Jean Paul Friedrich. *Levana; or, The Doctrine of Education.* Boston: D.C. Heath & Co., 1890, pp. 255-259.

dioptric line, which brings as distinct separations into the world of
matter as Kant has done by his categories into the world of mind,
may also be commenced early; for geometrical observations, unlike
philosophical, strain the mind to the injury of the body as little as
the external sense of sight. Sculptors and painters study
mathematics as the skeleton of visible beauty without injury to their
sense of beauty: I know a little girl of two years and a half old who
recognised, in the full foliage of nature, the dry paper skeleton of
the mathematical figures which she had learned to draw in play. In
the same way these little beings have early developed powers of
calculation, expecially for the important part of mental arithmetic.
Why are they not also taught a multiplication table for the
reduction of the various kinds of money and yard measurements?

Philosophy is something quite different, indeed diametrically
opposite. Why should these lovers of wisdom and of wise men learn
it? A lottery ticket with a great premium has been occasionally
drawn from among this sex—a true born poetess; but a
philosopheress would have broken up the lottery. A woman of
genius—Madame Chatelet—may understand Newton in English,
and render him into French; but none could do that in German for
Kant or Schelling. The most spiritual-minded and intellectual
women have a way of their own, a certainty of understanding the
most profound philosophers, which even their very scholars de-
spairingly aim at—namely, they find every thing easy, especially
their own thoughts, that is feelings. In the ever-changing atmosphere of their fancy they meet with every most finely-drawn
skeleton of the philosophers; just like many poetical followers of
the new schools of philosophy who, instead of a clearly defined
circle, give us a fantastic wreath of vapour.

Geography, as a mere registry of places, is utterly worthless for
mental development, and of little use to women in their vocations;
on the contrary, that is indispensable which, teaching the enduring
living history of the earth—in opposition to that which is transitory
and dead—is at once the history of humanity, which divides itself
into nations as well as into contemporaneous historic periods, and
also that of the globe itself, which converts the twelve months into
twelve contemporaneous spaces. The mind of a girl attached to her
chair and her birthplace, like an enchanted princess in a castle, must
be delivered and led forth to clearer prospects by the descriptions of
travelers. I wish some one would give us a comprehensive selection
of the best travels and voyages round the world, shortened and
adapted for the use of girls; if the editor were well furnished with
Herder's patience and insight into the most dissimilar nations, I

know of no more valuable present to the sex. With regard to descriptions of places, every station requires a different one, a merchant's daughter one very unlike that provided for a princess.

Almost all this equally applied to petrified history, which only conducts from one past age into another. For a girl it can scarcely be too barren in dates and names. How many emperors in the whole history of German emperors are for a girl; On the other hand, it cannot be sufficiently rich in great men and great events, which elevate the soul above the petty histories of towns and suburbs.

Music, vocal and instrumental, is natural to the female mind and is the Orphean lute which leads her uninjured past many siren sounds, and accompanies her with its echo of youth far into the autumn of wedded life. Drawing, on the contrary, if carried beyond the first principles, which educate the eye and taste in dress more perfectly, steals too much time from the husband and children: therefore it is usually a lost art.

One foreign language is necessary, and at the same time quite enough, for the scientific explanation of her own. Unfortunately French pushes itself most prominently forward, because a woman really must learn it to comply with the necessities consequent on the billeting of French soldiers. I would wish—why should one not wish, that is, do every day of the year what one does on the first?— that a selection of English, Italian, Latin words were placed before every girl as an exercise in reading, so that she might understand when she heard them.

The talking and writing world has sent into circulation so large a foreign treasury of scientific words that girls, who do not, like boys, learn the words along with the sciences, should have weekly lessons in them out of a scientific dictionary, or translate into comprehensible phrases tales in which such anti-Campean words are purposely employed. I wish that for this end an octavovolume full of foreign words, with an explanatory encyclopaedia to them, were published. The best women read dreaming (the rest truly sleeping); they pass gliding as easily over the mountains of a metaphysical book as sailors do over the mountainous waves of the ocean. None of them ever thinks of asking the dictionary, nay, not even her husband, what any word means; but this vow of silence which regards asking questions as a forbidden game, this content- ment with dark thoughts, which possibly learns in the twentieth book the meaning of a scientific term used in the second, ought to be prevented. Else they will read books as they listen to men.

There is one charm which all girls might possess, and which

frequently not one in a provincial town does possess; which equally enchants him who has, and him who has it not; which adorns the features and every word, and which remains imperishable (nothing can exist longer) while a woman speaks;—I mean the pronunciation itself, the pure German indicating no birthplace. I entreat you, mothers, to take lessons in pure German enunciation and to rehearse them constantly with your daughters. I assure you—to place the matter on a firmer foundation—that a vulgar pronunciation always rather reminds one of a vulgar condition, because, in general, the higher the rank the better is the pronunciation, though not always the language. The higher ranks, contrary to Adelung's change of words, are not the best musical artists of language (composers), but they are the best deliverers of it (virtuosi).

Girls, unlike authoresses, cannot write too much. It is as though on paper, this final metamorphosis of their dear flax, they themselves experienced one, and, in the backward viewing of the rough and smooth external world, won space and rest for their own inner world; so often in letters and diaries do we find women, the most ordinary in conversation, reveal an unexpected spiritual heaven. But the theme on which and for which they write must not be one drawn from a learned caprice, but from the observation of wife—for their sensations and thoughts depend upon climate far more than those of boys; of course I speak of real letters and their own diaries, not mere exercises. From this cause—that an appointed goal marked and restrained their course—the author has received so many eloquent, profound and brilliant letters from feminine, nay, masculine, minds, that he has often exclaimed in vexation, "If only five authoresses wrote as well as twenty lady-letter-writers, or twenty authors as well as forty correspondents, literature would be of some value!"

BERTHA MARIA VON MARENHOLZ-BÜLOW
(1810–1893)

This well-educated German noblewoman met Friedrich Froebel in 1849. She happened upon Froebel on a small farm where he was preparing a class of young women to teach kindergarten. This chance encounter was the beginning of a long relationship based upon both work and friendship.

Froebel believed that the natural sensitivity of women suited them to be ideal teachers in his kindergartens. He opened a vast sphere for educated women in Germany and elsewhere in the world because he prepared only females for this work.

Von Marenholz-Bülow became Froebel's most tireless, effective disciple. Her only child had died of an illness she attributed to his severe education, so she was eager to disseminate Froebel's philosophy of kindness and play for the young. She accomplished her mission by several means: (1) writing extensively to explain Froebel's philosophy, (2) opening schools based on his philosophy, (3) lecturing widely, although this required travel at a time when it was considered unseemly for a lady to travel alone or with only a female companion. She gave lectures, taught courses, and demonstrated Froebel's teaching materials in England, Italy, Switzerland, France, Holland, and Belgium. Interestingly, she influenced Froebel, who relied upon her to critique his manuscripts.

The impact of von Marenholz-Bülow's work was felt in the United States. After he had heard her lecture and had viewed her demonstration, Henry Barnard, influential Connecticut educator, wrote enthusiastic reviews which fostered the founding of kindergartens in the United States. In Germany, von Marenholz-Bülow had been a co-worker of Mrs. Carl Schurz. Mrs. Schurz emigrated to Watertown, Wisconsin, where she established the first United States kindergarten.

Froebel was certain that women had adequate instinct and intuition to become successful teachers. For this reason he

objected to von Marenholz-Bülow's crusade for higher education of women. He claimed that higher education would give to
women useless knowledge and suppress their natural nature
for kindergarten teaching.

This excerpt from the baroness's book *Reminiscences of
Friedrich Froebel* (1877) includes a description of her initial
meeting with Froebel and an introduction to his educational
theory.

REMINISCENCES OF FRIEDRICH FROEBEL*

Chapter I

"My First Meeting With Froebel"

In the year 1849, at the end of May, I arrived at the Baths of
Liebenstein, in Thuringia, and took up my abode in the same house
as in the previous year. After the usual salutations, my landlady, in
answer to my inquiry as to what was happening in the place, told
me that a few weeks before, a man had settled down on a small farm
near the springs, who danced and played with the village children,
and therefore went by the name of "the old fool." Some days after
I met on my walk this so-called "old fool." A tall, spare man, with
long gray hair, was leading a troop of village children between the
ages of three and eight, most of them barefooted and but scantily
clothed, who marched two and two up a hill, where, having
marshalled them for a play, he practised with them a song
belonging to it. The loving patience and *abandon* with which he did
this, the whole bearing of the man while the children played various
games under his direction, were so moving, that tears came into my
companion's eyes as well as into my own, and I said to her, "This
man is called an 'old fool' by these people; perhaps he is one of
those men who are ridiculed or stoned by contemporaries, and to
whom future generations build monuments."

The play ended, I approached the man with the words, "You
are occupied, I see, in the education of *the people.*"

"Yes," said he, fixing kind, friendly eyes upon me, "that I
am."

---

*From Mann, Mrs. Horace (trans.). *Reminiscences of Friedrich Froebel by
Baroness B. von Marenholz-Bülow.* Boston: Lee and Shepard, publishers,
1891, pp. 1-4.

"It is what is most needed in our time," was my response. "Unless the people become other than they are, all the beautiful ideals of which we are now dreaming as practicable for the immediate future will not be realized."

"That is true," he replied; "but the 'other people' will not come unless we educate them. Therefore we must be busy with the children."

"But where shall the right education come from? It often seems to me that what we call education is mostly folly and sin, which confines poor human nature in the strait-jacket of conventional prejudices and unnatural laws, and crams so much into it that all originality is stifled."

"Well, perhaps I have found something that may prevent this and make a free development possible. Will you," continued the man, whose name I did not yet know, "come with me and visit my institution? We will then speak further, and understand each other better."

I was ready, and he led me across a meadow to a country-house which stood in the midst of a large yard, surrounded by outhouses. He had rented this place to educate young girls for kindergartners. In a large room, in the middle of which stood a large table, he introduced me to his scholars, and told me the different duties assigned to each in the housekeeping. Among these scholars was Henrietta Breyman, his niece. He then opened a large closet containing his play-materials, and gave some explanation of their educational aim, which at the moment gave me very little light on his method. I retain the memory of only one sentence: "Man is a *creative* being."

But the man and his whole manner made a deep impression upon me. I knew that I had to do with a true MAN, with an original, unfalsified nature. When one of his pupils called him Mr. Froebel, I remembered having once heard of a man of the name who wished to educate children by *play*, and that it had seemed to me a very perverted view, for I had only thought of *empty* play, without any serious purpose.

As Froebel accompanied me part of the way back to Lieben-stein, which was about half an hour's distance from his dwelling, we spoke of the disappointment of the high expectations that had been called forth by the movements of 1848, when neither of the parties was right or in a condition to bring about the desired amelioration.

"Nothing comes without a struggle," said Froebel, "opposing forces excite it, and they find their equilibrium by degrees. Strife creates nothing by itself, it only clears the air. New seeds must be planted to germinate and grow, if we will have the tree of humanity blossom. We must, however, take care not to cut away the roots out of which all growth comes, as the destructive element of to-day is liable to do. We cannot tear the present from the past or from the future. Past, present, and future are the trinity of time. The future demands the renewing of life, which must begin in the present. In the *children* lies the seed-corn of the future!"

Thus Froebel expressed himself concerning the movements of the time, always insisting that the historical (traditional) must be respected, and that the new creation can only come forth out of the old.

"That which follows is always conditioned upon that which goes before," he would repeat. "I make that apparent to the children through my educational process." (The Second Gift of his play-materials shows this in concrete things.)

But while Froebel, with his clear comprehension, cast his eyes over the movements of the time, neither joining with the precipitate party of progress nor with the party of reaction that would hinder all progress, he was counted by those in authority among the revolutionists, and condemned with his kindergartens. He repeated again and again: "The destiny of nations lies far more in the hands of women—the mothers—than in the possessors of power, or of those innovators who for the most part do not understand themselves. We must cultivate women, who are the educators of the human race, else the new generation cannot accomplish its task." This was almost always the sum of his discourse.

UNITED STATES

EMMA WILLARD (1787–1870)

Emma Willard, Catharine Beecher, and Mary Lyon, three women who achieved extraordinary success in the development of female seminaries, are among the six nineteenth-century American authors whose works are included in this volume.

Willard's education began in a Connecticut boarding school, then continued at an academy. Even in her early years she was known for her enthusiasm for learning. At the age of seventeen she taught at a district school, after which she attended a private school to study reading, writing, arithmetic, geography, French, drawing, painting, and needlework.

Her first teaching assignment began in 1806 at the Academy of Berlin where she had been a student. Her success there led to an appointment to manage the female academy at Middlebury, Vermont. In 1814 she moved from there to open a boarding school, which, in 1821, was named Troy Female Seminary. Later, the school was re-named Emma Willard School.

Willard's valuable contribution to teacher preparation was apparent in the consistent requests to hire her students. Her work in obtaining public grants to support the education of women is a lesser known achievement.

Her two major educational goals were to make available to girls an education equal to that available to boys, and to promote the education of increasing numbers of women.

"Sketch of a Female Seminary" is from *A Plan for Improving Female Education* (1819), which Willard published at her own expense.

268

From considering the deficiencies in boarding schools, much may be learned, with regard to what would be needed, for the prosperity and usefulness of a public seminary for females.

I. There would be needed a building with commodious rooms for lodging and recitation, apartments for the reception of apparatus, and for the accommodation of the domestic department.

II. A library, containing books on the various subjects in which the pupils were to receive instruction; musical instruments, some good paintings, to form the taste and serve as models for the execution of those who were to be instructed in that art; maps, globes, and a small collection of philosophical apparatus.

III. A judicious board of trust, competent and desirous to promote its interests, would in a female, as in a male literary institution, be the cornerstone of its prosperity. On this board it would depend to provide,

IV. Suitable instruction. This article may be subdivided under four heads.

    1. Religious and Moral
    2. Literary
    3. Domestic
    4. Ornamental

1. *Religious and Moral.* A regular attention to religious duties would, of course, be required of the pupils by the laws of the institution. The trustees would be careful to appoint no instructors, who would not teach religion and morality, both by their example, and by leading the minds of the pupils to perceive, that these constitute the true end of all education. . . .

2. *Literary Instruction.* To make an exact enumeration of the branches of literature, which might be taught, would be impossible, unless the time of the pupils' continuance at the seminar, and the requisites for entrance, were previously fixed. Such an enumeration would be tedious, nor do I conceive that it would be at all promotive of my object. The difficulty complained of, is not, that we are at a loss what sciences we ought to learn, but that we have not proper advantages to learn any. Many writers have given us excellent advice with regard to what we should be taught, but no legislature has provided us the means of instruction. Not however,

---

*Willard, Emma. *A Plan for Improving Female Education.* [Vermont?]: The Author, 1819. Reprinted in Goodsell, Willystine (ed.). *Pioneers of Women's Education in the United States.* New York: AMS Press, 1931, pp. 59-79.

to pass lightly over this fundamental part of education, I will mention one or two of the less obvious branches of science, which, I conceive should engage the youthful attention of my sex.

It is highly important, that females should be conversant with those studies, which will lead them to understand the operations of the human mind. The chief use to which the philosophy of the mind can be applied, is to regulate education by its rules. The ductile mind of the child is intrusted to the mother: and she ought to have every possible assistance, in acquiring a knowledge of this noble material, on which it is her business to operate, that she may best understand how to mould it to its most excellent form.

Natural philosophy has not often been taught to our sex. Yet why should we be kept in ignorance of the great machinery of nature, and left to the vulgar notion, that nothing is curious but what deviates from her common course? If mothers were acquainted with this science, they would communicate very many of its principles to their children in early youth. . . . A knowledge of natural philosophy is calculated to heighten the moral taste, by bringing to view the majesty and beauty of order and design; and to enliven piety, by enabling the mind more clearly to perceive, throughout the manifold works of God, that wisdom, in which he hath made them all. . . .

3. *Domestic instruction* should be considered important in a female seminary. It is the duty of our sex to regulate the internal concerns of every family; and unless they be properly qualified to discharge this duty, whatever may be their literary or ornamental attainments, they cannot be expected to make either good wives, good mothers, or good mistresses of families: and if they are none of these, they must be bad members of society; for it is by promoting or destroying the comfort and prosperity of their own families, that females serve or injure the community. To superintend the domestic department, there should be a respectable lady, experienced in the best methods of house-wifery, and acquainted with propriety of dress and manners. Under her tuition the pupils ought to be placed for a certain length of time every morning. A spirit of neatness and order should here be treated as a virtue, and the contrary, if excessive and incorrigible, be punished with expulsion. There might be a gradation of employment in the domestic department, according to the length of time the pupils had remained at the institution. The older scholars might then assist the superintendent in instructing the younger, and the whole be so arranged, that each pupil might have advantages to become a good domestic manager by the time she has completed her studies.

This plan would afford a healthy exercise. It would prevent that estrangement from domestic duties, which would be likely to take place in a length of time devoted to study, with those, to whom they were previously familiar; and would accustom those to them, who, from ignorance, might otherwise put at hazard their own happiness, and the prosperity of their families.

These objects might doubtless be effected by a scheme of domestic instruction; and probably others of no inconsiderable importance. It is believed, that housewifery might be greatly improved, by being taught, not only in practice, but in theory. Why may it not be reduced to a system, as well as other arts? There are right ways of performing its various operations; and there are reasons why those ways are right; and why may not rules be formed, their reasons collected; and the whole be digested into a system to guide the learner's practice?

It is obvious, that theory alone, can never make a good artist; and it is equally obvious, that practice unaided by theory, can never correct errors, but must establish them. . . .

In the present state of things, it is not to be expected, that any material improvements in housewifery should be made. There being no uniformity of method, prevailing among different housewives, of course, the communications from one to another, are not much more likely to improve the art, than a communication, between two mechanics of different trades, would be, to improve each in his respective occupation. But should a system of principles be philosophically arranged, and taught, both in theory and by practice, to a large number of females, whose minds were expanded and strengthened by a course of literary instruction, those among them, of an investigating turn, would, when they commenced housekeepers, consider their domestic operations as a series of experiments, which either proved or refuted the system previously taught. They would then converse together like those, who practice a common art, and improve each other by their observations and experiments; and they would also be capable of improving the system, by detecting its errors, and by making additions of new principles and better modes of practice.

4. The *Ornamental* branches, which I should recommend for a female seminary, are drawing and painting, elegant penmanship, music, and the grace of motion. Needle-work is not here mentioned. The best style of useful needle-work should either be taught in the domestic department, or made a qualification for entrance; and I consider that useful, which may contribute to the decoration of a lady's person, or the convenience and neatness of her family.

But the use of the needle, for other purposes than these, as it affords little to assist in the formation of the character, I should regard as a waste of time.

The grace of motion, must be learnt chiefly from instruction in dancing. Other advantages besides that of a graceful carriage, might be derived from such instruction, if the lessons were judiciously timed. Exercise is needful to the health, and recreation to the cheerfulness and contentment of youth. Female youth could not be allowed to range unrestrained, to seek amusement for themselves. If it was entirely prohibited, they would be driven to seek it by stealth; which would lead them to many improprieties of conduct, and would have a pernicious effect upon their general character, by inducing a habit of treading forbidden paths. The alternative that remains is to provide them with proper recreation, which, after the confinement of the day, they might enjoy under the eye of their instructors. Dancing is exactly suited to this purpose, as also to that of exercise; for perhaps in no way, can so much healthy exercise be taken in so short of time. It has besides, this advantage over other amusements, that it affords nothing to excite the bad passions; but, on the contrary, its effects are, to soften the mind, to banish its animosities and to open it to social impressions.

It has been doubted, whether painting and music should be taught to young ladies, because much time is requisite to bring them to any considerable degree of perfection, and they are not immediately useful. Though these objections have weight, yet they are founded on too limited a view of the objects of education. They leave out the important consideration of forming the character. I should not consider it an essential point, that the music of a lady's piano should rival that of her master's; or that her drawing room should be decorated with her own paintings, rather than those of others; but it is the intrinsic advantage, which she might derive from the refinement of herself, that would induce me to recommend to her, an attention to these elegant pursuits. The harmony of sound, has a tendency to produce a correspondent harmony of soul; and that art, which obliges us to study nature, in order to imitate her, often enkindles the latent spark of taste—of sensibility for her beauties, till it glows to adoration for their author, and a refined love of all his works.

5. There would be needed, for a female, as well as for a male seminary, a system of laws and regulations, so arranged, that both the instructors and pupils would know their duty; and thus, the whole business, move with regularity and uniformity.

The laws of the institution would be chiefly directed, to

regulate the pupil's qualifications for entrance, the kind and order of their studies, their behaviour while at the institution, the term allotted for the completion of their studies, the punishments to be inflicted on offenders, and the rewards or honours, to be bestowed on the virtuous and diligent.

The direct rewards or honors, used to stimulate the ambition of students in colleges, are first, the certificate or diploma, which each receives, who passes successfully through the term allotted to his collegiate studies; and secondly, the appointments to perform certain parts in public exhibitions, which are bestowed by the faculty, as rewards for superior scholarship. The first of these modes is admissible into a female seminary; the second is not; as public speaking forms no part of female education. The want of this mode, might, however, be supplied by examinations judiciously conducted. The leisure and inclination of both instructors and scholars, would combine to produce a thorough preparation for these; for neither would have any other public test of the success of their labors. Persons of both sexes would attend. The less entertaining parts, might be enlivened by interludes, where the pupils in painting and music, would display their several improvements. Such examinations, would stimulate the instructors to give their scholars more attention, by which the leading facts and principles of their studies, would be more clearly understood, and better remembered. The ambition excited among the pupils, would operate, without placing the instructors under the necessity of making distinctions among them, which are so apt to be considered as invidious: and which are, in our male seminaries, such fruitful sources of disaffection.

Perhaps the term allotted for the routine of study at the seminary, might be three years. The pupils, probably, would not be fitted to enter, till about the age of fourteen. Whether they attended to all, or any of the ornamental branches, should be left optional with the parents or guardians. Those who were to be instructed in them, should be entered for a longer term, but if this was a subject of previous calculation, no confusion would arise from it. The routine of the exercises being established by the laws of the institution, would be uniform, and publicly known; and those, who were previously acquainted with the branches first taught, might enter the higher classes; nor would those who entered the lowest, be obliged to remain during the three years. Thus the term of remaining at the institution, might be either one, two, three, four, or more years; and that, without interfering with the regularity and uniformity of its proceedings.

The writer has now given a sketch of her plan. She has by no means expressed all the ideas, which occurred to her concerning it. She wished to be as concise as possible, and yet afford conviction, that it is practicable, to organize a system of female education, which shall possess the permanency, uniformity of operation, and respectability of our male institutions; and yet differ from them, so as to be adapted, to that difference of character, and duties, to which early instruction should·form the softer sex.

It now remains, to enquire more particularly, what would be the benefits resulting from such a system.

Benefits of Female Seminaries

In inquiring, concerning the benefits of the plan proposed, I shall proceed upon the supposition, that female seminaries will be patronized throughout our country.

Nor is this altogether a visionary supposition. If one seminary should be well organized, its advantages would be found so great, that others would soon be instituted; and, that sufficient patronage can be found to put one in operation, may be presumed from its reasonableness, and from the public opinion, with regard to the present mode of female education. It is from an intimate acquaintance, with those parts of our country, whose education is said to flourish most, that the writer has drawn her picture of the present state of female instruction; and she knows, that she is not alone, in perceiving or deploring its faults. Her sentiments are shared by many an enlightened parent of a daughter, who has received a boarding school education. Counting on the promise of her childhood, the father had anticipated her maturity, as combining what is excellent in mind, with what is elegant in manners. He spared no expense that education might realize to him, the image of his imagination. His daughter returned from boarding school, improved in fashionable airs, and expert in manufacturing fashionable toys; but, in her conversation, he sought in vain, for that refined and fertile mind, which he had fondly expected. Aware that his disappointment has its source in a defective education, he looks with anxiety on his other daughters, whose minds, like lovely buds, are beginning to open. Where shall he find a genial soil, in which he may place them to expand? Shall he provide them male instructors? —Then the graces of their persons and manners, and whatever forms the distinguishing charm of the feminine character, they cannot be expected to acquire.—Shall he give them a private tutoress? She will have been educated at the boarding school, and

his daughters will have the faults of its instruction second-handed.
Such is now the dilemma of many parents; and it is one, from which they cannot be extricated by their individual exertions. May not then the only plan, which promises to relieve them, expect their vigorous support.

Let us now proceed to inquire, what benefits would result from the establishment of female seminaries.

They would constitute a grade of public education, superior to any yet known in the history of our sex; and through them, the lower grades of female instruction might be controlled. The influence of public seminaries, over these, would operate in two ways; first, by requiring certain qualifications for entrance; and secondly, by furnishing instructresses, initiated in their modes of teaching, and imbued with their maxims.

Female seminaries might be expected to have important and happy effects, on common schools in general; and in the manner of operating on these, would probably place the business of teaching children, in hands now nearly useless to society; and take it from those, whose services the state wants in many other ways.

That nature designed for our sex the care of children, she has made manifest, by mental, as well as physical indications. She has given us, in a greater degree than men, the gentle arts of insinuation, to soften their minds, and fit them to receive impressions; a greater quickness of invention to vary modes of teaching to different dispositions; and more patience to make repeated efforts. There are many females of ability, to whom the business of instructing children is highly acceptable, and who would devote all their faculties to their occupation. They would have no higher pecuniary object to engage their attention, and their reputation as instructors they would consider as important; whereas, whenever able and enterprising men, engage in this business, they consider it, merely as a temporary employment, to further some other object, to the attainment of which, their best thoughts and calculations are all directed. If then women were properly fitted by instruction, they would be likely to teach children better than the other sex; they could afford to do it cheaper; and those men who would otherwise be engaged in this employment, might be at liberty to add to the wealth of the nation, by any of those thousand occupations, from which women are necessarily debarred.

But the females, who taught children, would have been themselves instructed either immediately or indirectly by the seminaries. Hence through these, the government might exercise an intimate, and most beneficial control over common schools. Any one, who has turned his attention to this subject, must be aware, that there is great room for improvement in these, both as to the modes of teaching, and the things taught; and what method could be devised so likely to effect this improvement, as to prepare by instruction, a class of individuals, whose interest, leisure, and natural talents, would combine to make them pursue it with ardour. Such a class of individuals would be raised up, by female seminaries. And therefore they would be likely to have highly important and happy effects on common schools.

It is believed, that such institutions, would tend to prolong, or perpetuate our excellent government.

An opinion too generally prevails, that our present form of government, though good, cannot be permanent. Other republics have failed, and the historian and philosopher have told us, that nations are like individuals; that, at their birth, they receive the seeds of their decline and dissolution. Here deceived by a false analogy, we receive an apt illustration of particular facts, for a general truth. The existence of nations, cannot, in strictness, be compared with the duration of animate life; for by the operation of physical causes, this, after a certain length of time, must cease; but the existence of nations, is prolonged by the succession of one generation to another, and there is no physical cause, to prevent this succession's going on, in a peaceable manner, under a good government, till the end of time. We must then look to other causes, than necessity, for the decline and fall of former republics. If we could discover these causes, and reasonably prevent their operation, then might our latest posterity enjoy the same happy government, with which we are blessed; or if but in part, then might the triumph of tyranny, be delayed, and a few more generations be free.

Permit me then to ask the enlightened politician of my country, whether amidst his researches for these causes, he cannot discover one, in the neglect, which free governments, in common with others, have shown, to whatever regarded the formation of the female character.

In those great republics, which have fallen of themselves, the loss of republican manners and virtues, has been the invariable precursor, of their loss of the republican form of government. But is it not in the power of our sex, to give society its tone, both as to manners and morals? And if such is the extent of female influence, is it wonderful, that republics have failed, when they calmly suffered that influence, to become enlisted in favour of luxuries and follies, wholly incompatible with the existence of freedom?

It may be said, that the depravation of morals and manners,

can be traced to the introduction of wealth, as its cause. But wealth will be introduced; even the iron laws of Lycurgus could not prevent it. Let us then inquire, if means may not be devised, to prevent its bringing with it the destruction of public virtue. May not these means be found in education?—in implanting, in early youth, habits, that may counteract the temptations, to which, through the influence of wealth, mature age will be exposed? and in giving strength and expansion to the mind, that it may comprehend, and prize those principles, which teach the rigid performance of duty? Education, it may be said, has been tried as a preservative of national purity. But was it applied to every exposed part of the body politic? For if any part has been left within the pestilential atmosphere of wealth, without this preservative, then that part becoming corrupted, would communicate the contagion to the whole; and if so, then has the experiment, whether education may not preserve public virtue, never yet been fairly tried. Such a part has been left in all former experiments. Females have been exposed to the contagion of wealth without the preservative of a good education; and they constitute that part of the body politic, least endowed by nature to resist, most to communicate it. Nay, not merely have they been left without the defence of a good education, but their corruption has been accelerated by a bad one. The character of women of rank and wealth has been, and in the old governments of Europe now is, all that this statement would lead us to expect. Not content with doing nothing to promote their country's welfare, like pampered children, they revel in its prosperity, and scatter it to the winds, with a wanton profusion: and still worse,—they empoison its source, by diffusing a contempt for useful labour. To court pleasure their business,—within her temple, in defiance of the laws of God and man, they have erected the idol fashion; and upon her altar, they sacrifice, with shameless rites, whatever is sacred to virtue or religion.

* * *

But while, with an anguished heart, I thus depict the crimes of my sex, let not the other stand by and smile. Reason declares, that you are guiltier than we. You are our natural guardians,—our brothers,—our fathers, and our rulers. You know that our ductile minds, readily take the impressions of education. Why then have you neglected our education? Why have you looked with lethargic indifference, on circumstances ruinous to the formation of our characters, which you might have controlled?

But it may be said, the observations here made, cannot be applied to any class of females in our country. True, they cannot yet; and if they could, it would be useless to make them; for when the females of any country have become thus debased, then, is that country so corrupted, that nothing, but the awful judgments of heaven, can arrest its career of vice. But it cannot be denied, that our manners are verging towards those described; and the change, though gradual, has not been slow: already do our daughters listen with surprise, when we tell them of the republican simplicity of our mothers. But our manners are not as yet so altered, but that, throughout our country, they are still marked with republican virtues.

The inquiry, to which these remarks have conducted us is this —What is offered by the plan of female education, here proposed, which may teach, or preserve among females of wealthy families, that purity of manners, which is allowed, to be so essential to national prosperity, and so necessary to the existence of a republican government.

1. Females, by having their understandings cultivated, their reasoning powers developed and strengthened, may be expected to act more from the dictates of reason, and less from those of fashion and caprice.

2. With minds thus strengthened so they would be taught systems of morality, enforced by the sanctions of religion; and they might be expected to acquire juster and more enlarged views of their duty, and stronger and higher motives to its performance.

3. This plan of education, offers all that can be done to preserve female youth from a contempt of useful labour. The pupils would become accustomed to it, in conjunction with the high objects of literature, and the elegant pursuits of the fine arts; and it is to be hoped, that both from habit and association, they might in future life, regard it as respectable.

To this it may be added, that if housewifery could be raised to a regular art, and taught upon philosophical principles, it would become a higher and more interesting occupation; and ladies of fortune, like wealthy agriculturalists, might find, that to regulate their business, was an agreeable employment.

4. The pupils might be expected to acquire a taste for moral and intellectual pleasures, which would buoy them above a passion for show and parade, and which would make them seek to gratify the natural love of superiority, by endeavoring to excel others in intrinsic merit, rather than in the extrinsic frivolities of dress, furniture, and equipage.

5. By being enlightened in moral philosophy, and in that, which teaches the operations of the mind, females would be enabled to perceive the nature and extent, of that influence, which they possess over their children and the obligation, which this lays them under, to watch the formation of their characters with unceasing vigilance, to become their instructors, to devise plans for their improvement, to weed out the vices from their minds, and to implant and foster the virtues. . . .

Thus, laudable objects and employments, would be furnished for the great body of females, who are not kept by poverty from excesses. But among these, as among the other sex, will be found master spirits, who must have pre-eminence, at whatever price they acquire it. Domestic life cannot hold these, because they prefer to be infamous, rather than obscure. To leave such without any virtuous road to eminence, is unsafe to community; for not unfrequently, are the secret springs of revolution, set in motion by their intrigues. Such aspiring minds, we will regulate by education, we will remove obstructions to the course of literature, which has heretofore been their only honorable way to distinction; and we offer them a new object worthy of their ambition; to govern, and improve the seminaries for their sex.

LYDIA SIGOURNEY (1791–1865)

Having the advantage of belonging to a family of wealth and culture, Sigourney was provided a traditional education which included Latin and Greek. This background enabled her to open a select school for young ladies in her home town of Norwich, Connecticut. After four years, she moved to Hartford where she opened another successful school for girls. The 1819 closing of her fashionable school had a fortunate consequence—it created a need for Catharine Beecher to open a school.

Although marriage brought an end to Sigourney's teaching career, it did not prevent her from continuing to write prose and poetry. A prolific writer, she wrote nearly sixty volumes and in excess of two thousand articles. Moreover, her marriage and writing did not deter her from performing philanthropic work that earned community respect.

One letter has been selected from her interesting, lengthy volume *Letters to Young Ladies* (1833).

ADDRESS TO THE GUARDIANS OF FEMALE EDUCATION*

In preparing "Letters to Young Ladies," some reflections have arisen, which claim the attention of the guardians of their education —of those who either prescribe its limits, conduct its details, or rule the mighty engine of publick opinion. They are offered without apology, since the subject of education is now considered worthy to dictate the studies of the sage, the plans of the political economist, and the labours of the patriot. "The mind of the present age acting on the mind of the next," as it has been happily defined by a living writer, is an object of concern to every being endowed with intellect, or interest either through love or hope, in another generation.

*Sigourney, Mrs. L.H. *Letters to Young Ladies.* 3rd ed. New York: Harper & Brothers, 1837, pp. 9-16.

Nor has the importance of education in the abstract, been alone conceded. Practical researches for its improvement, signalized our age and incorporated themselves with its vigorous and advancing spirit. Our most gifted minds have toiled to devise methods for the instruction of the humblest grades of community, and to make useful knowledge the guest of the common people.

In this elevation of the intellectual standard, our sex have been permitted freely to participate. No Moslem interdict continues to exclude them from the temple of knowledge, and no illusion of chivalry exalts them to an airy height, above life's duties, and its substantial joys.

We are grateful for our heightened privileges. We hope that those who have bestowed them, will be no losers by their liberality. Still we believe that an increase of benefits may be made profitable both to giver, and receiver. We solicit them in the name of the blooming and the beautiful—those rose-buds in the wreath of our country's hope.

It is desirable that their education should be diffused over a wider space of time, and one less encumbered by extraneous objects, and that the depth of its foundation should be more correctly proportioned to the imposing aspect, and redundant ornament of its superstructure. Is it not important that the sex to whom Nature has intrusted the moulding of the whole mass of mind in its first formation, should be more correctly proportioned to the imposing aspect, and redundant ornament of its super-structure? Is it not important that the sex to whom Nature has intrusted the moulding of the whole mass of mind in its first formation, should be acquainted with the structure and developments of mind?—that they who are to nurture the future rulers of a prosperous people, should be able to demonstrate from the broad annal of history, the value of just laws, and the duty of subordination—the blessings which they inherit, and the danger of their abuse? Is it not requisite, that they on whose bosom the infant heart must be cherished, should be vigilant to watch its earliest pulsations of good or evil?—that they who are commissioned to light the lamp of the soul, should know how to feed it with pure oil?—that they in whose hand is the welfare of beings never to die, should be fitted to perform the work, and earn the plaudit of Heaven?

That the vocation of females is to teach, has been laid down as a position, which it is impossible to contravert. In seminaries, academies and schools, they possess peculiar facilities for coming in contact with the unfolding and unformed mind. It is true, that only a small proportion are engaged in the departments of publick and systematick instruction. Yet the hearing of recitations, and the routine of scholastick discipline, are but parts of education. It is in the domestick sphere, in her own native province, that woman is inevitably a teacher. There she modifies by her example, her dependants, her companions, every dweller under her own roof. Is not the infant in its cradle, her pupil? Does not her smile give the earliest lesson to its soul? Is not her prayer the first messenger for it in the court of Heaven? Does she not enshrine her own image in the sanctuary of the young child's mind, so firmly that no revulsion can displace, no idolatry supplant it? Does she not guide the daughter, until placing her hand in that of her husband, she reaches that pedestal, from whence, in her turn, she imparts to others, the stamp and colouring which she has herself received? Might she not, even upon her sons, engrave what they shall take unchanged through all the temptations of time, to the bar of the last judgment? Does not the influence of woman rest upon every member of her household, like the dew upon the tender herb, or the sunbeam silently educating the young flower? or as the shower, and the sleepless stream, cheer and invigorate the proudest tree of the forest?

Admitting then, that whether she wills it or not, whether she even knows it or not, she is still a teacher—and perceiving that the mind in its most plastick state is yielded to her tutelage, it becomes a most momentous inquiry what she shall be qualified to teach. Will she not of necessity impart what she most prizes, and best understands? Has she not power to impress her own lineaments on the next generation? If wisdom and utility have been the objects of her choice, society will surely reap the benefit. If folly and self-indulgence are her prevailing characteristicks, posterity are in danger of inheriting the likeness.

This influence is most visible and operative in a republick. The intelligence and virtue of its every citizen have a heightened relative value.—Its safety may be interwoven with the destiny of those, whose birthplace is in obscurity. The springs of its vitality are liable to be touched, or the chords of its harmony to be troubled, by the rudest hands.

Teachers under such form of government should be held in the highest honour. They are the allies of legislators. They have agency in the prevention of crime. They aid in regulating the atmosphere, whose incessant action and pressure causes the life-blood to circulate, and return pure and healthful to the heart of the nation.

Of what unspeakable importance then, is *her* education, who gives lessons before any other instructor—who pre-occupies the unwritten page of being—who produces impressions which only death can obliterate—and mingles with the cradle-dream what shall be read in Eternity. Well may statesmen and philosophers debate how *she* may be best educated, who is to educate all mankind.

The ancient republicks overlooked the value of that sex, whose strength is in the heart. Greece, so susceptible to the principle of beauty, so skilled in wielding all the elements of grace, failed in appreciating their excellence, whom these had most exquisitely adorned. If, in the brief season of youthful charm, she was constrained to admire woman as the acanthus-leaf of her own Corinthian capital, she did not discover that, like that very column, she was capable of adding stability to the proud temple of freedom. She would not be convinced that so feeble a hand might have aided to consolidate the fabrick, which philosophy embellished, and luxury overthrew.

Rome, notwithstanding her primeval rudeness, seems more correctly than polished Greece, to have estimated the "weaker vessel." Here and there, upon the storm-driven billows of her history, some solitary form towers upward in majesty, and the mother of the Gracchi still stands forth in strong relief, amid imagery over which time has no power. But still, wherever the brute force of the warrior is counted godlike, woman is appreciated only as she approximates to sterner natures: as in that mysterious image which troubled the sleep of Assyria's king—the foot of clay derived consistence from the iron, which held it in combination.

In our own republick, man, invested by his Maker with the right to reign, has conceded to her, who was for ages in vassalage, equality of intercourse, participation in knowledge, dominion over his dearest and fondest hopes. He is content to "bear the burden and heat of the day," that she may dwell in ease and affluence. Yet, from the very felicity of her lot, dangers are generated. She is tempted to be satisfied with superficial attainments, or to indulge in that indolence which corrodes intellect, and merges the high sense of responsibility in its alluring and fatal slumbers.

These tendencies should be neutralized by a thorough and laborious education. Sloth and luxury must have no place in her vocabulary. Her youth should be surrounded by every motive to application, and her maturity dignified by the hallowed office of rearing the immortal mind. While her partner toils for his stormy portion of that power or glory, from which it is her privilege to be sheltered, let her feel that in the recesses of domestick privacy, she still renders a noble service to the government that protects her, by sowing seeds of purity and peace in the hearts of those, who shall hereafter claim its honours, or control its destinies.

Her place is amid the quiet shades, to watch the little fountain ere it has breathed a murmur. But the fountain will break forth into a rill, and the swollen rivulet rush towards the sea;—and who can be so well able to guide them in right channels, as she who heard their first ripple, and saw them emerge like timid strangers from their source, and had kingly power over those infantwaters, in the name of Him who caused them to flow.

And now, Guardians of Education, whether parents, preceptors, or legislators—you who have so generously lavished on woman the means of knowledge—complete your bounty, by urging her to gather its treasures with a tireless hand. Demand of her as a debt, the highest excellence which she is capable of attaining. Summon her to abandon selfish motives, and inglorious ease. Incite her to those virtues which promote the permanence and health of nations. Make her accountable for the character of the next generation. Give her solemn charge, in the presence of men and of angels. Gird her with the whole armour of education and of piety— and see if she be not faithful to her children, to her country, and to her God.

CATHARINE BEECHER (1800-1878)

Beecher did not share Emma Willard's early intense love of intellectual subjects; rather, she enjoyed such performance skills as dramatics, painting and drawing. Her father was the eminent clergyman, Lyman Beecher, who tutored each of his many children. Catharine, the eldest, continued her formal education at Miss Pierce's highly regarded Litchfield School.

The death of her fiancé prompted Beecher to seek a way to serve mankind; she chose the profession of teaching as a means to fulfill her goal. In 1822 she founded a seminary for girls in Hartford, then established three schools in the West, among them the successful Milwaukee, Wisconsin, academy which was to become Milwaukee-Downer College.

Recognizing the growing need for teachers, Beecher encouraged women to enter the profession; however, she cautioned that, with the sole exception of the classroom, a woman's place was in the home. She founded "The American Woman's Education Association" to improve the quality of teaching.

Aware that writing was another avenue for improving the educational lot of women, Beecher wrote extensively on the subject of pedagogy. A brief excerpt follows from "Essay on the Education of Female Teachers," which she read in 1835 at the annual meeting of the American Lyceum.

"ESSAY ON THE EDUCATION OF FEMALE TEACHERS"*

The topic proposed for consideration in this essay cannot properly be presented, without previously adverting to certain

---

*Beecher, Catharine. "Essay on the Education of Female Teachers," Paper read at the annual meeting of the American Lyceum, 1835. Reprinted in Goodsell, Willystine (ed.). *Pioneers of Women's Education in the United States.* New York: AMS Press, 1931, pp. 168-187.

difficulties in regard to female education; and, in the same connection, suggesting the most practicable methods of securing their remedy.

One of the first objects that need to be attempted in regard to female education, is to secure some method of rendering female institutions permanent in their existence, and efficient in perpetuating a regular and systematic course of education. This is secured for the other sex, by institutions so endowed that the death or removal of an individual does not hazard their existence or character. They continue year after year, and sometimes for ages, maintaining the same system of laws, government, and course of study. But in regard to female institutions, every thing is ephemeral; because, in most cases, every thing depends upon the character and enterprise of a single individual. A school may be at the height of prosperity one week, and the next week entirely extinct. Communities seem almost entirely dependent upon chance, both for the character and the perpetuity of schools. If good teachers stray into their bounds, they are fortunate; if poor ones, they have no remedy. Thus the character, the conduct, and the continuance of those who are so extensively to mould the character of the future wives and mothers of this nation, are almost entirely removed from the control of those most deeply interested.

One method which tends to remedy this evil is, the investment of property in buildings, furniture, and apparatus devoted to this object, under the care of a suitable corporate body. It thus becomes the business of certain responsible men, that the property thus invested shall secure the object for which it has been bestowed. But this method alone will not avail, for though the probabilities are greater that endowed institutions will be well sustained, it is often found that they do fail in securing a systematic and perpetuated plan of education. There needs to be added a well devised plan of government and course of study, together with that division of labor existing in colleges, which secures several able instructors to the same institution, and in such a way that the removal of any one teacher does not interrupt the regular system of the institution.

That this can be accomplished in regard to female seminaries, as well as those for the other sex, is no longer problematical, for it has already been done; and what has been, can be done again. One female institution, at least, can be referred to, in which a regular system of government and instruction has been carried on for a course of years, until an adequate number of teachers and pupils has been fitted to perpetuate the system, so that as one teacher after another was called away, others were prepared to take their places;

and thus the whole number of teachers, from the principal and the lowest monitor, has been repeatedly changed, and yet the same system and course of study have been preserved; while there is as fair a prospect of future perpetuity as is afforded by most of our colleges.

Another object to be aimed at in regard to female education is, a remedy for the desultory, irregular, and very superficial course of education now so common in all parts of our country. When young men are sent to obtain a good education, there is some standard for judging of their attainments; there are some data for determining what has been accomplished. But, in regard to females, they are sent first to one school, and then to another; they attend a short time to one set of studies, and then to another; while everything is desultory, unsystematic, and superficial. Their course of study is varied to suit the nations of parents, or the whims of children, or the convenience of teachers; and if a young lady secures a regular and thorough course of education, it is owing either to the uncommonly good sense and efforts of parents, or to the rare occurrence of finding teachers sufficiently stationary and persevering to effect it.

The remedy for this evil (in addition to what is suggested in previous remarks) is to be sought in cooperating efforts among the leading female schools in the country, to establish a uniform course of education, adapted to the character and circumstances of females, to correspond with what is done in colleges for young gentlemen. The propriety of giving titles of honor to distinguished females who complete such a course, may well be questioned. It certainly is in very bad taste, and would provoke needless ridicule and painful notoriety. But if leading female institutions combine to establish a regular course of study, which is appropriate and complete, it will prove an honor and advantage to young ladies to have it known that their education is thus secured; and it will also prove an advantage to the schools that thus gain the reputation of sending out uniformly well educated pupils. Other schools will gradually adopt the same plan; and thus the evils alluded to will, to a great extent, be remedied. These measures will have the same effect on female education, as medical and theological schools have upon those professions. They tend to elevate and purify, although they cannot succeed in banishing all stupidity and empiricism.

Another object to be aimed at in regard to female education is, to introduce into schools such a course of intellectual and moral discipline, and such attention to mental and personal habits, as shall have a decided influence in fitting a woman for her peculiar duties. What is the most important and peculiar duty of the female sex? It is the physical, intellectual, and moral education of children. It is the care of health, and the formation of the character, of the future citizen of this great nation.

Woman, whatever are her relations in life, is necessarily the guardian of the nursery, the companion of childhood, and the constant model of imitation. It is her hand that first stamps impressions on the immortal spirit, that must remain forever. And what demands such discretion, such energy, such patience, such tenderness, love, and wisdom, such perspicacity to discern, such versatility to modify, such efficiency to execute, such firmness to persevere, as the government and education of all the various characters and the tempers that meet in the nursery and school-room? Woman also is the presiding genius who must regulate all those thousand minutiae of domestic business, that demand habits of industry, order, neatness, punctuality, and constant care. And it is for varied duties that woman is to be trained. For this her warm sympathies, her lively imagination, her ready invention, her quick perceptions, all need to be cherished and improved; while at the same time those more foreign habits, of patient attention, calm judgment, steady efficiency, and habitual self-control, must be induced and sustained.

Is a weak, undisciplined, unregulated mind, fitted to encounter the responsibility, weariness, and watching of the nursery; to bear the incessant care and perplexity of governing young children; to accommodate with kindness and patience to the peculiarities and frailties of a husband; to control the indolence, waywardness, and neglect of servants; and to regulate all the variety of domestic cares? The superficial accomplishments of former periods were of little avail to fit a woman for such arduous duties; and for this reason it is, that as society has been advanced in all other improvements, the course of female education has been gradually changing, and some portion of that mental discipline, once exclusively reserved for the other sex, is beginning to exert its invigorating influence upon the female character. At the same time the taste of the age is altered; and, instead of the fainting, weeping, vapid, pretty play-thing, once the model of female loveliness, those qualities of the head and heart that best qualify a woman for her duties, are demanded and admired.

None will deny the importance of having females properly fitted for their peculiar duties; and yet few are aware how much influence a teacher may exert in accomplishing this object. School is generally considered as a place where children are sent, not to form their habits, opinions, and character, but simply to learn from books. And yet, whatever may be the opinion of teachers and parents, children do, to a very great extent, form their character under influences bearing upon them at school. . . .

Nor is the course of study and mental discipline of inferior consequence. The mere committing to memory of the facts contained in books, is but a small portion of education. Certain portions of time should be devoted to fitting a woman for her practical duties; such, for example, as needlework. Other pursuits are designed for the cultivation of certain mental faculties, such as *attention, perseverance,* and *accuracy.* This for example, is the influence of the study of the mathematics; while the conversation and efforts of a teacher, directed to this end, may induce habits of investigation and correct reasoning, not to be secured by any other method. Other pursuits are designed to cultivate the taste and imagination: such as rhetoric, poetry, and other branches of polite literature. Some studies are fitted to form correct moral principles, and strengthen religious obligation: such as mental and moral philosophy, the study of the evidences of Christianity, the study of the Bible, and of collateral subjects. Other studies are designed to store the mind with useful knowledge: such for example, as geography, history, and the natural sciences. The proper selection and due proportion of these various pursuits, will have a decided influence in forming the mental habits and general character of the pupils.

Another important object in regard to female education is, the provision of suitable facilities for instruction, such as are deemed indispensable for the other sex, particularly apparatus and libraries.

While the branches now included in a course of education for females of the higher circles have increased, till nearly as much is attempted, as, were it properly taught, is demanded of young men at college, little has been done to secure a corresponding change, in regard to the necessary facilities to aid in instruction.

To teach young men properly in chemistry, natural philosophy, and other branches of science, it is deemed necessary to furnish a teacher for each separate branch, who must be prepared by a long previous course of study, who shall devote his exclusive attention to it, and who shall be furnished with apparatus at the expense of thousands of dollars; while, to aid both teachers and pupils, extensive libraries must be provided, and all at public expense.

But when the same branches are to be taught to females, one teacher is considered enough to teach a dozen such sciences, and that too without any apparatus, without any qualifying process, and without any library.

If females, are to have the same branches included in their education as the other sex, ought there not to be a corresponding change to provide the means for having them properly taught; or are our sex to be complimented with the intimation that a single teacher, without preparatory education, without apparatus, and without libraries, can teach young ladies what it requires half a dozen teachers, fitted by a long course of study and furnished with every facility of books and apparatus to teach young gentlemen? We certainly are not ambitious of such compliments to the intellectual superiority of our sex. It is true such extensive public endowments are not needed for females as for the other sex, because their progress in many of the sciences never needs to be so extensive; but, if these branches are to constitute a part of female education, is not *something* of this kind demanded from public munificence, that all be not left to the private purse of the teacher, who must furnish it from slender earnings, or remain unsupplied?

But the most important deficiency, and one which is equally felt by both sexes, is the want of a system of moral and religious education at school, which shall have a *decided influence* in forming the character, and regulating the principles and conduct, of future life. . . .

In regard to education, the world is now making experiments, such as were never made before. Man is demanding disenthralment, alike from physical force, and intellectual slavery; and, by a slow and secret process, one nation after another is advancing in a sure, though silent progress. Man is bursting the chains of slavery, and the bonds of intellectual subserviency; and is learning to think, and reason, and act for himself. And the great crisis is hastening on, when it shall be decided whether disenthralled intellect and liberty shall voluntarily submit to the laws of virtue and of Heaven, or run wild to insubordination, anarchy, and crime. The great questions pending before the world, are simply these: are liberty and intelligence, without the restraints of a moral and religious education, a blessing or a curse? Without moral and religious restraints, is it best for man to receive the gift of liberty and intelligence, or to remain coerced by physical force, and the restraints of opinions and customs not his own?

The master spirits of the age are watching the developments as they rise, and making their records for the instruction of mankind.

And what results are already gained? In England, the experiment has been made by the sceptical Brougham; and, at great expense, knowledge has gone forth with increasing liberty, and all who have witnessed the results are coming to the conviction, that increase of knowledge, without moral and religious influence, is only increase of vice and discontent. And what are the results of the experiment in France? The statistics of education show, that the best educated departments are the most vicious, and the most ignorant are the freest from crime. And, in that country, where the national representatives once declared that Christianity should be banished, and the Bible burnt, and the Sabbath annihilated, we now find its most distinguished statesmen and citizens uniting in the public declaration, that moral and religious education must be the foundation of national instruction. Victor Cousin, one of the most distinguished philosophers of the age, and appointed by the King of France to examine the various systems of education in Europe, has reported, as the result of his investigations, that education is a blessing, just in proportion as it is founded on moral and religious principles.

Look, again, at Prussia! with its liberal and patriotic monarch, with a system of education unequalled in the records of time, requiring by law that all the children in the nation be sent to school, from the first day they are seven years of age, till the last day they are fourteen, with a regular course of literary and scientific instruction, instituted for every school, and every teacher required to spend three years in preparing for such duties; while, on an average, one teacher is furnished for every ten pupils through the nation. The effects of merely intellectual culture soon convinced the monarch and his counsellors that moral and religious instruction must be the basis of all their efforts; and now the Bible is placed in every school, and every teacher is required to spend from one to two hours each day, in giving and enforcing instruction in all duties of man towards his Creator, towards constituted authorities, and towards his fellow-men.

And what is the experience of our own country? Those portions of the nation, most distinguished for the general diffusion of education, are those in which moral and religious influences have been most extensively introduced into schools, and have pervaded all the institutions of society. But, in those portions of our country the increase and jealousy of religious sects, and other combining causes, have had an influence in banishing the Bible, and moral and religious influence, more and more from public schools. And now we hear the widely extended complaint, that common schools are dangerous places for children while parents, who are most regardful of the moral influences exerted upon their children, are more and more withdrawing them from what they deem such contaminating influence.

Thus, in those parts of our country which have been most moral and intelligent, the education of the lower classes is deteriorating, as it respects moral and religious restraints, while the statistics of education, coming from other parts of the nation, are most appalling. We find that in one of our smallest middle states, thirty thousand adults and children are entirely without education and without schools. In one of the largest middle states, four hundred thousand adults and children are thus destitute. In one of the best educated western states, one-third of the children are without schools; while it appears, that, in the whole nation, there are a million and a half of children, and nearly as many adults, in the same deplorable ignorance, and without any means of instruction. At the same time, thousands and thousands of degraded foreigners and their ignorant families, are pouring into this nation at every avenue. All these ignorant native and foreign adults are now voters, and have a share in the government of the nation. All these million children, in a very few years, will take the same stand; while other millions, as ignorant and destitute are hastening in their rear. What is the end of these things to be; How long will it take, at this rate, for the majority of votes, and of the physical force of the nation, to be in the hands of ignorance and vice? That terrific crisis is now before us; and a few years will witness its consummation, unless such energetic and persevering efforts are made as time never saw.

Here, we have no despotic monarch to endow seminaries for teachers, and to send every child in the nation to school for seven successive years, to place a Bible in every school, and enforce a system of moral and religious instruction. It is the people who must voluntarily do it, or it will remain undone. Public sentiment must be aroused to a sense of danger; the wealthy and intelligent must pour out their treasures to endow seminaries for teachers; moral and religious education, and the best methods of governing and regulating the human mind, must become a science; those who have had most experience, and are best qualified in this department, must be called upon to contribute their experience and combined efforts, to qualify others for these duties; men of talent and piety must enter this as the noblest and most important missionary field; females who have time and talents, must be called to aid in the effort; seminaries for teachers, with their model schools, must be established in every state; agents must be employed to arouse and enlighten the people; and, when the people are sufficiently awake to the subject, legislative and national aid must be sought.

The object aimed at is one immense and difficult enough to demand the highest exercise of every energy and every mode of influence. If Prussia, with her dense population, finds one teacher for every ten children needful, the sparseness of population in our wide territories surely demands an equal supply. At this rate, *ninety thousand* teachers are this moment wanted to supply the destitute; and to these must be added every year *twelve thousand,* simply to meet the increase of population. But if we allow thirty pupils as the average number for every teacher, then we need *thirty thousand* teachers for present wants, and an annual addition of *four thousand* for increase of population. And yet, what has been done—what is now doing—to meet this enormous demand? While Prussia, for years, has been pouring out her well educated teachers from her forty-five seminaries, at the rate of one every ten pupils; while France is organizing her Normal schools in all her departments for the education of her teachers; what is done in America,—wealthy, intelligent, and free America,—whose very existence is depending on the virtuous education of her children? In New England, we hear of one solitary institution for the preparation of teachers; and, in New York, eight are just starting into being; and this is all! Now, at this moment, we need at least thirty thousand teachers, and four thousand every year in addition, just to supply the increase of youthful population. . . .

When we consider, the claims of the learned professions, the excitement and profits of commerce, manufactures, agriculture, and the arts; when we consider the aversion of most men to the sedentary, confining, and toilsome duties of teaching and governing young children; when we consider the scanty pittance that is allowed to the majority of teachers; and that few men will enter a business that will not support a family, when there are multitudes of other employments that will afford competence, and lead to wealth; it is chimerical to hope that the supply of such immense deficiencies in our national education is to come chiefly from that sex. It is woman, fitted by disposition, and habits, and circumstances, for such duties, who, to a very wide extent, must aid in educating the childhood and youth of this nation; and therefore it is, that females must be trained and educated for this employment. And, most happily, it is true, that the education necessary to fit a woman to be a teacher, is exactly the one that best fits her for that domestic relation she is primarily designed to fill.

But how is this vast undertaking to be accomplished? How can such a multitude of female teachers as are needed, be secured and fitted for such duties? The following will show how it *can* be done, if those most interested and obligated shall only *will* to have it done.

Men of patriotism and benevolence can commence by endowing two or three seminaries for female teachers in the most important stations in the nation, while to each of these seminaries shall be attached a model school, supported by the children of the place where it is located. In these seminaries can be collected those who have the highest estimate of the value of moral and religious influence, and the most talents and experience for both intellectual and moral education.

When these teachers shall have succeeded in training classes of teachers on the best system their united wisdom can devise, there will be instructors prepared for other seminaries for teachers to be organized and conducted on the same plan; and thus a regular and systematic course of education can be disseminated through the nation.

Meantime, proper efforts being made by means of the press, the pulpit, and influential men employed as agents for this object, the interest of the whole nation can be aroused, and every benevolent and every pious female in the nation, who has the time and qualifications necessary, can be enlisted to consecrate at least a certain number of years to this object. There is not a village in this nation that cannot furnish its one, two, three, or in some cases ten or even twenty, laborers for this field.

And, as a system of right moral and religious education gains its appropriate influence, as women are more and more educated to understand and value the importance of their influence in society, and their peculiar duties, more young females will pursue their education with the expectation that, unless paramount private duties forbid, they are to employ their time and talents in the duties of a teacher, until they assume the responsibilities of domestic life. Females will cease to feel that they are educated just to enjoy themselves in future life, and realize the obligations imposed by Heaven to live to do good. And, when females are educated as they ought to be, every woman at the close of her school education, will be well qualified to act as a teacher.

We need institutions endowed at public expense, and so constituted, that, while those who are able shall pay the full value of their privileges, those who have not the ability shall be furnished gratuitously with what they cannot purchase; while all who receive these advantages shall consider themselves pledged to devote themselves to the cause of education, and also to refund their expenses, whenever future earnings, or a change in their situation, will enable them to do it. And if men of wealth will furnish the means, if they will collect the talent and experience that are ready to engage in the enterprise, they will soon find multitudes of laborers hastening to the field. As things now are, few females of discretion and good sense would attempt, unaided, what their friends, and most of the community, would deem the Quixotic enterprise of preparing themselves to be teachers, and then set out to seek a situation in the destitute portions of our country. But let benevolent men unite in endowing institutions for those who are unprepared, and secure some organization of suitable persons, whose business it shall be to provide places for those who are prepared; let statistics of the wants of the country be sent abroad, and the cry go forth "Whom shall we send, and who will go for us?" and from amid the green hills and white villages of New England, hundreds of voices would respond, "Here am I, send me"; while kindred voices, through the whole length of the land, would echo the reply.

In behalf of such then it is, that the writer would address this intelligent and patriotic assembly, and through them the benevolent and philanthropic of the nation: Give us the opportunity of aiding to preserve the interests and institutions of our country. . . .

MARY LYON (1797-1849)

Mary Lyon's practical, frugal management of Mount Holyoke was a reflection of her childhood. Lyon's family was poor in material goods, but rich in its regard for learning. As a child, Lyon learned housekeeping, nursing, spinning, and sewing at home. She attended a district school, then, at the age of seventeen, an academy. Her social awkwardness and a lack of stylish clothing elicited peer ridicule; however, her friendliness quickly earned her respect even from those who had mocked her. Lyon attended the seminary operated by an outstanding teacher, Rev. Joseph Emerson, whose emphasis upon the study of prominent English authors instilled in Lyon a lifetime interest. Her studies at Emerson's seminary included philosophy, metaphysics, logic, theory, disputation, religious study, and diet. This constituted an unusually scholarly curriculum for women at that time.

Beginning as an informal teacher of children in homes where she boarded, Lyon devoted her adulthood to teaching. Her educational objective was to prepare students for practical aspects of future life, not to utilize a seminary as a "finishing" school. Specifically, she promoted the ideas of equivalent education for young men and women, non-denominational Christian schools, and education for girls who had little money. Keeping in mind this threefold goal, she raised contributions ranging from 6¢ to $1,000 to open Mount Holyoke Female Seminary in 1836 in South Hadley, Massachusetts. Her reputation as a teacher was such that she had to refuse entrance to four hundred girls the first year. The ensuing national demand for her alumnae was evidence that she had justified the faith the public had placed in her. The method of keeping tuition low by having students share in housekeeping chores was a unique facet of her seminary.

Letters and interviews solicited from seventy persons fifty years after her death are remarkable in their consistency in describing Mary Lyon as a teacher who set high academic

296

ideals, was loving but stern when necessary, took a personal interest in each student, was an eloquent speaker, and conducted inspirational morning Christian devotions. The letters extol her superb pedagogic skills and her missionary ardor.

The first of two reprinted excerpts is from an unpublished 1835 pamphlet in which Lyon defined the nature of the student and of the curriculum she intended for her seminary. The second, written two years later, is a detailed exposition of the nature and purpose of the recently opened Mount Holyoke Female Seminary.

UNPUBLISHED PAMPHLET*

It has been stated, that the literary standard of this Institution will be high. This is a very indefinite term. There is no acknowledged standard of female education, by which an institution can be measured. A long list of branches to be taught, can be no standard at all. For if so, a contemplated manual labor school to be established in one of the less improved of the western states, whose prospectus we chanced to notice some two or three years since, would stand higher than most of our New England colleges. Whether the institution was ever established we know not, nor do we remember its name or exact location. But the list of branches to be taught as they appeared on paper, we do remember, as for the time, it served as a happy illustration of a general principle, relating to some of our attempts to advance the cause of education among us. In a seminary for females, we cannot as in the standard of education for the other sex, refer to established institutions, whose course of study and standard of mental discipline are known to every literary man in the land. But it is believed, that our statement cannot be made more intelligible to the enlightened community, than by simply saying, that the course of study, and standard of mental culture will be the same as that of the Hartford Female Seminary—of the Ipswich Female Seminary—or of the Troy Female Seminary—or of some other institution that has stood as long, and ranked as high as these seminaries. Suffice it to say, that it is expected, that the Mount Holyoke Female Seminary will take the Ipswich Female Seminary for its literary standard. Of course there will be room for a continued advancement; as that institution

---

*Lyon, Mary. Unpublished pamphlet, 1835. Reprinted in Goodsell, Willystine (ed.). *Pioneers of Women's Education in the United States.* New York: AMS Press, 1931, pp. 246-266.

has been raising its own standard from year to year. But at the commencement, the standard is to be as high as the present standard of that seminary. It is to adopt the same high standard of mental discipline—the same slow, thorough, and patient manner of study; the same systematic and extensive course of solid branches. Though this explanation will not be universally understood, yet it is believed that it will be understood by a great many in New England, and by many out of New England—by those who have long been intimately acquainted with the character of that seminary, or who have witnessed its fruits in the lives of those whom it has sent forth to exert a power over society, which cannot be exerted by mere goodness, without intellectual strength. "By their fruits ye shall know them."

PRINCIPLES AND DESIGN OF THE MOUNT HOLYOKE FEMALE SEMINARY*

This institution is established at South Hadley, Massachusetts. It is to be principally devoted to the preparing of female teachers. At the same time, it will qualify ladies for other spheres of usefulness. The design is to give a solid, extensive, and well-balanced English education, connected with that general improvement, that moral culture, and those enlarged views of duty, which will prepare ladies to be educators of children and youth, rather than to fit them to be mere teachers, as the term has been technically applied. Such an education is needed by every female who takes the charge of a school, and sustains the responsibility of guiding the whole course and of forming the entire character of those committed to her care. And when she has done with the business of teaching in a regular school, she will not give up her profession; she will still need the same well-balanced education at the head of her own family and in guiding her own household.

1. This institution professes to be founded on the high principle of enlarged Christian benevolence. In its plans and in its appeals it seeks no support from local or private interest. It is designed entirely for the public good, and the trustees would adopt no measures not in accordance with this design. It is sacredly consecrated to the great Head of the church, and they would not seek for human approbation by any means which will not be well pleasing in his sight.

*Lyon, Mary. *Principles and Design of the Mount Holyoke Female Seminary,* 1837. Reprinted in Goodsell, Willystine (ed.). *Pioneers of Women's Education in the United States.* New York: AMS Press, 1931, pp. 278-303.

2. The institution is designed to be permanent. The permanency of an institution may be considered as consisting of two particulars—first, its perpetual vitality, and second, its continual prosperity and usefulness. The first is to be secured in the same manner that the principle of perpetual life in our higher institutions for young men has been so effectually preserved. A fund is to be committed to an independent, self-perpetuating board of trustees, known to the churches as faithful, responsible men; not as a proprietary investment, but as a free offering, leaving them no way for an honorable retreat from their trust, and binding them with solemn responsibilities to hundreds and thousands of donors, who have committed their sacred charities to their conscientious fidelity. Give to a literary institution, on this principle, an amount of property sufficient to be viewed as an object of great importance, and it is almost impossible to extinguish its vital life by means of adversity. How firmly have our colleges stood amidst the clashing elements around us, and the continual overturnings which are taking place in the midst of us!

The usefulness of this institution, like all others, must depend on its character. This may be very good for a time, where there is no principle of perpetual life, as is the case with some of our most distinguished female seminaries. Amidst all their prosperity, they have no solid foundation, and in themselves no sure principle of continued existence. Could we secure to our public institutions the continued labors of the same teachers through an antediluvial life, the preservation of the vital principle would be a subject of much less consequence. But in view of the present shortened life of man, rendered shorter still by disease and premature decay, and in view of the many changes which are ever breaking in upon the continued services of those to whose care these institutions are committed, every reflecting mind must regard it as of the very first importance to secure to them this principle, especially to a public seminary for the raising up of female teachers.

3. The institution is to be entirely for an older class of young ladies. The general system for family arrangements, for social improvement, for the division of time, for organizing and regulating the school, and the requirements for entrance, will be adapted throughout to young ladies of adult age and of mature character. Any provision in an institution like this for younger misses must be a public loss far greater than the individual good. Their exclusion from the institution will produce a state of society among the members exceedingly pleasant and profitable to those whose great desire is to be prepared to use all their talents in behalf

of the cause of education, and of the Redeemer's kingdom; and it will secure for their improvement the entire labors of the teachers, without an interruption from the care and government of pupils too immature to take care of themselves.

4. The young ladies are to take part in the domestic work of the family. This also is to be on the principle of equality. All are to take part, not as a servile labor, for which they are to receive a small weekly remuneration, but as a gratuitous service to the institution of which they are members, designed for its improvement and elevation. The first object of this arrangement is, to give to the institution a greater degree of independence. The arrangements for boarding all the pupils in the establishment will give to us an independence with regard to private families in the neighborhood, without which it would be difficult, if not impossible, to secure its perpetual prosperity. The arrangements for the domestic work will, in a great measure, relieve it from another source of depressing dependence—a dependence on the will of hired domestics, to which many a family in New England is subject.

The other object of this arrangement is to promote the health, the improvement, and the happiness of the pupils; their health, by its furnishing them with a little daily exercise of the best kind; their improvement, by its tending to preserve their interest in domestic pursuits; and their happiness, by its relieving them from that servile dependence on common domestics, to which young ladies, as mere boarders in a large establishment, are often subject, to their great inconvenience. The adoption of a feature like this, in an institution which aims to be better endowed than any other existing female seminary in the country, must give it an attitude of noble independence, which can scarcely fail to exert an elevating influence on its members.

This cause is the humble, but firm and efficient patron of all other branches of benevolence. What the present generation is beginning to accomplish for the salvation of the world it seeks to preserve and carry forward with increasing rapidity. Whatever of conquest is now gained it seeks to secure forever from the encroachments of the enemy. It seeks to lay the foundation strong, on which, under God, the temple with all its increasing weight, is to rise, and be sustained, and to secure it from injury and decay. It looks abroad on a world lying in wickedness. It beholds with painful interest the slow progress of these United States in carrying the blessings of salvation to the two hundred millions, who are the estimated proportion of the inhabitants of this benighted world to be converted to God through our instrumentality. And as it attempts in vain to calculate the time when the work shall be accomplished, it would fain increase its progress a hundred fold, by training up the children in the way they should go. It has endeavored to fix an eye on the distant point of futurity, when, according to a fair and reasonable computation, this nation, with all its increasing millions, and the inhabitants of the whole earth, shall be supplied with faithful, educated ministers of the gospel. And as it inquires in vain, "When shall these things be?" and as it attempts, in vain, to count up the millions on millions who shall go down to everlasting death before that time *can* arrive, it would fain strive, with unparalleled efforts, through the children of our country, greatly to multiply the numbers of ministers during the next generation, and to carry forward the work in an unexampled and increasing ratio through the generations which shall follow.

The object of this institution penetrates too far into futurity, and takes in too broad a view, to discover its claims to the passing multitude. We appeal in its behalf to wise men, who can judge what we say. We appeal to those who can venture as pioneers in the great work of renovating a world. Others may stand waiting for the great multitude to go forward, but then is the time when these men feel themselves called upon to make their greatest efforts, and to do their noblest deeds of benevolence. Thus we hope it will be on behalf of this institution.

We commend this enterprise to the continued prayers and efforts of its particular friends, of all those who have enlisted in its behalf, and have given of their time, their influence, and their substance. We would invite them to come with us around the same sacred altar, and there consecrate this beloved institution, as first fruits, to the Lord, to be devoted forever to his service.

This enterprise, thus far, has been under the care of a kind Providence. It has not been carried forward by might, nor by power; but in every step of its progress the good hand of God has been upon it. Let all its friends bring in the tithes and the offerings, and let them commit the disposing of the whole to Him who can accomplish the work which his own hands have commenced, and he will pour out upon this institution, and the cause with which it is connected, and upon the children and youth of our country, and of the world, a blessing, that there shall not be room enough to receive it.

The enterprise of founding this seminary was commenced nearly five years ago. More than three years were occupied in the preparing the way, in raising the funds, and in erecting the building now occupied. It was ready for the reception of scholars November 8, 1837.

The original plan was to provide for two hundred. Only the first building has yet been erected. This can accommodate only ninety. Though it is a noble edifice, and well adapted to its end, it is but a beginning. Full one half of the funds must yet be raised. In order to finish the plan, at least twenty thousand dollars more will be needed for the buildings, besides perhaps five thousand dollars or more for furniture, library, and apparatus.

This seminary is specific in its character, and, of course, does not provide for the entire education of a young lady. Such a provision may be found expedient in foreign countries, where all systems can be brought under the rigid rules of monarchy, without being subject to the continual encroachments and changes necessarily resulting from a free government. But in our country it is doubted whether female seminaries generally can attain a high standard of excellence till they become more specific and less mixed in their character.

1. *Religious Culture.* This lies at the foundation of that female character which the founders of this seminary have contemplated. Without this, their efforts would entirely fail of their design. This institution has been for the Lord, that it might be peculiarly his own. It has been solemnly and publicly dedicated to his service. It has been embalmed by prayer in many hearts and consecrated around many a family altar. The donors and benefactors of this institution, with its trustees and teachers, have felt a united obligation to seek, in behalf of this beloved seminary, "first the kingdom of God and his righteousness." Endeavors have been made to raise the funds and to lay the whole foundation on Christian principles, to organize a school and form a family that from day to day might illustrate the precepts and spirit of the gospel. Public worship, the Bible lesson, and other appropriate duties of the Sabbath, a regular observance of secret devotion, suitable attention to religious instruction and social prayer meetings, and the maintaining of a consistent Christian deportment, are considered the most important objects of regard, for both teachers and scholars. The friends of this seminary have sought that this

might be a spot where souls shall be born of God, and where much
shall be done for maturing and elevating Christian character. The smiles of Providence and the influences of the Holy Spirit have encouraged them to hope that their desires will not be in vain.

2. *Cultivation of Benevolence.* This is implied in the last particular, but it needs special care in a lady's education. While many of the present active generation are fixed in their habits, and will never rise above the standard of benevolence already adopted, the eye of hope rests with anxious solicitude on the next generation. But who shall take all the little ones, and by precept, and still more by example, enforce on them the sentiments of benevolence, and, aided by the Holy Spirit, train them up from their infancy for the service of the Redeemer? Is there not here an appropriate sphere for the efforts of women, through whose moulding hands all our children and youth must inevitably pass?

How important, then, is it that the education of a female should be conducted on strictly benevolent principles! and how important that this spirit should be the presiding genius in every female school! Should it not be so incorporated with its nature, and so wrought into its very existence, that it cannot prosper without it? Such a school the friends of this seminary have sought to furnish. They would have the spirit of benevolence manifest in all its principles, and in the manner of conferring its privileges, in the mutual duties it requires of its members, and in the claims it makes on them to devote their future lives to doing good.

3. *Intellectual Culture.* This trait of character is of inestimable value to a lady who desires to be useful. A thorough and well-balanced intellectual education will be to her a valuable auxiliary in every department of duty.

This seminary has peculiar advantages for gaining a high intellectual standard. The age required for admission will secure to the pupils, as a whole, greater mental power, and the attainments required for admission will secure to the institution a higher standard of scholarship.

4. *Physical Culture.* The value of health to a lady is inestimable. Her appropriate duties are so numerous and varied, and so constant in their demands, and so imperious in the moment of their calls, as will render this treasure to her above price. How difficult is it for her to perform all her duties faithfully and successfully, unless she possesses at all times a calm mind, an even temper, a cheerful heart, and a happy face! But a feeble system and a nervous frame are often the direct antagonists of these indispensable traits in a lady's character. A gentleman may possibly

live and do some good without much health; but what can a lady do, unless she takes the attitude of an invalid, and seeks to do good principally by patience and submission? If a gentleman cannot do his work in one hour, he may perhaps do it in another; but a lady's duties often allow of no compromise in hours. If a gentleman is annoyed and vexed with the nervousness of his feeble frame, he may perhaps use it to some advantage, as he attempts to move the world by his pen, or by his voice. But a lady cannot make such a use of this infirmity in her influence over her children and family—an influence which must be all times under the control of gentleness and equanimity. Much has been said on this subject, but enough has not been *done,* in our systems of education, to promote the health of young ladies. This is an object of special regard in this seminary.

The time is all regularly and systematically divided. The hours for rising and retiring are early. The food is plain and simple, but well prepared, and from the best materials. No article of second quality of the *kind* is every purchased for the family, and no standard of cooking is allowed but that of doing every thing as well as it can be done. The day is so divided that the lessons can be well learned, and ample time allowed for sleep; the hour for exercise in the domestic department can be secured without interruption, and a half hour in the morning and evening for secret devotion, also half an hour for vocal music, and twenty minutes for calisthenics. Besides, there are the leisure hours, in which much is done of sewing, knitting, and ornamental needlework; and much is enjoyed in social intercourse, in walking, and in botanical excursions. This institution presupposes a good degree of health and correct habits. But little can be done in this seminary, or any other, for those whose constitution is already impaired, or whose physical habits, up to the age of sixteen, are particularly defective. This institution professes to make no remarkable physical renovations. But it is believed that a young lady who is fitted for the system, and who can voluntarily and cheerfully adopt it as her own, will find this place favorable for preserving unimpaired the health she brings with her, and for promoting and establishing the good physical habits already acquired.

5. *Social and Domestic Character.* The excellence of the female character in this respect consists principally in a preparation to be happy herself in her social and domestic relations, and to make all others happy around her. All her duties, of whatever kind, are in an important sense social and domestic. They are retired and private and not public, like those of the other sex. Whatever she does

beyond her own family should be but another application and illustration of social and domestic excellence. She may occupy the place of an important teacher, but her most vigorous labors should be modest and unobtrusive. She may go on a foreign mission, but she will there find a retired spot, where, away from the public gaze, she may wear out or lay down a valuable life. She may promote the interest of the Sabbath school, or be an angel of mercy to the poor and afflicted; she may seek in various ways to increase the spirit of benevolence and the zeal for the cause of missions; and she may labor for the salvation of souls; but her work is to be done by the whisper of her still and gentle voice, by the silent step of her unwearied feet, and by the power of her uniform and consistent example.

The following elements should be embraced in the social and domestic character of a lady:

(a) *Economy.* Economy consists in providing well at little comparative expense. It necessarily implies good judgment and good taste. It can be equally manifested in the tasteful decorations of a palace and in the simple comforts of a cottage. Suppose all ladies possessed this in a high degree, how much more would be found in families of comfort and convenience, of taste and refinement, of education and improvement, of charity and good works!

This institution, it is well known, is distinguished for its economical features. Economy, however, is not adopted principally for its own sake, but as a means of education, as a mode of producing favorable effects on character, and of preparing young ladies for the duties of life. The great object is to make the school really better. An economical character is to be formed by precept, by practice, and by example. Example has great effect, not only in furnishing a model for imitation, but also in proving that economy is practicable, which is one of the most essential requisites for success. Let a young lady spend two or three years, on intimate terms, in a family distinguished for a judicious and consistent illustration of this principle, and the effects cannot be lost.

(b) *A Suitable Feeling of Independence.* There are two kinds of dependence, very unlike in their nature, but both inconsistent with the highest degree of domestic bliss. To one of these ladies in cities and large towns are more particularly subject; but it is an evil from which ladies in the country are not wholly exempt. It is a feeling of dependence on the will of servants. Every lady should be so educated, as far as it can be done, that she will feel able to take care of herself, and, if need be, of a family, whatever may be her situation in life, and whatever her station in society. Otherwise, if she remains in these United States, she may be rendered unhappy by constantly feeling that her daily comforts are at the control of her servants, who in such cases are often unfaithful, unreasonable, and dissatisfied. The withering effects of family perplexities on the social character is well known to every observer of domestic life. On the other hand, how much happiness often results from a suitable feeling of independence. A lady in one of our large cities, who is distinguished for having faithful servants, considers the secret as lying in her feeling of independence. If one, in a fit of caprice, proposes leaving her, she has only to say, "You may go to-day. If need be, I can take care of my own family until your place is supplied."

Against this kind of dependence this institution seeks to exert its decided influence. The whole aspect of the family, and all the plans of the school, are suited to cultivate habits entirely the reverse. In the domestic independence of the household all have an interest. The daily hour for these duties returns to each at the appointed time, and no one inquires whether it can be omitted or transferred to another. No one receives any pecuniary reward for her services, and no one seeks with her money to deprive herself of the privilege of sharing in the freedom, simplicity, and independence of her *home*.

There is another kind of independence entirely different in its nature, but equally essential to a high degree of domestic happiness. This is the result of economy already considered. It is the power of bringing personal and family expenses fairly and easily within the means enjoyed. The whole system adopted in this seminary is designed to give a living illustration of the principle by which this power is to be gained. This ability will be of immense value in active life. It will prepare one to sustain the reverses of fortune with submission, or to meet the claims of hospitality and charity with promptness. This kind of independence might be to the great cause of benevolence like an overflowing fountain, whose streams will never fail.

(c) *Skill and Expedition in Household Duties.* Let a young lady despise this branch of the duties of woman, and she despises the appointments of the Author of her existence. The laws of God, made known by nature and by providence, and also by the Bible, enjoin these duties on the sex, and she cannot violate them with impunity. Let her have occasion to preside at the head of her own family and table, and she may despair of enjoying herself, or of giving to others the highest degree of domestic happiness. Does she seek to do good by teaching? The time, we hope, is not far distant, when no mother will commit her daughters to the influence of such a teacher. Does she seek to do good in the Sabbath school? How can she enforce all the duties to God and man in their due proportion while she condemns one of the most obvious laws of her nature? Would she endeavor to show the poor and the ignorant how to find the comforts of life? How can she teach what she has never learned? Does she become the wife of a missionary? How does her heart sink within her, as her desponding husband strives in vain to avoid the evils resulting from her inefficiency!

This institution is not designed to conduct this branch of a young lady's education. It would not take this privilege from the mother. But it does seek to preserve the good habits already acquired, and to make a favorable impression with regard to the value of system, promptness, and fidelity in this branch of the duties of woman. . . .

1. *In Furnishing a Supply of Female Teachers.* Teaching is really the business of almost every useful woman. If there are any to whom this does not apply, they may be considered as exceptions to a general rule. Of course, no female is well educated who has not all the acquisitions necessary for a good teacher. The most essential qualifications are thorough mental culture, a well-balanced character, a benevolent heart, an ability to communicate knowledge and apply it to practice, an acquaintance with human nature, and the power of controlling the minds of others.

But it is not enough that a great number of ladies are well educated. They must also have benevolence enough to engage in teaching, when other duties will allow and when their labors are needed. Female teachers should not expect to be fully compensated for their services, unless it be by kindness and gratitude.

There are many other chords in female hearts which will vibrate much more tenderly and powerfully than this. There is a large and increasing number of educated ladies, who will make the best of teachers, but who can be allured much more by respectful attention, by kindness and gratitude, by suitable school-rooms and apparatus, and other facilities for rendering their labors pleasant and successful, than they can by the prospect of a pecuniary reward.

The spirit of this seminary is suited not only to increase the number of educated ladies, but to enforce on them the obligation to use their talents for the good of others, especially in teaching. It is hoped it may also lead them to be more willing to take any school and in any place where their services are most needed.

2. *In Promoting the Prosperity of Common Schools.* Whoever will devise means by which reading, spelling, arithmetic, geography,

and grammar shall receive as thorough attention in common schools as they deserve, and whoever will throw inducements before the older female scholars to remain in them longer and attend thoroughly to these branches, as an example to others, will do much to elevate their standard. Such an influence this seminary seeks to exert.

3. *In Counteracting Certain Errors Which Have Prevailed to Some Extent in Female Education.*

First Error. Tasking the mind too early with severe mental discipline.—The evils of this course are beginning to be felt by careful observers of the human mind and of human character. When the effort is attended with the greatest success, there is generally the greatest injury. The most discouraging field which any teacher was ever called to cultivate is the mind of a young lady who has been studying all her days, and has gone over most of the natural and moral sciences without any valuable improvement, until she is tired of school, tired of books, and tired almost of life. As this institution proposes to conduct young ladies through a regular intellectual course, after the age of sixteen, its influence will be against this error.

Second Error. Deferring some parts of education till too late a period.—Among the things neglected till too late a period are the manners, the cultivation of the voice, included singing, pronunciation, and all the characteristics of good reading, gaining skill and expedition in the common necessary mechanical operations, such as sewing, knitting, writing, and drawing, and acquiring, by daily practice, a knowledge and a love of domestic pursuits. To these might be added some things which depend almost entirely on the memory, such as spelling, and others which are suited to lay the foundation of a literary taste, such as a judicious course of reading, practice in composition, etc. Those who are to attend to instrumental music, the ornamental branches, and the pronunciation of foreign languages, must commence early.

Third Error. Placing Daughters too young in a Boarding-school or large Seminary.—A common boarding-school is not a suitable place for a little girl. She needs the home of her childhood, or one like it. Direct individual attention, such as can be given by no one who has the care of many, is the necessary means of forming her character, of cultivating her manners, of developing her affections, and of nurturing all that is lovely and of good report. She wants the uninterrupted sympathies of a mother's heart. She needs a constant and gentle hand, leading her singly along in the path of safety and improvement. Perhaps the evils of a boarding-house are

most unfavorable on her character just as she is entering her teens.
Who can guide this self-sufficient age but the mother, who has gained a permanent place in her affections and a decided influence over her life? Who but the mother, who first taught her to obey, can lay on her the necessary restrictions without exposing her to form the unlovely trait of character gained by complaining of those whom she should love and respect, and who deserve her gratitude?

4. *In Giving Just Views of the Advantages of large female Seminaries.* Such institutions furnish peculiar privileges, which cannot be secured by smaller schools; but in most cases they have not been able to produce their legitimate results. They have often suffered for the want of accommodations and other facilities for successful operation, from their temporary and unsettled existence, from their want of system, and sometimes from too public a location, and too public an aspect in their features. Their efforts also to accommodate all ages and all classes often prevent their having any fixed or determinate character. This institution seeks to avoid all these evils, and to develop the real advantages of a large seminary.

In order that a lady may have the most thorough education, she should spend a number of years in close intellectual application after her mental powers have acquired sufficient strength, and her physical system sufficient maturity, and after she has all the necessary preparation. This must be during the best part of her life, when every year is worth more than can be estimated in gold and silver. Facilities for success should be given her, which will be an ample reward for the sacrifice of so much time. Whoever has undertaken to organize a school has had abundant evidence that all these points cannot be gained where the number is not large. This seminary is able now to secure all these advantages in some degree, but not so perfectly as it will when the two hundred can be received.

The influence of a large seminary on the social character is also important. The very discipline necessary to preserve little girls from exposure to injury, and to cultivate the principles of virtue and loveliness, is attended with some necessary evils which will need a pruning hand at a maturer age. Not the least prominent of these is a narrowness of soul, giving her limited views of others.

The spirit of monopolizing privileges is to some extent the effect of giving to a little girl all that individual care and affectionate attention which her cultivation demands. A large seminary, and more especially a large family, have a tendency to remove this. The young lady needs to feel herself a member of a large community, where the interests of others are to be sought equally with her own. She needs to learn by practice, as well as by principle, that individual accommodations and private interests are to be sacrificed for the public good; and she needs to know from experience that those who make such a sacrifice will receive an ample reward in the improvement of the community among whom they are to dwell.

5. *In giving the Claims of large female Seminaries an ackowledged Place among the other Objects of public Benevolence.* The claims of those for the other sex were admitted two hundred years ago; and the colleges, academies, and theological seminaries, all over the land, show that the wise and the good have not been wary in well doing. How ridiculous would be the attempt to found colleges in the manner that some female seminaries have been founded! Suppose a gentleman, having a large family depending on him for support, finds his health not sufficient for the duties of his profession. Casting his eye around, he looks on the office of a president of a college as affording more ample means, and a more pleasant and respectable situation for his family, than any other he can command. But a new college must be founded to furnish him the place. He selects a large village in New England, or at the west, or at the south, as may best favor the accomplishment of his object, and where he can find buildings which he can buy or rent on some conditions, though they may be far from being adapted to such an end. He purchases his apparatus, or has none, and procures professors on his own responsibility. Thus prepared, he commences, making his charge to the students such as will meet the rent of buildings, furniture, and apparatus, and the salaries of his professors, besides furnishing a handsome support to his own family. What could such a college do to encourage thorough and systematic education in our country? But this is scarcely a caricature of the manner in which some female seminaries have been founded.

We cannot hope for a state of things essentially better till the principle is admitted that female seminaries, designed for the public benefit, must be founded by the hand of public benevolence, and be subject to the rules enjoined by such benevolence. Let this principle be fully admitted, and let it have sufficient time to produce its natural effects, and it will be productive of more important results than can be easily estimated. Then our large seminaries may be permanent, with all the mutual responsibilities and cooperation which the principle of permanency produces.

THOMAS WENTWORTH HIGGINSON (1823-1911)

Higginson who had a varied career as clergyman, editor, writer, and soldier, contended that we are human first, and sexually distinctive second. He insisted that both masculine and feminine viewpoints are essential to the achievement of a well-rounded education. He ranked second in his class at Harvard, graduating at the age of seventeen. Higginson suggested that some women should teach at Harvard and Yale, while some men should teach at Smith and Vassar.

His essay, "Ought Women to Learn the Alphabet?" was printed in an 1859 issue of the *Atlantic Monthly*. Higginson included in the essay a brief historical review of female education. The following selection on "Study and Work" is from that essay, later published in his *Women and the Alphabet*.

VI

*STUDY AND WORK**

"Movet me ingens scientiarum admiratio, seu legis communis aequitas, ut in nostro sexu, rarum non esse feram, id quod omnium votis dignissimum est. Nam cum sapientia tantum generis humani ornamentum sit, ut ad omnes et singulos (quoad quidem per sortem cujusque liceat) extendi jure debeat, non vidi, cur virgini, in qua excolendi sese ornandique sedulitatem admittimus, non conveniat mundus hic omnium longe pulcherrimus."
—ANNAE MARIAE A SCHURMAN EPISTOLAE. (1638)

"A great reverence for knowledge and the natural sense of justice urge me to encourage in my own sex that which is most worthy the aspirations of all. For, since wisdom is so great an ornament of the human race that it should of right be extended (so far as practicable) to each and every one, I have not perceived

---

*From Higginson, Thomas Wentworth. *Women and the Alphabet*. Cambridge: Printed at The Riverside Press, 1900, pp. 213-217.

311

why this fairest of ornaments should not be appropriate for the maiden, to whom we permit all diligence in the decoration and adornment of herself."

Why is it, that, whenever anything is done for women in the way of education, it is called "an experiment,"—something that is to be long considered, stoutly opposed, grudgingly yielded, and dubiously watched,—while, if the same thing is done for men, its desirableness is assumed as a matter of course, and the thing is done? Thus, when Harvard College was founded, it was not regarded as an experiment, but as an institution. The "General Court," in 1636, "agreed to give 400£ towards a schoale or colledge," and the affair was settled. Every subsequent step in the expanding of educational opportunities for young men has gone in the same way. But when there seems a chance of extending, however irregularly, some of the same collegiate advantages to women, I observe that respectable newspapers, in all good faith, are apt to speak of the measure as an "experiment."

It seems to me no more of an "experiment" than when a boy who has usually eaten up his whole apple becomes a little touched with a sense of justice, and finally decides to offer his sister the smaller half. If he has ever regarded that offer as an experiment, the first actual trial will put the result into the list of certainties; and it will become an axiom in his mind that girls like apples. Whatever may be said about the position of women in law and society, it is clear that their educational disadvantages have been a prolonged disgrace to the other sex, and one of which women themselves are in no way accountable. When Francoise de Saintonges, in the sixteenth century, wished to establish girls' schools in France, she was hooted in the streets, and her father called together four doctors of law to decide whether she was possessed of a devil in planning to teach women,—"*pour s'assurer qu'instruire des femmes n'etait pas un oeuvre du demon.*" From that day to this we have seen women almost always more ready to be taught than was any one else to teach them. Talk as you please about their wishing or not wishing to vote: they have certainly wished for instruction, and have had it doled out to them almost as grudgingly as if it were the ballot itself.

Consider the educational history of Massachusetts, for instance. The wife of President John Adams was born in 1744; and she says of her youth that "female education, in the best families, went no farther than writing and arithmetic." Barry tells us in his "History of Massachusetts," that the public education was first provided for boys only; "but light soon broke in, and girls were allowed to attend the public schools two hours a day." It appears from President Quincy's "Municipal History of Boston," that from 1790 girls were there admitted to such schools, but during the summer months only, when there were not boys enough to fill them,—from April 20 to October 20 of each year. This lasted until 1822, when Boston became a city. Four years after, an attempt was made to establish a high school for girls, which was not, however, to teach Latin and Greek. It had, in the words of the school committee of 1854, "an alarming success"; and the school was abolished after eighteen months' trial, because the girls crowded into it; and as Mr. Quincy, with exquisite simplicity, records, "not one voluntarily quitted it, and there was no reason to suppose that any one admitted to the school would voluntarily quit for the whole three years, except in case of marriage!"

How amusing seems it now to read of such an "experiment" as this, abandoned only because of its overwhelming success! How absurd now seem the discussions of a few years ago! —the doubts whether young women really desired higher education, whether they were capable of it, whether their health would bear it, whether their parents would permit it. An address I gave before the Social Science Association on this subject, at Boston, May 14, 1873, now seems to me such a collection of platitudes that I hardly see how I dared come before an intelligent audience with such needless reasonings. It is as if I had soberly labored to prove that two and two make four, or that ginger is "hot i' the mouth." Yet the subsequent discussion in that meeting showed that around even these harmless and commonplace propositions that battle of debate could rage hot; and it really seemed as if even to teach women the alphabet ought still to be mentioned as "a promising experiment." Now, with the successes before us of so many colleges; with the spectacle at Cambridge of young women actually reading Plato "at sight" with Professor Goodwin, —it surely seems as if the higher education of women might be considered quite beyond the stage of experiment, and might henceforth be provided for in the same common-sense and matter-of-course way which we provide for the education of young men.

And, if this point is already reached in education, how long before it will also be reached in political life, and women's voting be viewed as a matter of course, and a thing no longer experimental?

HELOISE EDWINA HERSEY (1855-1933)

Although this work of Hersey was chosen for its own worth, her name holds sentimental appeal for a book which focuses on the education of women. The first Heloise is, of course, the medieval nun (1101-1164) who became a beloved, skillful teacher of girls following her tragic, brief marriage to Peter Abelard. The second Heloise is the title character in Rousseau's novel, *The New Heloise* (1760), which was inspired by his unrequited love affair with the sister of a prominent French salonist. The third Heloise is the author of the final work in this book.

In addition to an 1876 B. A. degree from Vassar College, Heloise Hersey was awarded honorary degrees from Bowdoin in 1921 and Tufts in 1922. From 1878 to 1883, she was professor of English at Smith College. From 1877 to 1899, she was principal of Miss Hersey's School for Girls in Boston.

The "Newest Heloise" wrote a collection of letters published in 1901 in a book named *To Girls.* A letter titled "The Educated Woman" is reprinted here. Ideally for the intent of this book about women, Hersey rhetorically asks the difference between an educated and uneducated woman, then proceeds to respond to the question. At the end of this letter, she concisely describes her concept of an educated woman, then exhorts the present generation of women to perform her miracles.

After studying the Hersey item, the reader might benefit from pondering the gestalt of 2,500 years of the education of women. Articles in this classics book have given descriptions of existing female education, along with dreams of longed-for female education in Ancient Greece, Early Christian Era, Middle Ages, Renaissance, Reformation, Enlightenment, and Nineteenth Century. Several provocative questions center around the education of girls and women: (1) Have women contributed to their own educational oppression at any time in history? If so, when and how? (2) Other than the twentieth

314

most desirable to have been a woman? (3) What changes have occurred in the past three quarters of a century? (4) What changes are likely to occur in the future?

Surely, Heloise Hersey would be in agreement with Plato's assertion that

> . . . the female sex must share with the male, to the greatest
> extent possible, both in education and in all else.*

THE EDUCATED WOMAN†

My Dear Helen: The difference between an educated and an uneducated woman? Yes, I think I know it, though I don't wonder that you are puzzled in comparing the qualities which you see in your Aunt Lizzie and those of Miss Johnson, freshly arrived from abroad, in all the glory of a European Ph.D.

Your aunt was educated, as the phrase goes, in an old-fashioned, fashionable boarding-school, where she was taught little except Americanised French, English history, needlework, and dancing; and yet you think her a more useful and delightful member of society than Miss Johnson, who reads seven languages, and took high honours with a thesis on quaternions.

Now, when I was a Sophomore in college, I had perfectly clear ideas as to what constituted feminine education. (We used to call it "The Higher Education" in those days, and took it for granted that that phrase referred to women, and not to men.) There was no doubt in my mind then that this education rested solidly upon a college degree. Modern science was its prime essential. History and French and music and *belles-lettres* had been well enough for our grandmothers, but scarcely counted toward the end which we modern women wished to gain. Now I have revised that judgment. To explain my present point of view, I must go back a little, to the real aim of education.

Education, like religion, we may say reverently, is to be known by its fruits. The ability to pass examinations and to take high honours, to wrest a degree from a reluctant university, to carry through a difficult piece of original research,—none of these is the test. They are promise, not fulfilment; blossom, not fruit; the road, not home. In other words, education is not an end in itself, but the

---

*R.G. Bury (trans.). *Laws*. London: William Heinemann, Ltd., 1942, p. 61.
†From Hersey, Heloise Edwina. *To Girls. A Budget of Letters*. Boston: Small, Maynard & Co., 1901, pp. 1-19.

means to an end. So much that is delightful in the way of friendship and social life and pleasant class-room rivalries is associated with the years in college dormitories that there is danger of our forgetting the actual significance of these things. It is really slight.

Suppose I take you into my confidence, and tell you the actual test which I apply relentlessly to find out if a woman is well educated. It is this: Is she skilled in the art of living? Such a test, you see, would make difficult work for a board of examiners; but, after all, it is not so troublesome to apply as you might suppose.

You know well enough the distinction between amateur acting and that of the professional. We take pleasure in two amateur performances in the course of a winter, but a constant succession of them would be pretty painful. In point of fact, the third-rate professional gives more pleasure in the long run than the first-rate amateur. This is because he knows how to use all his powers, and he makes the most of them. He may even turn his weaknesses to his advantage. (Witness Sir Henry Irving's impersonation of Louis XI.) The professional's performance is all of a piece; and, although it may never reach any very high level, it has a certain consistency and completeness which make upon us the impression of reality.

Now education should turn the amateur in the art of living into the professional. My educated woman has all her powers at her command. They are not scattered by an emergency. Her temper is no more likely to play her false than her reasoning power, and her heart and her hand are equally steady and equally generous.

For example, my friend Mrs. Smithson lost all her servants in a cold snap last winter because the water-pipes froze and her temper got the better of her. Whether the accident was her fault or that of the cook does not matter for the argument. The catastrophe demonstrated that in so far, she was not an educated woman, although I believe she has written an admirable essay in Browning's *Sordello*. The Harvard students who "plunged" in the stock market a few weeks ago, and lost a year's allowance and more, were not educated, and probably hardly on the road to education. Mary Knowles went to bed last winter and stayed there for a fortnight on being told by her father that she must give up her pony and dogcart in the family retrenchment of expenses. She is attending one of the most expensive schools in Boston, but so far she has not taken the first step toward being educated.

On the other hand, Stevenson, who never got a degree from the University of Edinburgh, made his frail body do the bidding of his iron will all his life. Shakespeare knew small Latin and less Greek, but his eye was trained to see and his heart to feel and his hand to

paint. The schooling which Abraham Lincoln had was hardly one
year, but no statesman of our century has had a firmer grasp of
large issues.

One need not go to the history of great men to see this
illustrated. The girl who meets a family crisis bravely and effective-
ly, or who can take a moribund branch of the Girls' Friendly
Society and restore it by her skill to life and vigour, or who can set
a poor family on its feet by advice and help at the right moment, or
who can be nurse, housemaid, secretary, friend, daughter, by turns,
and each with a good heart, this girl has already gathered the fruit
of education, whatever may have been her technical training.

How to come by these powers is the next question, and a very
important one. Some people seem to be born with them, but I fancy
none ever is. Some men seem to be born athletic, but I have never
found one who had not some history of training to tell. Now the
process of education which on the whole has seemed to be most
successful in getting desirable results is a twofold one. The first half
of it has an ugly name, and it is not a favourite in girls' boarding-
schools. It is Discipline. Discipline consists in doing some one thing
over and over and over again, and, when that is done, beginning the
very same thing anew. It makes less difference than we suppose
whether the task on which this labour is expended is Greek,
algebra, history, or French. People talk about the "disciplinary
studies," meaning thereby mathematics and the classics; but in my
scheme of education there is no study which is not disciplinary. If
there is such a one, it surely does not belong in the curriculum of
anybody under twenty-five years of age.

This doing the thing over and over again results finally, of
course, in being able to do it with extreme rapidity, accuracy, and
perfection. In many cases these go so far that the act becomes really
automatic. There is no better illustration of this than your experience, for instance, in learning to play the piano. The five-finger
exercise, which at first took all your attention, presently required no
attention; and after a year or two the finger and the brain began to
act together, and the work which had been so difficult and
thankless became a delight.

There are good reasons why one should try to get this
discipline out of the subjects which have been used for the purpose
for centuries. Latin, for example, is better for the desired end than
Chinese, because wise men have given their minds to the Latin
tongue, and have developed all its capacities for discipline. I heard
a clever business man say that his world was divided into two
classes of men, those who had studied Latin and those who had not,

and there was, and would always be, a definite difference in their points of view. I had never put it quite so sharply, but I think that is substantially true. There must always be a wide difference between a man that has seen a great city and one that has never seen one, between the man that has been to Europe and one that has not been. The outlook gets broadened, changed. A man need not necessarily be better, but he is different. So with the student of Latin. His attitude toward the use of words is altered by even a slight knowledge of Latin, and the English dictionary becomes a better friend.

If it is true that doing the thing over, doing it well, doing it patiently and doing it persistently, is the main thing in the requirement of training, you will see that where it is done, or under whose direction, is of little consequence. Now we are approaching one of the reasons, at least, why your Aunt Lizzie seems to you to be better educated than our friend, the Ph.D. Even from the delicate needlework which she learned to do at her fashionable boarding-school she gained the power of attention, of patience, and of taste. Nobody can tell whether practice in Greek paradigms or in the use of logarithms would have been better. Suffice it to say that the end of education was attained. Of course, embroidery should not take to-day the place of history. None the less, we are bound to give it due credit for its good results in the past.

Our educated woman must have a sense of proportion, and it is never too early to acquire that. Her study of geography, her reading of French, her knowledge of history, her investigations in biology, all should tend to show her the world as it is. Siberia should not be too far for her sympathy to reach. China's customs should not seem to her so odd as to turn her world upside down. England should not be merely a set of shrines sacred to literary associations, but a living island where history is a-making in this very year of our Lord. Even to the girl country born and bred the problems of the great municipal life of New York should be important and interesting; and, in short, the material for education might well be so chosen that, when it has been assimilated, our young woman can declare, without exaggeration, that nothing human is alien to her.

One more word about this disciplinary process. I believe it can be made perpetually interesting. Now I don't mean easy. I have no patience with easy education. The kindergarten method has no place in education after the child can read. I have gone into a school-room where the children sat in easy-chairs, and listened to the teacher's explanation of easy subjects, illustrated by the stere-

opticon, when I despaired of education. At the end of the day the
teacher was exhausted, and the children had the pleasantly bored
expression which is the most discouraging that one can see on a
child's face. I recall a school which was well ventilated by loose and
rattling windows, and half heated by a stove that smoked. In it
there was the buzz of recitations all day long, in every subject from
the primer to Cicero's Orations. There was not a single modern
appliance; and yet a student, working with an antiquated lexicon
and a text without a note or illustration, somehow managed to get
a picture of Rome, the Forum, the Senate, and the struggling
factions more vivid than any stereopticon ever gave. She was never
bored with hard work; and, if her fingers sometimes ached with the
cold and her eyes smarted with the smoke, she found a cure for
these ills, without knowing why, in the intellectual activity which is
really the highest joy of life. It would be a curious commentary on
our modern enthusiasm for education if it should prove to be a
cheapener of the noblest of mind and spirit; and if we should
discover, by and by, as its fruit, not skill in the art of living, but the
peevish discontent with that eternal condition of wholesome life
imposed in the garden of Eden: "In the sweat of thy face shalt thou
eat bread."

I said that discipline was half of education. If it were all, a
convent or a monastery would be the best place to put the young
life for its training: routine is there reduced to its perfection. But the
girl whose education has had in it nothing richer than subjection to
routine will show little skill when she comes to actual life with its
complicated problems and its sudden emergencies.

It is easy to define the methods of discipline. It is difficult even
so much as to describe this other half of the process. Edward Thring
has, perhaps, put the matter better than any one else,—"the
transmission of life from the living, through the living, to the
living." This is the second and the crowning element in education:
it is a hard saying; it makes way but slowly. Many a college
professor ignores or decries it. In many a lecture-room a phono-
graph delivering the same lectures would be as useful to the student
as is the teacher. Those who hold that teaching is but an inferior
species of lecturing are many, and they abound especially in what
we call "the higher institutions of learning." They would have us
believe that a personal relation between teacher and student is
subversive of all sound educational results. Let us once for all get
this matter cleared up. Lecturing is dealing with books, facts,
subjects. The more excellent the arrangement, the more lucid the
exposition, the better satisfied may the lecturer be. He may fairly

judge of his success by his own state of mind at the end of his lecture: any one else may judge of it by reading the syllabus of the lecture carefully. Teaching, on the other hand, is dealing with the minds and hearts of the students; and the only test of success in this art is the condition in which those hearts and minds are found at the end of an hour or a year. If the note-book has gained pages of notes, but the brain has felt no thrill of inspiration, the hour is a failure; if the memory has been tested, but the heart has not been quickened, the teacher may well be discontent; if the student has caught glimpses of the teacher's pet hobby, but the teacher has not been able to discern and reach the causes of the student's difficulties, there may have been much talk, but there has been little vitalising work.

Of course here, as in every great principle of life, there are possibilities of absurdity and exaggeration. The personal note is as sensitive to forcing as any other note in the gamut of experience. Personal relations of every sort have in themselves a tendency to degenerate if they are not consciously held up to a high standard. There is no place more trying to the weakness of human nature than the slight elevation on which the attractive teacher finds herself when she enters upon her work. The raised platform invites to the pleasing indulgence of striking an attitude and receiving worshippers. We all of us know the gushing teacher who loves her "dear girls," and who has tears for their little faults, blind eyes for their large ones, and no real influence in moulding their characters. In no soft paths shall my teacher and pupil walk hand in hand. The Hill Difficulty is to be climbed alone. The voice of inspiration, of encouragement, of admonition, will generally come from the cloud-capped summit. So coming, woe be to it if it have not the accent of sincerity,—a large sincerity! The least suspicion of a pose, a hint of flippancy, the shadow of a mock knowledge on the part of the teacher, will destroy the efficacy of any offered aid. So we come at last to this serious and sobering conclusion. A genuine personal relation between teacher and student is the vital spark of education. The nature of that relation must of necessity be determined by the elder and stronger. Life, life, life, it must have and must give. Truth-telling must be its very substance. Loyalty must repay truth, even when the truth is bitter. That a teacher should give a death stab to vanity or deceit in the student, should bear the pain with a smiling face, and reach out grateful and affectionate hand of friendship in return,—this is an experience that should make each party to it glad and proud.

Thus far I have spoken of this vitalising process as if it must always come from the mind of the teacher; but there are many other sources from which it is drawn. Great books are life-givers. When Tennyson was fourteen years old, he heard of Byron's death; though he had never seen the poet, he said "I thought the whole world was at an end. I thought everything was over and finished for every one,—that nothing else mattered. I remember I walked out alone, and carved 'Byron is dead!' into the sandstone." Ten years later he wrote of Byron and Shelley, "However mistaken they may be, they yet did give the world another heart and new pulses; and so we are kept going." Millions of human souls owe to the poets, the philosophers, the stirring writers of the lives of great men, "another heart and new pulses." Such inspiration has come in the very highest degree from the Bible. From whatever source the stimulus comes, it is traceable at last to the contact of the human spirit with some other and greater human spirit. It is the transmission of life from the living (who live though they are dead) to the living. So I think we may trace in every well-regulated character the two processes of education,—its discipline and its personal inspiration. This last may have come from one teacher, from many teachers, from one's parents, from a friend, or from great books. Somewhere in the life of the well-educated man or woman we shall find that this glorious spiritual flame has touched it and set its torch alight.

You will be asking me now for some practical test which may be applied, that we may find out whether or not this twofold work is going on. Is there any way in which I may tell if one of my girls is being educated? I think I know one test. Let the poet help me to it with a parable. Once upon a time a fair lady dwelt at Camelot. She wrought a wondrous web, and she dreamt of shadows as she saw them in a mirror. One day she broke away from work and mirror and dream; and, seeking the world in which lived the knight of her ill-fated love, she died at his feet, her hungry heart fed only by one glance of pity from his eye. So runs the world-old tale of the Lady of Shalott. Yet, once again, there lived a lady deep in a wood. She, too, wove a magic garment. Till it was finished, she could never go forth into the world. One day the last thread was set in its golden fringe. Bearing it proudly on her arm, she made her way out of the forest. All unknown to her a noble prince came riding toward the very path by which she was emerging. He was close upon her. In another instant they would have been face to face, but a wretched beggar sprang from the roadside with hands stretched out for alms. In an instant she had thrown over him the magic robe, and it had wrought its charm. Henceforth she was doomed to see in him, and in him alone, all manly beauties, virtues, powers, and to

322 follow him throughout the world. Now here are two exquisite parables of the life, the fate, the nature, of a woman. She dies for love of the unattainable. She is blind, and loves the base with a devotion and loyalty worthy of a nobler object. From these mediaeval failures the education of our time is pledged to deliver us. Our modern girl may no longer die for love of that which is out of reach. She may not to-day even live cherishing a love for that which is beneath her. She must live and choose and love, and she must choose to love the highest. Tell me what a woman loves, and I will tell you whether she has learned the fine art of living. First, she must love noble books, because they are the life-blood of the most vital of human souls. Then she must love beauty wherever it is found,—in nature, in character, in good causes, in art. She shall love beauty enough to work for it with heart and mind, she shall protect it, she shall be able to create it, she shall imbue other souls with her own zeal for it. Then she shall love humanity even when it is unlovely, because, when the worst is said of man, it remains true that he was made in the image of God, and for the saving of him it was worth while that the Son of God should die. Finally, she shall love her country. She shall love it in peace and in war, in times of good report and in times of evil report. If she once loves her own country, I do not fear that she shall lack what is to-day called "the higher patriotism." I do fear that that may sometimes be found to be no patriotism at all. Books, beauty, humanity, her country,— these are noble loves. Woe to her who substitutes for them self, pleasure, "our social circle." The new Elaine is bred neither in cloister nor in forest, but on the edge at least of the full, rich life of the city. She comes forth with no magic web, but with the clearest of eye, the most apprehensive of minds, the steadiest of wills. She is surefooted and strong-hearted. She is no sentimentalist, she is no agnostic, she is no indifferentist. She is intellectual, and she is lovable. She knows how to listen and how to speak. She is brave, and she is true. The women of my generation dreamed of a world made new by reason of our new liberties. Our dream has but partly come to pass. The girls of the future must make the miracle for which we hoped the commonplace of every day,

"They to the disappointed earth shall give
The lives we meant to live,—
Beautiful, free, and strong;
The light we almost had
Shall make them glad;
The words we waited long
Shall run in music from their voice and song;

Unto our world hope's daily oracles
From their lips shall be brought;
And in our lives love's hourly miracles
By them be wrought."